To the rangers, the caring, enthusiastic
and knowledgeable stewards of these
parks and preserves

In Mills Canyon.

PENINSULA TRAILS

OUTDOOR ADVENTURES ON THE SAN FRANCISCO PENINSULA

Jean Rusmore · Frances Spangle · Betsy Crowder

WILDERNESS PRESS
BERKELEY

FIRST EDITION January 1982
Second printing March 1982
Third printing December 1983
SECOND EDITION January 1989
Second printing May 1989
Third printing April 1990
Fourth printing April 1991
Fifth printing February 1993
Sixth printing May 1995
THIRD EDITION May 1997

Design by Thomas Winnett and Peter Browning
Maps by Larry Van Dyke and Ben Pease
Cover photos © 1997 by Frank S. Balthis
Cover design by Larry Van Dyke

Library of Congress Card Catalog Number 96-46624
International Standard Book Number 0-89997-197-0

Manufactured in the United States of America

Published by Wilderness Press
            2440 Bancroft Way
            Berkeley, CA 94704
            (800) 443-7227
            FAX (510) 548-1355

            Write, call or fax us for a free catalog

Cover photos: Coast Redwood Forest, Butano State Park;
               Gray Whale Cove *(inset)*

Library of Congress Cataloging-in-Publication Data

Rusmore, Jean.
    Peninsula trails : outdoor adventures on the San Francisco
Peninsula / Jean Rusmore, Frances Spangle, and Betsy Crowder. -- 3rd
ed.
        p. cm.
    Includes index.
    ISBN 0-89997-197-0
1. Outdoor recreation--California--San Francisco Peninsula-
-Guidebooks. 2. Hiking--California--San Francisco Peninsula-
-Guidebooks. 3. Trails--California--San Francisco Peninsula-
-Guidebooks. 4. San Francisco Peninsula (Calif.)--Guidebooks.
I. Spangle, Frances. II. Crowder, Betsy, 1926–   . III. Title.
GV191.42.C2R87 1996
917.94'9--dc21   96-46624
                                                   CIP

Foreword

For more than 25 years San Francisco Peninsula residents have worked collaboratively with each other and dozens of private and government agencies to realize a vision of interconnected, permanently protected lands. These lands, an urban-rural boundary, afford a refuge for plants and animals, provide low-intensity recreational opportunities, and promote continued agricultural use. The results of this vision define the uniqueness of the San Francisco Peninsula landscape and give us a sense of continuity and place.

Peninsula Trails, by Jean Rusmore, Frances Spangle and Betsy Crowder, invites you to experience the results made possible by the hard work of hundreds of people. It is your guide to the Peninsula's growing treasure-trove of protected park and open space lands. *Peninsula Trails* provides a way for you to know why the effort to safeguard this place is worth it.

Building on the excellent work done for the second edition of *Peninsula Trails*, Rusmore and Crowder have walked all these trails, and they describe the special features of each route with care and accuracy. Even a casual reading of *Peninsula Trails* inspires you to make plans to leave the traffic and noise behind and head for the hills. Using this book allows you to take a spontaneous walk when you have only a couple of hours, or to plan a day-long hike. While you'll still have your own surprises—a special view, a bobcat sighted down the trail, or a drift of wildflowers—*Peninsula Trails* will keep you from having the unfortunate surprise of a trail that ends too soon or one that climbs too steeply. If you seek a special kind of experience, *Peninsula Trails* is sure to guide you to it.

Besides hiking and writing books, the authors are active in the effort to protect the Peninsula's remaining open lands. Rusmore and Spangle are co-authors of the first two editions of *Peninsula Trails*, and of *South Bay Trails*. Rusmore is the author of *The Bay Area Ridge Trail*. Crowder is an elected member of the Board of the Midpeninsula Regional Open Space District, an agency that owns and manages many of the lands covered in these pages. Both Rusmore and Crowder are active in many local organizations, including the Committee for Green Foothills, Greenbelt Alliance, Sierra Club, Sempervirens Fund, California Native Plant Society, and Peninsula Open Space Trust, all of which work to save lands on the Peninsula.

Currently the Peninsula Open Space Trust is spearheading a major effort to raise private funds to acquire strategically located lands. These acquisitions will complete trail and wildlife corridors, protect magnificent redwood forests and oak woodlands, restore miles of streams, and create new public beaches. It is an effort that will require the help of thousands of supporters.

Being part of the effort to save land is deeply satisfying. Under what other circumstances can you create a legacy that you can fully enjoy now and know will be there for generations to come? How exciting to walk out from a forest through a beautiful spring meadow, or stand on a cliff overlooking the Pacific and be able to say "I saved this. I made sure this place would always be just as it is today." With your help, perhaps the next edition of *Peninsula Trails* will include a vista trail that you made possible!

Audrey C. Rust
Executive Director, Peninsula Open Space Trust

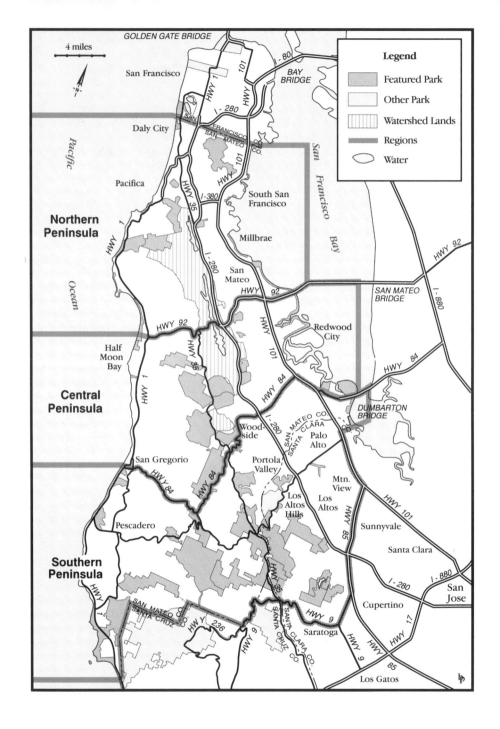

Peninsula Parks and Open Space Preserves

Contents

Hiking in the backcountry entails unavoidable risk that every hiker assumes and must be aware of and respect. The fact that a trail is described in this book is not a representation that it will be safe for you. Trails vary greatly in difficulty and in the degree of conditioning and agility one needs to enjoy them safely. On some hikes routes may have changed or conditions may have deteriorated since the descriptions were written. Also trail conditions can change even from day to day, owing to weather and other factors. A trail that is safe on a dry day or for a highly conditioned, agile, properly equipped hiker may be completely unsafe for someone else or unsafe under adverse weather conditions.

You can minimize your risks on the trail by being knowledgeable, prepared and alert. There is not space in this book for a general treatise on safety in the mountains, but there are a number of good books and public courses on the subject and you should take advantage of them to increase your knowledge. Just as important, you should always be aware of your own limitations and of conditions existing when and where you are hiking. If conditions are dangerous, or if you're not prepared to deal with them safely, choose a different hike! It's better to have wasted a drive than to be the subject of a mountain rescue.

These warnings are not intended to scare you off the trails. Millions of people have safe and enjoyable hikes every year. However, one element of the beauty, freedom and excitement of the wilderness is the presence of risks that do not confront us at home. When you hike you assume those risks. They can be met safely, but only if you exercise your own independent judgement and common sense.

Preface

The first edition of *Peninsula Trails* covered the existing parks and preserves on the east side of the Santa Cruz Mountains. The second edition also included those westside parks and preserves that adjoin the Skyline ridge. Recent land purchases and easements still farther west opened up two new trail corridors, one connecting Long Ridge Open Space Preserve to Portola Redwoods State Park and another linking Pescadero Creek County Park with Big Basin Redwoods State Park. Now this expanded third edition of *Peninsula Trails* encompasses all the parklands in San Mateo County—from north to south and from Bay to coast—and some in Santa Clara County.

In 1995 Betsy Crowder joined the *Peninsula Trails* partnership. Since then we have hiked through every park and preserve, beach, Bayland and marsh, on loop and round trips, exploring and marveling at the rich variety of landscape and the magnificent heritage of natural beauty showcased in the Peninsula's public parklands. We hope that our readers also will enjoy the first-hand experience of walking, running or leisurely riding the trails we've described and will come to appreciate, treasure and care for these public open spaces. Here are more than 60,000 acres of public parklands at the fringes of bustling urban centers, yet wild enough to offer solitude, majestic views and opportunities to relax and re-create.

Introduction
The Peninsula Bayside, Mountain and Coastside Setting

Geography

The Santa Cruz Mountains are part of the Coast Ranges of California. They run northwest to southeast, extending from Montara Mountain near San Francisco to Mt. Madonna near Watsonville. A natural divide splits the range into two parts at the Highway 17 pass going to Santa Cruz. The Spaniards called the southern section the Sierra Azul (blue mountains) and the northern part, the Sierra Morena (brown or dark mountains). The area covered by this guide centers on the Sierra Morena and includes land from the San Francisco Bay on the east to the Pacific Ocean on the west. The highest mountain in the Sierra Morena is appropriately called Black Mountain.

The east side of the Santa Cruz Mountains, steeper than the west, is cut into deep canyons by streams running generally at right angles to the main axis. San Mateo, Belmont, Redwood and Cordilleras creeks are the main streams flowing east in central San Mateo County. The San Francisco Watershed drains into the Crystal Springs reservoirs and San Mateo Creek. The large drainage basin of San Francisquito Creek and its tributaries is fed by streams from Woodside and Portola Valley. Along with Los Trancos Creek, it forms a natural boundary between San Mateo and Santa Clara counties.

In Santa Clara County are Matadero, Adobe and Permanente creeks. At the south edge of the area covered by this guide is Stevens Creek, which rises near the Skyline ridge, flows south between Monte Bello Ridge and the Skyline ridge, then bends around the southeast end of Monte Bello Ridge and turns due north on its way to the Bay.

The upper reaches of these creeks, which still flow more or less untrammeled down through the mountains and the foothills, are some of the main delights of our mountainside parks. Where these creeks meandered across the Bay plain, they were once the dominant features of the landscape, being bordered by huge oaks, bays, alders and sycamores. Now they have all but disappeared from sight in the flatlands, being mostly confined to concrete ditches and culverts and bordered by chain-link fences. Two happy exceptions are the lower reaches of Los Trancos and San Francisquito creeks, which still retain their parklike tree borders as they wind through Portola Valley and the undeveloped lands of Stanford University. They are the sites of popular creekside trails.

The western slopes of the Santa Cruz Mountains are a different world from the eastern side. Very few roads cross the summit; most follow old Indian trails or Spanish routes, or are remnants of former logging roads. Originally thickly forested with redwoods and Douglas firs, the canyons and ridges now support a second or third growth of these trees, interspersed with live oak, black oak, tan oak, bay laurel and smaller shrubs and trees. In some places remnant groves of giant redwoods were spared the ax and saw. Toward the Coastside some areas formerly ranched are still open grassland.

We are fortunate that our state and county were urged, by foresighted citizens, to buy so much land for public parks. A glance at the map shows that a greater acreage of public lands lies west and south of the Skyline than on the Bayside. It is to enable the reader to explore these wonderful public lands from the Skyline to the Coast that this guide book has been expanded.

Westflowing creeks are generally larger and longer than Bayside streams, due to the heavier rainfall on the Coastside and the greater distance from the mountains to the sea. Major creeks are San Pedro in Pacifica, Pilarcitos in Half Moon Bay, and, farther south, Purisima, Tunitas, San Gregorio, Pescadero and Gazos. Some present-day trails follow the routes of early roads beside these creeks.

Geology

The Santa Cruz Mountains were formed over the millenia by the uplifting, folding and faulting of rocks. Frequent earthquakes in the area tell us that forces deep within the earth continue to reshape the land.

The San Andreas Fault, which extends the length of California, is the most conspicuous feature of the Peninsula landscape. It runs northwest-southeast roughly parallel to the main ridge of the Santa Cruz Mountains. Linear valleys lie along the fault, and the main ridge of the mountains stands west of it. Monte Bello Ridge and the lower hills stand to the east.

A dramatic vantage point from which to view this fault is the top of Los Trancos Open Space Preserve on a fault saddle between the Skyline ridge and Monte Bello Ridge. You can see the rift valley running south

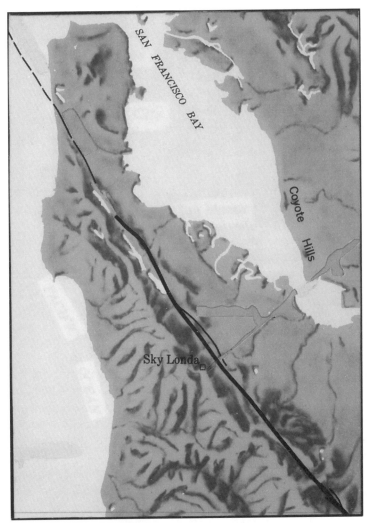

The San Andreas Fault

toward Loma Prieta and Mt. Umunhum and north up the Crystal Springs Valley as far as San Andreas Lake, about 25 miles in each direction.

In the 1890s Andrew Lawson, a noted California geologist, saw these straight valleys and recognized them as typical of a rift zone. He named the fault for the northernmost of the rift-valley lakes. The great earthquake of 1906, centered a few miles offshore and west of San Francisco's Lake Merced, made the San Andreas Fault famous around the world.

The Santa Cruz Mountains are very young geologically. The oldest exposed rocks on the Peninsula were formed only 150 million years ago, whereas the oldest known rocks on earth are four billion years old. In spite of its youth, Peninsula geology is extremely complex because the area lies at the boundary between the Pacific and the North American plates. These plates have been and are still moving very slowly past each other. The movements of these large blocks of the earth's crust are explained by the modern concept of plate tectonics.

From the concept of plate tectonics, and the kind of bedrock formation found in the Santa Cruz Mountains, the following geologic history can be inferred. Between 150 and 65 million years ago, massive quantities of lava flows, red ooze, sand and mud accumulated in complex layers on the Pacific Plate in a location west of what is now the California coast. These deposits on the ocean floor were hardened to rock, partly crushed and thoroughly mixed as the edge of the Pacific Plate was pushed under the North American continent, thus moving what is called the *Franciscan Complex* to its present location on the east side of the Pilarcitos and San Andreas faults. This complex is composed of shale, siltstone, limestone, sandstone, chert and greenstone, occurring sometimes as a melange and sometimes as discrete beds. Outcrops of these rocks occur on Sweeney and Sawyer ridges, San Bruno Mountain, Belmont Hill and Monte Bello Ridge.

For the past several million years the San Andreas Fault has formed a boundary between the Pacific and the North American plates, the land west of the fault (the Pacific Plate) moving northwest in relation to the North American Plate, at an average rate of 1 to 2 inches per year. As a result of movements along the fault, granitic rocks originally formed about 90 million years ago in the area now occupied by Southern California underlie most of the land west of the San Andreas fault at depth, and are exposed on Montara Mountain.

Serpentine, the California state rock, occurs in outcrops along Sawyer Camp Trail, in road cuts along I–280 from Woodside north, in Edgewood Park and in scattered locations on Monte Bello Ridge.

The linear fault valleys of the Peninsula exist because rock broken by fault movements erodes more rapidly than rock farther from the fault. However, you can see other and more recent signs of faulting in the Peninsula. Where the fault crosses the ridge at the top of Los Trancos Open Space Preserve, the crushed rock has eroded to form a fault saddle. Sag ponds at the preserve result from horizontal fault displacements that shifted hillslopes, blocked ravines and created undrained depressions. Earthquake movements have changed streamcourses along upper Stevens Creek Canyon. Landslides occur frequently in the steep Santa Cruz Mountains; many were triggered by the 1906 quake and its prehistoric counterparts.

The San Andreas Fault Trail in Los Trancos Open Space Preserve is a good place to learn about the effects of fault movement. As a joint project of the Midpeninsula Regional Open Space District and Foothill College, geologists interpret for you evidence of earthquake activity along a self-guided trail through an area changed by the 1906 earthquake and earlier ones. After you have completed the trail and look straight down the rift valleys, you will sense the awesome force of the constant movement of the segments of the earth's skin as they float on top of the deeper mantle of semimolten rock.

The San Gregorio Fault runs northwest-southeast inland from the coast on the west side of the Santa Cruz Mountains. Its effects are seen in the shifts of creek directions near Butano State Park, at Fitzgerald Marine Reserve and near Mussel Rock.

Plant And Animal Life

Looking up at the Peninsula hills from several vantage points along I–280, it is possible to identify four of our main plant communities. (A plant community is a group of plants with similar tolerances and similar adaptations to environmental conditions.) First, you see the rounded forms of the oaks, madrones, bays and buckeyes of the mixed woodlands, which cover much of our hillsides. A noticeably different community is the open, rolling grasslands of mountainside meadows and foothill pasturelands, mostly imported annual grasses. Green in winter, dry and golden in summer, they are characteristic of California and other areas of Mediterranean climate, distinguished by winter rains and summer drought.

On the Skyline ridge you see the jagged silhouettes of firs and redwoods in the conifer forest. Although the redwoods were cut over in the 19th century, extensive stands have grown again. This third plant community covers thousands of acres in the Skyline ridge watersheds, parks and sheltered canyons. A fourth plant community, chaparral, thrives on hot, dry slopes. This dense growth of shrubs and trees is specially adapted to our winter rains and long, dry summers. Their leathery or waxy evergreen leaves, sometimes curled inward, conserve moisture, and their long taproots reach water deep below the surface. These plants form a scratchy thicket, unfriendly to the hiker but home to many species of wildlife. The Spaniards are said to have named the vegetation "chaparral" after a Spanish evergreen oak, the *chaparro*.

On the west side of the Santa Cruz Mountains, a thick forest is nurtured in the canyons and on the upper slopes by the heavy winter rainfall (up to 60 inches in wet years; about 45 inches in normal years) and by the summer fog. This fog is formed when cold water beside the coast upwells to the surface and chills the moisture-laden air above, causing condensation. The rising hot air inland creates a partial vacuum, into which foggy air flows. This encourages the lush growth of giant coast redwood trees in

L. to R. blue oak, coastal live oak, black oak, valley oak.

southern San Mateo County, and nurtures associated Douglas fir, oak and bay laurel trees and herbaceous plants. On the coast itself, the winds are strong and the salt spray pervasive, so that most of the coastal terraces and bluffs are either grasslands or coastal scrub, a softer version of inland chaparral.

After you note the general appearance of these plant groupings from a distance, you will be surrounded by a great variety of trees, shrubs and flowers on the trail. More than 1700 species grow in the Santa Cruz Mountains and their western and eastern flanks.

You will also see and hear unnumbered birds, and if you look closely you will notice lizards, salamanders and the myriad spiders and insects of the earth. Larger animals, once so plentiful, are now rarely seen, though you may have the pleasure of catching sight of a deer in the woods, a squirrel in the trees or an occasional rabbit in the brush. Larger mammal predators such as gray foxes, coyotes, bobcats, and even an occasional mountain lion live in the wild areas. Footprints in the wet earth by a stream or in the dust on a sunny trail will tell you there is still animal life nearby. Small holes in the ground and tunnels underfoot are probably all you will see of the many burrowers, such as badgers, voles, field mice and gophers. In thick woodlands you may find the three-foot-high piles of sticks that are the homes of woodrats.

In this guide we mention some of the trees, flowers and creatures you may encounter, but we can touch only briefly on a few of the many species. Fortunately for those whose curiosity is aroused, there are many excellent publications that focus on the plants and wildlife of the Bay Area and California. See Appendix II.

California buckeye has spikelike blossoms.

The Peninsula's and Coastside's Past

Although humans have lived on the Peninsula for 3000 years (some think for much longer), it is only in the past 200 years that they have significantly changed the natural landscape. Spanish newcomers in the 18th century hunted game with their guns, brought herds that grazed the hills, and introduced annual grasses that supplanted the native bunch-grass. By the mid-19th century, Anglos from the East were changing the face of the Peninsula, logging over the forests and farming the valleys and foothills.

But it was not until the mid-20th century that the settlements that were scattered down the length of the Peninsula suddenly spread over the valley, reshaped the hills and replaced woodlands and orchards with houses, roads and shopping centers.

However, the Peninsula Bayside, which three decades ago was seem-ingly about to be engulfed in buildings, is now witnessing renewed efforts toward containing its urban spread. Public and private groups are setting aside parks, preserves and trail corridors that complement the increasingly dense settlement patterns of the Bayside. An expanding system of public greenbelts now gives us the opportunity to walk through the lovely foothill landscape, follow a stream, or climb a trail up our steep mountains to thousands of acres of forest on both sides of the Skyline ridge. Public beaches and a coastal trail offer access to the length of the San Mateo County Coast. The total size of public parklands in the area covered by this book is more than 60,000 acres.

Earliest Inhabitants

The first people to walk these hills were the Ohlone Indians, a tribe of hunters and gatherers who lived along the Bay and Pacific shores and in the foothills between San Francisco and Monterey. When the first Euro-pean explorers came onto the Peninsula, they found their way criss-crossed by trails worn by the Indians as they went from their villages to the shores of the Bay, into the hills and across the mountains to the coast. The explorers came across small tribelets of these Indians living in reed huts in villages built beside creeks west of the Bayside marshes and below the first rise of the hills. Our first Peninsula cities were built on some of these same pleasant sites. Before the Spanish era the Peninsula supported one of the densest Indian populations in the country. Nearly 10,000 Ohlone Indians lived between San Francisco and Monterey.

The Ohlones lived well without cultivating the land. They thrived on the incredible bounty of Peninsula woodlands, streams and shores. Elk, deer, antelope, coyote, fox, bear and mountain lion roamed the hills, along with plentiful small game. Birds, particularly waterfowl, filled the air in sky-darkening numbers. Acorns, the staple of the Indians' diet, were gathered from the thick stands of oak in the hills and on the valley floors. Families returned to ancestral groves year after year to harvest. Welcome seasonal additions to their diet were the plentiful grass and flower seeds, roots, fruits and berries. They also used the bountiful supply of fish and shellfish from the Bay, the creeks and the ocean. Indeed, when early explorers were offered gifts of food, they commented that Indian fare was palatable, even tasty.

Although the tribelets traveled between Bay and foothills most of the year to gather food, they did not stray far from the small territories they considered their own. Spring and summer migrations for hunting and gathering were not extensive. A few groups made longer expeditions to trade with other groups for beads, salt, pine nuts, obsidian, abalone shells and wood for bows. Regular trade routes crossed the hills between Bay and ocean.

From the great size of the shell mounds found along the Peninsula it is believed that the Indian population lived here with little change for thousands of years. Theirs was a successful culture that provided well for these people, who lived in relative peace with their neighbors and in harmony with the land.

Save for the periodic burning of the native bunchgrasses and underbrush in the meadows to keep them open for better hunting and acorn-gathering, and the paths worn by centuries of their footprints, the Indians had little impact on the land or the animals around them. Early Europeans reported that the Indians moved among the wildlife and small game without arousing their fears. As Malcolm Margolin states in *The Ohlone Way*, "animals and humans inhabited the very same world, and the distance between them was not very great."

The coming of the European, with his guns, horses and cattle, changed all this. The antelope, elk and bear soon disappeared, and other animals retreated from sight. Changes in the land were profound. Cattle grazing and the inadvertent introduction of European oat grass nearly eliminated the native perennial grasses. For the Indians, change was swift and complete with the advent of the Spanish missions.

The Spanish-Mexican Period

Two centuries after Europeans first explored the California coast by ship, the overland expedition of Gaspar de Portolá discovered San Francisco Bay in 1769. This event paved the way for permanent Spanish settlement. Mission Dolores and the Presidio of San Francisco, as well as Mission Santa Clara, were founded in 1776. A year later, the Pueblo of

Guadalupe in San José was built. Mission Santa Cruz on the Coastside was founded in 1791.

After the founding of these missions and their supporting ranches and outposts, the Padres baptized the Indians and drew them into the mission system. By the end of the 18th century, most of the Indians had been moved from their villages to missions and ranches, their families broken up, their old ways lost. The mission founders' dream of small farms run by Christian Indians did not come to pass. In just over half a century the stable Indian culture that had changed little over thousands of years disappeared. In the final tragedy these native people succumbed by the thousands to imported diseases to which they had little or no resistance.

In the brief period of Mexican rule the missions and their supporting farms were secularized, and the ensuing disruptions of mission life further demoralized the remaining Indians.

Then, with the Gold Rush came land-hungry Easterners, who gained title to the few remaining lands occupied by the Indians, displacing these first Americans who had lived in harmony on the Peninsula for so long. The United States census of 1860 listed only 62 persons on the Peninsula as Indians.

In the early Spanish days the entire Peninsula was divided into a few vast supporting ranches for the missions and the Presidio. Great herds of cattle and sheep grazed over the hills. Grains, vegetables and fruits from the ranches on the Bayside near San Mateo and from the coast north of Santa Cruz supplied these Spanish outposts.

When Mexico gained independence from Spain in 1821, the government secularized the missions and their ranches. To encourage settlement of the land the Mexican governors of California made grants of land to individuals. They divided the Peninsula into huge ranchos, as large as the 35,000-acre Rancho de las Pulgas. East of the Skyline ridge in the area covered by this guide were the Ranchos Guadalupe, BuriBuri, Feliz, Raimundo de las Pulgas, Martinez, Corte de Madera, Purissima de Concepción and San Antonio. To the west were the Ranchos San Pedro, Corral de Tierra, Miramontes, Cañada Verde y Arroyo de la Purisima, San Gregorio, Pescadero, Butano and Punta del Año Nuevo.

The brief flowering of these Mexican ranchos ended in 1848 when the American flag was raised over California. The Treaty of Guadalupe, intended to protect the titles of Mexican land grants, failed to do so. Hordes of Americans from the east, eager for land after the discovery of gold, poured into northern California. The great ranchos were soon divided and sold or even usurped by squatters.

On the Coastside American settlers took over the lands from the Mexican rancheros by fair means or foul. By 1853 Andrew Johnston had settled in a large house near present-day Half Moon Bay, having come by wagon over the mountains from San Mateo. In 1855 a toll road was built on this mountain alignment, making it easier to send farm produce to the Bayside towns. Other settlers moved north from Santa Cruz—the Moore family established a homestead in Pescadero and the Steele brothers started a dairy near Punta Año Nuevo. Butter and cheese, shingles and tanbark were shipped from a variety of rather precarious wharves and chutes.

Eventually tourists discovered the Coastside, and by 1907 the Ocean Shore Railroad was built south from San Francisco, reaching as far as Tunitas Creek. Another railroad worked north from Santa Cruz, but the two never met. The gap between Tunitas and Swanton (present-day Davenport) was crossed by Stanley Steamer. In 1920 storms washed out parts of the Ocean Shore Railroad and it never was reconstructed.

When modern-day roads were built along the alignments of the earlier railroad tracks, the Coastside settlements grew apace, mainly as "bedroom communities" for Bayside workers. Half Moon Bay is the only incorporated city on the Coastside, but the communities of Montara, Moss Beach, El Granada and Pescadero all are expanding as fast as their limited water supplies allow.

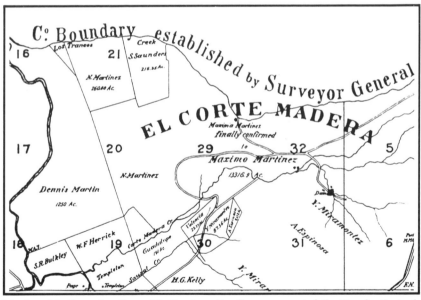

Maximo Martinez, together with Domingo Peralta, was granted the Rancho Corte de Madera, which took its name from the wood cut in the forests of present day Portola Valley. The Martinez home near Alpine Road was torn down in 1940.

Logging

The Spanish had dealt lightly with the forested Peninsula hills. The redwoods cut to build their missions they felled by ax. In fact, they later expressed concern over unrestrained logging by the Anglos. The greatly increased demand for lumber to build Gold Rush San Francisco brought the first major change to the Sierra Morena, particularly to that part known as the Pulgas Redwoods—the forest above present-day Portola Valley and Woodside. The new owners of these lands logged them heavily with whipsaws. They built sawmills powered first by water, then by steam engines. As many as 50 sawmills operated in these forests, turning out lumber to build San Francisco and then rebuild it after its fires. By 1870 the huge trees, some 10 feet or more in diameter, were gone. Hardly a redwood tree remained standing east of the Skyline, but logging continued in the vast forests on the western slopes. Most of the original giant trees were cut by 1900, but redwoods are fast-growing in this climate, and second-growth trees of marketable size still are being harvested on private lands.

Farming and Ranching

With the redwoods gone in eastern San Mateo County, some of the lower slopes of the mountains were planted with orchards and vineyards. Dairy farms and large estates covered the foothills. During the late 1800s in northern Santa Clara County, ranchers planted vineyards and orchards of plums, apricots, peaches, pears and cherries on the valley floor and in the lower foothills. This area became one of the most productive fruit-growing areas in the world. The scent of blossoming trees filled the air every spring. Ripening fruits on the trees and trays of apricots, peaches and prunes drying in the fields made summers colorful in the peaceful orchard country. On western slopes open land became livestock and dairy farms. Later, row crops of artichokes and Brussels sprouts were grown in large acreages and greenhouses containing flowers proliferated.

Urbanization

In eastern San Mateo County a century of settlement saw the gradual break-up of large estates and the burgeoning of towns. By 1863 tracks for the San Francisco and San Jose Railroad had been laid as far as Palo Alto and soon they extended to San Jose. By 1900 a string of suburban towns had grown up along the railroad, which shaped the growth of the Peninsula until the coming of the automobile.

The Santa Clara Valley orchards survived until the middle years of this century, when people poured into the Peninsula after World War II. Industry expanded in the valley, and orchard after orchard gave way to housing tracts. Towns grew until their borders touched to form the present unbroken urban band along the Bay.

Although houses had been built on the gentler slopes of the eastern foothills, the steeper hillsides, where road building was too difficult, remained wild. By the mid-1950s there were still many undeveloped hillsides, forested slopes and canyons in a relatively natural state. As the concept of public open space evolved, the precipitous canyons and oak-covered hills were seen as welcome breaks between subdivisions. These are the lands that have become parks and open-space preserves where miles of trails beckon hikers today. By the 1980s many forests and ranch-lands west of the Skyline were acquired for parks and preserves.

On the Coastside in the '90s the Peninsula Open Space Trust sold the remaining 1197 acres of former Cowell Ranch lands adjacent to Cowell Ranch State Beach to farmers who signed conservation easements permanently reserving the land for agriculture. Also on the Coastside, POST took an option in 1996 to purchase the 5638-acre Cloverdale Coastal Ranch, situated between Año Nuevo State Reserve and Butano State Park. Sempervirens Fund bought an undivided one-half interest in 1800 forested acres along Gazos Creek south of Butano State Park. Some of these large acreages may become dedicated parkland in the future.

In addition, several private citizens gave sizeable properties to POST, one of which, the Thysen Bald Knob piece, is now part of Purisima Creek Redwoods Open Space Preserve.

San Francisco Watershed Lands

The vast San Francisco Watershed lands in the heart of San Mateo County have remained wild since early logging ceased here, their hills spared from development and their reservoirs forming a sparkling chain of lakes. The Watershed deserves special mention because the Bay Area Ridge Trail plans include an important segment traversing the length of these lands. The thousands of acres east of the lakes are slated for some recreation use, including more trails.

The 23,000-acre Watershed belonging to the City of San Francisco lies between the wooded northern Santa Cruz Mountains and the lower hills to the east. It drains into upper San Mateo Creek, which was dammed in the 1890s. The resultant Crystal Springs Lakes and San Andreas Lake to the north are now water-supply reservoirs for San Francisco and much of the Peninsula.

The 15-mile linear valley running through the Watershed was formed over the millenia by movements along the San Andreas Fault. For perhaps thousands of years before the coming of the Spanish this valley was the site of Indian villages. From then until the dams were built, it was a place of small, fertile farms and a few inns. The Crystal Springs Hotel, built in 1855, a popular spa of its day, gave the lakes their name.

When San Francisco needed more water than local wells could supply, the city's Spring Valley Water Company began buying up lands in the Watershed and building reservoirs. In 1862 they dammed Pilarcitos Lake

14 PENINSULA TRAILS

in the northwest part of the Watershed, bringing water by gravity to San Francisco along a 32-mile wooden flume. Next they built the San Andreas Dam and the two Crystal Springs dams. The last of these dams, built across the gorge of San Mateo Creek, was completed in 1896, the engineering feat of its time. Although it is only 1,200 feet from the San Andreas Fault rupture of 1906, it withstood the earthquake.

When San Francisco's needs were again outpacing its water supply, the city acquired the private Spring Valley Water Company and started the ambitious project of bringing water from the Sierra Nevada. In 1934 O'Shaughnessy Dam at Hetch Hetchy was completed and a pipeline was built across the San Joaquin Valley. Sierra waters flowed into the Crystal Springs lakes through the Pulgas Water Temple, built to celebrate this event.

The entire Watershed now belongs to the City of San Francisco. The location of I–280 through the Watershed south of Highway 92 required prolonged negotiations that involved the federal government, the State of California, the City and County of San Francisco and San Mateo County. An agreement was finally reached in 1969 to place the freeway farther east of the lakes than originally proposed. This agreement granted two easements affecting the Watershed lands and guaranteed certain scenic and recreation rights in perpetuity to the people of the United States.

Roughly 19,000 acres on the west side of the lakes are designated as a scenic easement. They must remain undeveloped—preserved for watershed capacity, scenic quality and limited access. East of the lakes, 4,000 acres of the Watershed will continue to be set aside for scenic value and watershed purposes, but may also be used for recreation.

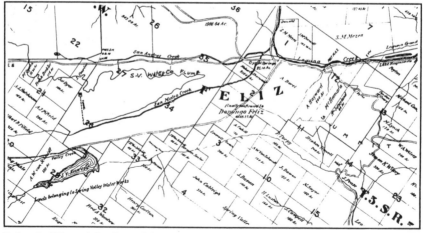

Before building of the Crystal Springs dams, San Mateo Creek flowed through the San Andreas Valley and was joined by Laguna Creek from the south.

Trail Planning

History

As the Peninsula became more urban, opportunities for walking, riding and picnicking diminished. Then NO TRESPASSING signs and houses appeared where once you could climb a fence to walk or picnic. The counties began to recognize the recreation value of some of the steep canyons, hillsides and once-cut-over lands.

In 1924 Santa Clara County acquired lower Stevens Creek Canyon, its first county park, which has been a favorite place for hiking and riding ever since. Also in 1924 the Spring Valley Water Company laid out 10 miles of equestrian trails near Lake Merced adjacent to northern San Mateo County, probably the earliest formal trails built on the Peninsula. According to a bulletin of the Spring Valley Water Company, "These trails were planned to give riders as great a diversity of scenery as possible while at the same time minimizing the danger of trespassing on Lake Merced, the golf courses and vegetable gardens." To this day these concerns remain for trail planners as they seek routes through the countryside that will not conflict with the interests of farmers and property owners.

Visitors who enjoy the parks protect the resources.

San Mateo County in the mid-1930s began requiring dedication of riding-trail easements as a part of land subdivisions. In the Woodside and Portola Valley area in particular, this requirement was used to prevent loss of pre-existing trail links when land was subdivided.

The continued interest in trails, particularly for riding, was manifested in the late Forties and early Fifties in a grand plan for a statewide California Riding and Hiking Trail system. In San Mateo County, with the support of horsemen's associations and hikers and with some funding by the state, trails were laid out over easements through private property along the Skyline ridge, through the San Francisco and Bear Gulch watersheds, and along the right-of-way of Skyline Boulevard and Cañada Road. The California Riding and Hiking Trail was marked by posts with gold symbols of horseshoes and hiking boots. Regrettably, in time, a number of easements through private property lapsed and freeway building obliterated parts of the trail near San Andreas Lake and below Crystal Springs Dam. But many miles of the trail survived, and San Mateo County's north-south trail corridor from San Andreas Lake to Wunderlich Park and Skylonda uses much of this same route.

The Forties saw the acquisition of Huddart Park and the development of riding and hiking trails there. San Mateo County, with trail-club cooperation, laid out still more hiking and riding trails on road rights-of-way along Cañada, Whiskey Hill and Portola roads through the present-day towns of Woodside and Portola Valley.

In a burst of trail-planning activity in the Fifties and Sixties, San Mateo County mapped over 400 miles of trails in the City/County Regional Plan for Parks and Open Space, adopted in 1968. Unfortunately, at that time neither the funding nor the support for trails was sufficient to bring these trails into being.

However, with funding from a federal pilot project to encourage trails in urban areas, three important trails were built in 1969—the Waterdog Lake and Sheep Camp trails from Belmont to Cañada Road and the Alpine Road Hiking, Riding and Bicycle Trail.

In the Seventies, with renewed appreciation for the remarkable potential for hiking and riding trails in the Peninsula mountains and foothills, conservation, hiking and riding organizations pressed for specific programs and funding for trails. Voters in San Mateo County adopted a Charter for Parks establishing a special tax for park purposes, and Santa Clara County voters passed a park bond issue. In 1974 a gift of Wunderlich Park's 942 acres of conifer forest and meadows provided hikers with many more miles of trails. The City of Palo Alto bought 1400 acres of hillside woodland, which have become the much prized Foothills Park. Other cities reserved canyons, streamsides and hillsides for public use.

But the citizens of the Peninsula, still concerned with the rapid disappearance of open space and the slow pace of park acquisition, proposed by initiative a Midpeninsula Regional Park District. Northern Santa Clara County voters formed this district in 1972 and were joined by voters in southern San Mateo County in 1976, after which the name was changed to Midpeninsula Regional Open Space District (MROSD).

The District's major purpose is to acquire and preserve foothill and Bayland open space to protect it from development, and to open it to public use consistent with protection of the environment. These lands provide protection for natural vegetation, wildlife and areas of scenic beauty. The District's goal is to help preserve a greenbelt of open space linking District lands with state and county lands. By 1996 the District had acquired 41,000 acres in San Mateo and Santa Clara counties and a corner of Santa Cruz County. This greenbelt is creating a system of regional trails with outstanding opportunities for hiking, riding, bicycling and running.

In 1994, the voters in southern Santa Clara County formed the Santa Clara County Open Space Authority (SCCOSA), a special district with a purpose similar to that of MROSD.

The Peninsula Open Space Trust, a nonprofit land conservancy, takes another approach to open-space acquisition. The Trust is dedicated to private and public preservation of open space in San Mateo and Santa Clara counties. Organized in 1977, the Trust has protected over 27,000 acres through purchase, gift and provision of local, private matching funds for public projects.

In 1995 the Santa Clara County Board of Supervisors adopted a Trails Master Plan that was the product of several years' work by citizens' committees and commissions. This plan identifies 522 miles of trails and trail corridors that in the future will link the county's urban areas and parks and connect with trails in adjoining counties.

San Mateo County's Trails Plan was adopted by the Board of Supervisors in March 1990; a revision was drafted in 1995 and awaits the public hearing process. This plan proposes a system of trails that would link county parks to other public parklands in this county and in adjacent counties.

Pressure for trails sparked state legislation for funding major trails to link state and county parks. Growing interest in regional trails led to bold programs initiated in 1987 for two Bay Area trail systems—the San Francisco Bay Trail and the Bay Area Ridge Trail. Statewide citizen action has spearheaded planning for the Coastal Trail and the Anza Trail.

Hostels and Overnight Camping

As long-distance trails take shape, more camping and hostel facilities will be needed. In the area covered by this guide, camping by reservation is possible at Huddart Park and at the MROSD camp on Black Mountain in Monte Bello Open Space Preserve. In the western part of San Mateo County there are many opportunities for overnight camping. Portola Redwoods and Butano state parks and Memorial, Sam McDonald, and

Pescadero county parks, now reachable by long trails from the Bayside, have camping facilities and trail camps. At Half Moon Bay State Beaches there are camping facilities. The Hikers' Hut in Sam McDonald County Park may be reserved for overnight accommodations by calling the Loma Prieta Chapter of the Sierra Club. The Jack Brook Horse Camp in Sam McDonald Park is also available to groups by reservation with San Mateo County Parks Department.

Hostelers in the '50s at the first West Coast youth hostel, still operating today.

Hidden Villa Hostel at the base of Black Mountain in Los Altos Hills, the first and oldest hostel in the West, is open September through May, but closes in summer to accommodate a youth camp. However, Welch-hurst Hostel in Sanborn-Skyline Park is just 4.3 miles south of Saratoga Gap. The Montara and Pigeon Point Lighthouse hostels provide accommodations for coastal travelers. Be aware that Youth Hostels are closed from 9:30 A.M. to 4 P.M. daily.

Trail Building and Maintenance

The success of trail programs depends to a great extent on careful operation and maintenance. The Santa Cruz Mountains Trail Association, user group organizations, Scouts, Sierra Club groups, the Trail Center and school groups are making valuable contributions in trail building and clean-up projects. They also perform an important role in disseminating trail information, and promoting a sense of stewardship for public land and respect for private property.

The Trail Center, a nonprofit organization established in 1983, recruits, trains and encourages volunteers to help public agencies build and maintain local trails. The Midpeninsula Regional Open Space District has an active Preserve Partners program in which volunteers work on trail maintenance together with district Open Space Technicians. See Appendix III.

Volunteers from the Trail Center help rangers build the Redwood Trail in Purisima.

Trails in The 1990s

Plans for four long trails in the Bay Area include segments of them in the area covered by this guidebook. With the completion of more than 200 miles of the proposed 400-mile Bay Area Ridge Trail and 170 miles of the San Francisco Bay Trail, trail users already have an unparalleled opportunity to explore our region at its highest elevations and at sea level along the Bayfront. Local pathways, like spokes of a wheel, will eventually connect our communities with both these encircling trail systems.

The Ridge Trail is being developed by the Bay Area Ridge Trail Council with the sponsorship of the National Park Service, state and local park departments, regional open-space districts and water agencies. In the area covered by this guide, it will link Peninsula trails from the Golden Gate National Recreation Area in San Francisco through San Mateo County's mountainside parks to Saratoga Gap. Already thirty-seven miles of trail in this corridor are completed, and only a few gaps remain.

The Bay Trail is being implemented by the Association of Bay Area Governments, the Metropolitan Transportation Commission, and the non-profit San Francisco Bay Trail Project.

The Coastal Trail along the San Mateo County Coastside, part of a Pacific Coast Trail from Canada to Mexico, is being implemented by federal, state and local jurisdictions. Local citizens assist in planning, implementation and trail maintenance. Some sections are completed and are described in the San Mateo Coast Beaches section of this book.

The Anza Trail, a National Historic Trail, follows the path of Captain Juan Bautista de Anza on his quest to find a land route from Mexico to San Francisco in 1776. Now this historic route is being marked by local agencies under the auspices of the National Park Service.

For information on these ongoing projects, see Appendix III.

The Volunteer Trail Patrol helps a visitor at Montebello OSP.

Information for Trail Users

The main purpose of this guide is to describe trips through our parks and preserves, giving a detailed account of each trail and information on elevation change, terrain, orientation, trip distance and hiking time. The authors have drawn on their own experience of hiking on all the trails in this guide. Their enthusiasms are, of course, subjective, but directions, trail distances and details of natural features are intended to be objective and concise.

Travel times are based on a moderate hiking pace, which averages about two miles an hour, taking into account the difficulty of the terrain and the elevation gain. Trip distances are stated as one way, loop or round trip. Trip times are those required to complete the trips as described. Of course, time for bicyclists or equestrians will differ from that for hikers.

Figures for elevation change tell the vertical footage gained or lost from the start to the highest or lowest point of the trip. These figures do not include minor elevation changes along the way. When the outward leg of a loop or a round trip is uphill, the elevation change is given as a gain; then, of course, the return leg will be an elevation loss. Conversely, when the outward leg is downhill, the elevation change is given as a loss.

To estimate the time required for a trip where the cumulative gain is more than 1000 feet or where there are steep climbs within a short distance, the authors used an old hiking rule: for every 1000 vertical feet gain, add ½ hour to the time that would be required on level ground.

These trails include not only long hikes in big federal, state and county parks and major open-space preserves, but also strolls on paths in some city parks, by the Bay and along the Coast that offer pleasant, brief respite from the urban scene. The many choices for trips in this area range from steep mountain climbs to gentle paths through the woods to level paths past tidal marshes and ocean beaches.

Trails for Different Seasons and Reasons in Appendix I groups trails for a variety of purposes and situations. These suggestions may help those unfamiliar with the Peninsula and its Coastside to find a suitable trail or perhaps inspire seasoned hikers to try new trails in our parks and open-space preserves. It is not an exhaustive list. Each user can add his favorites.

Every effort has been made to make this guide up-to-date, but new parks and preserves opening in the future undoubtedly will provide new trails.

Maps

On the Map of Peninsula Trails in the beginning of this book the general locations of parks, preserves and watersheds are shown. The map is divided into three sections—Northern, Central and Southern Peninsula—as delineated by the three major roads crossing from Bay to Coast, and corresponds with the table of contents. An enlarged map precedes each of these three sections in the text. Parks and preserves in each section are numbered from north to south and correspond to their place in the text. Separate maps of the San Francisco Bay Trail and the San Mateo Coast Beaches and Coastal Trail precede those sections of the book and are presented from north to south. A map also accompanies each park or preserve, and a listing of maps follows the contents.

Maps of all the parks and preserves, specially prepared for this book, show trail routes and entry points, main natural features, elevations, park facilities and parking areas for cars and horse trailers. These maps are a valuable reference for hikers, runners, bicyclists and equestrians, as well as for those who wish to picnic or just relax in public recreation sites.

Although most major parks and preserves offer maps of their trails, these are not always available. To secure more information, leaflets and maps, and free docent-led walks and tours in MROSD preserves, federal, state and county parks, write, phone or visit the agencies listed in Appendix III.

In addition to these public agencies, the Trail Center, a volunteer organization, serves as a source of information about local trails and trail activities. Among publications available are a four-county parks map and a trail map of the southern Peninsula; and books on trails, parks, open-space preserves and wildlife refuges in San Francisco, San Mateo, Santa Clara and Santa Cruz counties. A monthly activity schedule lists upcoming hiking, running, equestrian and bicycling events.

Excellent topographic maps are available from the United States Geological Survey headquarters and from many sporting-goods stores. The western district headquarters of the USGS is at 345 Middlefield Road, Menlo Park. The map sales and information office, Building 3, a fascinating place worth a trip in itself, is open from 8 A.M. to 4 P.M. A full-service map store, the Map Center, is at 63 Washington Street, Santa Clara. USGS maps are published in a 7.5-minute series. Some local trails are shown on these maps, but it is the topographic information that is of particular interest to the hiker—contours and natural features, such as wooded areas, clearings, creeks, lakes and mountains. Although "topos" are not necessary for hiking on the trails in this guide, they can add to your understanding of the terrain. After you have learned to read the contour lines, you can visualize the shape and elevation of the land they represent. Then you can tell by the spacing of the contour lines whether the grade on the trail will be steep or gentle. Generally these maps were prepared from aerial photos in the 1950s. Some were field-checked more recently, but the "cultural" information is often out of date.

The area of this guide is covered by quadrangles of the 7.5-minute series, listed here from north to south: San Francisco South, Montara Mountain, San Mateo, Half Moon Bay, Woodside, Pigeon Point, Palo Alto, Mindego Hill, Cupertino, La Honda, San Gregorio, Big Basin, Franklin Point and Año Nuevo.

Trail Rules, Etiquette and Safety

Park and open-space preserve regulations are few, but they are important. Based on common sense, they are necessary for your own safety and the protection of our parklands. To preserve the beauty of the natural setting, all plants, animals and natural features are protected. Leave them undisturbed for others to enjoy. Stay on the trail. Shortcuts across trail switchbacks break the trail edge and accelerate erosion. Don't smoke on the trail, and build no fires except where permitted in established fireplaces. Firearms and bows and arrows are prohibited.

- Hours: Generally open 8 A.M. to dusk; MROSD preserves open dawn to dusk. Fees for some state and county parks; subject to change.
- Trail closures: In wet weather trails often are closed to bicyclists and equestrians. Newly constructed trails are temporarily closed until treads harden.
- Dogs: Prohibited in all San Mateo County parks. In Santa Clara County dogs are prohibited except in some parks that permit dogs on a short leash in picnic areas, but never on trails. Midpeninsula Regional Open Space District permits dogs on leash in some preserves; call for information. State parks allow dogs on leash in campgrounds but not on trails.
- Hikers and runners: Yield to equestrians.
- Bicyclists: Observe closure signs; ride on designated trails only. Helmets required in all parks and preserves. Speed limit in MROSD preserves and Santa Clara County parks is 15 m.p.h; 5 m.p.h. when passing. Yield to equestrians and hikers.
- Equestrians: Observe closure signs. Indicate to other users when it is safe to pass.
- Safety: Travel with a companion rather than alone. List of organizations offering group trips is in Appendix III.

Some Hazards For Trail Users

Poison Oak: This plant, *Toxicodendron diversilobum*, is widespread through most of the Peninsula hiking country. You don't need to remember its Latin name, but you should learn to recognize this ubiquitous plant with its three-lobed leaves. A pretty cream-colored flower cluster is followed by white berries. It looks different according to the season and the environment where it is growing. In spring its gray branches send out reddish buds, then shiny, young, light-green leaves. In autumn it has rosy red leaves that are brilliant in the woods and along the roadsides. To touch the twigs or leaves is to court the outbreak of an uncomfortable, itchy, blistering, long-lasting rash.

Poison-oak plant.

Avoid it! Wear long sleeves and long pants for protection; bathe with cool water and soap when you get home. If you have unavoidably brushed against some poison oak, wash the area in the nearest stream or even use water from your canteen.

Rattlesnakes: Another, and far less common, hazard is the rattlesnake. It has a triangular-shaped head, diamond markings or dark blotches on its back, and from one to ten or more rattles (segments) on its tail—it adds a new rattle each time it sheds its skin. It is the only poisonous snake native to our hills; it inhabits many hillside parks, though it is rarely seen. The rattlesnake will avoid you if it possibly can. Just watch where you put your feet and hands, and stay on the trails.

Lyme Disease: A potentially serious illness can result from the bite of the Western Black-Legged tick, a ¼-inch-diameter insect. Ticks brush off onto you from grasses and trailside bushes. Wear long pants, tucked into boots or socks, and a long-sleeved shirt.

Mountain Lions: Sighting of these shy, native resident of wild lands have become more frequent due to increased use of their habitat by people. A mountain lion is about the size of a small German shepherd, with a thick tail as long as its body. It is recommended that trail users stand facing any mountain lion they encounter, make loud noises while waving their arms, and not run away.

Bobcats: Not hazardous to humans, they are about twice the size of a house cat with six-inch-long tails.

Feral Pigs: Imported from Europe, these animals have spread over many acres of wild lands since their introduction for hunting in the 19th century. While generally not dangerous to humans, they can be fierce when cornered.

Remember, wild animals normally avoid humans, if possible. Trail users must be careful not to entice them closer by giving them food, as they may lose their natural fear and cause problems.

Weather

The vagaries and variety of our local weather require some flexibility in planning hikes. Summer weather can vary from day to day, even from hour to hour where coastal fogs and winds influence the temperature. The Coastside, Skyline ridge and the northern Peninsula are often windy and dripping with fog in summer while the rest of the Peninsula is mild and sunny. In other seasons the mountains can be drenched in rain when the Bayside cities are merely cloudy. Fall, winter and spring are best on the Coastside, when fresh breezes bring clean air and crystal visibility.

Summer and fall bring sunny, hot days to the southern Peninsula. Midday hiking is best then in the cool, forested canyons. In any season, south- and west-facing slopes are the warmest. A winter hike on such slopes is delightful on a sunny day.

Although we all welcome the many clear, mild days of our incomparable climate, there are hikers who find particular joy in a bracing hike on a cold day. And there is even a unique pleasure in walking through the woods in the gentle rains of early spring when pale green new leaves begin to appear on the trees.

What To Wear

Walking is surely the prime low-cost sport. The rewards are unrelated to the outlay for equipment, since the only essential is comfortable, sturdy footgear. The many available walking and running shoes with good treads are fine for Peninsula trails. Some hikers still prefer boots for the protection they give on rough terrain and on wet trails. As for clothing, some experienced hikers suggest that you "dress like an onion," so you can peel off layers as needed. A sweater and a windbreaker provide against the extremes of weather and temperature you may encounter during a day. If you are susceptible to poison oak or are not yet familiar with it, a long-sleeved shirt and long pants offer protection to sensitive skin. With a hat for shade in summer and a scarf or warm cap for cold and windy days, you are well-equipped for enjoying the trail.

Put the extra clothing in a light, inexpensive day pack, add a snack or lunch, a canteen of water and perhaps this guidebook. Binoculars for birds, a magnifying glass for flowers, lichen and insects, and a flower or bird guide won't add much weight. An all-purpose bandana and pocket knife come in handy. Water is a must, since streams are infrequent and their water is unsafe to drink.

Even in dense fog, hikers enjoy Peninsula trails.

Map Legend

═══	Freeway	ⓟ	Parking
───	Road	ⓟ̸	No parking
------	Hiking & equestrian trail*	ⓛⓟ	Limited parking
··········	Hiking-only trail	ⓔⓟ	Equestrian parking
∘∘∘∘∘∘∘	Proposed trail	■	Restroom
—··—	Park boundary	▲	Picnic area
—·—	Watershed boundary	△	Campground
—···—	Stream	✳	Park office or headquarters
➡	Park entrance		
►	Trail entry point	□	Other structure
I RR02	Gate/ Gate Number	★	Seasonal footbridge (removed in winter)

* See text for bicycle information

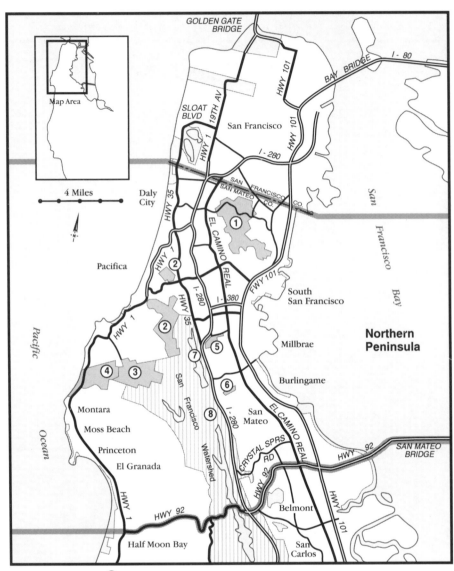

① Numbers in circles refer to Northern Peninsula text

Northern Peninsula Parks

Northern Peninsula
From the San Francisco County Line to Highway 92

Circled #   Park or Trail Name in Text
on Map

1	San Bruno Mountain State and County Park
2	Sweeney Ridge
3	San Pedro Valley County Park
4	McNee Ranch
5	Junipero Serra County Park
6	Mills Canyon Nature Area
7	San Andreas Trail
8	Sawyer Camp Trail

Northern Peninsula

From the San Francisco County Line to Highway 92

San Bruno Mountain State and County Park

San Bruno Mountain rises starkly from the Bay to an elevation of 1314 feet, dominating the northern Peninsula landscape, its bare, steep flanks creased by narrow ravines and a few wooded canyons. The cities of San Francisco, Brisbane, South San Francisco, Colma and Daly City surround the mountain.

From the top of this seemingly barren mountain rising above the cities encircling it, you see the other Bay Area landmark mountains, the Pacific Ocean, the skyscrapers of San Francisco and the ships on its great Bay.

In 1978 the mountain became San Bruno Mountain Park with the purchase by the State of California and San Mateo County of 1500 acres and the gift of 500 acres by the property owner. Later additions brought the park's total to 2266 acres, which are managed by San Mateo County.

Guadalupe Canyon Parkway, running generally east-west across the park, leads to the park entrance. North of the parkway is a relatively level area known as the Saddle, where visitors find beautiful views and attractive picnic areas screened by native oaks and sheltering low walls. A day camp nestles in the center of the Saddle and trails loop around the perimeter.

South of the parkway, trails ascend the mountain's steep sides and a road to the summit leads to trails along its high ridges. Superb views from this mountaintop make it a fine place to take visitors for an orientation to the Bay Area, all laid out before you.

More than 11 miles of trails take the visitor over the mountain's varied terrain on short, easy nature trails accessible for the physically limited, on moderate loop hikes, and on longer trips up the mountain. Although the ridges of the mountain are exposed to the prevailing winds and fog from the ocean, and buffeted by the storms of winter, the ravines in the lee of the main ridgeline are often sunny and relatively warm. After winter rains clear, the superb 360° views are worth a trip to the mountain with windbreaker, binoculars and camera. Even in blustery weather, the hiking is good if you are prepared with proper clothing.

Considered an outliner of the Santa Cruz Mountains, San Bruno Mountain geologically is an elevated fault block composed largely of a dark gray Franciscan rock with the catchy name of graywacke (three syllables). You can see jumbled outcroppings of this rock above Guadalupe Canyon Parkway as you come up the canyon from the west.

History

Some evidence of Indian habitation has been found in Buckeye Canyon and shell mounds are known along the edge of the Bay below. A few years after the Portolá expedition discovered San Francisco Bay in 1769, Captain Fernando Rivera, the principal officer of Father Francisco Palou's exploring party, climbed the mountain with four of his men to watch the sunrise. Man has since greatly altered the land they saw around them, but the mountain itself remains very little changed. It is believed that the mountain was named for the patron saint of Captain Bruno Heceta, who commanded an inland party mapping the Bay and the surrounding lands.

From Spanish times the mountain was considered good pasture, and from those times until World War II cattle grazed these grassy slopes.

In one of the early grants of the Mexican regime, in 1836 Governor Luis Arguello bestowed on Jacob Lesse, a naturalized Mexican citizen, the Rancho Cañada de Guadalupe, Concepción y Rodeo Viejo. The ranch took in the whole mountain, Visitacion Valley and the old rodeo grounds near the Bay. Over the years the ranch changed hands many times as it was traded, sold and divided, until 1872 when the Visitation Land Company secured the largest holding. In 1884 H. W. Crocker acquired the company's 3814 acres. This large holding remained for nearly a century in the Crocker Estate, until the establishment of the park.

The Mountain's Special Flora

The mountain, so dun-colored from a distance after its grasses dry up, is at close view colorful and lively with a great variety of plants, lichen-covered rocks and fern-lined canyons. In spite of over a century of grazing, San Bruno Mountain is a botanical island with vegetation typical of that which once covered the San Francisco hills. A great number of native species of plants grow on the mountain—384 have been counted, including some rare and endangered species and a few unique to this special environment.

Nearly 50 varieties of grasses grow here, half of them native, including many of California's perennial bunchgrasses. In the grasslands from February on, you can see impressive displays of wildflowers—sheets of pearly everlasting, colonies of goldfields, clumps of Johnny jump-up, slopes covered with Douglas and coast irises and steep hillsides of brilliant, showy, red California fuchsias. The mountain's most extensive and varied displays of annual flowers are found on some 150 acres of the April Brook slopes known as the Flower Garden.

Four rare butterflies, among them the endangered Mission blue, the San Francisco silverspot and the San Bruno elfin, live and feed on the plants of San Bruno Mountain.

Habitat Conservation Plan

Long years of concern over potential effects of construction on the mountain's flora and its rare and endangered species led to a landmark decision in 1982. Known as the Habitat Conservation Plan, it granted developers a 30-year permit to build on some of the endangered species' habitat in return for their funding programs to enhance the species' chances of survival on the park lands.

This plan sets up an annual fund, the San Bruno Mountain Habitat Conservation Trust Fund, which will be used to eliminate invasive gorse and eucalyptus and to seed host plants, such as lupine and goldfields, for food and refuge for the endangered species.

Gorse elimination projects are ongoing; 1995 saw the beginning of eucalyptus removal. Time will tell how well these fragile native species can survive in limited space and in close contact with urban development. In the meantime, building moves right up to the boundaries of the park.

Jurisdiction: State of California and San Mateo County—415-363-4020.

Facilities: Trails for hikers, one for bicyclists and another for physically limited. Picnic areas, barbecues, meadow play area, restrooms and day camp.

Rules: Open 8 A.M to sunset. No dogs allowed in park. Bicycles allowed on Radio Road and Saddle Loop Trail only.

Maps: San Mateo County *San Bruno Mountain Park* and USGS topo *San Francisco South.*

How To Get There: From I-280: (1) Southbound—Take Eastmoor Ave exit and turn left on Sullivan Ave, which parallels freeway. At first street on left, turn left onto San Pedro Rd, which goes over freeway. Across Mission St San Pedro Rd becomes East Market St, which becomes Guadalupe Canyon Pkwy. Park entrance is on north side of parkway. (2) Northbound—Take Mission St exit. At first stop sign, turn left onto Junipero Serra Blvd, then right on San Pedro Rd and follow directions above. From Hwy 101: Take Bayshore Blvd, turn west on Guadalupe Canyon Pkwy and go 1.5 miles to park entrance on right.

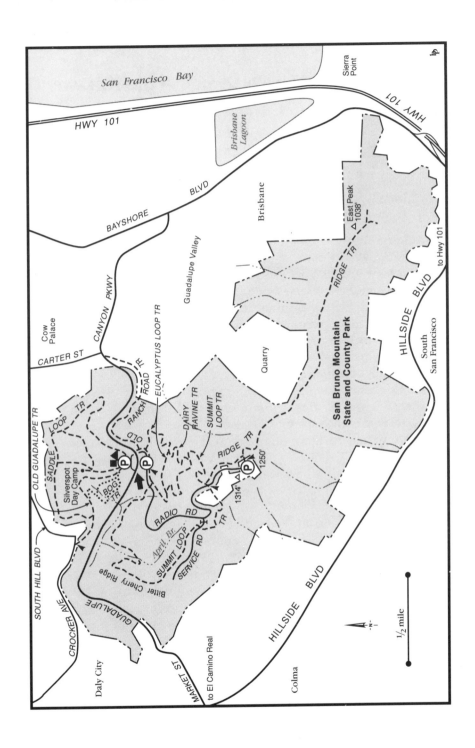

San Bruno Mountain State and County Park

Two Trips on the North Side of the Parkway

Trip 1. Saddle Loop Trail

Circling the northern Saddle area of the park, this is an invigorating hike when fresh breezes sweep in from the Pacific. Views stretch beyond San Francisco to its dramatic setting of Bay and mountains.

- **Distance:** 2.7-mile loop.
- **Time:** 1½ hours.
- **Elevation Gain:** 150′

TRAIL NOTES

Marked off in ½-mile segments, this loop is a longtime favorite of joggers. Now open to bicyclists too, it is becoming an even more popular trail. Starting on the Old Guadalupe Trail on the west side of the north parking area, follow this former ranch road lined with eucalyptus and Monterey cypress. It traverses the side of a ravine, where moisture-loving plants grow by the path. On foggy days the aroma of eucalyptus leaves is intensified when they are crushed underfoot.

In 0.8 mile veer right past new subdivisions crowding the park boundary, to climb into open grasslands where you have long views out to the Pacific Ocean and Pt. Reyes. If the day is very clear, the Farallon Islands seem closer than their 30-mile distance.

The trail arcs right, staying close to the boundary of the park, with flowers brightening the way at most any season. Particularly brilliant in spring with goldfields, lupines and some rare species, this path even in summer is dotted with magenta farewell-to-spring and white yarrow.

Downtown San Francisco highrises puncture the skyline, and the Bay Bridge stretches across to Oakland. As your trail continues to its highest point, the view spreads toward the South Bay shoreline. From about the halfway point of this loop, a service road cuts straight back to the park entrance, passing the pleasant Silverspot Day Camp area en route. As you continue around the Saddle Loop, the view changes to take in the full height and breadth of San Bruno Mountain. It beckons the hiker to cross the parkway and climb its trails to even wider views of the entire Bay Area.

Heading back to the parking area, you pass the gorse elimination projects. European gorse has taken over large areas of this saddle, threatening to wipe out the host plants for the rare and endangered butterflies. Because gorse seeds can live up to 25 years, gorse is very difficult to eradicate.

In small ravines coastal scrub harbors many bird species. You may recognize the quail's warning call and see wren-tits and song sparrows flitting from shrub to shrub. These birds and the rare plants and butter-

Looking north from San Bruno Mountain's summit.

flies of the mountain are now protected through the establishment of San Bruno Mountain Park.

Trip 2. Bog Trail

A short nature trail aligned on a gentle grade and having a stable surface skirts a little swale west of the park entrance. A bridge over an intermittent stream leads from it to the Old Guadalupe Trail. This 0.4-mile trail, accessible to the physically limited, offers an opportunity for all nature lovers to enjoy the riparian environment. A self-guiding pamphlet explains the plants and animals of this environment.

The Bog Trail, together with a section of the Old Guadalupe Trail (the first leg of the Saddle Loop Trip), makes a loop of less than a mile. Try this before sitting down to lunch at one of the picnic sites just beyond the old cypress trees at the park entrance.

Four Trips on the South Side of the Parkway

Trip 1. Eucalyptus Loop Trail

A relatively easy trail samples the lower slopes of the mountain with views up to its long ridgetop.

- **Distance:** 1-mile loop.
- **Time:** ½ hour.
- **Elevation Gain:** 170′

TRAIL NOTES

This trip is just right for a brisk walk before lunch. Before you set off, pause to learn about the natural wonders of the mountain from the exhibits on the display board by the trailhead at the south-side parking area. Here too, you can see the botanical garden, funded by the Habitat Conservation Trust Fund and planted and maintained by the volunteer group, Friends of San Bruno Mountain. At present three of the five plant communities found on San Bruno Mountain are represented—grassland, coastal dune scrub and wetland. The remaining two will be added later.

Then take the lefthand trail to begin this loop trip. When past the eucalyptus removal area and the botanical garden, you see the deeply furrowed sides of the mountain, dark green against the sky. Water rushes down the mountain in winter, carving still deeper furrows in the mountain's side. After a few bends in the trail, turn right at the first junction. Your way straightens out above the former eucalyptus grove to cross Dairy Ravine. High above, the long spine of the park extends for more than 2 miles southeast. Up close, the mountain has a magnificent profusion of poppies and goldfields glowing golden in spring and early summer.

A right turn at the next junction takes you into the trees and thence back to the trailhead. For lunch you can take the footpath through the underpass to the north-side picnic area by the old Monterey cypresses that mark the north entrance to the park.

Trip 2. Dairy Ravine Loop

Climbing higher on the mountain, this trip zigzags up and down the sides of Dairy Ravine past trailside gardens of remarkable beauty.

- **Distance:** 1¾-mile loop.
- **Time:** 1 hour.
- **Elevation Gain** 325'

TRAIL NOTES

In return for the extra elevation gain and extra mileage, this loop offers the delights of coming upon a different rock garden at every turn. Lichen-covered rocks shelter gray-green sedums, their tall flower stalks bearing coral and yellow blossoms.

Starting from the trailhead on the south side of Guadalupe Canyon Parkway, take the left branch of the Eucalyptus Loop Trail (see Trip 1 above) and at the first junction bear left onto the Dairy Ravine Trail. This ½-mile-long trail climbs the east side of Dairy Ravine in wide switchbacks to meet the Summit Loop Trail at the head of Dairy Ravine. When you meet the Summit Loop Trail, veer right on it, and see the San Francisco skyline looming in the distance. Below are the old cypress trees in Dairy

Ravine. The name and these trees are all that remain of the dairy farm that once operated at the foot of the ravine.

The trail crosses over and makes a switchback above the steep east side of Cable Ravine, then descends quickly through waist-high cream bush, coffee berry and snowberry to meet the Eucalyptus Loop Trail. Here you take a left turn to return to the south-side parking area.

Trip 3. Summit Loop Trail

This mountaintop climb takes you past the Flower Gardens of April Brook Ravine, along the west ridge for its views, and down the steep north face below the summit.

- **Distance:** 3.1-mile loop.
- **Time:** 2 hours.
- **Elevation Gain:** 725'

TRAIL NOTES

Although you can complete this trip in two hours, you may want to linger longer in spring to enjoy the views and the flowers at every step of the way. From the trailhead on the south side of Guadalupe Canyon Parkway, take the path to the right through the eucalyptus grove.

After crossing the road, you soon come out into dense, waist-high growth—tall cow parsnip with its flat clusters of white blossoms, pink-flowered honeysuckle and California bee plant with its small, dull red flowers. Along the way you come across the many wet places in the trail where even in summer water is seeping from springs above.

You are soon at the ravine where April Brook flows into willow-bordered Colma Creek. It's a protected little swale that catches the noontime sun. The brook is heavily lined with sword ferns, and big clumps of

Summit of San Bruno Mountain, from northwest of Guadalupe Parkway.

coastal iris edge the trail. In winter, you can distinguish the coastal iris from the Douglas iris, also found on the mountain, by the former's straplike leaves that are green on both sides; in contrast, Douglas iris leaves are shiny green on top and dull-grayish green below. Come back in April and May to see the long-petaled flowers in shades of blue.

But even in winter you can see the promise of spring in the emerging foliage of California poppies, lupines and other annual flowers. Stone outcrops by the trail form rock gardens of such satisfying design as to serve as models for our domestic landscaping efforts. Needlepoint-textured, orange and gray lichen cover the rocks; pink-hued succulents, small polypody ferns and thick-leaved daisies fill the crevices.

The trail crosses April Brook Ravine and ascends via switchbacks to Bitter Cherry Ridge, where the skyscrapers of San Francisco and the blocks of Daly City homes come into view. East of April Brook in the sloping meadow below Radio Road is the Flower Garden, a carpet of color from early March through May.

At the very top of the ridge the trail joins a paved road, which you cross and look for the continuation of the trail on the south side. Keep to the narrow trail going uphill and avoid an old jeep road that contours around to a lower destination. Southwest and far below are the cemeteries of Colma, with lawns, lakes and headstones.

The first stretch of the trip on the south side goes through a brilliant summer garden of knee-high golden yarrow, contrasted with purple pennyroyal, crimson pitcher sage, white yarrow, and pink owl's clover. If you look back over this sea of blooms, you will see up the coast all the way to Pt. Reyes. A few steps farther around the east side of the hill the stony slopes are encrusted with low, pink-edged succulents and gray-leaved, lemon-yellow-blossomed Indian paintbrush. Below the next bend in the trail the saucer of a telephone relay rises like a giant white bloom from this stony garden.

A switchback in the trail takes you up to Radio Road, where above you rises a spindly forest of antennas springing from the commercial communications installations in an enclave of private property. Cross the road and start north down the mountain in wide switchbacks with ever-changing vistas and a succession of trailside gardens as varied as the views. Just 400 feet down the Summit Loop Trail you pass the Ridge Trail going east. You could turn here and walk out to the East Peak and back, thus extending your trip by 5 miles.

Continuing down the Summit Loop Trail, you pass a rocky promontory where rare varieties of huckleberry and manzanita form ground-hugging mats. This species of manzanita, found only on San Bruno Mountain, is now sold in nurseries as a drought-resistant ground cover. From the promontory you can see down the flank of the mountain to the

Bay. After a hairpin turn you look east to Blue Blossom Hill, mantled with deep-blue wild-lilac blossoms in early spring.

At the next trail junction you can choose the east or the west ridge above Dairy Ravine. Both have fine views and remarkable flower displays, long after the spectacular spring show. To stay on the Summit Loop Trail bear left (west). On this long traverse you pass a series of little gardens in a sheltered spot. Low-growing pink daisies are blooming along with blue brodiaeas, accented with crimson sage, and a patch of pennyroyal is splashed with some scarlet paintbrush. Here and there are clumps of iris edged with monkey flower.

At the next trail junction, veer left and follow the Eucalyptus Loop Trail around a big bend down to the parking area.

Trip 4. Ridge Trail to East Peak Vista

An invigorating hike goes out to East Peak for commanding views of the Bay Area and far out over the Pacific Ocean.
- **Distance:** 4.8 miles round trip from summit; 8 miles round trip from lower, south-side trailhead.
- **Time:** 2½ hours from summit; 4½ hours from lower trailhead.
- **Elevation Loss:** 310' from summit; **gain** from lower trailhead 725'.

TRAIL NOTES

Drive up Radio Road to begin this trip at the east end of the summit parking area. Or, for a more challenging 8-mile hike, start at the lower, south-side parking area and take the Summit Loop Trail up to the Ridge Trail, which is on the northeast side of the summit. Then follow the Ridge Trail, contouring east below the mountaintop, to join the trail from the summit parking area to the East Peak. In either case, this trip calls for windbreakers against the usual mountaintop winds and sturdy shoes for the often rocky Ridge Trail.

Only ¼ mile out on the trail you can begin to take in the wonderful panorama. You stand with the San Francisco skyline in view in one direction, the Bay in front of you, and over your shoulder the blue Pacific Ocean. Right at your feet is the mountain, its grassy slopes flowering in early spring. You can see down into the steep ravines, the first to the southwest, Sage Ravine, grayed with artemisia. The northeast slopes tend to be brush-covered or wooded. Past the quarry, rock outcroppings, tall chaparral and trees cover Buckeye Ravine.

On either side hawks ride the updrafts. You may see one make its swift glide for a ground squirrel in the grass below. If it has a wing spread of 4 feet or more and a tail that shows reddish orange against the sky, it is a red-tailed hawk, the most common kind on the mountain.

By late February wildflowers begin to bloom through the grass, earlier here than elsewhere on the Peninsula. Clumps of California poppies and ground-hugging Johnny jump-ups color the ridgetop. Creamy yellow wallflowers blow in the breeze on ten-inch stems, and blossoms of white milkmaids are sprinkled down the shadier northeast slopes.

The East Peak, unmarked except by the transmission towers, is a good place to turn back. The ridge falls off rapidly a little beyond, which makes for a very steep climb back. Returning to the summit, the ocean is before you. On a clear day you can see Pt. Reyes on the northwest horizon.

San Francisco and beyond, seen from the Saddle Loop Trail.

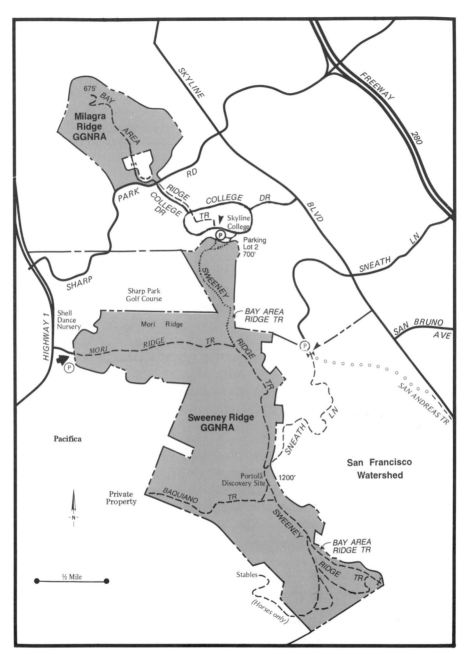

Sweeney Ridge

The Sweeney Ridge addition to the Golden Gate National Recreation Area takes in the high ridge just north of Montara Mountain. Its grassy hilltop commands sweeping views of ocean and Bay. From this site

Gaspar de Portolá's scouts first saw the expanse of water we know as San Francisco Bay.

In 1980 the Golden Gate National Recreation Area expanded its jurisdiction south from Marin County and San Francisco to include 26,000 acres of land within San Mateo County. Much of this land was already in public ownership, though not some thousand acres along Sweeney Ridge. The GGNRA purchased this land in 1982 to "preserve the natural, cultural and recreation values of the ridge." Included in this acquisition was the Portolá Discovery Site, already owned by the City of Pacifica and San Mateo County. In 1987 the GGNRA assumed jurisdiction of San Mateo County's adjacent Sweeney Ridge Skyline Preserve and Milagra Ridge Preserve less than a mile north.

In addition to their place in history as the spot from which Europeans first saw San Francisco, these wind-swept, foggy heights were grazing lands for Spanish ranches. By 1875 these lands, ideal for dairy farming, were acquired by the enterprising Richard Sneath, for whom the lane is named. He operated his dairy here until well into the 1920s. His barns were on Sneath Lane at El Camino Real.

From the rounded ridgetop, steep slopes and narrow, brush-filled canyons descend. At the northwest end of the preserve Mori Ridge reaches beyond Highway 1 to Mori Point. Sweeney Ridge's hogback is flanked east and south by San Francisco Watershed lands; west is the City of Pacifica. Only a few thousand feet from the southern boundary of the preserve is San Pedro Valley County Park.

Described here are three trips, one from each of the present access routes to the preserve. The quickest and most direct for those living on the Bayside is the approach from Skyline Boulevard on Sneath Lane. From the north there is a direct route from Skyline College to the ridgetop. From Pacifica, a trail up Mori Ridge leaves Highway 1 just north of Vallemar. A new trail from the existing San Andreas Trail beside San Andreas Lake is planned to reach the ridge, and another proposed route through the San Francisco Watershed would connect to the ridge from the south.

Sweeney Ridge is a key segment of the San Francisco Bay Area Ridge Trail, which extends from the southern Sweeney Ridge boundary with the San Francisco Watershed north through the Skyline College campus and on through Milagra Ridge.

Jurisdiction: Golden Gate National Recreation Area—415-556-8642; 415-239-2366.
Facilities: Trails for hikers, equestrians and bicyclists; portable toilet near old Nike site.
Maps: GGNRA *Sweeney Ridge*, USGS topo *Montara Mountain*.
Rules: Open from 8 A.M. to dusk; no dogs on trails.

How to Get There: There are 4 access points: (1) Sneath Lane trailhead—From Skyline Blvd (Hwy 35) in San Bruno go 2 miles west on Sneath Lane to off-street parking at gate; (2) Mori Ridge trailhead—Going north on Hwy 1 in Pacifica, pass Reina del Mar Ave, turn abruptly right into Shell Dance Nursery and continue past nursery buildings to parking at end of dirt road; going south on Hwy 1 in Pacifica, make sU-turn at Reina del Mar Ave. and go north, following directions above; (3) Skyline College—From Skyline Blvd. in San Bruno go west on College Dr, turn left at college entrance and proceed to parking lot 2 (several spaces reserved for GGNRA trail use); (4) North entrance, Milagra Ridge—From Hwy 1 or from Skyline Blvd, take Sharp Park Rd, turn north on College Dr Extension N. and continue to roadside parking at Milagra Ridge gate.

SamTrans buses reach Skyline College from Pacifica, Daly City BART and Serramonte-Tanforan.

Trip 1. From Sneath Lane to the Discovery Site

Up the lane to the Discovery Site and down Sweeney Ridge to its south end is a bracing hike with superb views.

- **Distance**: 1.8 miles one way from Sneath Lane parking area to Discovery Site, and a 2½-mile loop from Discovery Site to south end of preserve and back, altogether a 6.1-mile round trip.
- **Time:** 3¼ hours round trip.
- **Elevation Gain:** 700'

TRAIL NOTES

From the Sneath Lane trailhead, access point (1), enter through the stile to the paved service road through the San Francisco Watershed lands and descend by a willow-bordered watercourse that flows into San Andreas Lake. Close by is the proposed junction with the San Andreas Trail extension. The road soon starts its rise in and out of ravines that furrow the eastern slopes. From the outer bends of the road you catch glimpses of San Andreas Lake below. The grade is easy and the only traffic an occasional official vehicle or a few bicycles.

Partway up you will see a yellow stripe in the center of the pavement, making a "fog line" to guide cars and bicycles when dense fog blankets the hills. A word of caution about the ridge on foggy days: A walk in the fog is a bracing experience, but stay on roads or well-defined trails. When visibility is close to zero, a hiker can become disoriented and find himself lost on these moors.

Where the service road reaches the ridgetop, you are in the GGNRA. Turn left for the Discovery Site, which is marked by a dark granite cylinder. Carved around it are the outlines of the landmarks in the sweeping views around you, such as Mt. Tamalpais, San Bruno Mountain, Mt. Diablo and Montara Mountain.

From this point on the ridge Gaspar de Portolá's scouts saw "a great estuary . . . extending many leagues inland." They were in search of Monterey Bay, however, and felt misgivings that that bay and the ship they wished to rejoin might lie behind them. It was only several years later, and after subsequent expeditions, that the Spaniards recognized the importance of San Francisco Bay and its magnificent harbor.

From the Discovery Site the Sweeney Ridge Trail heads south toward the boundary of the preserve. For more than a mile you go over grasslands, past rock outcroppings and through patches of coastal scrub. In spring this is a flowery way, with carpets of goldfields, patches of blue lupine and great clumps of blue coastal iris. On fine days you can see forever. The dark outline of Montara Mountain is before you, and on either side the ocean and the Bay. As you go along, listen for the sharp cries of a kestrel, a small hawk with white undersides that searches the meadows for field mice and gophers.

Toward the south end of the preserve are a spring-fed marsh and a small reed-rimmed pond. The trail splits at the marsh; our route goes left of the marsh. Follow this trail to the southeast corner of the preserve, where a gate for equestrians with permits leads into the San Francisco Watershed. You pass through a thicket of coastal scrub enlivened by apricot-colored monkey flowers, white heads of pearly everlastings and here and there clumps of bright red and yellow Indian paintbrush. The trail going right at the marsh is an equestrian trail that takes off steeply downhill to stables at the end of Linda Mar Valley.

At the Watershed gate, our route turns north back to the Discovery Site where the Baquiano Trail, named for Portolá's scout, heads left (southwest). This trail goes down a ridge to end a mile below at private property beyond the preserve boundary. Ranger-led walks up into the preserve from Pacifica are available occasionally.

Trip 2. Up Mori Ridge to the Discovery Site

This trail heads straight up the steep grassy slope of Mori Ridge to superb views of the coast.

- **Distance:** 5 miles round trip.
- **Time:** 3½ hours.
- **Elevation Gain:** 1000'

TRAIL NOTES

From the Mori Ridge trailhead, access point (2), go to the preserve entrance gate where a service-road trail begins a steep, steady ascent up a grassy slope. Views open out over the Pacific Ocean and north to the

Farallons, Pt. Reyes and Mt. Tamalpais. In the foreground the suburban community of Pacifica contrasts with the austere outlines of Pedro Point.

In spring the grasslands are bright with flowers. You will be glad to stop the stiff climb now and then to look at them more closely. A half-hour's hike brings you to scattered old plantings of Monterey pines. One by the trailside provides a welcome shady stop on a bright day. Often, however, this exposed ridge is swept by winds and fog.

Soon you are on a gentler slope where grasses give way to low bushes. On Sweeney Ridge is one of the best examples of the lively combination of low shrubs and flowers called coastal scrub. In spring and summer this scrub takes on a brilliance that belies the harsh, negative connotation of its name. It blooms then with white pearly everlastings; patches of blue coast iris; Indian paintbrush in red and yellow; daisies in yellow, lavender and white; yellow yarrow; coffeeberry; greasewood and blue wild lilac. The ever-present poison oak is red and rose by the end of summer.

After about an hour, you reach an intersection with the Sweeney Ridge Trail, the Bay Area Ridge Trail route. Here the ridge flattens out and San Francisco comes into view, including the antenna on Sutro Heights and the towers of the Golden Gate Bridge. East are San Bruno Mountain and beyond, the East Bay Hills. At this intersection you bear right (southeast) on the Sweeney Ridge Trail (left goes north to Skyline College.) Shortly you skirt an old Nike site with blocky cement buildings and battered fences. Your trail continues for a mile on a paved, level road that is the upper end of Sneath Lane, leading to the Discovery Site.

Trip 3. Sweeney Ridge Trail from Skyline College to the Discovery Site

This route takes you quickly to a ridgetop from which there are wide views. However, after ½ mile you make a steep descent into and out of a ravine—losing 300 feet in elevation before you make the final gentle climb past the Nike site to the Discovery Site.

- **Distance:** 4 miles round trip.
- **Time:** 2 hours.
- **Elevation Gain:** 500', plus loss and gain of 300' in the ravine.

TRAIL NOTES

On a clear day the view is unlimited, all around the compass. However, this bald hilltop can get the full force of the wind from the ocean, so be prepared. On the other hand, if the day is clear and warm, take a lunch to this hilltop, where you can look down at the coast from Mussel Rock to San Pedro Point. Pacifica is below you, and the green of Sharp Park Golf Course contrasts with the deep blue of the ocean. White breakers curl into the sandy curves of the beaches.

But if the Discovery Site is your destination, continue down into and out of the ravine ahead on a re-aligned trail for hikers only, which was completed in 1996 and take the Sweeney Ridge Trail to the Discovery Site.

A segment of the Bay Area Ridge Trail descends a canyon where an endangered butterfly lives.

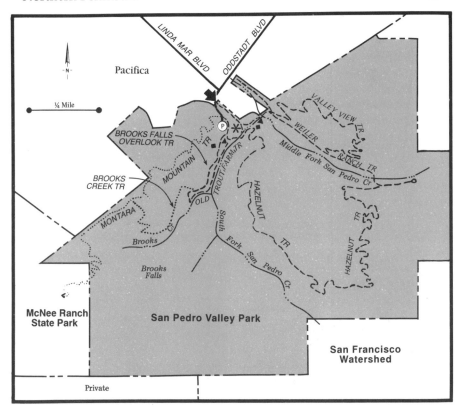

San Pedro Valley County Park

The park's 1050 acres include the narrow valley along San Pedro Creek's middle fork and the steep ridges draining the south fork. San Pedro Valley has a significant place in early Bay Area history as the site of Indian villages and the site of Gaspar de Portolá's camp from which his scouts climbed the ridge to get their first view of San Francisco Bay. An early outpost for Mission Dolores was in this valley, as was the adobe home of Francisco Sanchez, still standing and now a San Mateo County museum.

Park trails offer a number of easy, level strolls and some vigorous climbs to the ridges above the valley. The creeks run clear, and are still spawning grounds for the steelhead trout that migrate upstream to the park each winter. The creeks furnish a substantial part of Pacifica's water supply.

Jurisdiction: San Mateo County—415-363-4020.
Facilities: Visitor center, picnic tables and barbecues for families and groups; trails for hikers; self-guiding nature trail, wheelchair accessible. Wheelchairs for day use offered free.

Rules: Open 8 A.M. to dusk; bicycles permitted on Weiler Road only; no dogs; fee.
Maps: San Mateo County *San Pedro Valley Park*; USGS topo *Montara Mountain*.
How To Get There: From Hwy 1 in the south end of Pacifica turn east on Linda Mar Blvd and drive to the park entrance.

Trip 1. Up the South Fork of San Pedro Creek to the Old Trout Farm

From the picnic grounds a short, pleasant walk up the Old Trout Farm Trail beside the creek is just right to occupy the time before lunch.

- **Distance:** 0.8-mile loop.
- **Time:** Less than an hour.
- **Elevation Gain:** Relatively level.

TRAIL NOTES

Take time to explore the visitor center, which has something for the whole family. Children will enjoy display cases of the park's animals, and botany buffs delight in the well-mounted specimens of a surprising variety of plants. Photographs trace San Pedro Valley's long history.

Near the beginning of the trail look for the tanks that are all that remain of the trout farm washed away in the floods of 1962. Under overhanging trees by the rippling creek, the trail continues for almost a mile. Turn back when you will, or find the Brooks Falls Overlook Trail where stone steps start up the hillside, and follow that trail back to the picnic grounds.

Trip 2. North Ridge Loop

This trip climbs a west-facing slope on the Valley View Trail and then descends to join Weiler Ranch Road farther up the valley.

- **Distance:** 2-mile loop.
- **Time:** 1 hour.
- **Elevation Gain:** Valley View Trail 600'

TRAIL NOTES

Cross the creek on a bridge from the main parking lot to the left of the visitor center. Continue past the group picnic area under walnut trees. Turn right on Weiler Ranch Road, then almost immediately veer left on the Valley View Trail, which takes off uphill.

If you want a short level walk, continue on the road to one of the two picnic tables between the beginning and the end of the Valley View Trail. But for a brisk walk up the ridge before lunch, you can take the Valley View Trail and be back in less than an hour. In spring the meadow-side

Deer are among the frequent visitors to this park.

tables look out over a field of poppies, lupines, buttercups and wild mustard.

The Valley View Trail climbs a sunny slope, welcome in cool weather, through a eucalyptus grove and then fragrant chaparral. You can look south to the heights of Montara Mountain. In April blue coast iris blooms in clearings. From the ridgetop easy switchbacks bring you down to Weiler Ranch Road. For a longer walk you can follow this easy road to the upper end of the valley, where hills rise steeply to Sweeney Ridge a thousand feet above. An extension of the Valley View Trail is being planned to meet the Sweeney Ridge Trail in GGNRA.

Ocean fogs often roll in to shroud surrounding ridgetops, but San Pedro Mountain tempers winds from the west, sheltering the sunny valley. The same mild climate that led the Ohlone Indians to build their village by the creek makes San Pedro Valley Park a place to return to in all seasons.

Trip 3. A South Ridge Loop Trip

After a climb up the high ridge on the Hazelnut Trail, return on a west-facing slope to the visitor center.

- **Distance:** 4.3-mile loop.
- **Time:** 3 hours.
- **Elevation Gain:** 800′

TRAIL NOTES

On the Weiler Ranch Road, walk about a mile up the valley and cross a bridge over the creek. Continue to the head of the valley, where the Hazelnut Trail turns off on your right. On it you make a wide swing west, then continue on switchbacks up the canyon wall. After a wide traverse east, you zigzag up a ridge, gaining 400 feet in elevation.

At the high point of the trail you come to a gentler grade in tall chaparral of coffeeberry, Montara manzanita, wild lilac and scrub oak. On this trail you are soon down on a high saddle between San Pedro Creek's middle and south forks. A huge eucalyptus grove dominates the northwest end of the flat just before you begin the steep pitch downhill.

As the trail turns down in earnest, it doubles back and forth through a thicket of hazelnut, the shrub that gives it its name. You are soon at the foot of the hillside and crossing a sloping, flower-filled little meadow behind the visitor center, the end of the trip.

Trip 4. Montara Mountain Trail

Climb the park's western ridge for dramatic ocean views.
- **Distance:** 5 miles round trip.
- **Time:** 3 hours.
- **Elevation Gain:** 1400'

TRAIL NOTES

After the 1987 purchase of a strategic parcel of land between the adjoining McNee Ranch State Park and San Pedro Valley Park, San Mateo County built this trail for hikers only. It crosses the steep southwestern slopes of the park and joins McNee Ranch State Park high on the saddle between San Pedro Mountain and Montara's peaks.

Leaving from just west of the visitor center, the trail zigzags uphill, at first traversing a eucalyptus grove on east-facing slopes. It then goes through coastal scrub--huckleberry, manzanita, ceanothus, chinquapin, silk-tassel bush and the ubiquitous poison oak. From notches in the hills one has glimpses of the ocean; higher up are splendid views of the coastline from Point Reyes to Half Moon Bay, and east to Sweeney Ridge and Mt. Diablo. In spring irises bloom beside the trail and waterfalls drop into steep-sided canyons. At the junction with the trail from McNee Ranch, a left turn onto this wide service road, open to bicyclists, leads to the North Peak of Montara Mountain, about 1 mile farther uphill. A right turn leads downhill through the state park to its gate at Highway 1.

Trip 5. Brooks Creek/ Montara Mountain Trails Loop

Find the falls and reach the ridge between two deep canyons.
- **Distance:** 2.4-mile loop.
- **Time:** 1¼ hours.
- **Elevation Gain:** 460'

TRAIL NOTES

Begin this trip on the hikers-only trail beside the restrooms at the picnic area west of the visitor center. Mount a few steps and turn left (west) on the Brooks Falls Overlook Trail, which makes a gentle climb along the base of the south-facing hillside. At each junction thereafter, bear right on the Brooks Creek Trail. You rise slowly up the hillside under tall pines, occasional redwoods, and many eucalyptuses. When you leave the forest and get out into the chaparral, the views across the canyon open up and you see the Hazelnut Trail's route on the opposite hill.

With sounds of water tumbling down the canyon and the scent of flowering shrubs and wildflowers in the air, you arrive at the much-heralded waterfall viewing area. If you want to see the waterfall, come right after a winter storm clears and you will see and hear the triple falls dropping down the sheer mountainside. The great force of the water creates its own mist, which sometimes shrouds the canyon wall. At other times, the stream isn't full enough to put on a big display. However, the hike to the bench is pleasant and the vegetation changes as you rise.

To complete the loop trail, keep climbing on the Brooks Creek Trail past the turn where the Brooks Falls Overlook Trail goes left to return to the visitor center. Beautiful specimens of gray-green silk tassel trees and mahogany-trunked manzanita crowd the trailside. Going into the head of a little ravine and around some switchbacks, you soon reach the ridgetop and join the Montara Mountain Trail. From vistas of a misty, forested canyon you switch to splendid views of the ocean and the flanks of Montara Mountain. Turn right (east) on this trail and steadily descend around bends and turns to the floor of the park.

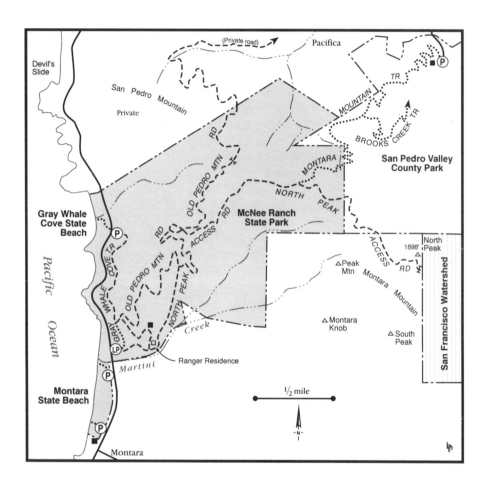

McNee Ranch

Rising steeply from rocky seacliffs, McNee Ranch's rugged slopes reach an elevation of 1500 feet near Montara Mountain's peaks. The 700-acre park includes the saddle between San Pedro Mountain and Montara Mountain. Over this saddle went the Indian trail followed by Gaspar de Portolá's party in 1769. Later it was the route of early wagon roads between coastal ranches. And in the 20th century the winding Old San Pedro Mountain Road carried automobiles over the saddle until it was abandoned for the cliff-side Devil's Slide route. Today the old road serves as a trail for hikers, equestrians and bicyclists.

Plans for McNee Ranch, which is a part of Montara State Beach, are in process at this writing. Meanwhile you can explore the park on informal paths along the lower hillsides, and on the trips described here following Old San Pedro Mountain Road and a service road up the mountain.

The State of California Department of Parks and Recreation purchased the McNee Ranch land in two parcels to accommodate a right-of-way for a possible Highway 1 bypass. In November 1996 citizens passed an initiative, Measure T, that substitutes a tunnel through San Pedro Mountain as the preferred route and gives it priority for federal and state highway funding. This route would preserve the park's trails and scenic values.

Jurisdiction: State of California, Department of Parks and Recreation—415-726-8819.
Facilities: Trails for hikers, equestrians and bicyclists.
Rules: Open from 8 A.M. to sunset.
Maps: McNee Ranch brochure, USGS topo *Montara Mountain*.
How To Get There: An entrance gate on Hwy 1 just north of Montara State Beach leads into park. There is ample parking at beach, on west side of highway. Cross with care.

The trips described start along the road leading east to the ranger's residence and then bear left to follow Old San Pedro Mountain Road. The lower part of this old road is badly gullied and eroded. However, you can find its start near the ranger's residence.

Trip 1. Old San Pedro Mountain Road North Across the Park

For fine views of the ocean and hills, this route takes you up to the saddle of San Pedro Mountain.

- **Distance:** 6.4 miles round trip.
- **Time:** 3½ hours.
- **Elevation gain:** 800′

TRAIL NOTES

From the entrance gate on Highway 1, walk ½ mile on the cypress-lined road to the ranger's residence, then bear left on Old San Pedro Mountain Road. The first section of this old road is less steep than the service road, and therefore much better for foot and bicycle travel. The old road you take upward was for many years the principal north-south highway along the coast. Its pavement is now worn and eroded, but yellow and blue bush lupine and sagebrush cover its banks. After 1.1 miles you join the service road, the North Peak Access Road, and continue upward on it.

From this junction you see below fields planted with rows of vegetables and flowers on the far side of Martini Creek. Above you tower

Montara's peaks, chaparral-covered and formidable. Broad Montara State Beach stretches south, and on a rise out of sight is Montara Lighthouse. Now an American Youth Hostel, it is an appealing place for an overnight stay while exploring the park.

A half mile past the junction, the steep North Peak Access Road turns to the right up the mountain to communications installations on its peaks, the route of our other trip in the park. Keep to the left on Old San Pedro Mountain Road, colloquially known as Old Pedro Mountain Road. A short section of this road is washed out beyond this junction, but it is possible to scramble down and back up to the old road level. From there the next ½ mile is on an easy grade.

It is worth the climb to reach the high flower garden that this old roadway becomes in late spring and summer. Its banks then bloom in brilliant variety, with red and yellow Indian paintbrush, purple pussy paws, orange wallflowers, blue-eyed grass, buttercups and more. West over the steeply descending hillside is the blue of the Pacific Ocean.

As you continue around the hillside, you come to large outcrops of granitic rocks. This light-colored igneous rock is exposed on this mountain and in only a few other places in the Bay Area, such as the Farallon Islands and Inverness Ridge. This is the same kind of rock you see at Yosemite Valley, formed beneath the surface many eons ago.

Old Pedro Mountain Road winds around the mountain, veers left at the Saddle Pass, the bypass section proposed for deep cuts, and continues to a gate marking the park's boundary. From the gate Old San Pedro Mountain Road passes through private property and down to San Pedro Valley, but you retrace your steps from the gate.

Trip 2. To Montara Mountain's North Peak

A steady, 3.8-mile climb brings you to rewarding top-of-the-world views.
- **Distance:** 7.6 miles round trip.
- **Time:** 4 hours.
- **Elevation Gain:** 1798'

TRAIL NOTES

Start from the Highway 1 entrance as in Trip 1, bear left at the ranger's residence, and continue to the point where the North Peak Access Road takes off right up Montara Mountain. On this steep service road you are soon in tall chaparral of wild lilac, coffeeberry, scrub oak, and here and there a few chinquapins—that sturdy tree with burrs and yellow-backed leaves that occurs on some dry slopes like these.

As you rise along the road and round the mountain, views are to the north and the east. After 0.9 mile you reach the junction with the Montara Mountain Trail coming up from San Pedro Valley County Park to the northeast. Beyond this junction you soon cross a flat where giant outcrops of granitic rock stand like great monuments. From this high plateau you are ½ mile from Montara's peaks. Now continue up the mountain to North Peak.

On a clear day, views from the mountaintop are awesome. Southeast are the green heights of Scarpers Peak and the ridges of the Santa Cruz Mountains. Below lie the coastal terrace of Half Moon Bay and its beaches. West and north you see Mt. Tamalpais across the Golden Gate, the Bay and the skyscrapers of San Francisco; east are the bridges, the East Bay hills and Mt. Diablo in Contra Costa County. Below are the slopes of adjoining San Pedro Valley County Park. The 1987 purchase of a key parcel of land makes possible the long-planned-for Montara Mountain Trail connection between these parks.

Trip 3. A Short Hike to Gray Whale Cove.

A springtime walk on a trail festooned with flowers.
- **Distance:** 2 miles round trip.
- **Time:** 1 hour.
- **Elevation Change:** Relatively level.

TRAIL NOTES

Just inside the entrance gate to McNee Ranch go left uphill (north) onto a trail that blossoms with myriad shades of spring wildflowers. On a clear, bright day the views up and down the Coast and out to sea are superb. The Gray Whale Cove Trail meanders along above Highway 1 traffic to the Gray Whale Cove parking area. Return the way you came for views south and east, especially the uncluttered, golden strand of Montara State Beach stretching a mile along the Pacific's edge.

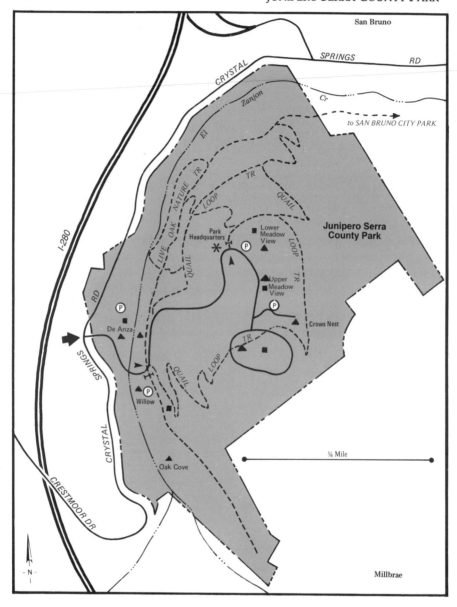

Junipero Serra County Park

This 100-acre wooded park in the curve of Junipero Serra Freeway (I-280), just minutes from homes in San Bruno, provides a quick retreat from the urban scene into protected meadows and woods. The park, situated on a long ridge that had been quarried for its Franciscan sandstone, offers several miles of trails, attractive picnic sites and a visitor center.

From the park entrance, meadows, picnic grounds and parking areas extend left and right. On weekends these are heavily used by families and groups who gravitate to the sheltered canyon. The entrance road winds uphill past park headquarters, the visitor center and the picnic tables, continuing to the very top, where still more picnic tables are nestled in a eucalyptus grove. This hilltop site offers spectacular views. From these wide views of mountains and Bay, the eye and the ear are drawn to the San Francisco Airport. Air-age, flight-minded children (and others too) delight in the bird's-eye view of planes taking off and landing.

At park headquarters, which serves as a visitor and information center, there are maps and exhibits about the park. A self-guiding nature trail through a wooded glade and a loop trail to the park's summit make good

From the upper meadow you can watch the airport.

warm-up trips before a picnic spread at one of the many picnic tables in this attractive setting.

Jurisdiction: San Mateo County—415-363-4020.
Facilities: Trails for hikers and a nature trail. Picnic areas with barbecues; covered shelters and group picnic areas available by reservation only; visitor center at park headquarters; youth-group camp by reservation.
Rules: Open 8 A.M. to posted closing hour. Fees.
Maps: San Mateo County *Junipero Serra Park*, USGS topo *Montara Mountain*.
How To Get There: From I-280: Southbound—Take Crystal Springs Rd exit, go under freeway, turn right on Crystal Springs Rd and go 0.7 0.7mile to park entrance on left. Park at lower picnic areas or continue to more parking on hilltop. Northbound—Take Hwy 35 (Skyline Blvd) exit, go 1mile to San Bruno Ave exit and turn east. Turn right (south)

on Crestmoor Dr, cross over I-280 where Crestmoor becomes Crystal Springs Rd and turn northeast. Go 0.4 mile to park entrance on right.

Trip 1. Hike to the Hilltop on the Quail Loop Trail

Gaining altitude quickly on a zigzag climb, this trip leads to flowers in grasslands and woods and to protected slopes on the park's east side.

- **Distance:** 1.4-mile loop.
- **Time:** 1 hour.
- **Elevation Gain:** 300'

TRAIL NOTES

To the right of the park entrance find the signed beginning of the Quail Loop Trail. You start climbing immediately, with oak trees overhead and patches of bright flowers at your feet. Early in spring false Solomon's seal plants droop with clusters of small white flowers, which later form panicles of red-brown berries. Switchbacks take you up the mountain, first out into an open grassy slope where sun-loving orange poppies and yellow mule ears dot the hillside. At the next switchback you are under the cover of oaks and toyons with ferns and snowberry underneath.

Toward the top of the hill you encounter Monterey pines and a large grove of mature eucalyptuses. Here the trail crosses the picnic grounds to reach the wide meadow beyond. On a clear day the brilliant Bay waters are set against the backdrop of East Bay cities and tree-topped hills. After taking in the sweep of Bay from north of San Francisco to its southern shores, continue on the Quail Loop Trail past the Crows Nest picnic shelter and bear left to descend across the meadow.

Fog rolling eastward over the hills.

At the first trail junction you could turn left to reach the visitor center at park headquarters, but instead stay on the Quail Loop Trail, which swings right. From the next trail junction the Quail Loop Trail goes left on a long traverse through woods of magnificent oaks back to the picnic areas near the park entrance.

If you would like to extend your trip, pass up the left Quail Loop Trail turnoff and continue on down the hill for about 1000 feet to the next trail junction. Park signs offer the choice of going to San Bruno City Park or back to the park entrance on the Live Oak Nature Trail. If you take the San Bruno option, this trail, following El Zanjon Creek down to the park and back, adds 3 miles to this hike.

If you ignore this side trip to San Bruno City Park, you will take the left turn to descend quickly on the Live Oak Nature Trail. In about 200 yards, take either leg of this trail to return to the meadows below.

Trip 2. Two Short Walks in the Canyon

The ½-mile Live Oak Nature Trail leaves the lower meadow parking area going left on the hillside just above El Zanjon Creek. The creek probably got its name from a Spanish word meaning "deep ditch" or "slough." Through an oak glade follow the trail in the shade of specimen liveoaks. In fall poison oak bushes put on a brilliant red-orange display in the understory. Now crossing open grasslands, you see east to Mt. Diablo, the main reference point for surveying in northern California. The trail circles back on the shady upper hillside, then drops down to return to its starting point.

Another short walk goes by the Willow Shelter to the right of the park entrance on a service road above El Zanjon Creek, past picnic tables in the shade of oak groves. From the end of this road it is just ⅓-mile back to the park entrance.

Mills Canyon Nature Area–Burlingame

Under Mexican rule Mills Canyon was part of Rancho Buri Buri, which included most of northeast San Mateo County, extending as far south as present-day City of San Mateo. In the early 1860s Darius Ogden Mills and his brother-in-law, Ansel Easton, each bought 1500 acres of Rancho Buri Buri. The division between their two holdings ran straight through this canyon. Most of Mills' estate was in contemporary Millbrae, but this land, including the upper part of this canyon which takes his name, was eventually annexed to Burlingame. The city acquired the canyon as a park and wildlife area and in 1978 volunteers built a delightful hikers-only, 2½-mile trail loop called the Ed Taylor Trail, in honor of the man who inspired the volunteers and led the first work parties. Dedicated in September 1983, the trail is maintained by local volunteers with the help of the City of Burlingame. The nature area is open from 8 A.M. to dusk. To get there from I-280 or El Camino Real in Burlingame take Trousdale Drive, then turn south on Sebastian Drive. In two blocks, turn right on Arguello Drive and go to the park entrance on the south side of the 3000 block.

A 2.5-mile loop trail through a tight little canyon in suburban Burlingame traverses open northwest slopes, then dips down into deep woods beside Mills Creek. On a summer day this canyon is a cool, sheltered place for a leisurely walk along a little watercourse, relatively unchanged since the early settlers came here. On fair winter days the southern sun shining on the northwest hillside will warm you while you enjoy the views down the canyon.

Start your trip by going downhill about 150 yards from the entrance on Arguello Drive to a small path cut into the hillside on the left. Follow this path through willows, coyote bushes and toyons for about 20 yards to a trail junction. The Creekside Trail turns off sharply to the right, while the Northwest Trail continues straight ahead on the upper hillside.

For the best views, take the Northwest Trail first, returning on the trail by the creek. On the Northwest Trail you follow a shady path under huge, high-branched live oaks. Descending along the upper edge of a tributary to Mills Creek, you then follow the north bank of Mills Creek upstream winding in and out of little ravines. After passing a tall, picturesque rock outcropping with lichen-covered ledges, you come upon a plank bridge with chain handrails that crosses to the south side of the creek, but you continue on the path upstream past mossy rocks and lacy wood ferns to a succession of miniature cascades and small pools. Before long the path to the main entrance turns uphill, and you leave this little creek, which below the park flows beside homes and schools, under streets and finally into the Bay at Burlingame's Shoreline Bird Sanctuary.

Trails on Northern Watershed Lands

San Andreas Trail

The wide, paved San Andreas Trail follows the eastern boundary of the San Francisco Watershed, giving views of the lakes and the wooded mountains. At Larkspur Drive it becomes a hiking and equestrian path, winding through the trees and underbrush in a fenced right-of-way until it reaches Hillcrest Boulevard.

Jurisdiction: San Mateo County—415-363-4020.
Facilities: Trail for hikers, bicyclists and equestrians.
Rules: Open dawn to dusk.
Map: San Mateo County *Mid-County Trails*; USGS topo *Montara Mountain*.
How To Get There: (1) North entrance: (a) Northbound—Take Skyline Blvd to a point ¼ mile south of San Bruno Ave, where signed trail entrance is on west side of road; (b) Southbound—Take Sneath Lane exit and continue south on frontage road to San Bruno Ave, where you turn right; at Skyline Blvd turn left and go ¼ mile to entrance. (2) South entrance: (a) Northbound—Take Millbrae Ave exit, go north on frontage road to Hillcrest Blvd, then west (left) under freeway to parking at trail entrance on right; (b) Southbound—Take Larkspur Dr exit, go under freeway and turn south on frontage road to Hillcrest Blvd; turn right under freeway to trail entrance.
By Bus: One of the few trails with good bus access. The south entrance can be reached by bus 33B on weekdays and Saturdays.

- **Distance:** 4.2 miles round trip.
- **Time:** 2 hours.
- **Elevation Change:** Relatively level.
- **Connecting Trails:** Proposed trail continuing north to San Bruno Ave, Sawyer Camp Trail south.

TRAIL NOTES
As you start down the 2.1-mile San Andreas Trail from the north

62   SAN ANDREAS TRAIL

Continued on map at left

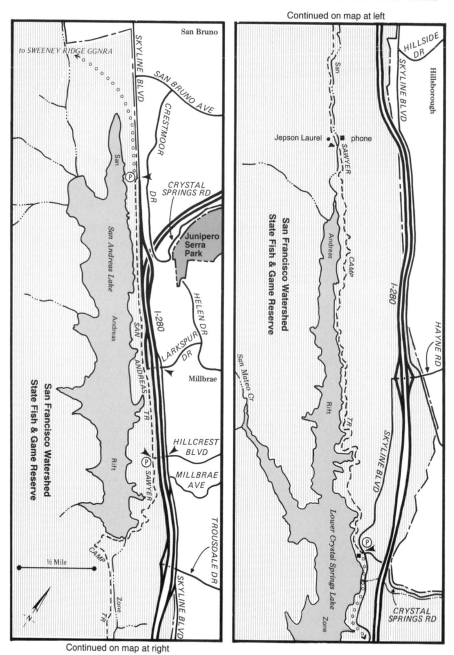

Continued on map at right

entrance, you can see directly in the west the spot on the ridge from which Gaspar de Portolá first saw San Francisco Bay in 1769. An extension of this trail will someday reach the trail to this "Discovery Site."

The San Andreas Reservoir now fills the valley, which for centuries before the coming of the Spaniards was the site of Indian villages. As

Portola's party was searching for a site for a mission and presidio in the northern part of the Peninsula, his diarist and historian, Father Francisco Palou, and his scout, Captain Fernando Rivera, went through this valley on November 30, 1774. Palou named it San Andres, honoring that saint's feast day.

Later, the earthquake-fault valley north of the present damsite was included in the Rancho Feliz, where Spaniards grazed cattle and grew wheat. There were no Spanish settlements here, reportedly because of trouble with bears. It is now surmised that the bear population may have exploded when the cattle provided an increased food supply.

With the coming of the Anglos in the 19th century the valley became a place of small farms and a dairy. In the mid-1880s farmers and herdsmen were still hunting down marauding bears and mountain lions that were attacking their cattle. San Francisco's Spring Valley Water Company began buying bought up the farms in the valley by in the late 1860s, and the lands have been kept as a watershed from that time. The bears are now gone, but the vast and still-wild watershed (also a State Fish and Game Refuge) harbors a great variety of animals, probably including wildcats and a few eagles.

The first 1½ miles of the San Andreas Trail are paved, from the Skyline Boulevard entrance to Larkspur Drive. From the end of this paved path to the Sawyer Camp Trail entrance at Hillcrest Boulevard, hikers and equestrians take a cleared and maintained 0.6-mile path in a wooded corridor next to the freeway. Runners use the trail frequently, perhaps because the forest floor is springy underfoot and the air fragrant with the scent of pine needles. Bicyclists must travel on Skyline Boulevard to Hillcrest Boulevard, where they turn right to the paved Sawyer Camp Trail.

In spite of the noisy presence of the freeway, you can enjoy the outlook to the west as the path winds through groves of Monterey pines and old plantings of cypresses, with vistas of the lake below and the western hills beyond.

Sawyer Camp Trail
Map on page 62

A historic road of singular beauty extends for 6 miles through the San Francisco Watershed lands past the sparkling San Andreas and Crystal Springs lakes. The road is paved, but open to hikers, equestrians and bicyclists only. The camp that gave the road its name was in a small flat in the San Andreas Valley where in the 1870s Leander Sawyer trained performing horses for circuses. Later he ran an inn here for travelers on their way to Half Moon Bay.

The sunny meadow by the creek where Sawyer had his camp had earlier been home to the Shalshone Indians (a tribelet of the Ohlones), who hospitably offered wild fruits and seed cakes to Gaspar de Portolá's expedition when it passed this way in 1769. During Sawyer's day, wagons pulled by teams of eight horses hauled wood over the road on their way to San Francisco and stage coaches used it as an alternative route to Half Moon Bay.

When San Francisco took over the Watershed lands, narrow, winding Sawyer Camp Road was kept open, and later fenced on either side for protection of the Watershed. In 1978 San Mateo County closed the road to motorized vehicles, and it is now Sawyer Camp Trail.

Jurisdiction: San Mateo County—415-363-4020.

Facilities: Trail for hikers, bicyclists and equestrians. Picnic tables, restrooms, water at Jepson Laurel picnic area and north end of trail, and telephones.

Rules: Open dawn to ½ hour after sunset.

Maps: San Mateo County *Jogging, Exercise and Bicycle Trails* and USGS topos *Montara Mountain* and *San Mateo.*

How To Get There: By Car From I-280: (1) North entrance at Hillcrest Blvd: (a) Southbound—Take the Larkspur Dr exit and go south on Skyline Blvd to Hillcrest Blvd, then west under freeway to trail entrance on right; (b) Northbound—Take Millbrae Ave exit and go north on Skyline Blvd, then west on Hillcrest Blvd to trail entrance. (2) South entrance at Crystal Springs Rd: (a) Southbound—Take Hayne Rd exit and go south on Skyline Blvd to parking beside entrance gate on west side of road; (b) Northbound—Take Bunker Hill Dr exit, cross over freeway, then go north on Skyline Blvd past Crystal Springs Dam to entrance gate.

By Bicycle: Use the same approaches from Skyline Blvd as for cars.

- **Distance:** 6 miles one way.
- **Time:** 3½ hours. A car shuttle is practical here. Shorter round trips on part of the trail from either end make good hikes.
- **Elevation Loss:** 400' from north to south.
- **Connecting Trails:** San Andreas Trail north. Crystal Springs Trail south. Note: The first 1.6 miles of the Crystal Springs Trail south of the Sawyer Camp Trail are not built at this writing, but the trail resumes at the Hwy 92/Skyline Boulevard intersection.

TRAIL NOTES

Entering the trail at the north end, you descend for the first ¾ mile from Skyline Boulevard to San Andreas Lake and its dam. The woods and lake are a pleasant introduction to the trail. Summer winds often ruffle the lake, and drifts of fog sweep over the hills. On the far side of the dam a commemorative plaque marks the hundredth anniversary of the dam's completion in 1869. The trail heads south along a shady walk between the creek and a hillside of bay trees. Fern-covered banks bloom with purple iris and scarlet columbine. Look here for the very rare shrub leatherwood, with its small yellow blossoms. It is found in only a few places in San Mateo County (one of them is Edgewood Park). The Indians used its tough, flexible branches for lacings.

In a small clearing along the way, about 30 yards west of the trail, is the venerable Jepson Bay Laurel, thought to be one of the oldest and largest in the state. It was named in honor of Willis Jepson in 1923. He was one of California's most noted botanists. The flowery little meadow around the tree was popular as a picnic spot in Mexican and early California times. Today the tree is fenced to protect it, and there is a picnic area nearby, and once again picnickers are enjoying this retreat beside the famous bay tree.

Here and there you will come to benches beside the trail for a place to rest, picnic, or enjoy the sound of a stream or a view of the lake. At about its halfway point the trail crosses San Andreas Creek where it enters Lower Crystal Springs Lake. From here on, it borders the east side of the lake, giving a succession of views out over the bright waters to the wooded Watershed hills. The Peninsula's own "Lake District" has a special enchantment whether mists are shrouding the mountains or the lakes are reflecting a blue sky.

A few hawks sail overhead. Grebes, ducks, and other waterfowl bob on the water, and the oaks by the trail are alive with countless small bird—countless except to the Audubon Society, which enumerates the species meticulously in its annual Christmas bird count; a recent count totaled 190 species. Bring your binoculars and favorite bird guide.

Along the road cuts you will see the greenish-gray serpentine, a rock that occurs through the foothills in San Mateo County. It is frequently found in major earthquake fault zones, and is associated with some of our finest wildflower displays.

The south end of the trail is on Skyline Boulevard at Crystal Springs Road, close to the Crystal Springs Dam across the gorge of San Mateo Creek. This is a good starting point for a 3-mile walk north by the lake, with vistas of the shimmering waters around each bend. Your return trip brings you new views as you retrace your steps. Walk here in late winter when clouds are moving across the sky and sunshine alternates with light showers. The hills are already green, drifts of magenta Indian warriors bloom under the trees, and the first buds of iris appear. This is one of the Peninsula's best walks for any time of the year.

The Sawyer Camp Trail is good for an early-morning family ride.

On the San Andreas Trail.

68

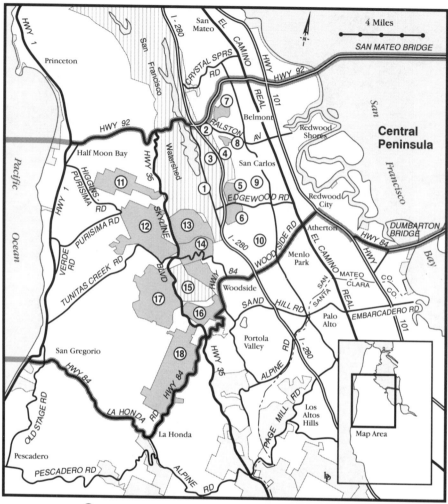

① Numbers in circles refer to Central Peninsula text

Central Peninsula

Central Peninsula
From Highway 92 to Highway 84

Circled # on Map	Park or Trail Name in Text
1	Crystal Springs Trail
2	Ralston Trail/I-280 Overcrossing
3	Sheep Camp Trail
4	Cross Country Running Course
5	Pulgas Ridge Open Space Preserve
6	Edgewood County Park
7	Laurelwood Park
8	Waterdog Lake Park and Trail/John S. Brooks Memorial Open Space Preserve
9	Big Canyon and Eaton Parks
10	Stulsaft Park
11	Burleigh Murray Ranch State Park
12	Purisima Creek Redwoods Open Space Preserve
13	Phleger Estate
14	Huddart County Park
15	Ridge/Skyline Trail
16	Wunderlich County Park
17	El Corte de Madera Open Space Preserve
18	La Honda Creek Open Space Preserve

Central Peninsula
From Highway 92 to Highway 84

Trails on Southern San Francisco Watershed Lands

Crystal Springs Trail

Bordering Upper Crystal Springs Lake, this trail traverses the linear valley on the San Andreas Rift Zone known by the Spaniards as Cañada de Raimundo, then continues through a corner of the Watershed and up through Huddart Park to the Skyline. Views of lakes, mountains and hills make this a beautiful trail for short trips along its segments. Connections with trails east and west make it a useful route for longer expeditions. The trail is part of San Mateo County's north-south trail corridor, and it provides access to the regional Bay Area Ridge Trail.

The Crystal Springs Trail follows the easement of the old California Riding and Hiking Trail between the boundary fence of the Watershed and Cañada Road, from Highway 92 to Huddart Park and up to the Skyline. Although the trail easement extends north to the Sawyer Camp Trail, a 1.6-mile segment from Highway 92 to Bunker Hill Road is not built.

The nearly 10-mile Crystal Springs Trail is covered in this book in three sections: (1) from Cañada Road at Highway 92 to Edgewood and Cañada roads, (2) from Edgewood Road to Huddart Park, and (3) through the park to the Skyline. This last segment is covered in the section on Huddart Park.

At the Pulgas Water Temple grounds there is a small parking area. No roadside parking is allowed within a mile on either side. However, the lovely water temple and its reflecting pool and grounds, open to pedestrians and bicyclists, make a fine destination from either end of the trail.

Jurisdiction: San Mateo County—415-363-4020.
Facilities: Trail for hikers and equestrians.
Rules: Open from 8 A.M. to ½ hour after sunset. No bicycles.

Maps: San Mateo County *Mid-County Trails*; USGS topos *San Mateo* and *Woodside*.

How To Get There: From I-280: (1) North entrance: (a) Southbound— Take Half Moon Bay exit to Skyline Blvd (Hwy 35), go south to Hwy 92, and then turn east. Turn south on Cañada Rd and go 0.2 mile to trail entrance on west side of road just opposite the Ralston Trail/I-280 Overcrossing Trail junction; (b) Northbound—Take Hwy 92 exit west to Cañada Rd. Turn south for 0.2 mile to trail entrance. (2) South entrance: Take Edgewood Rd exit, go west to Edgewood/Cañada Rd intersection, where there is parking. No parking at Raymundo Drive cul-de-sac entrance to Huddart Park. Note: Cañada Rd is closed to motor-vehicle traffic from the intersection of Hwy 92 to Edgewood Rd for "Bicycle Sunday," a popular event held on the first, third and fourth Sundays in the months of April through October.

Continued on map at left

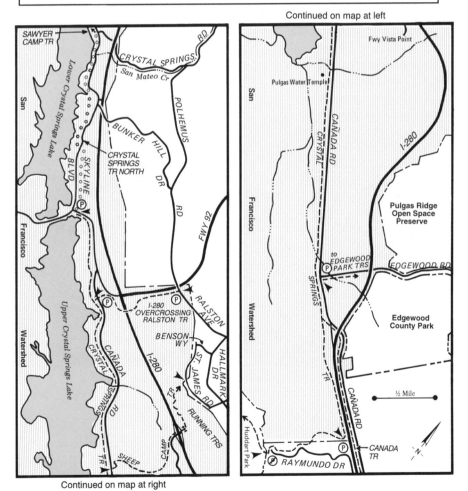

Continued on map at right

Crystal Springs Trail, and Ralston Trail/I-280 Overcrossing

Trip 1. Highway 92 to Edgewood and Cañada Roads

The first part of the trail to the Water Temple is close to the lake, where you can enjoy the blue waters and the flocks of birds. South from the Water Temple the trail takes you through the broad, parklike Watershed valley past spring wild-flowers against a backdrop of the wooded slopes of the Santa Cruz Mountains.

- **Distance:** 4 miles one way.
- **Time:** 2 hours.
- **Elevation Gain:** Relatively level.

TRAIL NOTES

Start your hike by going down the path departing from a point on Cañada Road 0.2 mile south of Highway 92 and just across the road from the western entrance to the Ralston Trail/I-280 Overcrossing. You can also walk north along this lakeside trail as far as the intersection of Highway 92 and Skyline Boulevard. This trail at times swings away from the road, coming close to the lake, or leads down below road level through oak groves.

The lake is a resting place for water birds in the Pac]ific Flyway, so take your binoculars. Even without them you will easily identify the big, brownish Canada geese that winter here. Flocks of them are often gathered along the shores. In the early morning and evening you may see herds of deer grazing in the fields or drinking at the water's edge.

Through this temple with its classic colonnades rush Sierra waters before flowing into Crystal Springs Lakes.

Soon after the trail leaves the lakeside it passes the point where the Sheep Camp Trail joins the east side of Cañada Road. From here to the Pulgas Water Temple the trail is on a bank above the road. The Water

Temple grounds, open to pedestrians and bicyclists from 8 A.M. to 4:30 P.M., include lawns for picnicking and sunning, and the Water Temple itself. At the end of a long reflecting pool is the classic little Pulgas Water Temple, where waters from high in the Sierra thunder into the sluiceway to the Crystal Springs lakes. Inscribed around the pediment are words from the Book of Isaiah, "I give waters in the wilderness and rivers in the desert to give drink to my people."

Continuing south you see on the valley floor to the west open fields and groves of stately oaks, a part of the Filoli estate, which once belonged to W. B. Bourn, president of the Spring Valley Water Company. The name for the estate was coined by Bourn from "Fight," "Love," and "Live" coined from "Fight for a just cause, love your fellow man, and live a good life." A later owner, Mrs. William Roth, changed the "fight" to "fidelity." Completed in 1917, Filoli was the last of the great mansions built in San Mateo County.

Bought by the Roth family in 1934, the estate was given by Mrs. Roth to the National Trust for Historic Preservation in 1975. It is now operated by the Filoli Center, a nonprofit organization. The mansion is hardly visible from the trail, but its beautiful formal gardens and the mansion itself, as well as its nature trails, can be visited on tours by arrangement with the Filoli Center.

From the Filoli gates our trail passes more oak-bordered meadows to reach the stone gates at the foot of Edgewood Road, the end of this trip. From there the Crystal Springs Trail continues on to Huddart Park.

Trip 2. Edgewood and Cañada Roads to Huddart Park

A short trip over a hill through the Watershed and down to West Union Creek in Huddart Park.

- **Distance:** 2.4 miles one way.
- **Time:** 1¼ hours.
- **Elevation Gain:** 200′

TRAIL NOTES

As you pass the stone gates at the foot of Edgewood Road, fields extend on either side of Cañada Road. Come this way in April and May to see some of the Peninsula's most dazzling displays of wildflowers. They thrive on the thin, magnesium-rich soil over serpentine rock outcroppings. Swatches of intense blue larkspur bloom against great drifts of cream cups, goldfields, poppies, lupines and owl's clover. Admire these flowers from the roadside paths, photograph or paint them, but do not cross the fence and walk among them. The fields have been set aside as a preserve in the Watershed, and these flowers, if left undisturbed, will continue to bloom year after year to amaze and delight our great-grandchildren.

The Crystal Springs Trail enters a redwood grove near West Union Creek.

Where Cañada Road turns east to cross under the freeway, the trail continues south beside the freeway for nearly a mile between wire fences, the freeway on one side and the Watershed lands on the other. It's not so attractive a stretch for walkers, but the cinderpath surface is popular with equestrians and joggers.

The Crystal Springs Trail emerges from the cinderpath at Runnymede Road at the Woodside Town boundary. From here another fenced trail goes across a corner of the Watershed and south on an easement to Raymundo Drive. From this point walk west on Raymundo Drive 0.2 mile to its cul-de-sac.

The trail leaves the south side of the cul-de-sac, descending into oak woods on switchbacks for 0.3 mile to the redwood groves beside West Union Creek. Here a footbridge takes you across to forested Huddart Park. The Crystal Springs Trail continues upstream by the creek, then turns up through the park on the 3½-mile trip to the Skyline described in the section on Huddart Park. Access to the Phleger Estate also is possible from this trail.

For groups with a backpack excursion in mind, there is a trail camp (by reservation) about 1¼ miles up the trail on the park's secluded north side. From there you can explore the miles of trail in the park, or climb up the mountainside to the Ridge/Skyline Trail and across to Purisima Creek Redwoods Open Space Preserve.

The Ralston Trail/I-280 Overcrossing
Map on page 71

A wide, mile-long pedestrian, equestrian and bicycle path and free-way overpass crosses high above 10-lane Junipero Serra Freeway, I-280, at its interchange with Highway 92. It connects the bike path on Ralston Avenue in Belmont to Cañada Road north of the Sheep Camp Trail junction.

Jurisdiction: San Mateo County—415-363-4020.
Facilities: Pedestrian, equestrian and bicycle path.
Rules: Open sunrise to sunset.
Map USGS topo *San Mateo*.
How To Get There: From I-280: (1) East entrance—Take Hwy 92 exit east, then take Ralston Ave exit. At first traffic signal, ⅛ mile east of Ralston/Polhemus/Hwy 92 interchange, park on south side of Ralston Ave. (2) West entrance: (a) Northbound—Take Hwy 92 west to Cañada Rd. Go south on it 0.2 mile to gate on east side. Parking is on either side of road. (b) Southbound—Take Half Moon Bay exit to Skyline Blvd (Hwy 35) and continue south to Hwy 92, then turn east to Cañada Rd. Go south on it 0.2 mile to gate on east side.

- **Distance:** 2 miles round trip.
- **Time:** ½ hour.
- **Elevation Loss:** 125′
- **Connecting Trail:** Crystal Springs Trail at Cañada Road.

TRAIL NOTES

This is no quiet country trail, but a paved, fenced path and concrete structure vaulting over the freeway. It is the only way to cross the freeway on foot, horse or bicycle at this point. From Ralston Avenue the path goes through a gate to the Watershed lands and descends along chaparral-covered slopes. It curves south and then rises steeply to the arched structure over the freeway. A swift drop on the other side and a sharp right turn take you down to Cañada Road. On the west side you can pick up the roadside Crystal Springs Trail.

An interesting 6.2-mile circle hike starting at the Ralston Avenue entrance combines the Overcrossing Trail, part of the Crystal Springs Trail, the Sheep Camp Trail and the upper part of the Waterdog Lake Trail. When the Waterdog Lake Trail reaches Hallmark Drive, walk north on it to Ralston Avenue, then west on the Ralston bike path to where you started. These trails are described more fully in their separate chapters.

Sheep Camp Trail

Map on page 91

This walk from the eastern crest of the Watershed winds downhill above Crystal Springs Lake to cross under I-280. On the far side the trail meanders through sheltered oak groves and small meadows to join the Crystal Springs Trail at Cañada Road.

Jurisdiction: San Mateo County—415-363-4020.
Facilities: Trail for hikers and equestrians.
Rules: Open 8 A.M. to sunset. No dogs or bicycles.
Maps: USGS topos *San Mateo* and *Woodside*.
How To Get There: From I-280 take Hwy 92 east to Ralston Ave, turn south on Hallmark Dr, west on Benson Wy and south on St. James Rd. Gate to Watershed is on right.

- **Distance:** 2 miles round trip.
- **Time:** 1 hour.
- **Elevation Loss:** 400'
- **Connecting Trails:** Waterdog Lake Trail east to Belmont; Crystal Springs Trail north to Highway 92 and south to Water Temple and Huddart Park; Cross Country Running Course and Watershed boundary trails on the east.

TRAIL NOTES

Enter through the green gates to the Watershed. Walk straight ahead on the graveled road over the grassy slope to the sign *Sheep Camp Trail. Cañada Road 1.6 km.* No sheep are in sight, but around the bend is a view of eight concrete lanes of the Junipero Serra Freeway, which would surprise its namesake, the Franciscan Father who trod a more modest path between his missions.

Keep going downhill on the road and cross under the freeway. As the road starts up the hill to the vista point, go instead through a gate on the right. From here a dirt-and-gravel road takes you away from the freeway roar into quiet oak woods with small meadows. About ½ mile from the gate you reach Cañada Road. On the far side is the Crystal Springs Trail, which goes south to Huddart Park and north to Highway 92. Just 0.4 mile south is the Pulgas Water Temple, a pleasant picnic destination.

For an interesting 6.2-mile loop trip on the Sheep Camp Trail and other trails in this area, see the description of the Ralston Trail/I-280 Overcrossing, page 75. Someday it may be possible to make a 9-mile loop hike using the Sheep Camp, Crystal Springs, Edgewood, Pulgas Ridge and Watershed boundary trails. Only a short connection from Pulgas Ridge Open Space Preserve to the Watershed boundary trail is missing at this writing.

Cross Country Running Course
Map on page 91

Considered one of the best running courses in the Bay Area, this course has a location on the eastern crest of the Watershed that makes it a good walking trail as well. Here is a chance to check your pace on carefully measured and marked loop paths.

Jurisdiction: San Francisco Water Department; maintained by College of San Mateo.
Facilities: Trails for runners, joggers and hikers. Drinking fountains.
Rules: Open to runners, joggers and hikers except during competition events. No dogs, no bicycles.
Maps: City of Belmont *Jogging Trails*, available at the Parks Department, USGS topo *San Mateo*.
How To Get There: From I-280 take Hwy 92 east. Take Ralston Ave exit, turn right on Hallmark Dr and past Wakefield Dr continue to Hallmark Park on right. Park on street. Enter course on path by tennis courts between Wakefield Dr and Paddington Ct.

- **Distance:** 0.5 to 7.5 miles.
- **Time:** 15 minutes to 4 hours, or as long as you like.
- **Elevation Change:** Relatively level.
- **Connecting Trails:** Sheep Camp Trail west to Cañada Road, Waterdog Lake Trail east to Belmont and Watershed boundary service roads to the west and southeast.

TRAIL NOTES

This championship course was started some 25 years ago by two College of San Mateo coaches. Although the course had to be rerouted because of the construction of I-280, its popularity has continued to increase. Local, regional and state high-school and community-college competitions are held during the months of September, October and November.

Care of the course is under the direction of the College of San Mateo track and cross-country coaches. Volunteers do cleanup, mowing and course conditioning. Walkers, hikers and joggers can use the course, but should respect competitions by staying off the course during races. Dogs are not allowed on Watershed lands and are particularly unwelcome along the running course. No smoking is allowed on Watershed lands.

From the start of the course at Hallmark Park the paths extend in loops west and south. The openness of the rolling hillsides and the views over Crystal Springs lakes to the Santa Cruz Mountains make this an exhilarating walk at any time of the year. In spring, poppies, lupines, daisies, blue-eyed grass and brodiaeas bloom at your feet. In summer, coastal breezes cool what could be a hot, sunny path. And with these breezes come drifts of fog curling over the mountains to the west.

For other walks along the Watershed ridge from Hallmark Park you can take the graveled service roads of the San Francisco Water Department that follow the Watershed boundary. Good for walks in wet weather, these surfaced roads extend more than a mile west and southeast. Going west from Hallmark Park you will come to the upper entrance to the Sheep Camp Trail at the St. James Road watershed gate.

Foothills Parks Adjoining Southern San Francisco Watershed

Pulgas Ridge Open Space Preserve

In the foothills west of San Carlos and just north of Edgewood Park is the 293-acre Midpeninsula Regional Open Space District preserve featuring a broad central meadow flanked by two wooded canyons. Cordilleras Creek originates in the preserve's canyons and then flows east to the Bay near the end of Whipple Road, picking up volume from the streams in Edgewood Park.

Formerly the site of a tuberculosis hospital owned by the City of San Francisco, the area was purchased by MROSD in 1983. Residents of San Carlos approved a local tax on their assessed valuation to help fund the purchase.

Jurisdiction: Midpeninsula Regional Open Space District—415-691-1200.
Facilities: Trails for hikers, bicyclists and equestrians. Cordilleras Trail accessible to wheelchairs.
Rules: Open dawn to dusk. Dogs allowed on leash, except in designated off-leash areas. Bicyclists on paved road only.
Maps: MROSD *Pulgas Ridge O S P*, USGS topo *Woodside*.
How To Get There: From I-280 take Edgewood Rd exit and go east 1 mile. Turn left on Crestview Dr and immediately left again on Edmonds Rd. Around first curve park at roadside turnout.

Trip 1. A Loop Trip to High Meadowlands

This trip on a surfaced road takes hikers and bicyclists to a grassy meadow for picnicking, sketching or kite-flying.

- **Distance:** 3-mile loop.
- **Time:** 1½ hours.
- **Elevation Gain:** 400′

TRAIL NOTES

From parking on Edmonds Road, walk through the entrance gate onto the 0.6-mile, fenced Cordilleras Trail on an easement beside the San Francisco Water Department road. This surfaced Cordilleras Trail, accessible to wheelchairs, now continues through a little glade on the east side of Cordilleras Creek, where Boy Scouts have installed a bench. For this trip take the existing paved road, the Hassler Trail, which curves left to reach the gated preserve entrance, and then meander uphill to circle the high meadow, where once the hospital buildings stood.

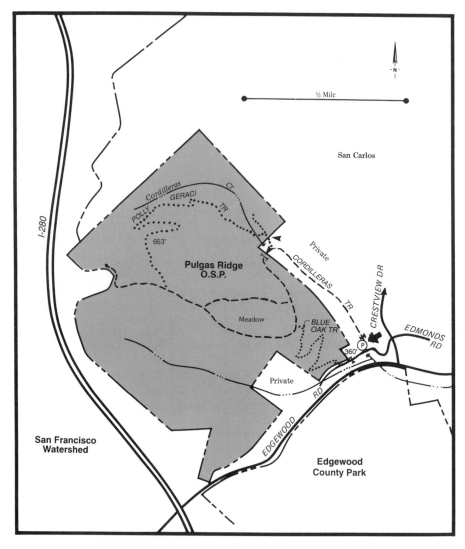

Pulgas Ridge Open Space Preserve

This sloping meadow, capped by tall eucalyptus, rimmed with oak woodland and filled with wildflowers in spring, is a place to picnic and enjoy the views of San Francisco Bay through a notch in the foothills. South are Edgewood Park's grasslands and wooded hilltop; west are the forested Santa Cruz Mountains.

In this area MROSD inaugurated in 1996 an experimental off-leash dog run fenced with split-rails. Signs caution both dogs and dog owners to be on their best behavior.

From the meadow walk farther along the paved road to the top of the preserve to look into the canyons on both sides of the ridge and out to San Francisco Bay. Then turn back and follow the road down around the other side of the meadow to return to the preserve entrance.

Trip 2. A Hikers Loop Trip

A loop trip for hikers only and their dog companions.
- **Distance:** 2½-mile loop.
- **Time:** 1½ hours.
- **Elevation Gain:** 100'

TRAIL NOTES

An alternate route to the ridgetop, the 1-mile Polly Geraci Trail, for hikers only, leaves the valley from the Cordilleras Trail at its junction with the paved road. The trail follows the creek near its west bank and then ascends on switchbacks through an oak forest. Ferns cover the hillside, and shade-loving flowers blossom here in spring.

As the trail rounds a ridge, leaving the creek far below, madrones and manzanitas appear in a tall chaparral cover. The ridge across the canyon comes into sight, along with rows of houses in a ridgetop subdivision in neighboring San Carlos. Then the trail rises to meet the road at the top of the preserve's high meadow.

Here you meet the Hassler Trail, a paved road, and follow it downhill through the dogs-off-leash area to the Blue Oak Trail (hikers only). Take this trail to the right (east) down switchbacks through a lovely, mixed oak forest. When the Blue Oak Trail emerges at the entrance road, turn left (northeast) to the parking area.

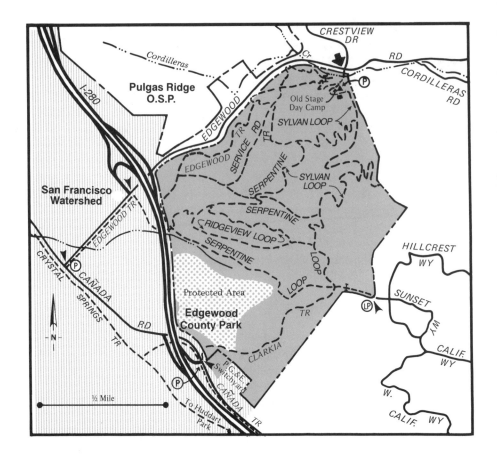

Edgewood County Park and Natural Preserve

This San Mateo County park of hilltops, gentle meadows, oak groves and canyons faces the green expanse of the Skyline ridge to the west and looks out over the Bay plain to the east. It adjoins Pulgas Ridge Open Space Preserve just across Edgewood Road, and the southern San Francisco Watershed lands across I-280. You can picnic here on a knoll listening to meadowlarks in the grass, climb a hill or walk in cool, secluded glades.

Edgewood Park's 467 acres, crowned by a wooded hill rising steeply from the surrounding meadows, had been set aside for a state college. After years of negotiation the land was finally acquired for a park by San Mateo County and the Midpeninsula Regional Open Space District in 1980. The county originally planned a golf course on the park's grasslands with trails on the periphery, but in 1994 changed plans and declared Edgewood a park and natural preserve. A new master plan for Edgewood Park, prepared by a citizen/staff committee in 1996, is under review.

From the park's main entrance on Edgewood Road, more than 7 miles of trail lead through wooded, fern-filled canyons to the rolling grasslands that surround the central wooded ridge. Beyond the entrance near the trailhead are a day camp and an amphitheatre beside Cordilleras Creek. Close by are attractive picnic sites nestled on terraces under the shade of huge oaks and redwoods, open to the public except during summer day-camp periods. Other entrances also open onto trails that reach the flower fields, the wooded hilltop and the northern canyons of the park.

This is a park for all seasons. Its closeness to the hundreds of thousands who live in neighboring communities makes it a good choice for short outings. In winter, rain-washed air and north winds bring clear views and cold days for brisk hiking. In spring, the meadows underlain with serpentine are thick with goldfields, poppies, cream cups, lupines and owl's clover. From March to June, volunteer members of the California Native Plant Society lead free weekend wildflower walks. On summer and fall days, shady oak groves provide good picnicking and inviting walks on the wooded northeast slopes.

Jurisdiction: San Mateo County—415-363-4020.
Facilities: Trails for hikers and equestrians. Picnic areas with barbecues, restrooms, day camp and amphitheatre.
Rules: Open from 8 A.M. to sunset. No dogs or bicycles.
Maps: San Mateo County *Edgewood Park* and USGS topo *Woodside*.
How To Get There: From I-280: (1) Main entrance on Edgewood Rd at Old Stage Day Camp—Take the Edgewood Rd exit and go east 1 mile; turn right at Edgewood Park and Day Camp sign, cross bridge to park. Overflow parking uses unpaved area beside Edgewood Rd. (2) West of I-280 on Edgewood Rd—Take Edgewood Rd exit, go west under freeway. Park on south side of Edgewood Rd near freeway or at Cañada and Edgewood roads. (3) Cañada Rd—Take Edgewood Rd exit, go west under freeway, turn south on Cañada Rd, go through freeway underpass and park beside Cañada Rd opposite PG&E switchyard. The Clarkia Trail entrance is immediately north of this installation. (4) Sunset Way—Follow directions for (3) above, but continue on Cañada Rd 1.2 more miles and turn left on Jefferson Avenue. Turn left on California Way (not West California Way) and then right on Sunset Way to park entrance at Hillcrest Way. Limited parking beside road.

Three Trips from the Park's Main Entrance

Starting from the Old Stage Day Camp entrance, you enter the park across a narrow old bridge over Cordilleras Creek framed by spreading valley oaks. Just beyond the bridge a rustic brown sign points to Old Stage Road, a section of a mid-1800s route to lumber mills and camps in Woodside. Ahead is the parking area and the trailheads for the Edgewood and Sylvan trails.

Trip 1. Loop Trip to the Wooded Hilltop That Crowns This Park

Take this trip across the park's wooded ridge for views over the Santa Cruz Mountains and out to the Bay.
- **Distance:** 5-mile loop.
- **Time:** 2½ hours.
- **Elevation Gain:** 600'

TRAIL NOTES

Start uphill on the Edgewood Trail to the right of the parking area on switchbacks that take you up the north side of a steep canyon. Shading your way are woods of buckeye, madrone and oak, with an understory of toyon, snowberry and poison oak.

Skirting a sloping meadow accented by immense spreading oaks, you continue uphill, crossing a service road to stay on the shady, tree-lined Edgewood Trail. At the next junction take the Serpentine Trail to your left. Now you traverse the steep canyon's rim and look across it to the southern San Francisco Bay and the East Bay hills. From a rocky outcrop beside the trail you can see into the canyon where once stood a Victorian house, part of the 1915 San Francisco Panama Pacific Exposition. It was disassembled and barged down to Redwood City, then reassembled on this site. Only the foundations of the house and vestiges of the garden walls remain today, artfully used to support terraced areas of the day-camp and picnic areas.

Continue around the hillside on the Serpentine Trail to its first intersection with the Sylvan Trail. If you turn left here, you will return to the park entrance and make this a 1½-mile loop trip. But if you stay on the Serpentine Trail, you first cross a high grassy plateau, then pass a turnoff to the Ridgeview Loop Trail on the right and another Sylvan Trail turnoff on the left. Unseen in the tall grasses are the homes of gophers, field mice and other rodents that make up the diet of the hawks you may see soaring overhead.

After the second Sylvan Trail junction you round two bends, leave the Serpentine Trail and turn right onto the Ridgeview Loop Trail. Under a canopy of live oaks and buckeyes you soon come to a fork in the trail. Take the right-hand fork and walk on over the wooded crown of this hill and out into the chaparral. From a wide clearing, views stretch up and down along fifty miles of the San Andreas Rift Zone. Looking northwest you see a vista relatively unchanged from early times (disregarding the multi-laned concrete ribbon by which you reached this idyllic spot). In San Francisco Watershed lands you see thousands of acres of unbroken forests, from the Skyline ridge to the lakes along the fault line.

To continue on your trip, follow the Ridgeview Loop Trail around the hill, bearing left at each trail intersection. Then, contouring around the south side of the hill, you look down on the serpentine grasslands, aglow with dazzling wildflower displays in spring.

At a saddle on the ridge you complete the Ridgeview Loop. Walk straight ahead for another 500 feet and turn left onto the Serpentine Trail at the junction where you left it. Along this short stretch of trail look for clumps of the low-growing blue-eyed grass, which blooms from early spring into summer.

Almost 3 miles from the beginning of your trip, you come to the Sylvan Trail on your right. Take it for a different way back. Around wide switchbacks you descend deep into a steep canyon. A spring high up the headwall feeds a perennial stream, which you cross and then follow along its fern-covered banks.

Picnic tables at the Old Stage Day Camp.

Emerging from the canyon, you pass the other leg of the Sylvan Trail on your left. Go straight ahead and downhill for 0.2 mile. Then pass to the right of the Old Stage Day Camp or take the lefthand trail, which curves around the camp's picnic tables and barbecues on the landscaped borders of Cordilleras Creek. The park entrance is just beyond the day camp.

For a shorter route to the park's central ridge take the Edgewood Trail just below Edgewood Road on the west side of I-280. This trail goes down the embankment to a fenced trail leading to a passageway under the freeway. After going through the passage, bear left at a service road. In

200 feet turn right and follow the trail to the Ridgeview Loop. Turn either left or right to circle the hilltop. This makes a 2¾-mile loop trip with an elevation gain of 430′.

Trip 2. A Summer Supper Hike

Some warm summer evening, take the Edgewood Trail out to the grassy knolls northwest of the park's wooded hilltop.
- **Distance:** 2 miles round trip.
- **Time:** 1 hour.
- **Elevation Gain:** 400′

TRAIL NOTES

Starting from the trailhead at the main park entrance, follow the Edgewood Trail and continue past the Serpentine Trail junction. Then, for the next ½ mile, there is little change of elevation as the trail contours around several steep-sided ravines.

When you get out into the grasslands, choose a trailside picnic spot with a view of the western hills. If your picnic supper is accompanied by a flutelike bird call, it may be the meadowlark's song filling the evening air. These once-common, pale-yellow birds with a black cravat are becoming rare as development continues to diminish their grasslands habitat.

Rare, too, except in some protected grasslands, are the lemon-yellow blossoms of mariposa lilies, which dot these meadows in early summer. Their centers blotched with magenta, these delicate, bowl-shaped flowers bloom in surprising profusion for flowers of such elegance.

The rosy glow of the summer sun setting over the Skyline ridge will remind you to allow time for the 1-mile hike back to your car in the lowering light.

Trip 3. A Shady Canyon Hike

Measured and marked as an exercise loop, the Sylvan Trail Loop circles the canyon south of the day camp. In shade for most of the way, it is a favorite warm-day trip for hikers and runners.
- **Distance:** 2-mile loop.
- **Time:** 1½ hours.
- **Elevation Gain:** 500′

TRAIL NOTES

This loop, closed to equestrians, starts by going straight ahead uphill from the parking area on the left of the greensward. In less than 0.2 mile you turn right on the Sylvan Trail and zigzag up the north side of the steep canyon. These switchbacks, at least 8 of them, take you through shady woodland to the edge of a high meadow, where you meet the

Serpentine Trail. Turn left on it, and weave in and out of the woods for ½ mile.

Now pick up the Sylvan Trail on your left and follow its wide switch-backs downhill. This trail at first descends an exposed, south-facing slope, but soon drops into deep woods. In season, watch for some of spring's first flowers, the deep-red Indian warriors, blooming under patches of oaks. Watch too for the part of the Sylvan Trail that arcs far back into the canyon to a perennial stream crossing. If you linger for a moment here in the depths of this canyon on the urban fringe, the only sounds to break the stillness are those of flowing water and woodland birds.

Then, continuing on for a few minutes, you pass the other leg of the Sylvan Trail and go straight ahead to the park entrance.

Trip 4. Trails to the Serpentine Meadows

For a spring wildflower pilgrimage take these short trails and glory in masses of colorful blossoms.

- **Distance:** 0.5 mile to 3½ miles round trip.
- **Time:** 1-2 hours, or linger as long as you can.
- **Elevation Gain:** From 100' to 400'

TRAIL NOTES

Either the Edgewood or the Clarkia Trail leads to the park service road, one leg of the Serpentine Loop that crosses the main flower display. The quickest way to reach the flower fields is from the trail below Edge-wood Road just west of I-280. This trail goes abruptly down an embank-ment to connect with the trail from Cañada and Edgewood roads.

A serpentine meadow in Edgewood Park.

Take the fenced trail south to the passage under the freeway and thence to the service road, the Serpentine Loop, in a grassy swale. Walk east for the best wildflower displays. Around the outcroppings of serpentine you will see goldfields, tidytips, cream cups, owl's clover, lupines and many more annuals. Where there is more moisture, look for blue larkspur. Bring your flower guide.

These serpentine meadows produce lovely carpets of flowers each spring. They are also home to the very rare checkerspot butterfly, found only here and on the extensions of this meadow west of the freeway, on San Bruno Mountain and on Jasper Ridge Biological Preserve. The presence of this butterfly, now on the federal list of threatened species, is marked on the accompanying map as protected area, the main habitat of the checkerspot.

If you have the time, walk along the length of the Serpentine Loop road and up on the Ridgeview Loop Trail, from where you can look down on the sea of color. In the shaded woodlands of this loop you will find different species, such as red Indian warriors, white milkmaids and blue hound's-tongue.

If you enter from Cañada Road, the Clarkia Trail contours around a south-facing hillside past some large serpentine outcrops and through a scattering of oak trees to reach the east end of the service road, the Serpentine Loop. As its name implies, you will find a show of magenta-colored clarkias here in early summer. This 0.75-mile trail, closed to horses in winter, circles the grasslands, and makes a good starting point for a trans-park trip.

Another entrance to the park's flower fields is from Sunset Way, but there is little parking there. For those with limited walking ability, this entrance offers a short route to an overlook of the colorful display.

White Fritillary in Edgewood.

City Parks and Trails in the Foothills

Many beautiful parks, large and small, dot the Peninsula landscape east of I-280. Nestled among residential neighborhoods, they provide a welcome green space, attractive children's play equipment and welcome meeting places within walking distance of many suburban dwellers. In previous editions of *Peninsula Trails* we described walks in Burlingame's Mills Canyon Nature Area, San Mateo's Laurelwood Park, Big Canyon Park in San Carlos and Redwood City's Stulsaft Park. In this third edition of *Peninsula Trails* we again call attention to these pretty havens of open space ranging from 40 to 250 acres and remind our readers of their local interest.

A special feature of this third edition is a complete write-up of those city parks in the foothills that connect to county, regional, state or federal parks. Belmont's Waterdog Lake Park and John S. Brooks Memorial Open Space is the only park that answers that criterion in the northern and central Peninsula. As San Mateo County and its cities plan for the future, it is quite possible that links will be created, thus forming a vast complex of public open space accessible to Bayside residents on foot, horse or bicycle trails.

In the area covered in this guide book trails from parks in four towns on the southern Peninsula—Portola Valley, Palo Alto, Los Altos Hills and Cupertino—reach parks and preserves in the foothills or on the Skyline. Some are paved off-road trails paralleling roads and others are unpaved paths that wander through residential areas, but all pass pockets of woodland, grassy meadows or small neighborhood open spaces.

Laurelwood Park—San Mateo

How To Get There: From I-280 take Hwy 92 east, exit east on De Anza Blvd and go to Glendora Dr. Parking is on east side of Glendora Dr, where two paths enter the park.

Pleasant paths through the 227-acre park surrounding Sugarloaf Mountain invite young and old to wander along the shaded canyon of Laurel Creek and climb its sunny hillsides. The City of San Mateo acquired Sugarloaf Mountain in 1988 and maintains a 1-mile loop trail and hillside paths. The park is open from sunrise to sunset, but occasionally closed for resource and fire protection. Besides trails for hikers, there are picnic tables, children's play equipment and a paved bicycle path.

The paved path from Glendora Drive enters the upper canyon in a sunny natural amphitheater where there are a small playground and a few picnic tables under wide-spreading oaks. This main path continues to Laurelwood Drive under the giant bay trees that gave the creek its name. Another path, a foot trail, descends on steps from Glendora Drive and then meanders through a handsome old grove of buckeye trees to reach the hillside on the north side of Laurel Creek, brightened by many-hued wildflowers each spring.

Buckeye trees blossom on the hill below Glendora Drive.

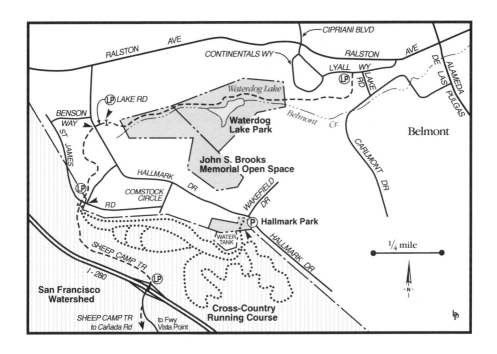

Waterdog Lake Park and Trail/John S. Brooks Memorial Open Space–Belmont

The trail through Belmont's wooded Diablo Canyon passes Waterdog Lake and comes out on the crest of the hill at the eastern boundary of the Watershed, where panoramic views of Crystal Springs Lakes and the Santa Cruz Mountains spread out before you. Here it joins a trail that leads to San Mateo County's long north-south trail.

Jurisdiction: City of Belmont.
Facilities: Trail for hikers, joggers. Lake for fishing and picnicking.
Rules: Open dawn to dusk. No swimming, no boating.
Maps: City of Belmont *Jogging Trails* and USGS topo *San Mateo*.
How To Get There: From I-280 take Hwy 92 east and turn on Ralston Ave to (1) East entrance: turn south on Lyall Way. Look for gate and sign just beyond Lake Rd intersection. (2) West entrance: turn south on Hallmark Dr, go west on Benson Way, and then south on St. James Rd. Find trail entrance across street from gate to Watershed, just past Rinconada Circle.

- **Distance:** 3 miles round trip.
- **Time:** 1½ hours.
- **Elevation Gain:** 300'

TRAIL NOTES

Enter the Waterdog Lake Trail through a narrow opening in a chain-link fence on the south side of Lyall Way at Lake Road. This trail was the old road over the hill to Laguna de Raimundo, now beneath the waters of Crystal Springs Lakes. In 1969 San Mateo County, using federal funds, rebuilt the road as an urban trail. Now, under the jurisdiction of the City of Belmont, the trail traverses the north side of Belmont's Waterlog Lake Park and John S. Brooks Memorial Open Space.

At first the trail winds up a hill past apartments; then, under a canopy of oaks you are in Cañada del Diablo, which the Spanish unaccountably called this lovely place. A walk of about ½ mile brings you to Waterdog Lake, a little reservoir that in earlier days was the water supply for Belmont, now a good stopping place for a rest, a picnic or even a morning of fishing.

From the dam at the end of the lake, the road climbs gently for another ½ mile along the north side of the John S. Brooks Memorial Open Space, with views across the wooded canyon, now rimmed with houses. In spring a roadside garden of blue lupine, yellow California poppies, scarlet Indian paintbrush and purple brodiaea graces your way.

When you emerge from the canyon at Hallmark Drive, cross the street to a gated easement, a steeper ½-mile stretch through oaks and behind backyards, to the highest point of the trail at St. James Road. Just across the street is a gate to the grassy slopes of the San Francisco Watershed.

Here you have several choices of other walks. You can follow the graveled service road to the left along the upper boundary of the Watershed. Or the Cross Country Running Course to the southeast may tempt you to stretch your legs. A third choice takes you south for a 1-mile walk on the broad Sheep Camp Trail to join the Crystal Springs Trail beside Cañada Road.

Big Canyon and Eaton Parks–San Carlos

How To Get There: From I-280 take Edgewood Road east, turn left (north) on Crestview Drive and then go right (east) on Brittan Ave. After 0.2 mile find the trail entrances on either side of the street. Big Canyon Park is marked by a prominent sign. There is on-street parking. From El Camino Real in San Carlos go west on Brittan Ave for 2 miles.

Trails in two city parks—Big Canyon and Eaton parks—climb to high vantage points and descend to meet at Brittan Avenue. Big Canyon is actually a small canyon of 28 acres with steep, narrow sides. One side is so shaded and cool that it supports a surprising variety of ferns, while the other side is a bright, sunny sagebrush slope. You enter the park from the north side of Brittan Avenue and climb a winding trail along its shady side to its upper reaches. From there are views of the cities of San Carlos and Redwood City and farther south the dark slopes of Black Mountain and Loma Prieta.

Across from Big Canyon Park on the south side of Brittan Avenue are sturdy railroad-tie steps that lead up to a mile-long trail built by Sierra Club volunteers. This trail meanders along below a subdivision on a north-facing hillside under live oaks and traverses open grasslands en route to Eaton Park. When spring wildflowers are in bloom and ferns grace the shady hillsides, this is a delightful, 2-mile round trip from Brittan Avenue.

Stulsaft Park–Redwood City

How To Get There: From I-280: (1) Main entrance—Take Woodside Rd northeast to Alameda de Las Pulgas, turn northwest and at Goodwin Ave turn left. Park on Recreation Way and walk to park entrance. Parking lot is closed. (2) Farm Hill entrance—Take Farm Hill Blvd north 1.3 miles to park entrance on right side. Limited parking on street.

Arroyo Ojo de Agua flows through Stulsaft Park.

This 42-acre Redwood City park is in a cool, green canyon with the Arroyo Ojo de Agua (Spring Pond Creek, or Stulsaft Creek) in its depths. Although the park is less a mile long, in a few minutes its paths can take you away from city streets and sounds into a quiet, wooded retreat where you find bird songs, deer tracks and the music of a running stream. Trips of 1 to 3 miles wind up the hillsides on both sides of the creek canyon. The many picnic tables and barbecues draw lively crowds on summer weekends, but during the rest of the year you may have the canyon almost to yourself.

Formerly the J. B. Shroeder estate, dating back to the 1880s, the land was later acquired by Martin Stulsaft and given to Redwood City in 1951. Traces of the former estate can still be seen in the bridge over the creek and the plantings of cultivated shrubs.

There are trails for hikers, playgrounds, picnic tables, barbecues, group picnic areas, a playing field, an amphitheater and restrooms. The park is open from 8 A.M. to sunset.

Mountainside Parks and Preserves on the Central Peninsula

Forests cover most of the steep slopes on both sides of the Santa Cruz Mountains' crest. Those on the east slopes in the watersheds and in Huddart, Phleger and Wunderlich parks are familiar to Baysiders as a backdrop of their communities.

Less familiar to Peninsula residents are the parks and preserves on the west slopes of the Santa Cruz Mountains encompassing the 8,700 acres opened to the public in the 1980s—Burleigh Murray Ranch State Park and Purisima Creek Redwoods, El Corte de Madera and La Honda Creek open space preserves. And seldom seen are the spectacular views of the Coastside and the ocean from high ridges in these preserves.

A century and a half ago majestic redwood forests extended from the Peninsula's valley floor over the ridge of the Santa Cruz Mountains and down the west slopes. In the forests on the east slopes, known to the Spanish as Pulgas Redwoods, Spanish soldiers, with the help of Indians, felled trees and dragged them by oxen to build missions in San Francisco and Santa Clara.

In 1840 the Mexican Governor of California, Luis Alvarado, granted to his friend John Coppinger the 12,545-acre Rancho Cañada de Raimundo, which included most of the Pulgas Redwoods, extending from the Woodside valley floor to the Skyline. During the decade in which Gold Rush San Francisco was built, the great trees were cut, and the lumber hauled down to the Embarcadero in Redwood City and sailed by schooner up the Bay to San Francisco.

By 1870 hardly a redwood tree remained uncut in the Pulgas Redwoods. Logging began then in the primeval forests along the Skyline and down the steep west slopes. Logging continued into this century until the old forests were almost completely cut over. In the years since, second-growth trees have been cut sporadically.

However, in the decade of the 1980s the Midpeninsula Regional Open Space District acquired much of these upper slopes west of the Skyline as preserves. The State of California purchased historic farmlands—the Burleigh Murray Ranch and lands extending to the Skyline ridge. And logging has ceased in Purisima Creek Redwoods, El Corte de Madera and La Honda Creek open space preserves. In 1995 the Peninsula Open Space Trust secured 1232 acres of the former Phleger Estate and this beautiful forest is now in the Golden Gate National Recreation Area.

In these preserves and parklands extensive trail systems are in place on old logging and farm roads. Trails in canyons, along creeks, and over the ridges are now open to hikers, equestrians and bicyclists.

Important trail links join these western parklands to the parks and trail systems on the east slopes that reach down to cities on the Bayside. A long-distance ridge trail extending north and south along the Skyline is part of the Bay Area Ridge Trail initiated in 1987. In the central section of San Mateo County, 12 miles of this trail system are already in place, many more are complete in the north and south sections of the county and a trail corridor has been designated to complete the gaps in the Ridge Trail through the county.

Future trail connections from Purisima Creek Redwoods and La Honda Creek open space preserves and Burleigh Murray Ranch State Park to the Coast may some day make it possible to walk from the Bay over the Santa Cruz Mountains to the ocean.

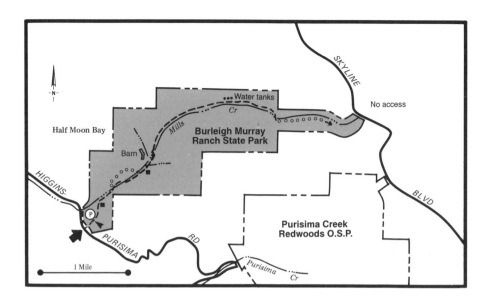

Burleigh Murray Ranch State Park

A historic ranch tucked away in a valley south of Half Moon Bay now belongs to the California State Park system. In the 1860s this was a working ranch, growing hay and grazing cattle. Perennial Mills Creek, named for Robert P. Mills, the first owner of the ranch, flows through the narrow valley. An arched stone bridge crosses the creek to an old barn and a bunkhouse remaining from the ranching days. The State of California received the donated property in 1983 and later added a parcel known as Rancho Raymundo to extend the park to Skyline Boulevard. The ranch is named for one of the last of many owners of the property, Burleigh Hall Murray.

The state is preserving the 1121-acre park for its historical interest, with an emphasis on interpreting early San Mateo County ranch life. The historic buildings, unparalleled on the north San Mateo County coast, will be restored—it is hoped—and the stone walls and the arch bridge preserved. Farming may be discontinued and the land restored to its natural state, with particular attention to protection of the sensitive riparian habitat.

Besides historic preservation, the major use of the park is day use for hiking, bicycling and horseback riding. An old farm road runs from the entrance on Higgins Purisima Road about 2 miles northeast, roughly following Mills Creek. This perennial stream rises near the Skyline ridge and flows through the heart of the park. A ½-mile loop trail on the north side of the creek is proposed for the future.

Jurisdiction: State of California, Department of Parks and Recreation—415-726-8819.

Facilities: Trails for hikers, equestrians and bicyclists. A picnic table is situated under the eucalyptus trees approximately ¾ mile from the park entrance; portable restrooms are at the parking area and above the creek crossing.

Rules: Open 8 A.M. to sunset. No dogs allowed.

Maps: USGS topos *Half Moon Bay* and *Woodside.*

How To Get There: From Hwy 1/92 intersection go south on Hwy 1 for 1.2 miles to Higgins Purisima Rd. Turn left (east) and go 1.7 miles to park entrance on left. Park in graveled area just inside gate.

A Hike on a Historic Ranch

Follow an old ranch road into a secluded coastal valley where a historic barn and bridge remain from early San Mateo County ranching days.

- **Distance:** 2 miles round trip to barn; 4 miles round trip to water tanks.
- **Time:** 1 hour round trip to barn; 2¼ hours round trip to water tanks.
- **Elevation: Gain** 680'

TRAIL NOTES

Leave the park entrance at the mouth of the valley on the farm road now used as a trail. As you near alder-bordered Mills Creek in the stillness of this secluded valley, you can hear the sounds of the stream accompanied by the songs of birds. Former farm fields border the trail and rounded hills rise on both sides of the canyon.

Upstream, where the valley narrows, you cross two bridges at a bend in the creek. Beyond in a semicircular meadow between the creek and the trail you find wildflowers blooming profusely in spring. On shady, north-facing road banks wild currant bushes blossom in winter.

One mile from the park entrance a small tributary enters the creek from the east and the trail veers left, following the creek into a broad flat near the old ranch headquarters. Past a 1930s bungalow that serves as a park residence, you cross a bridge from which you can note the original rock work lining the curve in the creek banks. Downstream is an arched stone bridge built with Italian masonry techniques dating back to the Romans. This bridge is often overgrown, but in late spring the area is usually cleared and the bridge is quite visible. On the far side of the creek is a great wooden barn dating from the 1890s, built to house 100 cows. Its roof now sags and its doors are wedged shut, but the state plans call for its restoration. A fine stone wall holds the bank beyond the barn.

Continuing on the road beyond the barn and its corrals, you pass a

A fine old stone bridge arches over Mills Creek.

small wooden bunkhouse by the creek. In a tangle of blackberry bushes stand pumps, outbuildings, cattle chutes and gates, all no longer used.

The trail continues up the narrowing valley between steep, chaparral-covered hills to the east and high, overgrown hayfields to the west. Then, about a mile above the barn, the old road used as a trail ends at the water tanks. However, in the future trail volunteers plan to clear this trail up the steep ridge to the next creek crossing. Someday it is hoped the trail will be continued up the steep ridge through the narrow Rancho Raymundo property to the Skyline. Heading back down the valley, you see the creek, rounded hills and valleys from a different perspective.

Visitors to this park should be aware that there is a shooting range near the park residence, reserved for police and sheriffs' practice.

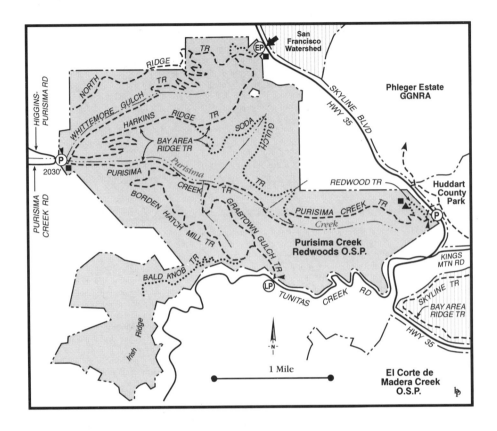

Purisima Creek Redwoods Open Space Preserve

This MROSD preserve is a 2633-acre treasure of redwood forests, clear–flowing streams, steep-sided canyons and long ridges. Its size and its rugged terrain make it a place to find both quiet seclusion and long trails for strenuous hiking trips. This northernmost redwood forest in San Mateo County is just minutes from the urban San Francisco Peninsula.

The preserve extends westward for 3 miles from the 2000-foot-high crest of the Santa Cruz Mountains. East across Skyline Boulevard are the San Francisco Watershed lands, Huddart Park, and the Phleger Estate. From the Skyline crest three ridges divide the preserve into two main canyons trending west. Between Harkins and Tunitas ridges flows Purisima Creek, the centerpiece of the preserve.

A beautiful, year-round stream fed by many tributaries, Purisima Creek rises along the Skyline ridge and flows west for 3 miles through the preserve. In the lower end of the preserve, large second-growth redwoods line its banks and side slopes. Leaving the preserve, Purisima Creek runs through rolling grasslands and the 2200-acre Cowell Ranch to reach the ocean in a waterfall over sandstone cliffs. The ranch, purchased in 1987 by the Peninsula Open Space Trust, included some bluffs and a beach which are now the Cowell Ranch State Beach.

Between Harkins Ridge and the next ridge north is Whittemore Gulch, where an intermittent creek flows through a lovely wooded canyon to join Purisima Creek at the preserve's west entrance.

In the 1860s, when redwoods were first cut here, the logs proved too large to drag up the steep canyons. Although the west end of the canyon was open, there was little need for lumber on the coastside and no port from which to ship it to San Francisco. Therefore, the trees were cut for shingles, which pack animals could haul out of the gulches over steep, winding trails. As many as eight shingle mills operated here during the late 1800s.

Logging was back-breaking, dangerous work, but some ingenious techniques were developed to hoist the heavy logs out of the canyon. One such device used a cable to operate a tramway rising one thousand feet from the creek to the ridgetop.

Lumbering ventures came and went in the narrow, steep canyon of the Purisima. Last logged in the 1970s, stands of second-growth redwoods now fill most of the canyon.

Then in 1982 MROSD bought 849 acres in Whittemore Gulch, and in 1984, assisted by the Save-the-Redwoods League, MROSD acquired an additional 1662 acres, including the headwaters of Purisima Creek. More recent purchases brought the total to 2633 acres. An additional 481 acres, southwest of Bald Knob, is managed by MROSD and it is anticipated that this eventually will become a part of Purisima Creek Redwoods Open Space Preserve. A few primeval redwoods remain; one is said to be 1200 years old. Purisima also harbors one of a few remaining critical habitats of the marbled murrelet, a seagoing bird now on the list of threatened species, which nests in old-growth trees.

Some of the most challenging hikes on the Peninsula are trips down Purisima's canyons and up its ridges. The old county road, now the Purisima Creek Trail, descends from Skyline Boulevard to follow the creek to the lower end of the canyon. New trails and old logging roads form a 21-mile trail network.

Some narrow trails are exclusively for hikers, others on logging roads are also open to horsemen and bicyclists. The ¼-mile Redwood Trail for the physically limited, funded by POST, meanders through tall redwoods along the Skyline ridge. From several turnouts for picnic tables one can look out toward the coast.

A short walk on an easy grade from the preserve's west entrance on Higgins Purisima Road reaches groves of the largest redwoods beside

From Skyline Boulevard the Redwood Trail gives
wheelchair users a trip through the forest.

Purisima Creek. Starting long loop hikes from this entrance gives you the advantage of gaining altitude while you and day are fresh.

Trails in Purisima Creek Redwoods link with adjoining Huddart Park and Phleger Estate trails, making it possible to walk from Bayside cities over the Santa Cruz Mountains to the west end of the preserve, only a few miles from the ocean. With advance reservations, backpacking groups can camp in Huddart Park. This route has been suggested as a city-to-sea trail, and with the addition of the new POST Bald Knob lands, this route looks more possible.

Be weather-wise when visiting Purisima Creek Redwoods Preserve. Because it is several miles back from the ocean, the preserve often has sun when fog hangs on the coast. However, on the days when fog sweeps in from the sea to reach the redwoods along the Skyline, condensed moisture falls from the tree branches like rain.

Jurisdiction: Midpeninsula Regional Open Space District—415-691-1200.

Facilities: Trails for hikers, equestrians and bicyclists; one trail for the physically limited, with picnic tables, restroom and special parking. Equestrian parking.
Rules: Open dawn to dusk. No bicycles on Soda Gulch or North Ridge foot trail. No dogs.
Map: MROSD brochure *Purisima Creek Redwoods O.S.P,* USGS topo *Woodside.*
How To Get There: There are four entrances: (1) Main entrance is on Skyline Blvd 4.5 miles south of Hwy 92; (2) Purisima Creek Trail entrance is 2.0 miles farther south; (3) Redwood Trail entrance and wheelchair parking are 0.2 mile south of Purisima Creek Trail entrance; (4) West entrance is off Higgins Purisima Rd, reached from Hwy 1 just 1.2 mile south of its intersection with Hwy 92 in Half Moon Bay.

Trip 1. Purisima Creek Trail

Follow the old 19th century Purisima Creek Road down a deep canyon beside Purisima Creek to the preserve's west entrance. Today's travelers can enjoy tall trees, beautiful flowers and the sight and sound of a yearround stream.

- **Distance:** 8.4 miles round trip.
- **Time:** 5 hours.
- **Elevation Loss:** 1600'

TRAIL NOTES

A steady descent from the Skyline ridge, this trail could be a one–way trip with a shuttle, or hikers could combine the first leg with the Harkins Ridge and the Soda Gulch trails to make a 10-mile loop trip.

Starting from the southern Skyline Boulevard entrance (2) opposite Huddart Park, go over the hiker's stile and down the wide trail through a redwood-and-fir forest. Note to the left of the stile the wheelchair gate to the specially surfaced Redwood Trail. Before long you come to switchbacks, where logging operations cleared the trees to make level platforms or landings. Wild lilacs, spring-flowering in shades of blue and purple, and young tan oak trees are thriving in this clearing. The climax trees, Douglas fir and redwood, will eventually shade out these hardy early plants.

After about a mile down the trail you begin to hear Purisima Creek, and before long you see it through the trees. Soon you are walking close to it. At a sharp turn in the trail, the Soda Gulch Trail takes off to the right up a heavily wooded canyon to join the Harkins Ridge Trail. At the next turn you cross the ever-widening creek, where clear pools are edged with fern fronds and horsetails.

Around the next bend on the south side is the site of a mile-long cable tramway that in the 1870s lifted logs from Purdy Pharis' shingle mill out of the canyon to a location near present-day Kings Mountain School. This ingenious device, a forerunner of modern cable-logging, had a short existence, but its location appeared on maps for many years.

From here to the west entrance the old road is close to the creek, which stair–steps down the canyon over rocks and under bridges of fallen logs. Some logs, still rooted, are sprouting new shoots. A heavy-timbered bridge crosses the creek to a trail leading to Grabtown, an old logging settlement on top of Tunitas Ridge. Where the canyon widens, two shingle mills operated in the early 1900s, some of the last in the canyon. This is an open, sunny place to stop for lunch and to speculate on the rugged life of those loggers, who had to deal with floods, fires and accidents.

The remaining 1.3 miles of your trip are less steep and more heavily wooded. Small streams trickle down the canyon sides, and flowers bloom at every season, from the deep red trillium of early spring to the lavender asters of fall. Soon your way is completely enclosed by forest. Some immense redwoods remain near the creek at the lower end of the preserve. On the north side is a grove of memorial trees, dedicated by a contributor to the Save-the-Redwoods League, which helped purchase this beautiful preserve.

Look for tall rush and western coltsfoot among rocks beside Purisima Creek.

Now you are near the preserve's west entrance. Before starting your return trip to Skyline Boulevard, find a log to sit on beside the creek to enjoy its clear waters and the light filtering through the redwood trees. You could shorten this hike by arranging a car shuttle at the west entrance. The west entrance is a popular and convenient way to the Santa Cruz Mountains for Coastside residents, and with its ample parking can be the starting point for Trips 1, 2 and 3 in reverse.

Trip 2. A Loop Trip from the North Ridge

This vigorous trip from the north ridgetop to the west entrance descends to Purisima Creek on the North Ridge and Harkins Ridge trails and returns on the Whittemore Gulch Trail.

- **Distance:** 6.8-mile loop.
- **Time:** 4½ hours.
- **Elevation Loss:** 1630'

TRAIL NOTES

Alternate routes of the North Ridge Trail leave the north Skyline Boulevard parking area: (1) hikers watch for the foot-trail turnoff about 100 feet from the entrance on the right, which bypasses the steep grade of the service road; (2) bicyclists and equestrians use the North Ridge service road for this 0.3-mile stretch to reach the Harkins Ridge Trail junction. The foot-trail zigzags 0.5 mile down the mountainside just below the ridgetop under Douglas firs, wide-spreading tan oak oaks, madrones and a scattering of live oaks. If the day is clear, the views west present a sweep of the San Mateo coast from Half Moon Bay north and south.

In 0.5 mile the foot trail intersects the service road, where all users go south on the Harkins Ridge Trail. On a bench created by early landslides, this path traverses the hillside above a steep canyon among clumps of sizable redwood trees and a thick stand of Douglas firs. Abundant flowers brighten the trailside—iris in spring, lavender asters, a purple mint and apricot-colored sticky monkey flower in late summer.

After a 0.6-mile contour around the canyon headwall, the route turns right on an old fire road down the spine of Harkins Ridge and descends more than 1300 feet in 2.1 miles. The ridge is predominantly chaparral–covered, although some tan oaks and bay laurels grow on the steep mountainside. Small stands of firs and redwoods on the north side of Harkins Ridge give late afternoon shade. From here we look north down into Whittemore Gulch, the route of our climb back to the Skyline ridge.

In 0.3 mile down Harkins Ridge the Soda Gulch Trail (for hikers only) takes off south to meet the Purisima Creek Trail in the canyon below. But you continue your descent on the Harkins Ridge Trail, passing knolls densely covered with ceanothus, which forms a showy blue cloud in spring.

After the trail arcs left off the open ridge, it makes 4 switchbacks into the cool shade of the Purisima Creek redwoods, then follows the creek downstream for ½ mile. Just a few steps before the bridge to the south side of the creek, you find the Whittemore Gulch Trail junction on the right.

About 300 feet beyond the bridge is the preserve gate at Higgins Purisima Road. You could leave a car here and avoid the hike back up the mountain, or you could start the hike here and do the steep climb first. In any case, step down to the creek to see its pools and cascades at close range.

The Whittemore Gulch Trail offers a 3½-mile return to the Skyline ridge. This trail's soils are heavily eroded, and it is closed in wet weather to bicyclists and equestrians, who should return on the Harkins Ridge Trail. In the lower gulch, redwoods deemed too small or irregular to cut in the logging days are now grown to handsome large trees. Alders and big-leaf maples fill openings among the redwoods and firs, and the canyon walls are lush with ferns. After crossing the creek, the trail passes close to the shell of a redwood tree, which we can estimate was at least 15 feet in diameter. There are venerable Douglas firs too. One old giant has sent out a branch that rises vertically after its first horizontal 8 feet, becoming an immense tree itself.

After 1½ miles, this well-designed trail leaves the canyon depths and zigzags more than a mile up the mountainside, crossing a thickly covered chaparral slope. Poison oak dominates the hillside, its fall colors brilliant reds and oranges. The southern exposure here is welcome on a winter's day, but can be hot in summer.

When you reach the old jeep road, the North Ridge Trail, turn right and follow it for ½ mile. Then watch for the trail junction where hikers turn left into the forest on the 0.5-mile foot trail on which they started their trip. Bicyclists and equestrians continue 0.3 mile uphill on the North Ridge service road.

Trip 3. Grabtown Gulch and Bald Knob Loop Trip

From the southern ridgetops of the preserve, this trip descends through the hardwood forests of Grabtown Gulch to the Purisima Creek Trail and returns on the Borden Hatch Mill Trail to Bald Knob.

- **Distance:** 7.4–mile loop.
- **Time:** 3 hours.
- **Elevation Loss:** 1200′ plus 500′ gain to Bald Knob.

TRAIL NOTES

There are two starting places for this trip: the first is on Tunitas Creek Road and the second is the west parking area on Higgins Purisima Road. To find the first trailhead, turn west off Skyline Boulevard just opposite Kings Mtn. Road. on winding Tunitas Creek Road and go 2 miles to a familiar MROSD brown metal gate with its sign FIRE LANE, DO NOT BLOCK on the right side. There are several turnouts for limited parking on the road downhill from the entrance. To reach the second trailhead see page 103 for directions.

Grabtown Gulch takes its name from the settlement that sprang up on a small flat near the trail entrance. It was the first level spot that logging wagons reached on their three- or four-day trip to the embarcadero at Redwood City. According to legend, a boy named it Grabtown because settlers grabbed whatever lodging or garden space became available.

This trail starts off gently over a little rise, staying along the flank of the ridge (possibly the Grabtown site) on which there are some private residences to the left just outside the preserve. When you reach the first little clearing, keep to the right and continue to a larger opening in the forest, a landing for logging operations. At this clearing trails take off left and right. You take the righthand fork, the Grabtown Gulch Trail; you'll return up the lefthand trail, the Borden Hatch Mill Trail.

First, you go down the 1.4-mile Grabtown Gulch Trail through Douglas firs and young redwoods that are beginning to overtake the tan oaks and madrones that sprang up after previous logging. At this stage of regrowth there is still plenty of space and light between trees for ceanothus, wild roses, toyon and honeysuckle. From openings in the trees it is possible to look out to the ocean—though it is often shrouded in fog.

Your trail continues downhill, cuts east across the ridge and then reverses direction to descend a very steep slope into Grabtown Gulch. You follow a path lined with ferns and ocean spray, where the creek is well below the trail. Continuing on the creek's shady east side, you can find 3-foot-tall orange tiger lilies in midsummer.

Shortly, Grabtown Gulch Creek enters Purisima Creek, which you cross on a reconstructed old logging bridge. You have reached the widest part of Purisima Canyon. Of the shingle mills that flourished here, no vestiges remain, but you can sit on the bridge to watch the water and listen to the birds at the confluence of these creeks.

To take the rest of the loop trip, continue down the canyon 0.3 mile to a trail on the left that climbs south on the ridge west of Grabtown Gulch, the Borden Hatch Mill Trail. This trail gains the 1000+ feet of elevation you lost as it snakes 2.1 miles up the north-facing side of the mountain below Bald Knob. You cross a tributary of Grabtown Gulch, sometimes quite damp in winter, and then meet the old patrol road out to Bald Knob, closed at the preserve boundary. To reach the new trail, for hikers only, bear left (east) at the old patrol road junction and continue about 0.2 mile toward the Grabtown Gulch Trail. Watch for an abrupt, sharp right turn onto the new Bald Knob Trail and follow it west along the southern border of the preserve.

On this trail, built and managed by MROSD on land gifted to POST, you wind through tan oaks and young, second-growth redwoods. Soon the summit of Bald Knob is visible through the trees. As the trail switchbacks around the south side of Bald Knob, redwoods give way to firs, some of giant proportions amid several huge stumps.

After about a mile, you walk through a dense grove of chinquapins searching for light in a tall fir forest and emerge onto grassy slopes dotted with young trees. Here is one of the most glorious vistas on the Coast. You are at the steep upper end of Irish Ridge which divides Tunitas Creek from Lobitos Creek. The view to the south and west encompasses the west side of the Santa Cruz Mountains sloping down to miles of surf breaking on the shore, with the Pacific Ocean spreading out to Hawaii and beyond. You have just traversed the south side of Bald Knob, which is private, but not bald. A dense grove of young firs is flourishing on its summit. The rough, gravel track down Irish Ridge is used for patrol only and is not for public use.

As you retrace your steps along the Bald Knob Trail, look down slope (south) to an open, brushy area to see the rooftops of private homes in the Kings Grove community. At the junction of this new trail with the Borden Hatch Mill Trail bear east and continue about 0.2 mile to the Grabtown Gulch Trail, go right (south) and return to the wide forest opening near Tunitas Creek Road and out to parking along this road.

To take this trip from the preserve's west entrance on Higgins Purisima Road, you add 1.4 miles to the trip, making a loop of 8.8 miles, but it has the advantage of doing the serious climbing at the beginning of the trip. Go 1 mile up the Purisima Creek Trail (described in reverse in Trip 1), turn right on the Borden Hatch Mill Trail and continue as described above, then return downhill on the Purisima Creek Trail to the west entrance.

Trip 4. The Bay Area Ridge Trail

Sample all the preserve's habitats on four different trails.
- **Distance:** 5.6 miles—hikers; 7.7 miles—bicyclists and equestrians.
- **Time:** 3½ hours.
- **Elevation Loss:** 1000'—hikers; 1400'—bicyclists and equestrians.

TRAIL NOTES

This route is one segment of the already completed 200 miles of the Bay Area Ridge Trail. Starting from the preserve's south entrance on the Purisima Creek Trail, as described in Trip 1, head downhill through a mixed forest of fir, redwood and tan oak trees. Descending steadily for 1.6 miles to the junction of the Soda Gulch Trail, hikers turn off on this narrow trail and bicyclists and equestrians continue on the Purisima Creek Trail to the Harkins Ridge Trail junction and ascend on it to the ridgetop (see Trip 1).

Although this hillside was logged sporadically into the 20th century, the redwood forest has regrown beautifully. A few trees of majestic size, scarred by fires of long ago, remain along the route, reminding us of this species' incredible vitality.

You follow the Soda Gulch Trail back into No Name Gulch and other little canyons where bridges cross small creeks that can become rushing torrents in winter. Springtime brings wildflowers with delightful splashes of color to brighten the trail—especially the clusters of rosy-red blossoms of Clintonia and the tall, delicate flowers of crimson columbine.

You then traverse a south-facing slope, drier and warmer, before returning to the cool shade of a deep redwood forest in Soda Gulch. Here are some of the largest redwoods on your trip, lovely circles or fairy rings of second-growth trees surrounding a space where an ancient tree once stood. After hiking deep into the upper reaches of Soda Gulch Creek, you cross a fine, sturdy bridge, and head west to emerge in chaparral. Climbing a bit you bend north and reach the Harkins Ridge Trail, on which you join the equestrians and bicyclists going right uphill (northeast).

From here you are following the route described in Trip 2 in reverse. After a steady 0.9-mile ascent on the Harkins Ridge Trail, hikers cross the service road to take the 0.5-mile foot trail segment of the North Ridge Trail, while equestrians and bicyclists bear right (east) to follow the unpaved North Ridge service road 0.3 mile uphill to the north preserve entrance.

You could have a shuttle car waiting here or return over the same route to make a long day's trip. From here to Sweeney Ridge there is a gap in the Bay Area Ridge Trail. Negotiations continue for use of a graveled service road through the San Francisco Watershed.

Spring-fed creeks flow through redwood groves.

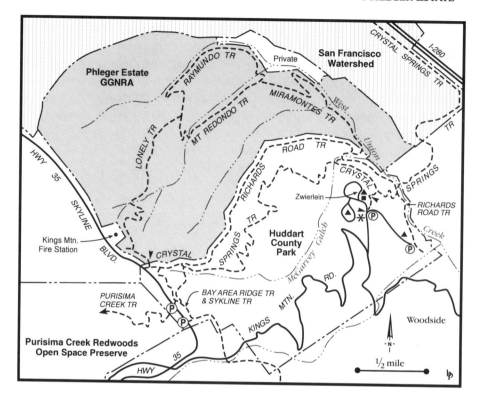

Phleger Estate

These 1232 acres of redwood and oak/madrone forest lie on the east side of the Skyline ridge immediately north of San Mateo County's Huddart Park. Situated at the southern end of the San Francisco Watershed, over which the Golden Gate National Recreation Area has a scenic easement, this newest addition to the GGNRA becomes a vital link in a 56-mile tapestry of permanent open space from San Francisco south to San Jose. Trails for hikers and equestrians ascend through the forest from Huddart Park to the Skyline ridge, gaining 1400 feet in elevation en route.

Once the domain of Herman and Mary Elena Phleger, who bought most of the land from George Eastman in 1935 and the balance in 1946, this property has changed little since that time. Redwood forests cut during the building and rebuilding of San Francisco after the Gold Rush are now achieving considerable girth and height. West Union Creek and its tributaries flow clear and clean and woodland spring wildflowers adorn the forest floor.

Ohlone Indians camped near here, hunted game and fished the waters of West Union Creek, leaving little impact upon the land. Loggers established camps and built the town of Union Creek nearby. They cut the giant trees, skidded them down U-shaped ditches, known as skid roads, to mills downstream, and then hauled the lumber by oxen to Redwood City to be barged to San Francisco.

In 1927 when George Eastman built his home, designed by San Francisco architect Gardner Dailey, this area of the Peninsula was sparsely inhabited. But as the Peninsula population grew, the Phleger lands became prize development property. With 1990 zoning there could have been 550 homes, each built on a 2½-acre parcel. From the earliest days of its founding, the private, non-profit Peninsula Open Space Trust had hoped to keep this key piece of land in open space.

After the death of Mrs. Phleger in 1990, POST met with her trustees to work out terms of a purchase. POST agreed to raise $14.5 million by August 1991, and to meet the total purchase price of $25 million by December 1994. A member of the POST Advisory Council, Gordon Moore, purchased the Phleger home and 24.5 surrounding acres, subject to a conservation easement restricting building, subdivision and commercial development. The Save-the-Redwoods League contributed $2.5 million and the Midpeninsula Regional Open Space District gave $6 million. Private donations made up another $3 million. After expanding the GGNRA boundaries to include this parcel, Congress appropriated the remaining $10.5 million through Land and Water Conservation Funds and by December of 1994, the Phleger Estate addition to the National Park Service was completed. It was the largest public-private acquisition in national-park history.

Jurisdiction: Golden Gate National Recreation Area—415-556-8642; 415-239-2366.
Facilities: Trails for hikers and equestrians.
Rules: Open 8 A.M. to sunset. Fee for parking at Huddart Park. No dogs, pets, fires, camping, vehicles, or bicycles.
How To Get There: From I-280 take Woodside Rd (Hwy 84) west 1.5 miles to Kings Mountain Rd, turn right, and go 1.5 miles to Huddart Park entrance on right side of road.

Climb to the Crest of the Santa Cruz Mountains

Make a circuit of the forested estate on four different trails.

- **Distance:** 8.8 miles.
- **Time:** 5 hours.
- **Elevation Gain:** 1400"

TRAIL NOTES

Two circle trips start on the Crystal Springs Trail in Huddart Park, one taking that trail uphill through the park and returning downhill through the Phleger Estate, the other going both up and down through the Phleger Estate. Described here is the latter route, starting from the trailhead south of the restrooms at the Zwierlein Picnic Area in Huddart Park. A signpost marking the Crystal Springs Trail points left (north) to the Phleger Estate and each turn thereafter is clearly marked.

This beautiful trail winds downward through redwoods and Douglas firs along banks lush with fern fronds and woodland shade-loving plants. After 0.2 mile you turn right on the Dean Trail and switchback downhill around a fairy ring of redwoods grown in a circle around the cavity where once an ancient redwood stood. In the depths of McGarvey Gulch you parallel the creek, but do not cross the first bridge over the creek. Follow the creek downstream (right) for 0.1 mile, and then turn sharp left to cross over it as it flows through a culvert. Now you head uphill on wide Richards Road, watching on your right for the Miramontes Trail, marked by a prominent sign THE PHLEGER ESTATE.

In spring the trailside banks are brightened by white violets and in summer by sticky monkey flower's apricot blossoms. Keeping West Union Creek on your right, you bear left at a fork, and soon come to a wooden sign hanging from a post topped by a metal cutout of a tired Indian warrior on his horse announcing that you are indeed on the Miramontes Trail. Follow the lovely, clear creek on its course over gravel bars, around meanders, and past pools beneath redwood roots or behind fallen trees.

After going through a metal gate in a fence, the trail starts uphill, switchbacking through an area of madrone trees and chaparral. Here on a flat are clusters of cream-colored Fremont lilies on tall stalks blooming in spring and healthy, ubiquitous poison oak bushes close to the trail.

At the next junction 1.4 miles from the entrance to the Phleger Estate, you come to a crossroads, again marked by the Indian warrior atop his horse. The Woodside Trail Club, which formerly built and managed these trails, originally installed distinctive trail markers which have been replicated by POST. Take the Mt. Redondo Trail uphill 0.8 mile along the south side of the steep canyon carved by a tributary of West Union Creek. Here you see very few old redwoods, but you travel under tall second-growth trees interspersed with Douglas firs and clumps of madrone and tan oak trees. Underfoot you may meet a five- or six-inch-long, slimy yellow banana slug, especially in rainy weather. Do avoid crushing this slow-moving, important decomposer of forest litter.

After a series of switchbacks in a predominantly madrone-tree forest, you come to yet another metal sign marking the junction of the Lonely and Raymundo trails with the Mt. Redondo Trail. To continue upward to the Skyline ridge, take the Lonely Trail left (southwest), and climb 0.6 mile up and around the heads of several small ravines before reaching a wooden bench in a small clearing. The bench, installed by POST, is inscribed with the words, "Rest and Be Filled with the Grace of the Forest"; take that advice and stop for a snack while enjoying the quiet broken only by sounds of woodpeckers and blue jays in the forest.

Climbing ever upward on the narrow trail, you traverse the steep canyonside of a West Union Creek tributary until you cross it in an opening in the forest. Look uphill on the right for another wooden bench—no inscription but quite a pleasant, cool place on a hot summer day. From here meander around and up more zigzags, pass an obscure gated trail on the right and then take another trail ambling left below the Skyline ridge on a much more gentle grade. After less than ½ mile on this trail with a much more gentle grade, you come to the upper Crystal Springs Trail entrance to Huddart Park. Now that you have achieved the summit of the Phleger Estate at 2000 feet, you can continue into Huddart Park and follow the beautiful Crystal Springs Trail downhill through vigorous second-growth redwoods to the Zwierlein Picnic Area where you started this trip. See Huddart Park Trip 1 in reverse, page 115.

However, if you retrace your steps on the Lonely Trail to its junction with the Mt. Redondo and Raymundo trails, you can peel off left (north) on the Raymundo Trail, and walk beside the banks of West Union Creek as it burbles along under alders, redwoods and occasional firs. Then after rejoining the Miramontes Trail you head back to the Crystal Springs Trail to complete a trip on all the estate's trails. You will have crossed or walked beside each of the three branches of West Union Creek on an 8.8-mile trip up, down and around this latest addition to the Golden Gate National Recreation Area.

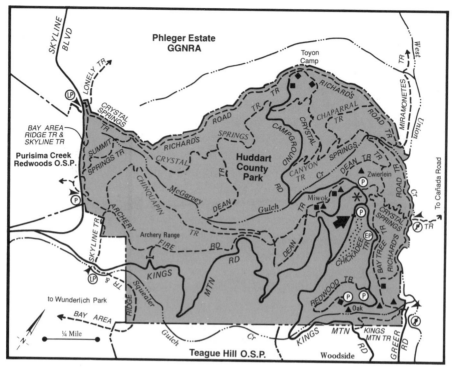

Huddart County Park

In Huddart County Park not only do stumps of the big redwood trees and vestiges of skid trails remind us of the early logging days, but many place names recall that era. Up on the mountain near the little logging town of Summit Springs, Frank King's Saloon flourished until the turn of the century, giving his name to the road that goes through the park. From Richards sawmill on the Skyline ridge, wagons carried lumber down a steep road that is now Richards Road Trail. Owen McGarvey had wood-cutting rights on the gulch that traverses the park and now bears his name.

But a far more significant heritage for us is the handsome second-growth redwood-and-fir forest and the woodland of oaks, madrones and California bay trees in this 973-acre park.

In addition to its picnic areas and playfields there are 18 miles of trails through its redwoods, along its creeks and up its mountainsides. A disabilities access and a nature trail with special parking offer short, easy walks. A group camp on the park's remote northern boundary is available by reservation.

Jurisdiction: San Mateo County—415-363-4020.

Facilities: Trails for hikers, equestrians and the physically limited. Equestrian parking. Picnic grounds, group camping facilities, children's play area.
Rules: Open 8 A.M. to sunset. Group picnics and camping by reservation only. Some trails open to hikers only. Trails may be closed to equestrians in wet weather. No pets, no bicycles on trails. Fees.
Maps San Mateo County *Huddart County Park*, USGS topo *Woodside*.
How To Get There: There are two entrances: (1) Main Entrance—from I-280 take Woodside Rd (Hwy 84) west 1.5 miles Kings Mountain Rd, turn right, and go 1.5 miles to main park entrance on right side of road. (2) Skyline Blvd entrance—turn right from Kings Mountain Rd. onto Skyline Blvd and go 0.3 mile. Use parking area on west side of Skyline Blvd, take short trail north and cross to Huddart County Park entrance.
Connecting Trails: From the upper park: the Ridge/Skyline Ridge Trail continues south to Wunderlich Park, and across Skyline Blvd are trails in Purisima Creek Redwoods O.S.P; from the lower park: the Crystal Springs Trail crosses West Union Creek to continue to Highway 92.

Trip 1. An All-Day Hike Circling the Park

This loop takes you from the Miwok Picnic Area down to West Union Creek and up the magnificent Crystal Springs Trail to the Skyline heights, ending with a downhill return on the Chinquapin Trail west of McGarvey Gulch.

- **Distance**: 8.2-mile loop.
- **Time**: 5 to 6 hours.
- **Elevation Gain**: 1500'

TRAIL NOTES
Starting at the Miwok Picnic Area, pick up the Dean Trail heading downhill. The trail swings down through redwoods for a little more than ½ mile to McGarvey Gulch. Walk across the McGarvey Gulch bridge upstream from West Union Creek and start up the Crystal Springs Trail. This is the loveliest route up through the park and a part of the County's north-south trail system.

At first in an oak-madrone woodland, you are soon in redwoods on the far side of McGarvey Gulch. On wide switchbacks the trail climbs past a sizable second-growth forest. Here and there are immense stumps from the ancient forest.

In ⅓ mile the trail leaves the gulch canyon, passing the Chaparral Trail on the right and the Canyon Trail on the left, and then zigzagging up to the edge of the Group camp area. If no camp is in session, find a table on which to spread out your lunch. Otherwise, continue on the trail, which soon crosses the service road (Campground Trail) to begin a 2-mile climb to the Skyline.

Redwoods, firs and madrones cover the mountainside and birds fill the air with their songs. The trail winds in and out of small canyons and crosses grassy meadows, beguiling the hiker with new vistas around each bend. Springs dampen fern-covered ravines, and in spring wildflowers bloom where small clearings let in the sun.

Picnic tables in the woods near the Dean Trail.

Eventually the trail climbs steeply to meet the Dean Trail. Here you could shorten the hike by returning to your starting point via the Dean Trail. But this trip continues up the ridge on comfortably graded switchbacks through a glade of madrones. Their summer leaf fall makes a rustling carpet underfoot in a delicately colored pattern of lemon-yellow, pink, and cream.

The trail levels off in a huckleberry flat under redwoods where the Crystal Springs and the Richards Road trails converge at the Summit Springs Trail. A log seat at this crossing is a good place to pause before finishing the last ½-mile climb to the Skyline.

From this intersection take the wide Summit Springs Trail (fire road) to the left and follow it toward Skyline Boulevard. The redwoods here have not been cut for over a century. Heavy winter rains (as much as 40 inches a season) and summer fog drip give these trees the moisture on which they thrive. Widely spaced trees, many of them 4 feet in diameter, have a handsome understory of shiny-leaved huckleberry and a ground cover of wood fern and oxalis. In spring you will find yellow violets, mauve mission bells and irises in many shades of blue and purple. For a short expedition to this part of the park, you can drive to the Skyline Boulevard entrance and get to this fine forest without the climb from below.

The Summit Springs Trail meets the Ridge/Skyline Trail, where you can cross Skyline Boulevard to Purisima Creek Redwoods O.S.P. But to continue this trip, take the Ridge/Skyline Trail southeast ⅛ mile farther, turn east on the service road (the Ridge/Skyline Trail) and follow it another ¼ mile. From this point the Ridge/Skyline Trail bears right to Kings Mountain Road, the service road (now becomes the Archery Fire Road) descends to park headquarters, and our route turns left (northwest) onto the Chinquapin Trail.

A team of horses pulling tanbark oak logs along Kings Mountain Road near the tollhouse.

Our return trip follows the 2-mile Chinquapin Trail, which veers north down a ridge in a handsome second-growth forest. A scattering of great stumps gives you a measure of the stately forest that grew on this mountainside until it was logged in the 1860s. The trail winds down a steep hillside into McGarvey Gulch, but before it reaches the creek it turns south to make a long traverse around the ridge and joins the Dean Trail about ¾ mile above the Miwok Picnic Area.

Trip 2. A Loop Through the Center of the Park

A half-day hike takes you up McGarvey Gulch and down the other side.
- **Distance:** 4.3-mile loop.
- **Time:** 2½ hours.
- **Elevation Gain:** 400'

TRAIL NOTES

Find the Dean Trail west of the Miwok Picnic Area and head uphill. Less than a half-hour's walk along the side of McGarvey Gulch brings you to a bridge over the creek, a cool spot to linger on a hot day. In winter and early spring you can enjoy the creek waters cascading over mossy rocks. The logging road near the trail and the great redwood stumps remind us of past logging, but now second-growth trees reach high overhead. Where there is underground water near the creek, giant chain ferns are taking hold again and bigleaf maples are growing on the bank.

Leaving the creek, the Dean Trail contours around a ridge on an easy grade. In a half hour a hiker should reach an intersection with the Crystal Springs Trail. Turn right on it, and after rounding another bend the trail turns downward through a handsome redwood forest.

From here the trip down repeats in reverse the journey up the Crystal Springs Trail described in Trip 1. In 1.1 miles from the Dean Trail you come to the Toyon Group Camp. After passing it, there are another 1.3 forested miles to the lower end of the park. Turn up there on the other end of the Dean Trail to complete your trip to the Miwok Picnic Area.

Trip 3. A Loop Trip In Lower McGarvey Gulch

Explore the forest and the chaparral-covered slope in the park's lower, northeastern corner to find tall forests, wide vistas and a walk down the old road from Richard's lumber mill.

- **Distance:** 3.5-mile loop.
- **Time:** 2 hours.
- **Elevation Loss:** 360'

TRAIL NOTES

This easy trip takes its one steep stretch going downhill. Start from Werder Flat on the Campground Trail (a gated road used only for service vehicles). On a slight rise in grade you go into and out of McGarvey Gulch. A little less than ¼ mile past the creek, turn right down the Canyon Trail. You switchback down the side of McGarvey Gulch in a transitional forest where redwoods are growing high enough to shade out the madrones and tanbark oaks that took over after these slopes were logged.

From the Canyon Trail join the Crystal Springs Trail and go downhill a few hundred feet to pick up the Chaparral Trail. At this point you leave the forest to traverse a ridge where scattered oaks, madrones and a few toyons cast light shade. Native bunchgrass covers open areas along with spring-blooming iris and snowberry. In ½ mile the trail approaches the park's northern boundary, beside which Richards Road Trail makes its steep way from what was Summit Road down to West Union Creek. In the 1850s this road carried logs down to Whipple's sawmill on the creek.

You start down Richards Road Trail on an open ridge among shrubby manzanita and blue-blossomed wild lilac. The view is toward Emerald Lake Hills, topped by a cross, and to the Bay plain beyond. To the right of the trail and paralleling it, the old skid road where oxen dragged logs to the mill is visible.

Below the chaparral area, great canyon oaks meet above the trail. Then as you approach the creek through groves of redwoods, you pass the left turn-off to the Phleger Estate. Shortly the trail veers right to cross McGarvey Gulch Creek running in a culvert. After crossing over this culvert, immediately turn right (west) uphill on the Crystal Springs Trail, in 0.1 mile take the Dean Trail to the left, and make an easy climb through redwoods back to Werder Flat.

Trip 4. A Shady Walk by West Union Creek

A warm summer day is a good time to explore these cool trails by the creek.
- **Distance:** 2-mile loop.
- **Time:** 1½ hours.
- **Elevation Gain:** 500′

TRAIL NOTES

The park's creekside trails, shaded by spreading big-leaf maples and tall redwoods, are a peaceful retreat. But over a century ago, in the 1850s, three sawmills operated along West Union Creek, handling logs cut from forests extending to the Skyline above.

For an easy, leisurely walk by the creek and a short loop up into the forest, start from the Redwood Picnic Area in the southeast corner of the park. Go down (east) into the Meadow walk-in area through a pedestrian stile at the gate and pass tables filled on weekends with groups of picnickers.

At the north end of the meadow pick up the Richards Road Trail, which forms the north boundary of the park. This trail, a broad service road, continues its nearly level way up the creek. Sounds from the picnic area begin to fade as you round the first bend and enter the quiet of the tall forest.

West Union Creek runs year-round, though dry years leave the water level low. Ferns and lush shrubs line its banks. Here and there are inviting

A sunny meadow by West Union Creek draws summer picnickers.

spots for a creekside picnic. About one-half mile upstream from the Meadow on the Richards Road Trail you come to a crossroads to which the Crystal Springs Trail (which you take on the returning leg of the trip) descends from the flat above. Along this part of the trail by the creek are some of the park's largest trees.

Another ½ mile on the Richards Road Trail brings you to McGarvey Gulch Creek. Fed by springs along the Skyline, it flows down a deep-sided canyon through the center of the park. Here you turn uphill on the Crystal Springs Trail following the creek's south side for 0.1 mile. Continue on the Crystal Springs Trail past the Dean Trail for a lovely walk through the redwoods to the vicinity of the Zwierlein Group Picnic Area.

At the trail junction below the Zwierlein area continue on the Crystal Springs Trail, bearing left, and zigzag downhill. For a few minutes you go along an oak-and-madrone-covered ridge, then on many switchbacks descend into a steep canyon. Ferns carpet the hillside and small streams flow down to join the creek below. Again by West Union Creek turn right (south) on the Richards Road Trail. In another half-hour you are back at your starting place.

Trip 5. Chickadee Trail into the Forest

This pleasant, nearly level trail goes through tall chaparral and oaks and past fern-lined banks to reach a redwood grove.

- **Distance:** 1-mile loop.
- **Time:** ½ hour or more.
- **Elevation Gain:** Nearly level.

TRAIL NOTES

This self-guiding nature trail, designed for wheelchair use, has a well-compacted surface and a grade of less than 5%. For the sight-impaired there is a guide wire. A brochure is available at the trail entrance.

From a level parking space in the southwest corner of the main parking lot by the park entrance, the trail takes off around a hillside covered with wild lilac, coyote bush and toyon. A short bridge spans an old log chute left from early timber-cutting days. The path soon comes into the deep shade of redwoods. Here a bench, dedicated to former park planner Harry Dean, is strategically placed for viewing the Bay Area while resting before you retrace your steps. Or you can turn downhill and return on a lower trail through oak woods to the parking lot.

Though suitably graded and surfaced for wheelchairs, this trail also provides a pleasant short walk for those who would enjoy an easy trip into the forest.

Trip 6. Ridge/Skyline Trail Extension North

An 0.8-mile trail, built by Trail Center volunteers, contours through the redwood and fir forests along the west boundary of the park. A continuation of San Mateo County's Ridge/Skyline Trail, which is a segment of the Bay Area Ridge Trail, this trail extends from Huddart Park's Skyline Boulevard entrance (opposite the Purisima Creek Trail) north to the west end of the Crystal Springs Trail. From here you can take a trail into the Phleger Estate and explore its forests and streams. See the Phleger Estate, page 110.

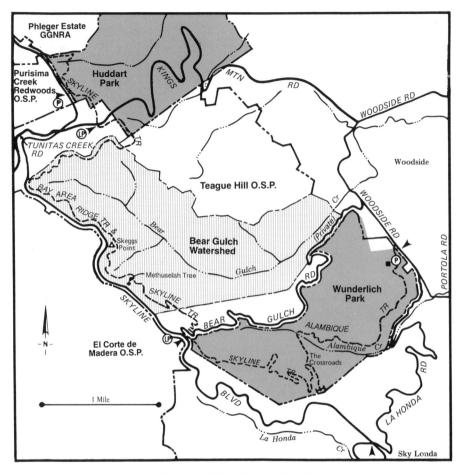

Ridge/Skyline Trail

Huddart and Wunderlich parks are linked by a beautiful and varied trail through the Bear Gulch Watershed. This long trail follows the Skyline ridge, where frequent fogs make it a cool trip in hot weather.

Jurisdiction: San Mateo County—415–363–4020.

Facilities: Trail for hikers and equestrians; last 0.6 mile restricted to equestrians.

Rules: Open 8 A.M. to sunset. No dogs or bicycles.

Maps: San Mateo County *Huddart Park* and *Wunderlich Park*, USGS topo *Woodside*.

How To Get There: (1) Huddart Park entrance—Take Skyline Blvd (Hwy 35) 6.5 miles south from Half Moon Bay Rd (Hwy 92) or 6.5 miles north from La Honda Rd (Hwy 84) to parking at Purisima Creek trailhead on west side of Skyline Blvd, then cross road to trail entrance; (2) Kings Mtn. Rd entrance—From Skyline Blvd. take Kings

Mtn. Rd 0.3 mile east to limited roadside parking; (3) Wunderlich Park entrance—Take Skyline Blvd 3 miles north of La Honda/Skyline Blvd intersection to entrance at Bear Gulch Road East (private, gated road); limited parking on west side of Skyline across from private road.

Connecting Trails: Crystal Springs and Chinquapin trails east in Huddart Park, Purisima Creek Trail west in Purisima Creek Redwoods OSP, Alambique Trail east in Wunderlich Park.

- **Distance:** 6.2 miles one way.
- **Time:** 3+ hours.
- **Elevation Loss:** 580'

TRAIL NOTES

The Ridge/Skyline Trail from the west boundary of Huddart Park to Wunderlich Park's west gate was dedicated and signed in 1989 as an official segment of the Bay Area Ridge Trail. The already completed 204 miles of this regional trail are planned to encircle the nine-county Bay Area along its 400-mile ridgetop route. Following the crest of the Santa Cruz Mountains, the Ridge/Skyline Trail passes under tall second-growth redwoods and Douglas firs, through two county parks, an open space preserve and a watershed. A part of the old California Riding and Hiking Trail, it is now also a segment of San Mateo County's north-south trail system.

With a car shuttle and a start at the north end, you will have fewer uphill climbs. Starting from Huddart Park's Skyline Boulevard entrance [entrance (1) in directions] hikers and equestrians follow the graveled service road southeast through open woodland to a park crossroads where you turn right (south) to continue on the Ridge/Skyline Trail. On the east side of this trail is lush redwood forest, and on the west is a large private inholding of several new homes on rolling grassland and evergreen forest. After 0.3 mile from your start, you reach Kings Mountain Road, which you cross to find the narrow path running beside the road, well-marked with Bay Area Ridge Trail signs.

Climbing under redwoods through low-growing huckleberries, you then swing south and cross a corner of Teague Hill Open Space Preserve in oak–madrone woodland. As the trail heads west it emerges on chaparral slopes at a sunny crossroads from which a watershed service road goes downhill. However, the Ridge/Skyline Trail continues straight ahead beside a property-line fence. Although the trail now runs through a fenced easement in the California Water Company's Bear Gulch Watershed, paralleling Skyline Boulevard, for the most part the fencing is barely apparent and does not give a closed-in feeling.

Circling around a meadow you come to a spectacular view south to Monte Bello Ridge. In spring and summer tall, yellow-flowered bush poppies brighten this spot. Soon the trail heads south, enters a forest of redwoods, then one of Douglas firs. As the trail contours around the ridges, you find redwoods growing especially tall in the deep, moist canyons below. Some of the Douglas firs are huge trees of the old-growth forest, but an occasional thicket of younger trees has sprung up, perhaps after some past fire.

From here to Wunderlich Park the trail often goes out on ridges some distance from Skyline Boulevard. At times it brings you close enough to hear the sounds of traffic, but most of the way all you hear is the wind in the treetops, the call of birds and, in summer, the fog drip hitting leaves on the forest floor.

At about the halfway point you come to a part of the forest where very large redwoods once grew. Note the size of some old stumps—6–8 feet in diameter. Look for slots cut into the trees about 6 feet off the ground, signs of the early logging method. Loggers wedged boards in these slots to support the planks they stood on while sawing the trees. Uphill from the trail you may catch a glimpse of the "Methuselah" tree, one of the few surviving giants of the old forest on the east slope of the Santa Cruz Mountains. According to a sign at its base, it is 14 feet in diameter and 1800 years old. Its crown was lost in some long-ago storm, but its lower branches are still flourishing. You can picture the awesome size of the old forest as it was before the coming of the Anglo lumbermen.

The trail continues in and out of canyons, here and there giving you a view out over the Bay. Wildflowers seen include many of the less common ones of the deep conifer forest. You can't miss the Clintonia in late spring, with its deep rosy-red blooms borne in clusters on 20-inch stalks above large basal leaves. Its unusual bright-blue berries glisten in the summer sun. But you will have to watch very closely for the rare coral–root orchid, a brownish plant bearing flowers on foot-high stalks without any green leaves. The cool, shaded forest environment prolongs the plentiful spring flower blooms into early summer.

In fall you will find the snowberry's inedible white balls on shrubs beside the trail, and the yellow leaves of the big-leaf maple reflect the light in golden hues. This trail is seldom dusty because the tall redwoods capture the fog, which then drips down to the forest floor.

Nearing Wunderlich Park the trail descends in switchbacks that takes it around a subdivision. After this detour, you climb back out of the canyon to reach the park's west gate at Bear Gulch Road, the end of the Ridge Trail route. This road is currently private, but the county has retained an easement on it for future trail use. From the west gate the old California Riding and Hiking Trail, the Skyline Trail, goes 2.7 miles east, downhill, to the southern boundary of Wunderlich Park (described in

Trip 1 of that park, see page 128). From the park boundary a 0.6–mile trail on an easement for equestrians only continues to Skylonda.

Across Skyline Boulevard is an entrance to El Corte de Madera Open Space Preserve, a possible trailhead for the continuation of the Bay Area Ridge Trail. At this writing, the route between the Ridge/Skyline Trail and La Honda Creek Open Space Preserve has not been determined.

The Methuselah tree.

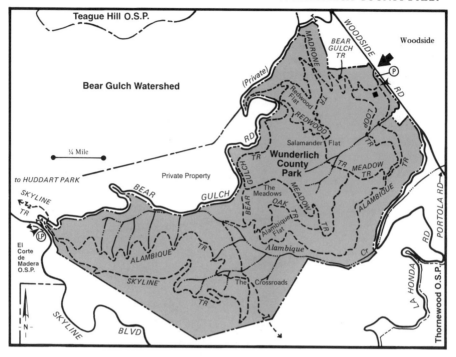

Wunderlich County Park

The Pulgas Redwoods covered most of the mountainside of present-day Wunderlich Park. These forests, part of the Rancho Cañada de Raimundo, were heavily logged during the 1850s and 60s. After the timber was cut, some of the lower hills were cleared for farming, but on the steeper mountainsides redwoods began to grow again.

The upper reaches of Wunderlich Park extend along the Skyline ridge at an elevation of about 2200 feet. East of the ridge the hillside falls away steeply, and the slope then flattens somewhat at a large meadow halfway down the mountainside. From this meadow smaller ridges and ravines descend to the lower park boundary along Woodside Road, making a total elevation change of nearly 1800 feet. Alambique Creek runs diagonally across the park, fed by streams in the precipitous wooded ravines to the north.

Alambique, which is the Spanish word for "still," reportedly was the site of a distillery in logging days. For a year the creek supplied water power for the Peninsula's first sawmill, until a steam boiler was installed. A plaque marks the site at the intersection of La Honda and Portola roads. Early residents drew their water from Alambique Creek, eventually piping it to the reservoir at Salamander Flat.

In 1872 Simon Jones bought 1500 acres of the Rancho Cañada de Raimundo and turned some of the cutover land into a working ranch he named Hazelwood Farm. (You will see the graceful shrub, hazelnut, as an understory in the forests along the trails.) Vestiges of the orchards, vineyards and olive groves Jones planted remain on the lower slopes of the park.

For the next owner, James A. Folger II, who bought the farm in 1902, it became the site of excursions, carriage trips, and weekend campouts in the woods. He built the handsome stable near the park entrance and a mansion that still stands, though not within the park. This historic stable still retains the flavor of its former elegance. The graceful design, the redwood paneling and the marble fireplace in the tack room recall the days when well-cared-for horses and carriages provided the transportation to trains and to mountain retreats. An application has been made to register the stable as a historic building.

These lands changed hands again in 1956 when Martin Wunderlich acquired much of the Folger estate. In 1974 he generously gave 942 acres to San Mateo County for open space and park use.

In 1978 San Mateo County completed the present extensive trail system, using the old ranch roads and logging roads and constructing a few new trails for loop trips, making this an outstanding park for hikers and equestrians. These 15 miles of trail, well laid out and clearly marked, lead through a mountainside wilderness of forest and meadow that can challenge hikers and horsemen with all-day trips to the Skyline or delight casual walkers with an hour or so of strolling under the trees.

It is possible to hike all day virtually without retracing any steps. A circle trip into the park from the main entrance on Woodside Road to "The Meadows" or from the Skyline Boulevard entrance down to "The Crossroads" and back is a good half-day's hike. Shady Alambique, Salamander and Redwood flats, 2 miles or less from the park office, are fine summer destinations. A segment of the Skyline Trail, crossing the upper park along the Skyline ridge, is designated part of the Bay Area Ridge Trail.

Once you have sampled some of these trails, you will want to return often to explore other routes. Following are more detailed descriptions of four suggested trips.

Jurisdiction: San Mateo County—415-363-4020.
Facilities: Trails for hikers and equestrians. At the parking area there is drinking water (none elsewhere, so carry your own) and a chemical toilet.
Rules: Open 8 A.M. to sunset. No pets or bicycles allowed.
Maps: San Mateo County *Wunderlich Park* and USGS topo *Woodside*.
How To Get There: (1) Main entrance on Woodside Rd: From I-280 take Woodside Rd (Hwy 84) southwest for 2 miles. Look for park sign

on right. (2) Upper entrance on Skyline Blvd: Follow directions above, but continue on Woodside Rd to right turn uphill onto La Honda Rd. Turn right off La Honda Rd at Skyline Blvd and go 3 miles to park entrance on east side of Skyline Blvd near entrance to Bear Gulch Road East (private). Limited parking on both sides of Skyline Blvd.

Trip 1. Figure-Eight Loop Trip to Skyline Ridge From Park Office

An ambitious all-day hike through the varied terrain and different ecosystems of the park includes sheltered, sunny meadows and cool streamsides. This hike follows the Alambique Trail to the Skyline ridge, then returns by the Skyline, Alambique, and Bear Gulch trails.

Distance: 10⅓-mile loop.

Time: 6 to 7 hours.

Elevation Gain: 1080'

Connecting Trails: Ridge/Skyline Trail north to Huddart Park; trails west in El Corte de Madera O.S.P.

TRAIL NOTES

The Alambique Trail starts on the south side of the main parking lot (1) on page 127 along a former ranch road. For the most part, it is an easy grade. For a short stretch you go up a hill through a redwood grove, but before long you note the invading "exotics"—eucalyptus, acacia, scotch broom, and other survivors of the ranch plantings, now gone wild. A project is under way to eradicate the eucalyptus and replant with redwoods, but you can see that that battle is far from won.

Rounding the ridges and climbing, the Alambique Trail goes through open mixed woodland. Some deciduous black oaks and the familiar combination of toyons, canyon oaks, and madrones are a friendly habitat for birds. Veteran birders will recognize many species, but even the novice will enjoy their songs and identify at least the insistent call of the scrub jay and the flash of its blue wings through the oaks.

The old road continues through the mixed woodland, where in late spring Douglas iris show their blue, purple, or creamy blooms along the banks. After passing the Loop and Meadow trails on the right, the Alambique Trail enters the redwoods above Alambique Creek, which forms the boundary of the park here.

The redwoods near the creek have grown again to a good size since the logging of a century ago, making Alambique Flat a cool, shady place to pause on a hot day. A side trip down to the creek over the soft duff shows you a sample of the redwood plant community. Note the size of the stumps of the old trees of the virgin forest cut in the 1850s. Huge trees (the largest some 8 feet or more in diameter where the water is most plentiful) were widely spaced but their high crowns nearly touched.

After leaving Alambique Flat you soon come to a junction with the Oak and then the Bear Gulch trails on the right, but you continue up the creek on the Alambique Trail. Soon you cross the creek and turn left to start a climb out of the canyon along the forested hillside to "The Crossroads," where the Alambique and Skyline trails intersect, 2.8 miles from the start of your trip.

You could take the Skyline Trail from here to the summit, but instead stay on the Alambique Trail, on which it's 2.4 miles and a good hour's walk to the top. This part of the trail winds in and out of steep ravines, which support sword fern and woodwardia, the 4-foot-tall, feathery, giant chain fern. In the grove of big redwoods near the summit is an old loading platform from which logs were put on wagons for the mills below. As the trail goes through the cuts for powerlines, you have a fine view northward to San Bruno Mountain, the San Francisco skyline and Mt. Tamalpais in Marin County. Just beyond here is the gate to Skyline Boulevard at Bear Gulch Road. Note the trail connection going north—the Ridge/Skyline Trail.

Turn left (east) at the trail convergence and follow the Skyline Trail through a forest of the park's most magnificent Douglas firs, which escaped the logger's saw of the last century. Soon the trail borders a long meadow where bunchgrass mixes with sedges and imported oat grasses. In spring the meadow is thick with flowers—baby blue eyes, rosy wild hollyhocks and blue and purple lupines. The sloping terrain faces southeast, a welcome warm exposure for winter morning hikes. As you look down the meadow, the Bay and East Bay hills are before you. There are fine spots here for eating the lunch you carried uphill.

Leaving the meadow, the trail leads again into fir forest, which is interspersed with huge specimens of madrone. Out from under the trees the trail emerges on a sunny ridge through a grove of chinquapin, a relative of the oak not commonly seen in San Mateo County but found in several of our hillside parks.

A hairpin turn brings you back into shady forest with an understory of buckeye, hazelnut and gooseberry. Just ahead is "The Crossroads." From here retrace your steps along the Alambique Trail to the Bear Gulch Trail, on which you turn left, uphill, to "The Meadows." Once an expanse of rolling grasslands, these meadows now are overgrown with invasive broom and native coyote brush. The best views, shady or sunny resting spots, flowers in spring and hawks overhead are now found on a knoll east of the Bear Gulch Trail and north of the Meadow Trail.

Leaving "The Meadows" by the Bear Gulch Trail, you go along a narrow track under Douglas firs. Some of the fallen trees give an idea of

The trail to the hilltop above "The Meadows."

their great size at maturity, nearly 200 feet in height and 6 or more feet in diameter. In early spring this trail segment is adorned with patches of the bold blue-flowered hound's tongue and a sprinkling of the little white blossoms of milkmaids. Hazelnut branches with pale green buds just showing make a lacelike tracery against the dark forest.

The trail soon crosses some old skid roads, those chutes where oxen dragged redwood logs down to the sawmills below. For a while the trail goes down the canyon close to Bear Gulch Road East on the northern boundary of the park, and then it veers away through Redwood Flat, a grove of tall second- and third-growth redwoods. Now the stump sprouts growing in circles around cut trees are as tall as 100 feet, making a lofty redwood grove again.

From Redwood Flat the trail winds down ravines through a fir forest, crosses the Madrone Trail, zigzags downhill for ¾ mile, passes the Loop Trail and then goes another ¼ mile along brushy hillsides back to the stables and the parking lot.

Trip 2. Loop Trip to the Meadows

This trip climbs gently to "The Meadows," the park's center, and returns by way of Salamander Flat, the site of a little reservoir in the redwoods.

- **Distance:** 2.2-mile loop.
- **Time:** 3 hours.
- **Elevation Gain:** 950'

TRAIL NOTES

After leaving the park office on the Bear Gulch Trail, you walk 0.2 mile along the lower slopes of the park through brush and oak woodlands. Then turn left onto the Loop Trail and make a gentle traverse to the Alambique Trail, which you follow for a very short distance before turning off to the right on the Meadow Trail. This is an old ranch road through the eucalyptus grove and orchards planted in Jones' farming days. Beyond the Redwood Trail junction you are in a handsome stand of toyon and madrone, where flowers bloom beside the Meadow Trail. In spring look for purple shooting stars, yellow wood violets and magenta Indian warriors. Under a canopy of tall black oaks you go uphill for ½ mile. In summer the monkey flower's apricot blossoms brighten the banks and golden stars edge the trail.

At the next trail junction turn left on the broad Oak Trail, which is shaded by oak woodland for another ½ mile. Next you turn right on a very short stretch of the Alambique Trail. Follow the narrow track through a madrone, oak and fir woodland which filters the light falling on the ground cover of low-growing poison oak (fortunately kept away from the trail).

The Bear Gulch Trail leads to many places.

At the next junction, turn right on the Bear Gulch Trail, which goes through a small clearing and an oak glade before coming out in "The Meadows," where invasive plants have crowded the grasslands.

At the top of the meadow, where perhaps there has been less plowing, you may find mounds where the grass grows in tufts, a sign that some of the ancient bunchgrass has survived here. This is one of the native perennial grasses that once covered the hills of California before being displaced by the annual European oat grass that now gives our state the famous golden look in summer.

Old clumps of bunchgrass are deep-rooted and may persist for hundreds of years (some say even thousands), spreading outward in circles. Indians burned it off in the fall to improve hunting. Although the Spaniards found the native grass to be good forage, the oat grass they inadvertently brought with them thrived in the dry California summers and soon took over.

After exploring "The Meadows," leave on the Meadow Trail going east and stroll more than ½ mile through rolling grasslands bordered by large madrones and spreading oaks. Sweeping views to the southeast show the broad flanks of Black Mountain, with the bare slopes of Monte Bello Ridge on its northwest.

From the grasslands the trail makes a switchback bringing you back into oak woodlands, though eucalyptuses now have a good foothold here. You descend rapidly for ¼ mile to the Meadow/Oak Trail junction. Take the Meadow Trail left and retrace your steps downhill for ½ mile of the trail you took on your way up. This brings you to the intersection of the Redwood Trail, on which you turn left.

From the sunlight of the intersection of the Meadow and Redwood trails you enter the deep shade of redwood forest. The soft forest duff muffles your footsteps on the narrow trail and the air is cool on even the warmest day. For ¾ mile the Redwood Trail crosses the park, contouring along the hillside at about the 1100-foot elevation line. It goes in and out of small ravines where moss-covered rocks line streams that cascade down the mountain after winter rains. After a ¼-mile walk you reach Salamander Flat, in a thick grove of big trees. An oval reservoir fed by springs up the hill was once a water supply for the farm below; later it was reportedly used as a swimming pool, but now it is fenced. The deep shade of Salamander Flat is an inviting place to lunch on the stump of a giant redwood or pause for a while on a hot day.

To return to the park entrance from Salamander Flat, pick up the Madrone Trail going right, downhill. Keep the reservoir on your right. In wet weather the reservoir overflows its dam, creating rivulets along an old wagon road. The hiker takes the wagon road, too, passing fences and hand-fashioned gate posts left from the farming days of the park's past.

About ½ mile from Salamander Flat, the Madrone Trail intersects the Bear Gulch Trail and you turn right onto it, then descend the last ¾ mile to the park office and the parking lot.

Trip 3. Circle Trip to "The Crossroads" from the Skyline Entrance

You can swing down the Alambique Trail to "The Crossroads" and return by the Skyline Trail on a 4-mile loop through the heart of the upper park.

- **Distance:** 4-mile loop.
- **Time:** 2½ hours.
- **Elevation Loss:** 700'

TRAIL NOTES

Starting from Skyline Boulevard on the Alambique Trail, you can go downhill at a good clip around bend after bend on the old ranch road. On this, the remotest trail in the park, you may hear deer crashing through the brush, but no sounds of civilization reach you. For more details of these trails see Trip 1, above.

When you get to "The Crossroads," you are in one of the coolest canyons of the park, a delightful woodsy destination for a hot day. Here you pick up the Skyline Trail and start uphill. (The other segment of the Skyline Trail descends ¼ mile to the park's south boundary.) On the varied terrain of your uphill trip you will walk along a ridge covered with oaks and madrones, traverse the edge of a long, sloping meadow and then reach the upper park entrance under giant Douglas fir trees.

Trip 4. A Short Loop Trip in the Lower Park to Salamander and Redwood Flats

This walk takes you to a small reservoir and shady redwood groves before circling back on the Bear Gulch Trail switchbacks.

- **Distance:** 3¼-mile loop.
- **Time:** 1¾ hours.
- **Elevation Gain:** 600'

TRAIL NOTES

This trip is in shade all the way, a delightful hot-weather walk. All the trail segments are described in earlier trips.

Starting from the park office, follow the Alambique Trail to the Meadow Trail junction and turn right. Follow the Meadow Trail for ⅓ mile, then turn right again on the Redwood Trail, which takes you on a gentle traverse at the 1100-foot elevation line. You pass through both Salamander and Redwood flats, good stopping places for a leisurely lunch.

Turn right at the Bear Gulch Trail junction, from which the remainder of the trip is downhill, a quick 1.4 miles on easy switchbacks. At trail's end you might notice the handsome stone walls along the old roads and beside the stable, which attest to an early craftsman's art.

*Horses still occupy the handsome stable built in Wunderlich
at the end of the 19th century.*

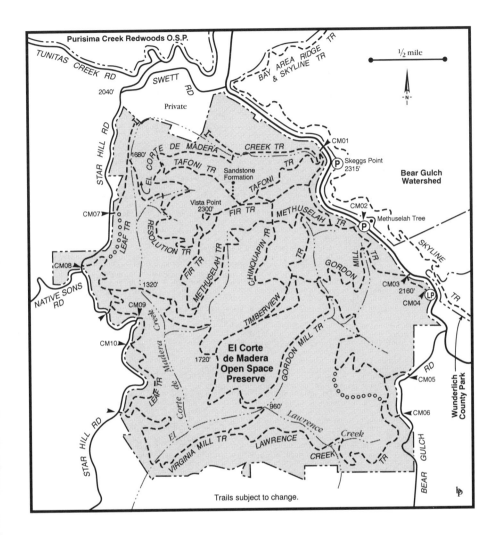

El Corte de Madera Open Space Preserve

The 2788 forested acres of El Corte de Madera Open Space Preserve, which include most of the drainage basin of El Corte de Madera Creek, lie west of Skyline Boulevard between Star Hill, Swett and and Bear Gulch roads. The creek rises from springs near the Skyline and flows between high ridges on the west side of the preserve, to be joined by its main tributary, Lawrence Creek, which flows through the southeast side. The preserve, from its 2400-foot-high point, Sierra Morena, to the canyon where the creek leaves the lower boundary at an elevation of 700 feet, is a place of high ridges and precipitously steep, deep canyons. From some of these high ridges, views between the trees of Coastside and ocean are breathtaking.

The primeval forests of El Corte de Madera's canyons and ridges were logged in the most accessible areas as early as the 1860s, starting first near the creek close to the Skyline. Logging of the old forest continued into this century, and second-growth forests have been cut sporadically since then. After the Midpeninsula Regional Open Space District acquired these lands in 1985, even limited timber cutting ceased by 1988. Although signs of logging are evident along certain roads, a handsome second-growth forest now covers the canyons and ridges.

Old logging roads, sometimes steep, form the basis for an extensive trail network for hikers, equestrians and bicyclists. A former owner allowed a motorcycle club, the Pits, to use the land, and remnants of these trails can be seen striking off from the district-designed trails. In spring 1996 the District, after a study by a citizens' task force, adopted a revised trails plan which at this writing is being implemented. By the fall of 1996 two new trails were completed, and other revisions in 1997 will improve the preserve for all its visitors. Today many trails are named and signed, and the trailheads are numbered. A spectacular 9-mile loop trip combines the Gordon Mill and Lawrence Creek trails. Other trails explore the Sierra Morena ridgetop.

Jurisdiction: Midpeninsula Regional Open Space District—415-691-1200.

Facilities: Trails for hikers, equestrians and bicyclists.

Rules: Open dawn to dusk. No dogs. All trails except foot trail to Sandstone Formation open to bicyclists and equestrians.

Maps: USGS topo *Woodside*.

How To Get There: On Skyline Blvd there are three entrances: (1) at gate CM03 (Gordon Mill trailhead) 3.7 miles north of Skyline Blvd/Hwy 84 intersection (Skylonda) and (2) at gate CMO2 (Methuselah Tree trailhead), 0.7 mile farther north. Limited parking on west side of road near preserve gate. (3) Skeggs Point Caltrans Vista Point 1 mile farther north, on east side of Skyline Blvd. Park at Skeggs Point, walk 100 yards north and cross road to preserve entrance at gate CMO1.

Trip 1. A Loop Trip to Sandstone Formation, Vista Point and Shady Valley

Try old logging roads and a new trail for an overview of this varied preserve's northern trails.

- **Distance:** 4.8 miles round trip.

- **Time:** 2½ hours.
- **Elevation:** Gain 300′

TRAIL NOTES

From the Skeggs Point entrance at CMO1 take the MROSD patrol road (not the gated, paved road on the left) which veers uphill and around a sharp bend. At this bend the road splits, its two branches being old logging roads that now serve as trails. Stay left on the upper road, the Tafoni Trail, for this trip. The lower road, the El Corte de Madera Creek Trail, on which you will return, turns right to follow the creek.

On the Tafoni Trail you continue around a hillside for 1.2 miles, skirting the north side of a ridge and rising gently to reach a multiple-trail junction—one trail goes to your left toward the Methuselah trailhead; the middle trail, the Fir Trail, bears slightly right (west) to the vista point; and the third trail, the Tafoni Trail, on which you have been traveling, goes right (northwest) to the Sandstone Formation.

For views of the Coastside and ocean, take the Fir Trail for 0.3 mile to a fork. There you take the trail on the right, signed VISTA POINT, to the end of a ridge, and through the rapidly encroaching trees on the slope below you can see the rolling grasslands running down to the Coast. Here is a good place to picnic and rest in the shade of some young Douglas firs, with chaparral, tan oaks and madrones bordering the wide trail that circles the vista point.

The weathering process called Tafoni creates columns and honeycomb patterns on sandstone rocks.

Return the way you came, rejoining the Fir Trail, to reach the multiple-trail junction you passed earlier, and bear left on the Tafoni Trail toward the Sandstone Formation, which gives the trail its name. After only 200 yards you find a narrow footpath on your right (for hikers only) that leads down to the outcrops. You will soon see the picturesque cliffs jutting up some 50 feet above the wooded hillside. Rainwater and carbon dioxide from the air combine to form a weak acid which slowly erodes the calcium-carbonate cement, binding the individual sand grains in sandstone. Over many years this weathering process has produced the honeycomb surface on the rocks and created some picturesque columnar structures. Climbing on these rocks can damage the formation, so examine them with your eyes, not your hands or feet.

For a longer trip along this ridge, retrace your steps on the narrow footpath to the Tafoni Trail you left and bear right (northwest) downhill on it for 0.9 mile under oaks and firs to the end of the road. Here at a trail junction, you meet the El Corte de Madera Creek Trail. You bear right (north) on it; the other segment of this trail goes sharp left downhill and west. On the El Corte de Madera Creek Trail you trend gently downhill (east) along a forested hillside past numerous burned-out redwood stumps, some of them remnants of giant trees that stood right across what is now the trail. Walking through a former tree trunk gives you an eerie feeling. Young redwoods are taking over in the tan oak forest, and the trail winds among them down the ridgeside.

Now descending north along the course of a small creek that is dry most of the year, you quickly reach the upper part of the preserve's main creek, El Corte de Madera. Here is probably the site of one of the earliest sawmills in the canyon, a water-powered mill operated by Ambrose Saunders in the 1860s. In most years this creek still trickles in late August, and moisture-loving plants thrive here—brilliant red-blossomed monkey flowers, orange tiger lilies and in late summer, six-foot-tall elk clover topped with a puff of delicate white flowers.

You now turn right, uphill (east) toward the preserve entrance. Young redwoods grow in this valley, but as you ascend the old logging road, the continuation of the El Corte de Madera Creek Trail, firs gradually replace the redwoods. As you pass the last redwood, you begin to hear the noise of Skyline Boulevard traffic. When you reach the junction with the Tafoni Trail on which you started, turn left and proceed a short distance to gate CM01.

Trip 2. Westward Ho!

Find the reason for the Resolution Trail's name.
- **Distance:** 5½-mile loop.
- **Time:** 3 hours

- **Elevation Loss:** 480'

TRAIL NOTES

For this delightful trip leave the Skeggs Point parking area and enter the preserve at CM01 on the Tafoni Trail. After just a hundred yards veer off right on the El Corte de Madera Creek Trail and follow the old logging road on the north side of the creek's headwaters. You are taking the last part of Trip 1 in reverse, being watchful for the trail's left jog as it leaves the creek canyon and begins a long, gradual ascent around the nose of the ridge surmounted by the Sandstone Formation. Rounding this ridge and heading a bit south, you come to fork where the Tafoni Trail goes off left (south) uphill, and the El Corte de Madera Trail continues right and slightly downhill.

Bending south and then west you contour under high canopies of madrone, tan oak and some old redwoods, most of them fire-scarred and many multi-trunked. Occasional shiny-leaved huckleberry shrubs and spring blooming iris grace the trailside, but the forest understory is relatively open. The well-graded trail is a pleasure to follow, thanks to many volunteers and the rangers who built retaining walls, put in drain pipes and deftly lined the trailside with sandstone rock. If you look uphill as you round a nose of the ridge, you can see a huge sandstone outcrop, a smaller version of the ones you visited in Trip 1.

When you come to the foot of a wide ravine, the El Corte de Madera Trail turns abruptly right (west), rounds the shoulder of a ridge, and drops down to a trail junction in a small clearing. Now you turn left (south) onto the Resolution Trail, leaving the creek and its namesake trail. However, you can hear the creek in the canyon below, especially after heavy rains, as it gathers volume and turns south on its way to join San Gregorio Creek beyond the preserve boundary and south of La Honda Road.

You climb gradually up a west-facing ridge beside some of the largest redwoods on the preserve. Some are merely burned-out shells of ancient giants, others are still living, nurse trees for sprouts that have grown to several feet in diameter. The best trees are downhill from the trail and in ravines where water is more plentiful.

But where is the reason for the trail's name? In a stand of mahogany-barked madrone at the head of a small gulch is the site of a 1953 airplane crash. The plane, en route to San Francisco, was named the *Resolution* after one of Captain Cook's four ships that explored the Pacific. All aboard were lost.

Beyond this point the trail continues gradually uphill, bends into a ravine where dense stands of tall firs and redwoods flourish, then reaches a west-facing chaparral thicket. If the day is clear, you can look out to the Coast, perhaps see a freighter in the shipping lanes offshore. Shortly you nip into conifer woods again and then emerge in a wide clearing at the junction with the Fir Trail. Take this trail left (northeast) and follow it past the junction with the trail to the vista point and on to the multi-trail junction you met in Trip 1. Here you pick up the Tafoni Trail, on which you can visit the Sandstone Formation, or head northeast on it back to gate CM01 and the Skeggs Point parking area.

Trip 3. A Loop Trip into the Preserve's Southern Canyons

A long, challenging loop trip on the main haul road down the steep canyon of the main tributary of El Corte de Madera Creek.

- **Distance:** 9-mile loop.
- **Time:** 5 to 6 hours.
- **Elevation Loss:** 1600'

TRAIL NOTES

From gate CM03 on the west side of Skyline Boulevard 3.7 miles north of Highway 84 start down the Gordon Mill Trail, an old timber haul road, now a patrol road. This day-long trip follows the broad, well-compacted old logging road for 2½ miles down the steep canyonside above the creek. After 1.5 miles down the haul road, you pass a road going left, downhill, the leg of your return trip.

Handsome second-growth redwoods and firs cover the ridges, in spite of extensive logging over the past century. Continue 1.2 miles on the Gordon Mill Trail in and out of ravines to the creek crossing at the lower end of the preserve. Watch on your left for the Lawrence Creek Trail, which you take for ¼ mile to the bridge over Lawrence Creek. This tributary of El Corte de Madera Creek is a refreshing sight on a hot day. Its clear waters cascade over mossy rocks and pause in pools above and below the bridge. Thimbleberries and huckleberries grow near its banks, and tiger lilies bloom here in late summer.

At the end of the bridge is the stump of an immense tree 6 feet in diameter, a remnant of the old forest. From the creek crossing you begin a long 2.5-mile climb on the Lawrence Creek Trail up the side of a ridge to Bear Gulch Road, a gain in elevation of more than 1000 feet.

Near Bear Gulch Road, firs rather than redwoods dominate, some of great size and age. Just before you make the last climb to reach the road at gate CM06, look for a relatively undeveloped, short but steep trail on your left on which you can bypass a segment of the old logging road from gate CMO5. (If you elect to skip this bypass, continue to gate CM06, take Bear Gulch Road north to the logging road at gate CM05 and go west on it.) On the bypass trail turn left (west) when you meet the old road, and go down into a steep-sided, verdant canyon. The next 1.3 miles are a delightful trip through second-growth forest with a ground cover of sword fern and huckleberry. At little flats along the way you have vistas across nearby canyons. As the road steepens, deep water bars across the road slow your descent.

In the canyon bottom you cross a tributary creek where logging activities and grading for roads once disrupted the channel. But in ¼ mile you reach the larger Lawrence Creek, which you followed down the canyon at the start of the trip. A few hundred yards uphill, bear right (northwest) on the Gordon Mill Trail, the main haul road. From here it is little less than an hour's trip back to the entrance gate, after a day within the enclosing walls of this vast canyon.

Other trips in El Corte de Madera Open Space Preserve will be possible after the fall of 1996 when MROSD completes the first construction phase of a new trails plan that was adopted in June 1996. Contact MROSD for updated maps and look for a later update to this edition of *Peninsula Trails* for descriptions.

New growth redwood fronds have a distinct sheen.

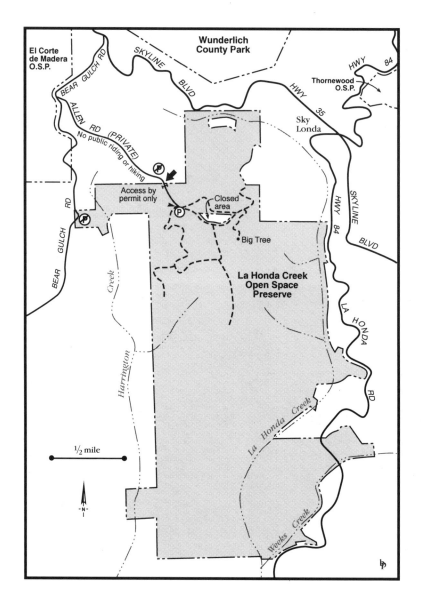

La Honda Creek Open Space Preserve

La Honda Creek Open Space Preserve includes 2043 acres of steep forests slopes and grasslands. The preserve takes in a sweep of meadow descending from private Allen Road south along the canyon of La Honda Creek to its intersection with Weeks Creek. The eastern slopes of the preserve are heavily forested; The central and western parts are steeply-rolling grasslands, with the drainage basins of Harrington and San Gregorio creeks in the near view, and the Pacific Ocean far to the west. This preserve is now open only with special permit; the present entrance via Allen Road is through private property and no riding or hiking is permitted on it. Only a few trails on the upper part of the preserve are open at this writing, but a trails plan, which may include a parking area in the southern part of the preserve (the former McDonald "Rocking Martini" Ranch), is being prepared by MROSD. The loop trip described here is not signed, but it takes the visitor to remarkable vistas, lovely meadows and handsome forests in this preserve.

Jurisdiction: Midpeninsula Regional Open Space District—415-691-1200.
Facilities: Trails for hikers and equestrians.
Rules: At this writing the preserve is open by permit only, which can be obtained from MROSD office. No bicycles or dogs permitted.
Maps: MROSD map *La Honda Creek O.S.P*, USGS topos *Woodside* and *La Honda*.
How To Get There: On Skyline Blvd go 2 miles northwest of Skyline Blvd/Hwy 84 intersection and turn south on Bear Gulch Rd. Go 0.5 mile down this narrow, winding road, turn left on private Allen Rd and go 1 mile to locked gate at preserve boundary. Directions for opening this gate are included in permit. A designated parking place is 0.2 mile beyond gate.

A Trip Down the Meadows for a Bird's-Eye View of the Coastside

This trip descends the meadows to the lower end of the preserve and returns across the pasture and through the woods on the west side of the preserve.

- **Distance:** 3-mile loop.
- **Time:** 1½ hours.
- **Elevation Loss:** 300'

TRAIL NOTES

From the designated parking area walk east on the paved road up a rise through a redwood grove and past a little clearing edged with a few Douglas firs of magnificent proportions. The road soon veers south to a barn and a private residence. An enclave of private property is uphill from the road. Leave the paved road and go right down a ranch road between the barn and a corral, then go up through a wooden gate to a meadow beyond.

A few steps from the gate along the ranch road one of the dramatic vistas of the coastside ranches and ridges opens up. A sloping pasture is edged on the east by tall, dark oaks, firs and redwoods. To the south you can see the hills along San Gregorio Creek and forested Butano Ridge. Far west are the gleam of white surf and the blue ocean beyond.

In less than a mile the ranch-road trail enters a patch of forest at the foot of the meadow. Here are a few towering old redwoods passed by in early logging. You emerge quickly into a lower meadow and to more views. In spring these grasslands are bright with wildflowers and the woods are bordered with blue irises. There are no trails here, and you will on the one side be stopped by a dense forest, or on the other by a precipitously steep hillside that falls off into the canyon of Harrington Creek. You will find any number of good picnic sites in the meadow.

Retrace your steps to the upper meadow, where you turn left on a path crossing to a service road on the west side of the preserve. Watch for the path across the pasture about halfway up to the hilltop. The path heads west, descending gradually down a ridge to pick up a service road, which you take uphill.

This winding road through a pleasant succession of woods and clearings gives you a chance to enjoy the variety of oaks, madrones, firs and redwoods along the way. You can see the 4- and 5-foot stumps of redwoods cut in early logging and compare them with the sizable second growth.

In a half hour you come out on a hillside clearing below a ridge and above a wooded canyon that drains into Harrington Creek. Around a bend are the parking area and your car.

From La Honda's meadows you have sweeping views of the
west slope of the Skyline ridge.

Southern Peninsula

Highway 84 to Saratoga Gap and Highways 9 and 85

Mountainside Preserves and Parks on the Skyline Ridge

A vast complex of public land in parks and preserves now encompasses much of the Skyline area on either side of the crest of the Santa Cruz Mountains from Skylonda/Highway 84 south to Saratoga Gap/Highway 9. More than 10,000 acres of conifer forests, oak/madrone woodlands, grasslands, canyons and streamsides are open to trail users.

These public lands and the trails therein now extend east to more than 5000 acres of regional, county and city parks in the foothills and on the urban Bay plain. An additional 17,000 acres of state and county parks lie southwest in the forest parks along Pescadero Creek—Portola Redwoods State Park and Pescadero, Memorial and Sam McDonald county parks—and on Little Butano Creek, Butano State Park.

A network of trails in these mountainside preserves and parks offers an outstanding variety of trips, from a short outing along the ridges to an invigorating day-long trip into deep canyons. Overnight trips connecting the Bayside with the Coastside are now possible. A hiker can stay at a hostel at Hidden Villa or a backpack camp on Monte Bello Ridge en route from the cities by the Bay to the parks by the ocean. Trail connections now exist via Ward Road, the Skyline-to-the-Sea Trail and the new Basin Trail to the county and state forest preserves. Vacationers can camp in Portola Redwoods State Park and the Pescadero Creek County Park complex and then continue to Big Basin Redwoods and Butano state parks and on to the Coastside via routes along Waddell and Gazos creeks. These links make possible vacation-sized expeditions through the Santa Cruz Mountains from trailheads only a half hour from the Peninsula's urban plain.

Hikers, equestrians, and bicyclists can now follow the Bay Area Ridge Trail for 16 miles along the crest of the Santa Cruz Mountains from Windy Hill to Saratoga Gap. Two 1-mile gaps in this trail to be closed by the end of 1997 will make an unbroken trail along this section of the Central Peninsula Skyline. South from Saratoga Gap the Ridge Trail route continues another 6 miles through Santa Clara County parks on the east and Castle Rock State Park on the west.

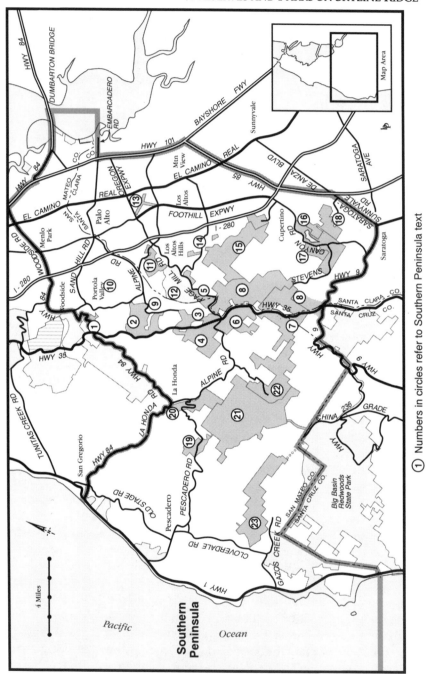

**Southern Peninsula from
Highway 84 to Saratoga Gap
and Highways 9 and 85**

Southern Peninsula
From Highway 84 to Saratoga Gap
and Highways 9 and 85

Circled # on Map	Park or Trail Name in Text
1	Thornewood Open Space Preserve
2	Windy Hill Open Space Preserve
3	Coal Creek Open Space Preserve and Upper Alpine Road
4	Russian Ridge Open Space Preserve
5	Los Trancos Open Space Preserve
6	Skyline Ridge Open Space Preserve
7	Long Ridge Open Space Preserve
8	Monte Bello and Saratoga Gap Open Space Preserves and Upper Stevens Creek County Park
9	Town of Portola Valley
10	"The Loop"—Through Portola Valley, Woodside and Menlo Park
11	Arastradero Preserve
12	Foothills Park
13	Arastradero/Foothill Expressway Hub Trails
14	Town of Los Altos Hills
15	Rancho San Antonio County Park and Rancho San Antonio Open Space Preserve, Duveneck Windmill Pasture Area and Town of Los Altos Hills Trails
16	Stevens Creek County Park
17	Picchetti Ranch Area, Monte Bello Open Space Preserve
18	Fremont Older Open Space Preserve
none	Pescadero Creek County Park Complex
19	Memorial County Park
20	Sam McDonald County Park
21	Pescadero Creek County Park
22	Portola Redwoods State Park
23	Butano State Park

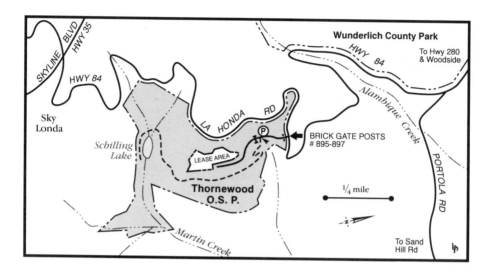

Thornewood Open Space Preserve

Thornewood Preserve came to the Midpeninsula Regional Open Space District as a gift. The property, now 109 acres, was developed by Julian and Edna Thorne in the 1920s, and was adjacent to the much larger August Schilling estate. Both properties were part of the Mexican Rancho Cañada de Raimundo, which was purchased by lumberman Dennis Martin in 1846.

The Thornes built a summer house designed in quite unusual style by Gardner Dailey (who also designed the home on the Phleger Estate and the ballroom at Filoli). After Julian's death, Edna maintained the elaborate gardens with the aid of her head groundsman, François Richard, to whom she gave a 2-acre life estate. Mrs. Thorne bequeathed the remainder of the property to the Sierra Club Foundation, stipulating that it should be kept as a "nature preserve." Finding it impossible to maintain, the Sierra Club Foundation donated the property to MROSD in 1978.

By 1982 the District had acquired a part of the adjoining former Schilling property, including a small lake, and had leased the house to a private party. Today, the area outside the leasehold and the life estate are open to the public. An 8-car parking lot lies just inside the gate and a short trail leads to Schilling Lake. Yearly the historic house has been opened to the public for docent-guided tours, date and time varying. Call MROSD for details.

Jurisdiction: Midpeninsula Regional Open Space District—415-691-1200.

Facilities: Trails for hikers, equestrians, bicyclists and dogs on leash.
Rules: Open dawn to dusk.
Maps: MROSD map *Thornewood OSP*, USGS *Woodside*.
How To Get There: From I-280 take Woodside Rd (Hwy 84) southwest 4 miles through Town of Woodside. After passing junction with Portola Rd (on left), Woodside Rd becomes La Honda Rd and you continue on it uphill for about a mile to brick gateposts #895 and 897 on your left.

A Trip through the Woods to a Historic Lake

A short, shady trail, just right for children, winds downhill to reach Schilling Lake, a remnant of August Schilling's property.

- **Distance:** 1.4 miles round trip.
- **Time:** 40 minutes.
- **Elevation Loss:** 80'

TRAIL NOTES

Starting from the small parking lot inside Thornewood's brick gateposts, walk 100 feet south along the driveway (which leads to the private leaseholding) and take the trail on your left. You meander in and out of a thick, second-growth forest, grown since the logging took place in the 1800s and the cleared gardens were abandoned some thirty years ago. The trail winds downhill, sometimes on the remnants of an old road, once part of the Schilling spice king's estate. After 0.7-mile you reach the 1-acre

Thornewood historic house and garden, ready for public tours.

lake, held back by a small dam and, remarkably, the home of some beautiful white swans. Try to imagine this as a centerpiece of Mr. Schilling's extensive gardens, which once featured a redwood temple, a Stonehenge-like pergola and even fake rocks made of wood, wire and plaster.

While you return from the pond uphill, the way you came, you can cogitate on the fleeting nature of man's past "glories."

•

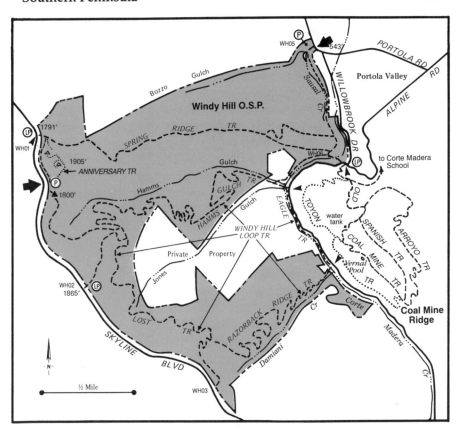

Windy Hill Open Space Preserve and Town of Portola Valley Trails on Coal Mine Ridge

This 1132-acre preserve includes the two bald knobs of Windy Hill and the long, grassy ridge extending from the Skyline to the floor of Portola Valley and many forested acres south of a private inholding. The upper grasslands of Windy Hill, familiar landmarks on the Midpeninsula mountains, stand out against the adjacent forested slopes. We watch Windy Hill from the Bay plain as it turns green in spring and as it is occasionally whitened by winter snows. In summer the wind and fog from the ocean sweep over this bare hill to give it the name it has been known by for 50 years or more.

Once part of an early Mexican land grant belonging to Maximo Martinez, known as El Corte de Madera ("the wood-cutting place"), these lands were also used for cattle grazing and hayfields. The Brown Ranch stood on the site of today's picnic area on Skyline Boulevard, and the Orton Ranch was located north at the head of Spring Ridge. Beautiful second-growth forests now clothe many slopes and fill the canyons of the preserve.

The first 537 acres of this preserve were donated to the Peninsula Open Space Trust in December 1979 and were later sold to the Midpeninsula Regional Open Space District. Additional purchases include the 429 acres of Spring Ridge, acquired in 1987. In 1995 POST purchased about 200 acres of the private inholding within the two arms of Windy Hill Open Space Preserve, which eventually will be transferred to MROSD. Located between clusters of county parks and MROSD preserves north and south along both sides of the Skyline ridge, Windy Hill Open Space Preserve is part of an expanding chain of public ridgelands on the Peninsula.

Approximately 14 miles of trails traverse Windy Hill's grassy slopes, climb its steep ridges and follow its stream canyons. From the main entrance on Skyline Boulevard, where a rustic fence encloses a picnic area, you can climb to the summit of Windy Hill for a 360° view—ocean, Bay, cities and distant mountains. Or you can take one of three long ridge trails that descend to Portola Valley, and return on a trail up another ridge.

Fund-raising headed by the Peninsula Open Space Trust (POST) brought donations from local citizens to the Windy Hill Endowment Fund to build the 8.4-mile Windy Hill Loop Trail. These funds also helped construct the Anniversary Trail up and around the Windy Hill knobs. The Windy Hill Loop Trail, one of the longest trails on the Peninsula, was laid out and constructed by volunteers, MROSD staff and the California Conservation Corps.

Kite-flying on Windy Hill is superb, though the wind will test the sturdiness of your kite. Others who take advantage of the ridgetop breezes include hang-gliders and para-sailors and those who operate their nonmotorized model gliders on Windy Hill with permits from MROSD.

Jurisdiction: Midpeninsula Regional Open Space District—415-691-1200.
Facilities: Trails for hikers and equestrians; bicycles on Spring Ridge Trail only. Picnic area.
Rules: Open dawn to dusk. Dogs on leash on the Anniversary, Spring Ridge, and Eagle trails only.
Maps: MROSD brochure *Windy Hill*, USGS topo *Mindego Hill*.
How To Get There: (1) Take Woodside/La Honda Rd (Hwy 84) or Page Mill Rd to Skyline Blvd. The main entrance is on the east side of Skyline Blvd 2.3 miles south of La Honda Rd. Two other entrances north and south of the main entrance are marked by brown pipe gates and hiking stiles. (2) Take Alpine or Sand Hill Rd toPortola Rd Preserve entrance is on west side of Portola Rd, ½ mile south of Portola Valley Town Center. Until parking area on Portola Rd is completed (scheduled for 1996), use pull-outs on Portola Rd just

north of Sequoias retirement home or park at Town Center. (3) Alpine Rd entrances: Take Alpine Rd south past Portola Rd to corner of Alpine and Willowbrook roads. Park on north side of Alpine Rd and walk up road to trail entrances on right side: (a) Spring Ridge Trail entrance (south end) and northeast connection to Hamms Gulch Trail, 0.1 mile beyond parking area; (b) Main Hamms Gulch Trail entrance, 0.3 mile farther at stone gates of Rancho Corte Madera; (c) Razorback Ridge Trail entrance, 0.6 mile still farther up road.

Trip 1. A Windy Hill Loop Trip

For hikers and equestrians only, this leg-stretching loop around the preserve starts from the Skyline ridge, descends 1120 feet to Corte Madera Creek and then climbs back up to the ridge on the Hamms Gulch Trail.

- **Distance:** 8.4-mile loop.
- **Time:** 5½ hours.
- **Elevation Loss:** 1120'
- **Connecting Trails:** Toyon and Old Spanish trails southwest on Coal Mine Ridge.

TRAIL NOTES

This spectacular trip starts from the picnic area at the main Skyline Boulevard entrance and follows the route of the Bay Area Ridge Trail south. Take the signed 0.6-mile connector trail on the right and contour around the knoll to the Lost Trail/Hamms Gulch Trail junction. Bear right there to cross a chaparral-covered shoulder of the ridge. Then, on an old road re-named the Lost Trail, you go around bends and into hollows below the crest of the Santa Cruz Mountains. Many viewpoint windows open up through the trees to reveal the valley below. Under madrones and oaks and across rivulets, this trail continues for 1.7 miles to the top of the ridge between Fitzpatrick and Damiani creeks, where a short connector trail ascends to gate WHO3 on Skyline Boulevard, the south end of the Ridge Trail in this preserve.

Then, turning left, you begin a series of downhill zigzags on the well-graded 2.5-mile Razorback Ridge Trail. Along the sides of small ravines and out onto shoulders of the ridge, the trail drops steadily downward under a high oak-and-madrone canopy. Hikers often find deer quietly making their way over the leafy forest floor.

At the lower end of the trail you join a dirt road and cross a bridge to Alpine Road. Paralleling the road beside Corte Madera Creek is the Eagle Trail, which you follow for 0.6 mile downstream, first along the pavement, then near the creek below the road. Cool and shaded in summer, it leads to a bridge over Corte Madera Creek at the stone-pillared, gated entrance to Rancho Corte Madera, a private inholding.

Go left across the old bridge with the moss-covered stones, then immediately go right and step onto the Hamms Gulch Trail. In a few feet you cross a wooden bridge over Jones Gulch. Just uphill from this bridge is a foot trail that leads right, meandering along Corte Madera Creek across private property, to join the Spring Ridge Trail near the Alpine/Willowbrook roads parking area. However, for this trip on the Windy Hill Loop, continue uphill on the Hamms Gulch Trail, built on the alignment of the old Brown Ranch Road, which takes today's trail users through magnificent oak, madrone and fir forests.

About a mile up the trail, at a break in the forest, you'll find a bench erected by MROSD rangers. From here you look across the wooded canyon of Hamms Gulch to the grasslands of Spring Ridge. Continuing uphill, the trail then climbs the south side of Hamms Gulch. On the side of this gulch grow immense Douglas firs. Some at least 6 feet in diameter have escaped the logging done early in this century.

The trail skirts around the trees and out of the forest, and then beyond a few bends you turn right on the trail that leads back to your starting point at the picnic area, the old Brown Ranch site.

Trip 2. To the Top of Spring Ridge

Climb up Spring Ridge to the Windy Hill Preserve heights, a 7-mile round trip. Or, hikers can make it a 9-mile loop by returning on the Hamms Gulch Trail.

- **Distance:** 7 miles round trip on Spring Ridge Trail, 9 miles on loop trip returning via Hamms Gulch Trail.
- **Time:** 4 hours round trip on Spring Ridge Trail; 5 hours on loop trip.
- **Elevation Gain:** 1260'

TRAIL NOTES

The long, grassy ridge rising to Windy Hill's summit provides delightful short trips to large, tree-bordered meadows, and serves as one leg of a long loop trip from the valley floor to the Skyline ridge and back. The trail follows an old ranch road right up the spine of bald Spring Ridge. The views from this expanse of high grasslands are superb. Start this uphill trip early and carry plenty of water on hot days.

From the main Portola Road entrance follow the tree-lined road to a left turn beside the little reservoir where Sausal Creek is impounded. If you want just a short outing, here is a pleasant site for a picnic in the shade of old eucalyptus trees near the water's edge. In winter, watch for brightly plumed wood ducks. A trail around the west side of Sausal Pond is planned for 1997.

Past the lake's marshy borders you find a weathered cattle chute on your left and occasional oaks arching over the trail. Where a side trail comes in from Alpine Road on the left, hikers note it for your return, if you come back down the Hamms Gulch Trail. At this trail intersection, your route up the ridge turns right and begins a series of steep rises and short, flat stretches. Curving left, then right, and ever upward, this old road keeps to the open slope. At the edges of wide meadows, clumps of oaks interspersed with maples and spring-flowering buckeyes fill the ravines.

The Spring Ridge Trail is the only one open to bicyclists in Windy Hill Preserve.

After about 2 miles, the trail arcs right and levels off and you pass through a line of weathered fence posts. Look for bluebird houses on posts in the grasslands. In this area are the springs that gave the ridge its name, and which watered the cattle that grazed here for many years. Uphill is a clump of Monterey cypresses that formerly sheltered the Orton ranchhouse. Only a few old fruit trees and a jumble of fallen logs remain to remind today's trail users of these early settlers. The wide trail curves north above the ranch site, makes a last gentle ascent, and then levels off north of Windy Hill to reach the Skyline Boulevard roadside parking at gate WH01.

Here you join the Bay Area Ridge Trail, which runs south through the preserve for 3.5 miles to its present termination at gate WH03. Plans are under way to extend the Ridge Trail south on an existing easement to join the Russian Ridge segment at Rapley Ranch Road.

To return to the valley floor, the shortest route (and the bicyclist route) is back down the Spring Ridge Trail. However, if hikers want a gentler grade and a different way back, they can follow the Anniversary Trail south from here up and over the Windy Hill knobs to the picnic area (see Trip 3). From there a 0.6-mile trail leads east to the Windy Hill Loop (see

Trip 1). At the first junction turn left and drop down into Douglas fir forest on the Hamms Gulch Trail, which you will follow for 2.4 miles back to the valley.

Shortly before reaching the foot bridge over Jones Gulch, you become aware of the paved driveway across the creek on your right leading to the private residences at Rancho Corte Madera. Then on your left, a foot trail (closed to bicycles and dogs), part of the Portola Valley Town trails system, leads down along Corte Madera Creek and winds through riparian vegetation to join the south branch of the Spring Ridge Trail. Turn left on it to reach your starting place at the Portola Road entrance. A right turn would take you to Alpine Road and limited roadside parking near the corner of Willowbrook Drive.

Trip 3. Summit Hike on the Anniversary Trail

Take this short trip on a segment of the Bay Area Ridge Trail for a top-of-the-world view of the Bay Area from Windy Hill's bald knobs.

- **Distance:** 1¼ miles round trip.
- **Time:** ½ hour.
- **Elevation Gain:** 127′

TRAIL NOTES

Leave the left (north) side of the Skyline Boulevard picnic area on the trail that celebrates the 10th anniversary of Windy Hill's purchase. This is an ideal place to take your out-of-town visitors, if the day is clear. A climb to the top will orient them with fixes on some Bay Area peaks—Black Mountain, Mt. Hamilton, Mt. Diablo and Mt. Tamalpais. West lies the Pacific Ocean; north, east and south are San Francisco Bay and its surrounding cities. The Anniversary Trail continues to the north roadside parking area at gate WH01 at the top of the Spring Ridge Trail.

The trip to the summit of Windy Hill is for hikers only, but equestrians and bicyclists can get breath-taking coastal views from the Fence-line Trail, which takes off from the Anniversary Trail less than 0.1 mile north of the picnic area. This route is a broad, unsurfaced, disked 0.3-mile trail that rounds the west shoulder of Windy Hill, offering splendid views of the San Mateo coastline. This trail and the Anniversary Trail are part of the 3.5-mile Bay Area Ridge Trail route through Windy Hill Open Space Preserve.

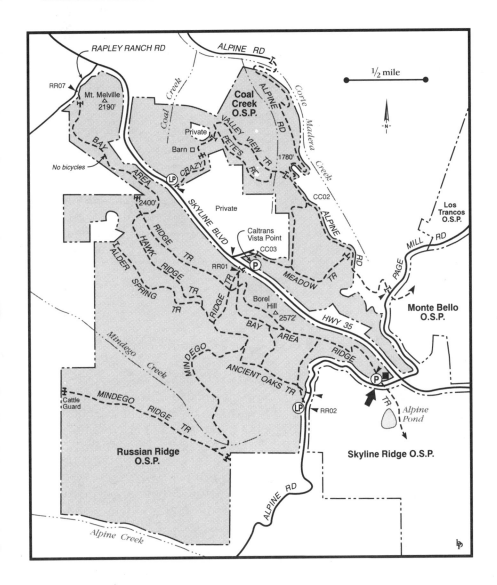

Coal Creek Open Space Preserve, Upper Alpine Road and Russian Ridge Open Space Preserve

Bordered on the west by Skyline Boulevard and on the east by Upper Alpine Road, crescent-shaped 493-acre Coal Creek Open Space Preserve is almost surrounded by other Midpeninsula Regional Open Space Preserves—Russian Ridge west across the Skyline, Monte Bello and Skyline Ridge south and Windy Hill less than a mile north.

Three lovely meadows lying just below the Skyline ridge are central attractions of this preserve. Their flowery slopes invite springtime outings. Groves of handsome oaks and madrones fringing their grasslands are right for summertime picnics–easy, short walks from Skyline parking, or longer walks up the hill from Upper Alpine Road. Birds, deer, bobcats and cottontail rabbits flourish in these meadows and forests.

These meadows, one in the north and two in the south, are linked by two old roads, now part of the preserve's trail system. Historic Crazy Petes Road and the Valley View Trail drop down from Skyline Boulevard and traverse oak-and-madrone woodlands above the preserve's steep, forested lower hillsides to end at Upper Alpine Road. This dirt road, closed to motor vehicles, links the two arms of Coal Creek Preserve, and makes a much-needed off-road hiking, riding and bicycling route between Portola Valley and Skyline.

Jurisdiction: Midpeninsula Regional Open Space District—415-691-1200.

Facilities: Trails for hikers, equestrians and bicyclists, dogs on leash.

Rules: Open dawn to dusk.

Maps: MROSD brochure *Russian Ridge/Coal Creek OSP*, USGS topo *Mindego Hill*.

How To Get There: Take Woodside/La Honda Rd (Hwy 84) or Page Mill Rd to Skyline Blvd. On the east side of Skyline Blvd are: (1) north entrance at Crazy Petes Rd, 6.1 miles south of Hwy 84, limited parking, stay clear of mailboxes; (2) south entrance at Caltrans Vista Point, 8.9 miles south of Hwy 84, 1.0 mile north of Page Mill Rd. Alternately, (3) take Alpine Rd from I-280 south for about 8 miles until you reach gate where road is closed. Park away from private driveways and go up dirt part of Upper Alpine Rd. (4) Take Page Mill Rd 8 miles south from I-280 to Monte Bello parking lot and take a trail southwest, paralleling Page Mill Rd, to gate MB05 to reach un-numbered, gated entrance to Alpine Rd on northwest side of Page Mill Rd.

Trip 1. Over the Meadow and Through the Woods

This loop trip traverses the southernmost meadow and follows Upper Alpine and Crazy Petes roads to the other end of the preserve. A leafy streamside and a sunny knoll make pleasant picnic destinations.

- **Distance:** 4-mile loop.
- **Time:** 2 hours.
- **Elevation Gain:** 400'
- **Connecting Trail:** Upper Alpine Road north and south.

TRAIL NOTES

Starting from the Caltrans Vista Point on Skyline Boulevard, walk north along the road 200 yards to the first driveway on the right. This unpaved road, the Meadow Trail, goes downhill to the preserve entrance at gate CCO3, identified by MROSD signs.

Under wide-spreading live-oak trees you descend past one private driveway to the top of a broad grassy meadow surmounted by a grove of immense madrone trees. In springtime this meadow is a beautiful swath of green, flecked with blues of lupines, gold of poppies and pinks of checker bloom. On an autumn day the authors saw a four-point buck standing in this meadow. Although such a sight is rare, you often see does along preserve trails.

From the trail junction at the top of the meadow a trail descends to the left, the return route on this loop trip. Now, however, you go straight ahead and slightly uphill from this junction through a forest of moss-covered madrones and oaks growing among large sandstone outcrops. Then the trail veers left and emerges in another large ridgetop meadow surrounded by oaks, both deciduous and evergreen, Douglas firs and big-leaf maples. In spring big, yellow-blossomed daisies, called mule ears, brighten these grasslands, and late into summer poppies bloom here.

Your path goes east across the length of the meadow, and then enters a grove of madrones and oaks. Wind downhill through these woods to reach Upper Alpine Road just below the culvert that carries a small creek under the road. You are now about half a mile below Page Mill Road. Turn left, downhill, on unpaved Alpine Road following the west edge of Corte Madera Creek Canyon. The trail passes under a canopy of deciduous black oaks where you find shade in summer and brightly colored leaves in fall.

About ½ mile down the canyon on the left is the gate to Coal Creek Preserve's middle entrance. Note it for the return trip, but go nearly ¼ mile farther, watching for Crazy Petes Road uphill on your left, marked with an MROSD sign. Leave Upper Alpine Road here and step over the stile to this historic road, now used as a trail. In 200 yards you cross a bridge over a boulder-strewn creek. Ferns, moss and moisture-loving dogwood line the banks of pools on either side of this bridge.

Beyond the bridge beneath wide-spreading madrones is a veritable thimbleberry terrace extending to a Y-shaped trail junction. Here Crazy Petes Road arcs left and the Valley View Trail goes right. This trip takes the Valley View Trail on the right and returns on Crazy Petes Road. In woods of live oak and madrone the trail narrows and curves around the mountain, with views north and east over the canyon of Corte Madera Creek. In about 15 minutes you come to a little knoll in a clearing that catches the sun in midday.

Gaining altitude now, the trail becomes a narrow, uneven path trending left through a miniature forest of long-leaved, lavender-flowered yerba santa. Shortly before reaching a gate you go left on Crazy Petes Road for the return leg of your journey.

This service road climbs through oak woodlands where vistas, framed by the trees, open up to the east. Passing an open hillside, where a few private homes sit outside the preserve, you now descend around a big curve and into the shade of the madrone woods. At the Y-shaped junction you meet the Valley View Trail again, and turn right to cross the bridge and rejoin Upper Alpine Road.

To finish this loop trip, first bear right here for ¼ mile to the next trail entrance on the right at gate CCO2. Go through the gate and begin a steady climb to the high grasslands. The trail may have been a construction road for a high-tension wire tower you pass under here. Beside the trail in spring, blue irises and purple lupines bloom, and later wild roses flower.

At the top of the meadow turn right on the unpaved road through the woods on which you started this trip, and return uphill to your car at the Vista Point. From here, looking beyond the meadows and forests of your hike, you see the Midpeninsula cities below, less than 10 miles from the preserves along the Skyline ridge greenbelt.

Two friends beneath oaks in Coal Creek Preserve.

Trip 2. A Short Hike to a Protected Meadow

Starting from Skyline Boulevard, hike ½ mile to sheltered grasslands above the urban scene.

- **Distance:** 1 mile round trip to meadow; 2½ miles round trip to knoll.
- **Time:** ½ hour round trip to meadow; 1¼ hours round trip to knoll.
- **Elevation Loss:** 200′ to meadow; 370′ to knoll.

TRAIL NOTES

With a sketch book, your favorite flower guide or bird book, and a snack in your daypack, start at the northern entrance to Coal Creek Preserve, ½ mile north of the Vista Point. There is limited parking where Crazy Petes Road intersects Skyline Boulevard.

Walk along Crazy Petes Road less than ½ mile to a point on your left where you can get down into the pasture near a big old barn (closed to the public). In the late 1990s a trail is planned to cross this meadow and extend north to Mt. Melville. In the meantime, there are pleasant places to enjoy your picnic in these sloping grasslands where Coal Creek originates.

You can walk another ¾ mile along Crazy Petes Road and continue to the protected knoll on the Valley View Trail, described in Trip 1, where the only sounds are those of birds in the trees, or possibly deer in the forest.

Trip 3. A Quiet Walk up Historic Upper Alpine Road to Skyline

A tree-shaded walk follows historic old Alpine Road up Corte Madera Creek to Page Mill Road about 0.7 mile below Skyline Boulevard. Along the way you pass three junctions of trails in the main part of Coal Creek Preserve, described in Trips 1 and 2.

This section of Alpine Road, now closed to motorized vehicles, is a quiet, winding way up a wooded mountainside where no traffic intrudes.

- **Distance:** 2½ miles one way.
- **Time:** 1¾ hours.
- **Elevation Gain:** 1000′

TRAIL NOTES

Alpine Road gets its name not from the heights of the Santa Cruz Mountains, which aren't really alpine, but from a pine tree, *El Pino*, (probably a Douglas fir) which grew beside the Pescadero Trail to the coast. The area near the intersection of the present Alpine Road and Portola State Park Road (3.1 miles southwest of Skyline Boulevard), called "El Pino" by Spanish Californians, became "Alpine." The name was first attached to the road west of Skyline, built in 1879. The part of the road we are walking on, built in 1894, was for some time called the Martinez grade, after the owner of Rancho Corte de Madera.

Before you start out on foot, you have a scenic drive up Corte Madera canyon, as Alpine Road leaves the open valley. The road beside the creek looks down into one of our loveliest streams. Maples, alders and bays shade its winding course, and wood ferns clothe its steep banks. In late fall and early winter, when the maples turn golden, this is an enchanting drive.

On the opposite side of the road from the creek, the steep canyon wall rises to Coal Mine Ridge, where you may glimpse thin veins of coal along the road cuts. Low-grade coal was once mined from this ridge.

About 3 miles from the Alpine/Portola Road intersection, just past Joaquin Road, you come to a fork in the road where a heavy metal gate bars the righthand fork. Park at one of several turnouts, crawl through the gate and start up unpaved Alpine Road. This road is owned and maintained by San Mateo County but runs through lands owned by MROSD and is bordered on the east by private lands.

A bicyclist leans into a curve on the old road.

The washed-out bridge over the creek at the first bend has been replaced by a culvert. Landslides on the road a bit higher up are repaired by the county after the rains. This wide, multi-use trail with an easy gradient is especially popular for bicycle riding.

Whether you take this road in winter after the first rains freshen the foliage and the cold turns leaves to gold, in the spring with the burst of pale new leaves and flowers along the way or at some less dramatic time of year, this is a fine, quiet old road where tall trees meet overhead and new views open up at each turn.

Hiking here in late fall or early winter, you will find that the shrubby willows that line the creek have turned yellow. The tall maples along the creek are golden, and other maples make bright splashes of color here and there on the hillsides where they mark springs that give them the moisture they need.

From the canyon the road climbs to a flat on a ridge covered with deciduous black oaks. Under the umbrella of this grove the light takes on a golden hue in the fall from the tawny yellow of their leaves. Many deer inhabit these woods, as you can see from their tracks on the road. In fall and winter, bucks, does and the fawns born the preceding spring stay together, and you can see the hoof prints of these family groups where they cross the road to the creek below. Occasionally you glimpse them as you round a bend.

From this flat the road continues up the ridge on an easy grade. In late fall and early winter madrones on the hills are heavy with red berries, and thick-clustered toyon berries are accented against their dark-green leaves. Black-headed Oregon juncos feast on wild cherries hanging down below shiny leaves.

The MROSD's Coal Creek Open Space Preserve borders Upper Alpine Road to the west almost up to the Page Mill Road intersection. Trails from Upper Alpine Road into Coal Creek Preserve, described in Trips 1 and 2, make good loop trips from the Alpine Road trailhead. An extension of this trip can be made in Monte Bello Open Space Preserve by taking the unnamed trail across Page Mill Road. See the chapter on Monte Bello Preserve for possibilities.

If you would like a short extension to a seldom-visited pond, cross Page Mill Road from the end of Upper Alpine Road, go through the stile at gate MB05, and walk 0.3 mile. You pass some weedy eucalyptus trees growing along an old swale, which is possibly a parallel to the San Andreas Fault trace farther east. The pond covers about 2 acres and is prime habitat for resting ducks. It is a charming spot for a picnic before retracing your steps down this historic old road.

Russian Ridge Open Space Preserve
Map on page 157

Russian Ridge Open Space Preserve's 1580 acres lie along the west side of Skyline Boulevard for about 3 miles north from the Page Mill/Alpine Road intersection through the Mt. Melville area and extend southwest into the deep canyons of Alpine and Mindego creeks. Trails run along the ridgetop parallel to Skyline Boulevard, surprising routes lead through beautiful wooded canyons and old ranch roads descend the west slopes. Spectacular views east of San Francisco Bay and the Diablo Range and west to the ocean over an expanse of ridges greet the visitor to Russian Ridge. Strong winds that bring clear skies can also carry dense fog, especially in summer.

Jurisdiction: Midpeninsula Regional Open Space District—415-691-1200.
Facilities: Trails for hikers, equestrians and bicyclists.
Rules: Open dawn to dusk. No dogs permitted.
Maps: MROSD brochure *Russian Ridge/Coal Creek OSP*, USGS topo *Mindego Hill*.
How To Get There: Take Hwy 84 from Woodside, Page Mill Rd from Palo Alto or Hwy 9 from Saratoga to three preserve entrances: (1) at Skyline Blvd/Alpine Rd intersection, with parking on northeast corner, (2) at Caltrans Vista Point 1 mile north of this intersection, and (3) at Rapley Ranch Rd ½ mile north of vista point with roadside parking on west side of Skyline Blvd.

Trip 1. A Bay Area Ridge Trail Trip for Those Clear Days When You Can See Forever

A trail along Russian Ridge for the length of the preserve has views out to the Pacific Ocean across ranchlands and forests little changed since American settlers moved to California over a century ago.

- **Distance:** 6.4 miles round trip.
- **Time:** 3¼ hours.
- **Elevation Gain:** 300'
- **Connecting Trails:** East to Coal Creek Preserve and Crazy Petes Road; south to trails in Skyline Ridge OSP.

TRAIL NOTES

From the Russian Ridge parking area at the northwest corner of Skyline Boulevard and Alpine Road, climb the steep rise to the ridge. After a long switchback you pass a trail that leads left (south) to a trailhead on Alpine Road. However, continuing along the Bay Area Ridge Trail route, go 0.2 mile to another junction where you can go right to the summit of Borel Hill (2572') or take the left fork, which winds along the west-facing slopes with canyon and ocean views. On either trail in early spring poppies, red maids, Johnny-jump-ups and lupines are in bloom and, by April, a profusion of goldfields covers these grasslands.

Few spots can beat this ridge for views that take in the Peninsula from Bay to ocean. If you take the Borel Hill trail on a clear day in winter, with binoculars you can see the snow-capped Sierra Nevada through the gap of Niles Canyon to the northeast and the Farallon Islands to the west. On a still, fogless evening in early summer when daylight lingers, this is a spectacular supper picnic site. Among the scattered rock outcrops are many places to spread out an evening meal and watch the sunset over the Pacific Ocean.

The lefthand trail follows a gentle meander along the west side of the ridge, passing a junction where a trail leads south to the Ancient Oaks Trail. (See Trip 3). However, the Ridge Trail curves north into the head of a swale, then bends west past sandstone outcrops that frame views of the grasslands, wooded creek canyons and forested ridges south and west.

From perches on scattered outcrops you see Mindego Hill rising west of Skyline.

Whichever Ridge Trail route you take, you reach the saddle near the Caltrans Vista Point entrance to the preserve. To complete this Russian Ridge segment of the Bay Area Ridge Trail, you briefly follow the Mindego Ridge Trail left (south) and then continue right (north) on the Ridge Trail. You are on a trail that gradually ascends the west side of the ridge. To the west stretch ranchlands, creek canyons and ridges, and the ocean lies beyond. In the morning light mists often hide the ocean, but late in the day the ocean waters glisten as they reflect the light of the late afternoon sun.

Southwest before you is Mindego Hill. In spring its green bulk stands out against dark ridges beyond. Mindego Hill is of volcanic origin, probably formed more than 135 million years ago. At that time it was submerged below the ocean as part of a range of mountains at the edge of the Pacific Plate. These mountains, now known as the Santa Cruz Mountains, have been moving northwest along the San Andreas Fault. In today's time frame, this trip traverses the eroded, worn-down remnants of these mountains little changed over the last century of cattle ranching.

Continuing 0.5 mile along the Ridge Trail toward a group of radio antennas, you come to a junction, where the 0.6-mile Hawk Ridge Trail leads left (west) and then south, downhill. You can take this trail for a shorter return to your starting point (see below). From this junction north to Rapley Ranch Road, the Ridge Trail is open to hikers and equestrians only. However, bicyclists can return south on the multi-use Hawk Ridge and Alder Spring trails and retrace their route back to the Alpine Road/Skyline Boulevard parking area.

On the northward Ridge Trail route, hikers and equestrians wind in and out of lovely woods with views alternating east and west. Surprisingly, a wooden deck appears beside the trail, inviting a sheltered lunch stop. Just beyond are some intriguing sculptures emplaced by a former owner. Enjoy these amenities, but respect the private residence by staying on the trail.

Winding down the ridge, the trail passes an ancient barn near the Rapley Ranch Road gate. At this writing there is no stile for horses to exit onto Rapley Ranch Road. Hikers crawl through the gate and walk 0.1 mile out to Skyline Boulevard. Plans to extend the Ridge Trail north to Windy Hill Open Space Preserve are in process at this writing. If you have arranged a car shuttle, you can end your trip here. Otherwise for variety, return to the Hawk Ridge Trail junction and take the Hawk Ridge and Alder Spring trails back to the Mindego Ridge Trail. Turn north on it and retrace your route to your starting point.

Trip 2. Down to Mindego Creek and to the Slopes of Mindego Hill

An old ranch road descends southwest, traversing pasturelands and winding in and out of canyons to reach one of Mindego Creek's main branches and to approach Mindego Hill.

- **Distance:** 6 miles round trip.
- **Time:** 3½ hours.
- **Elevation Loss:** 400'

TRAIL NOTES

Park at the Caltrans Vista Point, cross Skyline Boulevard and go through the gate onto the old ranch road that heads downhill. It passes both trails described in Trip 1 and turns southeast. It descends through grasslands and soon turns into a canyon shaded by oaks, madrones and Douglas firs. In half an hour you emerge into open pasture again, looking out across forests toward Mindego Hill's truncated summit.

Groves of buckeyes and oaks bordering the grassland below the road are tempting sites for a picnic stop or a welcome pause on the trip back up. Look for the intersection of the Ancient Oaks Trail uphill on your left. It is described in Trip 3.

A few minutes' walk farther down the trail brings you to a little flat beside a tributary of Mindego Creek. On one side of the flat, pasturelands furrowed by a century of grazing cattle rise steeply. On the other side, huge canyon oaks and tall laurels edge the creek, making a cool lunch spot for a hot day or a good place to turn around for a shortened trip. But to continue, cross the creek and go up over a little ridge and down to another branch of the creek. From here you make a brief climb to another ridge overlooking the canyon of Alpine Creek and the ridges to the south. A private road on the left, where public access is prohibited, leads out to Alpine Road. However, you follow the road northwest on the narrow ridge toward Mindego Hill.

Immense canyon live oaks line one side of the road. A mile walk along the ridge brings you to the fenced boundary of the preserve on the lower slopes of Mindego Hill. Turn back at this private property-line fence to retrace your steps to the Skyline.

Trip 3. Ancient Oaks Trail Loop

A shady trail winds through enormous canyon live oaks to emerge in grasslands with views of the world.

- **Distance:** 2.5 miles round trip.
- **Time:** 1¼ hours.
- **Elevation Gain:** 175'

TRAIL NOTES

Park at the roadside pullout on Alpine Road, 0.8 mile down Alpine Road from Skyline Boulevard, head uphill, cross the patrol road and go west following the Ancient Oaks Trail. From here it is 0.7 mile to the Mindego Ridge Trail. The trail rises across slopes with a superb view of Butano Ridge to the southwest. Shortly you pass a trail junction, but bear left here for 0.3 mile to a stand of huge oaks. These trees have multiple trunks rising from massive boles. Did they spout from the stumps of ancient trees after a long-ago fire?

In the grove you reach an unnamed trail on the right, on which you will return later. However continue left past more gnarled oaks, following the grassland border and maintaining splendid views even to the ocean on a clear day. Many young firs are growing among the oaks, probably seeded from large firs in the canyons below.

The trail goes down through the trees to the Mindego Ridge Trail, a patrol road, where in winter the roaring of Mindego Creek fills the air. If the trail is muddy, you will see the tracks of deer, coyotes, foxes and bobcats, which use human trails when they can. Walking northeast (right) on the Mindego Ridge Trail, you pass the Alder Spring Trail on your left, part of a loop in Trip 1. You can see Skyline Boulevard near the Caltrans Vista Point ahead, and you turn right (south) uphill on the Ridge Trail.

As you start uphill, take the foot trail which bears right, rather than the patrol road on the left, and curve across the southwest-facing grassy slope. After 0.5 mile, you pass an unnamed trail on your right. Mark this for your return trip, but continue straight a short distance, and then angle sharp left onto the patrol road to crest 2572-foot Borel Hill for the spectacular views described in Trip 1.

Retrace your steps from the Borel Hill summit to the Ridge Trail route on which you came, and turn left on the aforementioned unnamed 0.3-mile trail, which descends a grassy hillside and then enters a lovely oak forest. You soon reach the Ancient Oaks Trail, on which you go left (south) to your starting point at Alpine Road.

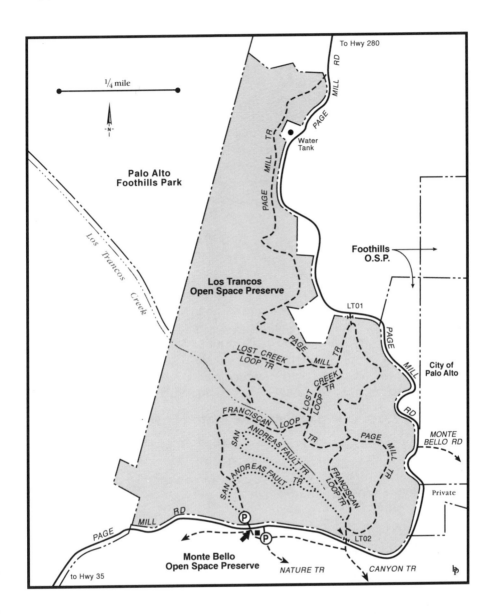

Los Trancos Open Space Preserve

Here is an enticing variety of trails over meadows and into canyons in this 274-acre preserve. A self-guiding fault trail explains earthquake phenomena, and a hike out to the far end of the preserve offers magnificent Bay views. Docents lead walks along the San Andreas Fault Trail; call MROSD for schedules.

Jurisdiction: Midpeninsula Regional Open Space District—415-691-1200.

Facilities: Self-guiding earthquake-fault trail and trails for hikers, equestrians and bicyclists.

Rules: Open dawn to dusk. No dogs. Some trails for hikers only.

Maps: MROSD brochure *San Andreas Fault Trail*, USGS topo *Mindego Hill.*

How To Get There: From I-280 take Page Mill Rd south for 7 miles and park at preserve entrance on right.

Trip 1. San Andreas Fault Trail

- **Distance:** 0.6-mile loop.
- **Time:** 1 hour.
- **Elevation Loss:** 240'

TRAIL NOTES

A self-guiding trail through a section of the fault zone shows you many signs of the violent movements of the earth in quakes of past centuries. With the District's information-packed brochure in hand, follow the yellow markers and learn all about plate movements, sag ponds, benches and scarps. Though it is only a short walk, you will want to spend at least an hour on this fascinating loop trail learning how the grinding action along the fault line affects the land.

Trip 2. Loop Trip on Franciscan and Lost Creek Trails

Descending into the cool, shady forest of the preserve's north-facing slope, this trip combines the Franciscan and Lost Creek Loop trails.

- **Distance:** 2.5-mile loop.
- **Time:** 1½ hours.
- **Elevation Loss** 400'

TRAIL NOTES

Start from the parking lot on the San Andreas Fault Trail, then turn left onto the Franciscan Loop Trail. As you cross the meadow on a clear day, you can see straight up the San Andreas Fault Zone to the Crystal Springs Lakes. Your trail soon descends into the woods under massive canyon oaks. In the fall deciduous oaks and big-leaf maples brighten the forest as their leaves turn golden.

You round the hill to cross a bridge over Los Trancos Creek, and then a short climb brings you to an open flat and a trail junction. Here you leave the Franciscan Loop Trail and begin the Lost Creek Loop. Keep to the left and go up a little rise through the woods. At the top of the rise the trail turns down to follow a ridge into the canyon of Los Trancos Creek.

Here and there firs tower above the oaks and you can see a scattering

Hikers beneath black oak on Earthquake Trail.

of these tall trees across the canyon as the trail descends toward Los Trancos Creek, mossy and fern-lined. Wild currant bushes show their pink blossoms very early in spring; later, mission bells, false Solomon's seal, star flower, trillium and wood fern grace the hillside.

As the creek drops into a narrow gorge, the trail veers away, traversing the hillside to follow a minor tributary. In the shade of large bays and oaks our trail climbs to a ridgetop. For a short stretch we join the Page Mill Trail on its way to the north meadow, then we turn right (west) on the Lost Creek Loop Trail up to the flat where it completes its loop.

From the flat take the Franciscan Trail. Bear right, following the trail down into a glade of bay trees. As you circle a low hill you pass a scattering of great craggy limestone outcrops and some ancient oaks that probably lost limbs in the violent shaking of the 1906 earthquake.

Ascending gradually to more open country, we reach the grasslands near the start of our trip and turn left on the Fault Trail to return to the parking lot. From early spring to summer this upper meadow is a bright exuberance of flowers. By fall the meadow has dried, leaving pale beige, gauzy-textured grasses with accents of dark seed pods from the small lavender and pink flowers of dwarf flax.

Trip 3. Page Mill Trail to the North Meadow

An easy trail along open countryside parallels Page Mill Road.
- **Distance:** 3½ miles round trip.

- **Time:** 1¾ hours.
- **Elevation Gain:** 200'

TRAIL NOTES

On the north side of Page Mill Road east of the main parking lot and across from Monte Bello Preserve's Canyon Trail is a stile for hiker, equestrian and bicycle access to this trail. In a minute turn right on this 1¾-mile trail, which keeps high above the canyon but below Page Mill Road. The trail turns briefly down into the woods, where you can examine a most remarkable stand of huge, ancient bay laurel trees, many with multiple trunks. These trees provide deep and welcome shade on a hot day.

Curving right around a hill past the Lost Creek Loop Trail junction, the trail comes out of the trees and emerges onto a series of rolling, grassy meadows that overlook the Bay. Canyon oaks and madrones rim these hilltop meadows, their dark foliage contrasting with the new light green grass in spring and the golden dry grass of summer and fall. Remains of an old orchard dot the hillside.

Continuing to the farthest north edge of the preserve, you will be looking for just the right spot to enjoy the view and watch hawks sail on the updrafts. While you won't see the small meadow creatures—mice, gophers and ground squirrels—you can see their myriad holes riddling the meadows.

In the northwest you will see the distant, dark shape of Mt. Tamalpais in Marin County. After taking in the exhilarating vistas and enjoying your knapsack lunch in the sun, retrace your steps at your leisure.

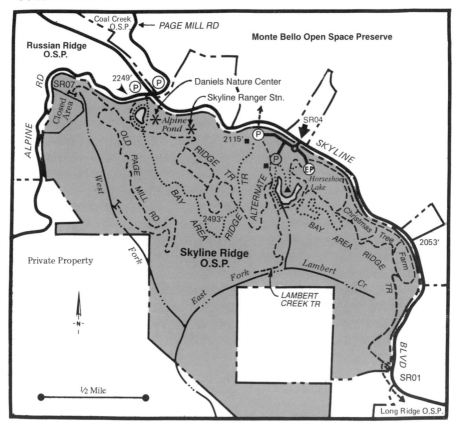

Skyline Ridge Open Space Preserve

Skyline Ridge Open Space Preserve lies along the western crest of the Santa Cruz Mountains in the heart of thousands of acres of public open space. Russian Ridge, Coal Creek, Monte Bello, and Long Ridge open space preserves and Upper Stevens Creek County Park surround Skyline Ridge Preserve. From its highest point, one can see south and west to the nearby forests of Castle Rock and Portola Redwoods state parks and Pescadero Creek County Park.

Skyline Ridge Preserve is rich in history, varied in landscape and easily accessible to a million Peninsula residents. Known to many Peninsula residents for its Christmas-tree farm, Skyline Ridge's 1612 acres also include two small reservoirs that lie in the valleys flanking a high central 2493-foot unnamed knoll. Rolling grasslands cover the preserve's more exposed heights and evergreen forests clothe its steep lower slopes.

Indians gathered acorns from oak forests and ground them on bedrock grinding stones that have been found here. As early as 1850, settlers built ranchhouses and raised cattle, hogs, horses, and hay along the crest of the Skyline ridge. In 1868 William Page built a road across the northwest corner of the preserve to link his mill in present-day Portola Redwoods State Park with the embarcadero in Palo Alto.

The most famous previous owner of the land was Governor James "Sunny Jim" Rolph, who used the modest farmhouse at Skyline Ranch as an occasional summer capital in the 1930s. Today a chestnut orchard and a Christmas tree farm occupy many acres on the east and south side of the preserve.

Parking areas in the north and center of the preserve provide access to 10 miles of trail, including two short trails for the physically limited. From the north parking area at Alpine Road and Skyline Boulevard the Bay Area Ridge Trail heads 3 miles south through the preserve. From here also one can quickly reach Alpine Pond, where the Daniels Nature Center features environmental exhibits and a viewing deck above the water. The nature center, built by private donations and contributions from POST, is open on Sundays staffed by volunteer docents. School groups can use the center by reservation. A short trail for the physically limited circles the pond and another trail follows Old Page Mill Road to the boundary of the preserve. The main entrance ¾ mile south along Skyline Boulevard offers ample parking for all visitors, including a horse trailer area and a handicapped parking lot near Horseshoe Lake. Starting from here are trails to the lake and to a few picnic tables above it, a trail into the canyon of Lambert Creek, and connections to the Bay Area Ridge Trail.

Jurisdiction: Midpeninsula Regional Open Space District—415-691-1200.

Facilities: Picnic area, observation deck, miles of trails for hikers, bicyclists, equestrians, and the physically limited.

Rules: Open dawn to dusk. No dogs.

Maps: MROSD brochure *Skyline Ridge OSP*, USGS topo *Mindego Hill*.

How To Get There: Take Hwy 84 from Woodside, Page Mill Rd from Palo Alto or Hwy 9 from Saratoga to two preserve entrances: (1) On northwest corner of Skyline Blvd/Alpine Rd intersection. Park here for trail entrances: (a) through an immense underpass leading to Alpine Pond for hikers and wheelchairs only, (b) 400' down Alpine Rd on left for bicyclists and equestrians, and (c) northwest uphill to Ridge Trail in Russian Ridge Preserve. (2) On Skyline Blvd ¾ mile southeast of this intersection.

Trip 1. A Trip Down Historic Old Page Mill Road

Hike down to Lambert Creek on the early logging route to Page's Mill.

- **Distance:** 5 miles round trip.
- **Time:** 2½ hours.
- **Elevation Loss:** 650'

TRAIL NOTES

From the preserve's north entrance at the corner of Skyline Boulevard and Alpine Road walk 400 feet down Alpine Road to the trail entrance on the left. Take this multi-use trail, which passes west of Alpine Pond, to its intersection with paved Old Page Mill Road. Turn right here, heading downhill (northwest) under tall old firs and past some sculptured sandstone outcrops. You are soon in a clearing with splendid views southeast over a succession of forested ridges.

At this clearing the now unpaved road arcs left, winding around the forested east side of the canyon of intermittent west Lambert Creek. On the way it crosses Lambert Creek tributaries cascading over sandstone boulders on the steep mountainside. About a mile downhill the road goes through some chaparral on a south-facing slope. Blooming at road's edge in summer are yellow bush poppies and magenta chaparral-peas. Around a sharp switchback look to your left to see the site of the former Glass Ranch, said to be a stagecoach stop on this route over the mountains to the Bay. No buildings remain today.

Back into the forest, now dominated by tall Douglas firs, you negotiate several more switchbacks to reach a washed-out bridge over the creek near the preserve boundary. Stop here and retrace your steps. Old Page Mill Road, long closed to the public, continues on to present-day Portola Redwoods State Park, where William Page milled logs that he transported up this canyon and on to Palo Alto's embarcadero. At this writing, plans to extend this trail to Portola Redwoods State Park are under way.

To begin your upward trip, retrace your same route to the chaparral area. Then continue uphill on Old Page Mill Road. When you reach the junction with trails circling Alpine Pond, you can continue on this old road to reach the ranger office on the site of the former ranch buildings. Or take the trail around the pond's east side to enjoy its blue waters rimmed with reeds. Nearby is a bedrock mortar used by Indians to grind acorns. Then follow the path through the underpass to the parking area.

Trip 2. A Loop Around Alpine Pond

A trail circling the pond leads to the Daniels Nature Center and to observation points from which to enjoy birds, fish, frogs, and insects.

- **Distance:** ½-mile loop.
- **Time:** ½ hour.
- **Elevation Change:** Nearly level.

TRAIL NOTES

From the preserve's north entrance at the corner of Skyline Boulevard and Alpine Road, hikers and wheelchair users take the trail through the underpass. About 100 feet inside the preserve take the trail to the right and follow it through a meadow which is filled with yellow buttercup blossoms in spring. At breaks in the lake's cattail-and-willow border on your left are several places where visitors can get close to the water and look for fish, frogs and waterskeeters.

Reed-rimmed Alpine Pond.

You can watch for red-wing blackbirds, barn swallows and marsh wrens from the shore, and look for raccoon and deer tracks in the mud at lakeside. Later you may want to picnic in the meadow or sit by the lake in the shade of tall willows.

After 0.3 mile around the pond you reach the Daniels Nature Center described above, and on weekdays you can relax on the deck while viewing the pond.

On a floating observation platform built over the pond or from the deck of the nature center, you can get a closer look at the aquatic life—fish and turtles are often visible. You may see a northern harrier hawk as it monitors the marshy lakeshore for unsuspecting frogs; other avian visitors are an occasional belted kingfisher and a great blue heron

Trip 3. The Bay Area Ridge Trail

Follow a segment of the Bay Area Ridge Trail down the length of the preserve.
- **Distance:** 6 miles round trip.
- **Time:** 3½ hours.
- **Elevation Gain:** 250' to Vista Point; **Elevation Loss** 90' to south end of preserve.
- **Connecting Trails:** Russian Ridge trails north, Monte Bello trails east, Long Ridge trails south.

TRAIL NOTES

This trail, formerly the Skyline Trail and now renamed a part of the Bay Area Ridge Trail, follows two alternatives from Alpine Pond to Horseshoe Lake. Bicyclists and equestrians take the high road over the preserve's central knoll; hikers contour around its southwest face on a lower alignment. Then, all can continue to the southeast end of the preserve on a multi-use trail. On the first segment after Horseshoe Lake, hikers may take a slightly longer, woodsy trail up and over a high ridge before rejoining bicyclists and equestrians on the rest of the route to the southeast end of the preserve.

Starting from the preserve's north parking area, hikers take either the underpass trail to the east side of Alpine Pond or the bicyclist/equestrian route from the trail entrance 400 feet south along Alpine Road. Both routes converge on Old Page Mill Road beyond Alpine Pond.

Massive canyon oaks shade the hikers' route on the Bay Area Ridge Trail.

From there bicyclists and equestrians go uphill, (east) pass former ranch buildings and take the old farm road going off to the left. They continue on it over the top of the preserve's summit and down to Horseshoe Lake (an elevation gain of 200' and loss of 400' in 1.4 miles.)

Hikers veer off south beyond the pond on a foot trail through a mature canyon-oak forest. Following an easy contour uphill, this trail traverses terraces where former owners of the preserve grew hay and pastured horses. It passes the low shed where other owners slaughtered hogs raised on this site. Then, as the trail gradually ascends the sloping grass-lands above the canyon of Lambert Creek, the views extend to miles and miles of forested ridges and rolling grasslands. Through a notch in the west the coast is visible on clear days.

As you reach the summit of the trip at an overlook chiseled out of a sandstone outcrop, you can look across to Butano Ridge, the prominent buttress above the Pescadero Creek canyon where Portola Redwoods State Park and Pescadero Creek County Park are situated. Beyond this long, high ridge lies Butano State Park.

Continue around the steep sides of the preserve's central knoll into heads of little ravines and out onto its rugged, imposing brow. You pass through stretches of dense chaparral and then into little oak and madrone woods. This trail, with a southwest exposure, is best taken on a sunny winter day or in the cool hours of a summer day.

Rounding the southernmost point of the ridge, you turn northeast and descend quickly to intersect the graveled farm road, the bicyclist/eques-trian route, that leads to Horseshoe Lake. Cross the farm road and dip into a forest of oak, bay and buckeye trees on a gently graded foot trail. Back into ravines where intermittent streams flow in rainy winters, you amble downhill past moss-covered tree trunks and sandstone outcrops. When you emerge on southeast-facing grassy slopes ablaze with orange poppies and blue lupines in spring, you can see east over the canyon of Stevens Creek to Monte Bello Ridge. Just before entering the parking area, take the 0.3-mile multi-use trail that cuts diagonally across the meadow to the shores of Horseshoe Lake, a two-armed reservoir that impounds the waters of East Lambert Creek.

Now, hikers, equestrians and bicyclists follow the same Bay Area Ridge Trail route across the dam and uphill around the east side of Horseshoe Lake. At the first trail junction, don't take the trail that keeps close to the lake's edge. Instead, take either the multi-use, former farm road straight ahead (east) or the hikers-only trail right (south). The wide, multi-use trail goes into the forest and proceeds 0.3 mile southeast under a high canopy of evergreen branches. The 0.6-mile, hikers-only route ascends on many switchbacks along the west side of a steep-sided ridge to reach a small plateau shaded by mature Douglas firs. Almost immediately the hikers' trail drops down the east side of the ridge, makes a few traverses and shortly joins the multi-use route.

From this junction the graveled farm road winds around small knolls, crosses gullies and passes the Christmas tree farm. There the formal plantings, set out in straight rows across the hillside, contrast markedly with the casual elegance of white oaks dotting the grasslands. Then you leave the farm road and follow a section of the old Summit Road through cool oak woodland. After ½ mile, you veer right onto a beautiful trail that traverses the fern-clad banks of a tributary of Lambert Creek. Gradually you climb to a walnut and chestnut orchard on a little knoll overlooking the southeast end of the preserve. If you come here in November, you can buy freshly harvested chestnuts from the orchard's former owners. In late 1996 MROSD installed a new 1-mile section of the Ridge Trail between this hilltop orchard and the Peters Creek bridge in Long Ridge Open Space Preserve. From there the Ridge Trail continues on an existing 3.8-mile leg to Saratoga Gap.

Unless you have a car shuttle waiting at one of the Long Ridge entrances or at Saratoga Gap, turn around here to complete your 6-mile round trip from the north entrance of Skyline Ridge Open Space Preserve. For variety, hikers can return on the bicyclist/equestrian route over the top of the preserve's central knoll.

Trip 4. Loop Hike Around the Shores of Horseshoe Lake

A short downhill trip from the ridge brings you to vistas of a forested canyon and to picnic sites beside the lake.

- **Distance:** 1½-mile loop.
- **Time:** ¾ hour.
- **Elevation Loss:** 115'

TRAIL NOTES

From the preserve's entrance on Skyline Boulevard ¾ mile southeast of Alpine Road, pick up the trail heading downhill into a valley surmounted on the west by the steep flanks of the preserve's summit. As you descend through this upper watershed of East Lambert Creek, the U-shaped lake comes into view, wrapped around a tree-topped knoll.

In ½ mile from the parking area you are at the south end of the lake, where you walk across the earthen dam on a farm road, then take a trail along the lake's marshy southeast rim. In the quiet of early morning or late on a summer day, you may catch sight of the deer, raccoons or foxes that inhabit the woods and meadows of this preserve. At any time of day you can watch the birds swooping down to the lake for insects. In winter a variety of migrating ducks rest at the lake.

Continuing on the path around the lake, you pass through a copse of moss-draped buckeyes and around the elbow of the east arm of the lake.

Trails circling Horseshoe Lake offer glimpses of wintering waterfowl.

Just before reaching the equestrian parking area, a footpath curves south. Take this path to reach a grove of hickory oaks on a knoll high above the lake. Here is a delightful, shady place to enjoy your daypack refreshments.

Then follow the trail north around the other arm of the lake, making a gentle descent to the main trail from the parking area.

Trip 5. Meander along Lambert Creek

A downhill saunter means an uphill return.
- **Distance:** 1.4 miles round trip.
- **Time:** 1 hour.
- **Elevation Loss:** 450'

TRAIL NOTES

This short trip is perfect for a late afternoon outing. With a backpack supper you can saunter along the creek's west bank until you find an appropriate picnic site.

Leave the Horseshoe Lake area just west of the bridge over the lake's outlet and turn due south on a wide track. For the first half mile you descend under oak, bay and fir trees that completely overarch the trail. Fern-draped banks, accented with showy, long-leaved, creamy-white and blue iris, extend high on the uphill side.

After ½ mile you step into a clearing after which the trail makes a wide curve east. Here is a marshy reed-choked-area where you can hear, but not see Lambert Creek. As the trail swings west, it comes a bit closer to the creek, but this marks the end of the trail.

The preserve closes at dusk; allow enough time to regain the 450-foot elevation loss and get to your car before the gates are locked.

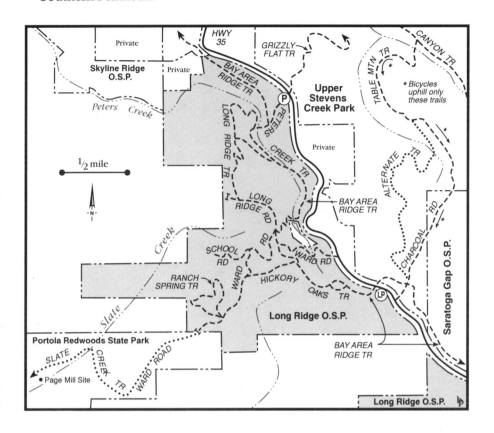

Long Ridge Open Space Preserve

Long Ridge Preserve extends along the heights of the Santa Cruz Mountains for 3 miles just west of Skyline Boulevard. Trails through 1551 acres of wooded hillside and open grasslands lead to dramatic vistas westward.

Peters Creek runs through Long Ridge Preserve, from its headwaters to the start of its descent into Devils Canyon, from whence it continues into Portola Redwoods State Park to join Pescadero Creek. Firs, oaks and madrones cover the eastern slopes, and magnificent spreading canyon oaks, known also as hickory oaks, dot the hillsides.

Twelve miles of trail in this preserve lead through a pretty Peters Creek canyon, up to Long Ridge and across high grasslands. A 3.4-mile segment of the Bay Area Ridge Trail traverses the preserve and a new segment of the Ridge Trail is planned to connect Long Ridge to Skyline Ridge Open Space Preserve.

Trails in a recently acquired section on Highway 9 southwest of Saratoga Gap will someday link to existing Long Ridge Trails.

Jurisdiction: Midpeninsula Regional Open Space District—415-691-1200.

Facilities: 12 miles of trail, all open for hikers, equestrians and bicyclists.

Rules: Open dawn to dusk.

Maps: MROSD *Long Ridge and Saratoga Gap O.S.P*, Portola Redwoods State Park brochure, USGS topo *Mindego Hill*.

Connecting Trails: The Grizzly Flat Trail and Charcoal Road in Upper Stevens Creek Park connect with the Canyon Trail going north in Monte Bello Preserve; the Saratoga Gap Trail going southeast to Saratoga Gap in Upper Stevens Creek Park. A planned segment of the Bay Area Ridge Trail will join this preserve to Skyline Ridge Preserve to the northwest. The Ward Road Trail leads to trails in Portola Redwoods State Park and Pescadero Creek County Park.

How To Get There: Take Skyline Blvd south from Page Mill Rd 3 miles or north from Saratoga Gap 3 miles to parking on west side at Grizzly Flat.

Trip 1. To the Ridge via the Long Ridge Trail

From the saddle on Long Ridge Road there are spectacular views westward to the coast.

- **Distance:** 4.6 miles round trip to the saddle; 2 additional miles round trip to Hickory Oaks Ridge.
- **Time:** 2 hours to saddle; 1 additional hour to Hickory Oaks Ridge.
- **Elevation Gain:** 400'

TRAIL NOTES

The trail heads across a grassy slope to a little valley where Peters Creek emerges from a narrow canyon and soon enters woods of oak and fir trees. Cross pretty little Peters Creek and shortly you will see the Long Ridge Trail turning right (north). Note this trail, which you can take on the return trip. However, continue now 0.4 mile along the Peters Creek Trail upstream as it passes through a narrow, steep canyon. Huge moss-covered boulders lie in the creek bed; laurels, firs and oaks meet overhead, and ferns line the banks.

You soon emerge from the canyon into a sunny little valley where the trail rises gently and the creek disappears beneath tall willows. An apple orchard, part of an old farm, grows between the willow-bordered creek and the hillside to the west. The trees are thriving in spite of neglect, and you may find a few apples in the fall.

As you continue along the trail by the orchard, watch for a sign marking a sharp right turn uphill. Here you take an old road leading 0.4 mile toward Long Ridge's summit. On an easy grade the trail takes you up a hillside under live oaks, madrones and tan oaks. From the treetops you will hear the calls of blue-black crested Steller jays, less raucous than the canyon jays of the foothills.

After a short climb you come to a crossroads in a small clearing where the trail branches left and right. If you turn right (north) here to circle the hill on the Long Ridge Trail, you can return to Peters Creek near the crossing you made on the way up. You can take this trail on the way back.

But to reach the ridgetop, turn left and wend your way south for 0.8 mile. Rock outcrops punctuate the steep hillside, and great canyon oaks and firs cast heavy shade. Suddenly you step out onto open grasslands at the ridgetop on Long Ridge Road. Here is a stone bench dedicated in May 1996 to commemorate author Wallace Stegner, a strong supporter of open space and wilderness. Wallace and Mary Stegner were part of a group who preserved and then sold the former Long Ridge Ranch to MROSD.—Before you stretches ridge after forested ridge to the Pacific Ocean. Grassy hills fall away precipitously from the crest of the ridge and clumps of spreading canyon oaks dot the hilltop. From here you can orient yourself to the ridges and canyons before you, much of which is in public parkland that you can explore with the help of this book. Due west in the great redwood canyon of Pescadero Creek is Portola Redwoods State Park. Its east boundary adjoins this preserve, reached via the Ward Road Trail (see Trip 3 following). Downstream are Pescadero Creek County Park and adjoining Memorial and Sam McDonald parks. Butano Ridge crosses the southwest horizon.

The trail ahead along the southwest-facing ridge leads to the Hickory Oaks Trail, which crosses a rolling, grassy slope to enter an oak forest and reach the preserve's southeast entrance on Skyline Boulevard.

On your return trip, retrace your steps along the crest of Long Ridge. At the crossroads continue north on the Long Ridge Trail. This trail makes one short switchback uphill before it circles west around and down through the woods. Watch for an opening in the trees by a patch of manzanita for a dramatic view down Devils Canyon and out to the sea.

In 20 minutes you will be back at the creek. Turn left to cross the creek and climb the short hill back to the preserve entrance.

Trip 2. Hike Through an Oak Forest

A short, easy walk takes you through a fine hickory-oak forest and across handsome meadows.

- **Distance:** 2 miles round trip.
- **Time:** 1 hour.
- **Elevation Gain:** 100′

- **Connecting Trail:** Across Skyline Boulevard in Upper Stevens Creek Park, Charcoal Road and the Table Mountain Trail lead north to the Canyon Trail in Monte Bello Preserve and the Saratoga Gap Trail goes southeast to Saratoga Gap. An 8-mile loop trip takes Charcoal Road, turns northwest on the Canyon Trail, turns south on the Grizzly Flat Trail and then crosses Skyline Boulevard to follow the Long Ridge trails back to this preserve entrance.

TRAIL NOTES

One and nine-tenths miles south on Skyline Boulevard from the main Long Ridge Preserve entrance at Grizzly Flat there is limited parking for the Hickory Oaks Trail. Go over the stile at the gated fire road to pick up the old ranch road, our trail through the woods.

In 100 yards the Hickory Oaks Trail turns right under wide-spreading trees for which the trail is named. From their massive, clear trunks, some up to 5 feet in diameter, grow huge horizontal and often contorted limbs. This oak, *Quercus chrysolepis*, also called canyon, gold cup and maul oak, has fine-grained hardwood which was prized for wagon wheels and farm implements.

Beyond the grove and uphill to the left (west) a side trail leads to a parklike meadow, rimmed with handsome trees and dotted with great, sandstone outcrops. Views down Oil Creek from the top of the meadow are worth the short detour. The western panorama of successive forested ridges creased by wooded canyons is an uncluttered pastoral scene to nourish your spirit. Returning to the road from the north side of the meadow, you continue for a pleasant 15-minute walk under more oaks before you rejoin the wide Hickory Oaks Trail to climb over rolling pasturelands that fall off to the forested canyons below.

In 0.5 mile you are at the junction with Long Ridge Road. From here you can retrace your steps or continue on to the Long Ridge Trail, as described in Trip 1.

Another trail at the junction leads down meadows and woodlands into Portola Redwoods State Park and its forested canyons. See Trip 3 following.

Trip 3. Downhill to Portola Redwoods State Park

With a car shuttle waiting at the state park, this is an easy trip. Two historic sites and a lovely creek walk make this a memorable trip.

- **Distance:** 8 miles one way to Portola State Park office.
- **Time:** 4 hours.
- **Elevation Loss:** 800′
- **Connecting Trails:** Pescadero Creek County Park Complex trails and the Basin Trail to Big Basin Redwoods State Park.

TRAIL NOTES

Starting from the south entrance on Skyline Boulevard, take the Hickory Oaks Trail northwest along the route described in Trip 2 above to the Long Ridge Road junction. Here you turn left (west), go 0.3 mile and arc southwest on Ward Road to begin your descent along this wide old ranch road. At first you amble along through broad grasslands gloriously green in spring, golden in summer and fall. Off to the east is the ridge where Highway 9 winds its curving way down along the west boundary of Castle Rock State Park, the approximate route of the Skyline-to-the-Sea Trail. To the southeast are the deep, lush, canyons of Oil and Waterman creeks, sometimes clothed in mist, sometimes so clear that individual trees are discernible.

Descending steadily, you reach a broad plateau where the Ranch Spring Trail circles the site of a ranch owned by the Panigetti family, from whom MROSD bought land in 1990. The loop trail swings around the plateau and into woods of black oak and Douglas fir, passes an old spring and returns to the main trail. At this remote ranch site you could pause on the sunny, south-facing grasslands to admire the views and to explore the pretty flat enclosed by venerable trees.

After another mile beside banks clothed with creeping manzanita bushes and lavender-flowered yerba santa, you reach the gate of Portola Redwoods State Park, beyond which bicyclists and horses are not permitted. Hikers walk around the gate and continue downhill, winding around the southeast-facing slope. After passing a forsaken farmsite on the left, you enter the shade of an evergreen forest, and go up a little rise. Look here on your right for the marked trail to Slate Creek and the Portola Redwoods.

Along this circuitous trail are old redwood logs, cut into three- to ten-foot lengths, evidence of an abandoned logging and shingle-making operation. After descending steps cut into the steep hillside, you cross Slate Creek to follow it through the cool redwood forest. This is an excellent, well-graded trail—a pleasure to walk on.

In less than ½ mile you'll find a large rustic sign declaring that William Page had a mill at this site, although there are no logs, buildings or old wagons to verify the fact. This was his second mill, the other being on Peters Creek downstream from the destination of the Peters Creek Loop Trail, one of the Portola Redwoods State Park trips in this book. A lunch stop here will give you time to ponder how Page hauled his lumber out of this canyon.

Shortly you pass the Slate Creek Trail Camp at the junction with the Peters Creek Loop Trail and continue 1.3 miles to the Slate Creek and Summit trails junction. Take either trail for a 1+ mile trip to the park visitor center, where your friends await your arrival.

Trip 4. The Bay Area Ridge Trail

Take the route of the regional trail that circles the Bay on its ridgetops.

- **Distance:** 6.8 miles round trip.
- **Time:** 4 hours.
- **Elevation Gain:** 150′

TRAIL NOTES

Combining parts of Trips 1 and 2, the 3.4-mile segment of the Ridge Trail route traverses the entire preserve. This multi-use trail starts on the Hickory Oaks Trail and turns uphill (north) on Long Ridge Road for 0.3 mile to its junction with the Peters Creek Trail. Here on the high ridge you can choose to follow the Ridge Trail up and around the preserve's west side through the grasslands on the Long Ridge Trail or to turn east on the Peters Creek Trail and switchback through oaks and madrones down to the little reservoir that holds back Peters Creek. From the dam you can follow the creek downstream through dense forest to a valley where an early settler planted an apple orchard. At the Peters Creek crossing, both routes converge and then climb out of the valley toward the Grizzly Flat parking area. Now a new 1-mile segment of the Ridge Trail extends north paralleling the east side of Peters Creek, then crosses two private roads and enters Skyline Ridge Open Space Preserve near an old chestnut orchard (see page 176).

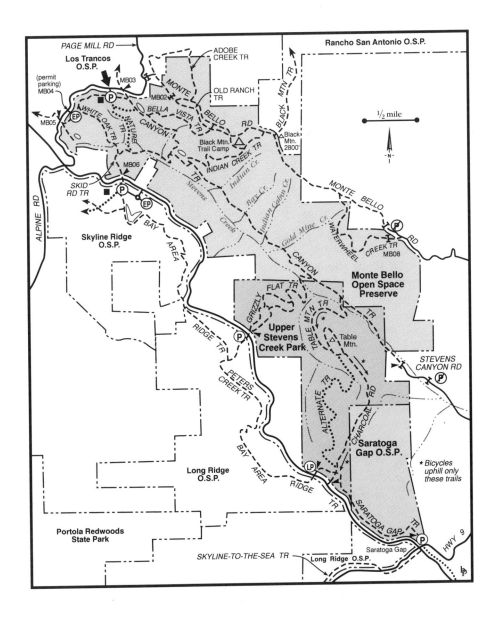

Monte Bello and Saratoga Gap Open Space Preserves and Upper Stevens Creek County Park

These 4664 acres of open space preserves and county park encompass most of Stevens Creek Canyon from Page Mill Road to Saratoga Gap and from Skyline Boulevard on the west to Monte Bello Ridge on the east. This aggregation of woodlands, streams, and grasslands is a magnificent near-wilderness treasure close to Peninsula cities. Trails into the vast canyon of upper Stevens Creek invite you to explore its depths and to climb the heights of Monte Bello Ridge.

Monte Bello Open Space Preserve's 2758 acres include the source and upper reaches of Stevens Creek, the west flanks of Black Mountain and some of the densely forested east side of the Skyline ridge. One of the first preserves acquired by the Midpeninsula Regional Open Space District, Monte Bello is just across Skyline Boulevard from Skyline Ridge and Long Ridge open space preserves and immediately southeast of Los Trancos and Coal Creek preserves. On the north side of Monte Bello Road the preserve adjoins Rancho San Antonio Open Space Preserve. Monte Bello's nearly 16 miles of trails serve as links between the parks and preserves north and south along the Skyline ridge, those east near urban areas and those west to the Coastside.

Upper Stevens Creek County Park's 1205 acres lie along the Skyline between Monte Bello and Saratoga Gap open space preserves. Its steep, rugged terrain is covered with dense woods of old-growth Douglas fir, madrone and big-leaf maple. Two long trails, the Grizzly Flat and Charcoal Road/Table Mountain trails, each with two alignments, rise through

The west side of Monte Bello Ridge.

the park from Stevens Creek to the Skyline and link with trails in the adjoining Long Ridge Preserve to the west.

Saratoga Gap Open Space Preserve's 701 acres extend northwest from Saratoga Gap on the east flank of the Skyline ridge. The Saratoga Gap Trail, a 1.7-mile segment of the Bay Area Ridge Trail, and a short section of Charcoal Road, cross the preserve. Notable along the Saratoga Gap Trail are great outcrops of lichen-covered, wind- and rain-carved sandstone. The preserve's steep wooded hillsides indented by stream canyons are a cool environment for summer hiking.

Jurisdictions: Midpeninsula Regional Open Space District—415-691-1200 and Santa Clara County—408-358-3741.

Facilities: Trails for hikers, equestrians and bicyclists and a nature trail for hiking only, accessible for ⅛ mile to physically limited. Most other trails open to equestrians and bicyclists. Restroom at Page Mill Road parking area. Equestrian parking by reservation at special parking area on Page Mill Road.

Rules: Open dawn to dusk. No dogs allowed. No bicycles or horses on Nature Trail.

Maps: MROSD brochures *Monte Bello OSP* and *Long Ridge/Saratoga Gap OSP*, Santa Clara County *Upper Stevens Creek Park* and USGS topos *Mindego Hill* and *Cupertino*.

How To Get There: There are 5 access points: (1) At Monte Bello O.S.P. main entrance on south side of Page Mill Rd 7 miles south of I-280; (2) on east side of Skyline Blvd 0.7 mile southeast of Page Mill Rd, limited roadside parking; (3) at Grizzly Flat in Upper Stevens Creek Park 3.1 miles from either Page Mill Rd or Hwy 9; (4) at Charcoal Rd on east side of Skyline Blvd 1.5 miles north from Hwy 9 and 4.7 miles south of Page Mill Rd, and (5) at Saratoga Gap on southeast corner of intersection of Hwy 9 and 35 (Skyline Blvd).

Monte Bello Open Space Preserve

Trip 1. Stevens Creek Nature Trail

Explore the headwaters of Stevens Creek to see ladybug wintering sites, creekside vegetation and the manifestations of movement along the San Andreas Fault Zone.

- **Distance:** 3-mile loop.
- **Time:** 1½ hours.
- **Elevation Loss:** 450'

TRAIL NOTES

More than the usual walking time is listed, to allow leisure to experience all the sights, sounds and smells of this delightful walk down the canyon by this lovely creek. Spring-fed, it flows year-round, unusual for these dry hills and most welcome in summer and fall.

From the parking area head out to the viewpoint above the canyon. Here on a bench commemorating Frances Brenner, a former Palo Alto council member, who did much to preserve these open-space lands, you can sit and appreciate the vastness of the near-wilderness below. Spread out before you is the watershed of Stevens Creek, and in fall the gold of big-leaf maples marks the course of the creek down the canyon. Firs of great height grow thickly on the eastern side of the canyon and oaks of immense breadth flourish on the warmer west-facing hills.

Four marked stations on the route tell salient facts about the linear valleys, sag ponds and pressure ridges created when stress along the San Andreas Fault was released by earthquakes. Other stations describe the intricate process of wood decomposition by beetles and ants, and the life cycle of the ladybug.

From the bottom of the canyon the Skid Road Trail climbs southwest on a pleasant grade to Skyline Boulevard. Directly across the road a stile leads to hiking and riding trails in the 1612-acre Skyline Ridge Open Space Preserve. However, the Nature Trail Loop turns left (east) after the last creek crossing and completes the loop on the Canyon Trail, passing oak-topped knolls, sag ponds and former walnut orchards.

If you want to learn more about this area's natural history, call the MROSD office for days and times of docent-led hikes.

Trip 2. Loop Trip to Black Mountain on Indian Creek and Bella Vista Trails

This trip from the Page Mill Road entrance descends into the canyon, then climbs steeply up the Indian Creek Trail to Black Mountain for spectacular views and wildflowers in season. You return on the Bella Vista Trail through the grasslands.

- **Distance:** 4½-mile loop.
- **Time:** 2½ hours.
- **Elevation Gain:** 840'
- **Connecting Trails:** Black Mountain Trail north to Duveneck Windmill Pasture Area of Rancho San Antonio Open Space Preserve.

TRAIL NOTES

Bring your wildflower guide and binoculars and choose a cool day or an early start. The Indian Creek Trail up the ridge has no shade for much of its length, so it can be very hot. From Page Mill Road take the Canyon Trail toward Saratoga Gap. After 1.2 miles turn left on the Indian Creek Trail. This old ranch road goes uphill, for a while shaded by oak trees.

On the Canyon Trail from Page Mill Road to Saratoga Gap.

Soon the trees are widely spaced, with only an occasional one for shade when you pause for breath. Then, for the rest of the trip to the top, the trail passes through treeless chaparral and grasslands.

As you pause on your climb, look back west at the series of mountain ridges stretching to the ocean. In ever-paler hues of blue and purple, their tops seem like small waves on the horizon. At times, the fog hangs in the valleys between the ridges; often fog blankets them. To the south you can see all the way to Mt. Umunhum, and to the north to San Bruno Mountain and Mt. Tamalpais.

In spring a brilliant succession of flowers blooms through the grass. In early summer yellow and black butterflies flutter about the purple blossoms of the shrubby, sticky-leaved yerba santa. On the open hillsides are patches of chia, its whorls of lavender flowers forming little globes on stiff stems. Its fine seeds were a delicacy of the Indian diet, ground for their pinole (seed cakes) and considered medicinally valuable.

Near the summit a poplar tree by the road marks an old spring and a cut-off trail to the backpack camp. Around the bend once stood the old red barn of the mountaintop cattle ranch and the houses that belonged to the Morrell family.

You are now on Monte Bello Road, the old route from Cupertino to Page Mill Road. It starts at Stevens Canyon Road, and winds up the northeast side of Monte Bello Ridge. No longer open to through traffic, but open to hikers, equestrians, and bicyclists, it follows the ridgetop, then makes a short descent to Page Mill Road. It provides access to two residences near Page Mill Road, to a City of Palo Alto water tank, to the antennas on Black Mountain and to MROSD lands, and serves primarily as a fire road.

This road makes a breath-taking, top-of-the-world walk over the high grasslands above Santa Clara Valley. In late June the deep magenta blossoms of farewell-to-spring that carpet the hilltop and the songs of meadowlarks in the grass are rewards for your climb. In fall you may encounter large herds of deer that congregate in this area.

If you have time, explore along the road to the southeast. In about ½ mile you reach the 2800-foot summit of Black Mountain, where an airway communication beacon and telephone relay towers stand. A hikers-and equestrians-only, 4-mile trail north down the mountainside connects with the Duveneck Windmill Pasture Area of Rancho San Antonio Open Space Preserve. See Trip 2, Duveneck Windmill Pasture Area, page 228.

Retrace your steps to the MROSD backpack camp, where there are a telephone and a portable toilet. With advance reservations you can spend the night here under the stars.

Then continue straight ahead (northwest) on Monte Bello Road or take the parallel Old Ranch Trail higher on the ridge. Here and there clumps of oaks shade the trail, but it is open most of the way, with views up the San Mateo County skyline. In June brilliant lemon-yellow mariposa lilies fill small meadows by the roadside. Although you can walk down the road to Page Mill Road, there is no parking at this junction and heavy traffic makes it risky to cross. Therefore, go just 0.4 mile on the Old Ranch Trail to the Bella Vista Trail junction in a gentle swale.

This trail, with steadier footing than continuing on Monte Bello Road, zigzags downhill on a moderate grade through steep grasslands, offering the great views that its name implies. It joins the Canyon Trail about one-half mile from Page Mill Road. Taking the Bella Vista Trail last on this loop trip makes for a safer descent that on the loose rock surface of the Indian Creek Trail.

For an interesting addition to this loop trip, from the Bella Vista/Old Ranch Trail junction go right (north) a few steps to the graveled Monte Bello Road and turn left (west). After 0.4 mile look on your right for the Adobe Creek Trail, a patrol road. Take this trail for a 1.4-mile loop north above the canyon of Adobe Creek. In spring you will see the tall candles of buckeye trees blooming; by fall the blossoms and leaves are gone and fist-sized nuts hang from the branch tips. Early summer brings bright orange monkey flowers.

As the trail makes a wide curve west, you have a spectacular view of the forested and chaparral-covered canyon of Adobe Creek. Here is the Hidden Villa Ranch, described in the Duveneck Windmill Pasture Area of this book. Farther to the north and east lies the Santa Clara Valley, with the huge hangar of Moffett Field a conspicuous landmark. This side hike is particularly good on a hot day because it is north-facing and shaded. Dropping down some 500 feet, you cross the upper end of the West Fork of Adobe Creek in a delightfully cool canyon.

Climbing again, you pass under power lines and find some rocky outcrops uphill from Monte Bello Road. These would make a good picnic spot. Look for a red-tailed hawk's nest of sticks and twigs on the power poles. Return southeast up Monte Bello Road to reach the Bella Vista Trail on your right, and continue as described above.

Trip 3. From Saratoga Gap to Monte Bello Preserve

This long trail, best done with a car shuttle, follows the San Andreas Rift Zone from Saratoga Gap to Page Mill Road. After dropping down to Stevens Creek, it leads up the quiet valley where the creek originates.

- **Distance:** 7.6 miles one way.
- **Time:** 5-6 hours.
- **Elevation Loss:** to Stevens Canyon 1400'
- **Elevation Gain:** to Page Mill Road 800'
- **Connecting Trails:** Skyline-to-the-Sea Trail from Saratoga Gap southwest to Castle Rock and Big Basin Redwoods state parks; Skyline Trail southeast to Sanborn-Skyline County Park; Los Trancos Preserve trails and Upper Alpine Road north across Page Mill Road; Skyline Ridge and Long Ridge open space preserves trails west across Skyline Boulevard; Ward Road connection to Portola Redwoods State Park on the west side of Skyline.

TRAIL NOTES

This trip can be taken in reverse, but by starting at Saratoga Gap, the trip's highest point, you walk the steep, exposed grade of Charcoal Road going downhill. For a car shuttle, leave one car at the Page Mill entrance and take another to the Saratoga Gap entrance. Bicyclists planning to do this trip must begin at the Page Mill Road end, because the Charcoal Road segment is open to uphill bicycle traffic only.

From the parking area, cross Highway 9 to the northeast corner of the intersection, where you'll find the signed entrance to Saratoga Gap preserve. Here too, is a Bay Area Ridge Trail sign marking the beginning of a continuous 12.6-mile trip northwest through four MROSD preserves and a county park. A stile in the wooden fence leads to the trail, which at first closely parallels Skyline Boulevard through a mixed woodland of firs, madrones, bays and oaks. These lands, too steep even for grazing, have remained virtually as they were before the coming of the Spaniards.

After 1.7 miles through a fragrant forest, the trail emerges in a clearing where the old Charcoal Road comes in from Skyline Boulevard. Across this opening a new trail takes off west through the woods to reach Skyline

Boulevard opposite the Hickory Oaks Trail in Long Ridge Open Space
Preserve.

From the east side of this clearing, a narrow path for hikers only,
known as the Alternate Trail, approximately parallels Charcoal Road on
its west side, then joins it at the north end of Table Mountain. If you follow
this delightful, narrow trail, it takes off to the left about 100 feet down
Charcoal Road and meanders through a woodland of black oaks, live
oaks and madrones with spring wildflowers dotting the trailside. Then
the trail passes through a section of dense chaparral—fragrant sage,
pink-blossomed pickeringia, some chinquapin and even the small,
prickly-leaved leather oak—which now covers the rocky soil following a
hot fire. The views open up north across a deep canyon and east toward
Black Mountain.

Then the Alternate Trail doubles back south, crosses to the east side of
the ridge and emerges on a south-facing slope with views southeast of Mt.
Copernicus and Mt. Hamilton. You descend steeply through a mature fir
forest, cross two little creeks and follow the second one on its east side up
to Table Mountain. Here the bedraggled remnants of a tree farm are being
replaced by healthy madrones and young firs. In a clearing the foot trail
joins the wide Table Mountain Road, but in about 1/10 mile the Table
Mountain Trail to Stevens Canyon ducks into the trees on the left (this
section of the trail is multi-use, quite narrow, eroded and full of switchbacks). You follow this trail with bicyclists and equestrians through meadows graced by iris of many shades of blue into the deep shade of tall firs,
and across a creek that tumbles into a steep ravine.

Soon you can hear Stevens Creek below in the canyon; go around a
couple of switchbacks and you will see it. When the creek is running full
in spring, it is a challenge to cross without getting wet. Here in this remote
canyon, you can believe reports that a few mountain lions still survive
here. On the far side a small flat makes an inviting picnic place where you
can lunch to the sounds of the creek.

If you had taken the Charcoal Road Trail from the ridgetop clearing,
you would have stayed right on the broad old farm road, built long ago
for cutting cordwood to make charcoal and for hauling it out of the forest.
This road leading north, downhill, into an oak woodland is a one-way
trail for bicyclists; they must ride uphill only. After a steep descent of
more than a mile, you pass an old road to the right and veer left on the
Table Mountain Trail. At Table Mountain you would join the narrow,
multi-use trail, down to Stevens Canyon described above.

After crossing Stevens Creek and starting uphill on the Canyon Trail
you cross a tributary, and begin to climb away from the creek. In less than
1/2 mile the Canyon Trail passes the Grizzly Flat Trail taking off to the left.
This trip continues straight and follows the former ranch road for about

View of Monte Bello Ridge from Russian Ridge.

3½ miles, all the way to Page Mill Road. This tree-canopied route crosses the little watercourses that furrow Monte Bello Ridge—Gold Mine, Indian Cabin, Bay and Indian creeks. The canyon gradually widens into more open, grassy slopes and a few meadows shaded by valley oaks. You go by occasional fragments of old orchards. The Canyon Trail passes the Indian Creek Trail, which leads right to Monte Bello Ridge.

Shortly past this trail intersection look for the left turnoff to the Stevens Creek Nature Trail. Here is another route to Skyline Boulevard, 1.3 miles away. This trail comes out across the road from Skyline Ridge Open Space Preserve and is described in Trip 3, below.

From this junction, the Canyon Trail passes the Bella Vista Trail on the right and continues through an area of sag ponds, which provide evidence that you are walking in the San Andreas Fault Zone. Over thousands of years, repeated earth movements along the fault have created both the benches that interrupt watercourses and the small, linear ponds—two signs of an active fault.

The knolls rising west of the trail beckon you to clamber up for a view of your hike along the earthquake valley to Saratoga Gap, where you started. Beyond, you see the trough where the San Andreas Fault goes west of Loma Prieta, where the 7.1 magnitude 1989 earthquake was centered. Mt. Umunhum, with its square tower remaining from World War II defenses, is conspicuous on the horizon.

As you near Page Mill Road, there are remnants of former ranching—orchards and old fences. Finally, after a day spent in the remote canyons and forests of Stevens Creek's headwaters, you are at the preserve entrance.

White Oak Trail Alternate to Upper Canyon Trail

As you return up the Canyon Trail, you can take a pleasant alternate to the west to return to the parking lot at Page Mill Road.

Just after passing the Indian Creek Trail turn left on the trail to the Stevens Creek Nature Trail. (Horses and bicycles are not permitted on parts of the nature trail, but should continue west for 0.9 mile to the junction of the Skid Road and White Oak trails). Take the White Oak Trail right (north) uphill through the grasslands. This narrow trail is named for the white oaks that dot its hillsides, and as you pause to catch your breath, look west and south for a different view of the Skyline Ridge.

After 1.3 miles you are at a junction with the trail coming in from the Upper Alpine Road Trail at gate MB05. Near this point is the equestrian permit parking lot at gate MB04. Turn right here and take the 0.3-mile trail back to the Monte Bello parking lot.

Upper Stevens Creek County Park

Map on page 187

Trip 4. Hike to Grizzly Flat

An easy trip on an old jeep road takes you 2 miles down through woods to a stately fir forest and a delightful creekside picnic spot in Upper Stevens Creek County Park.

- **Distance:** 4 miles round trip.
- **Time:** 2½ hours.
- **Elevation Loss:** 900'
- **Connecting Trail:** Canyon Trail in Monte Bello Preserve.

TRAIL NOTES

Follow directions to the Grizzly Flat parking area, access point 3 on page 189, and go through the opening in the fence. Two trails leave from this park entrance. The broad jeep road on the left is the well-used and better-graded route. If you take the righthand trail, which has recently been cleared, you will find some steep pitches and occasional rough footing. However, it is slightly shorter and provides variety, especially on the uphill trip.

Taking the lefthand trail, an old jeep road, you descend through oak and madrone woods where in summer the madrone leaves crunch pleasantly underfoot. About halfway down, the steep grassy slopes of Monte Bello Ridge come into sight on the far side of the canyon.

Black oaks and canyon oaks form a dense woodland here, but as you descend farther into the canyon you see increasing numbers of Douglas firs. Near the creek you find yourself in a forest of large firs and maples.

Although some wood cutting has occurred in the past in the upper part of this park, the lower canyon's great firs, 5 or 6 feet in diameter, are a fragment of virgin forest. Big-leaf maples filter the light at the bottom of the canyon, and a mosaic of the large, deeply lobed leaves of colts foot edges the stream. Here you will find choice sites for a picnic. The meadow above the creek is a ladybug wintering site and presently closed for rehabilitation.

If you veer left at Grizzly Flat, a narrow path around a thimbleberry thicket takes you to a crossing over Stevens Creek. Several sandy flats under maples and tanks edge clear pools in the creek protected by a high south wall clothed with five-finger ferns. This trail continues 0.4 mile uphill on many switchbacks to meet the Canyon Trail in Monte Bello Open Space Preserve.

For an 8-mile loop trip starting on the west side of the Grizzly Flat parking area in Long Ridge Open Space Preserve, follow its trails southeast, crossing Skyline Boulevard to pick up Charcoal Road and follow it down to the Canyon Trail, then climbing back uphill on this Grizzly Flat Trail.

This cool creekside is a fine destination for an early supper expedition in summer, but allow plenty of time for your return trip before dusk. At a leisurely pace you will take an hour and a half to get back up to Skyline Boulevard, a delightful trip in the shade of the hills. As you climb out of the canyon in the early evening, you will want to pause often to look out between the dark firs at tawny Monte Bello Ridge glowing in the setting sun.

City Parks and Trails in the Foothills of the Southern Peninsula

Town of Portola Valley

Map on page 151

Portola Valley has developed along the San Andreas Fault in the foothills of the Santa Cruz Mountains. The Mexican land grant of Rancho Corte de Madera (meaning cutting of timber) was divided into agricultural ranches acquired by Anglos in the late 1800s. By the end of World War II, the larger properties had been further divided and the area rapidly was becoming suburban.

Some of the subdivisions included horse trails in their design, but by 1964, when Portola Valley was incorporated, most of the land was private, fenced and inaccessible to hikers or equestrians. The Town adopted a Trails Plan in 1969, and as new properties subdivide, their designs must implement trails. The MROSD purchases of the Windy Hill and Coal Creek preserves, comprising about 1600 acres mostly within the town limits, gave residents easy access to trails in open space.

Portola Valley has some trails that are open to the public, and maps of these are available at Town Hall, 775 Portola Road. These include trails in the Portola Valley Ranch subdivision, close to Windy Hill, and the Larry Lane Trail in the Hayfields subdivision.

Remember, when you use Portola Valley town trails, you are going through private property. Although the trails are unfenced, it is your responsibility to stay on the trail and to comply with trail rules. Hard-working volunteers spend weekends constructing and maintaining these trails.

Following are three trips on the town trails and a long loop trip through the valley and into Menlo Park.

Jurisdiction: Town of Portola Valley—415-851-1700.
Facilities: Trails for hikers and equestrians, trailside benches.

Rules: Open dawn to dusk. Hikers only on Toyon Trail. No dogs, no bicycles.
Maps: Available from Portola Valley Town Hall, USGS topo *Mindego Hill.*
How To Get There: From I-280 take Alpine Rd exit south. Continue on Alpine Rd past Portola Rd junction to intersection of Willowbrook Dr, where there is limited parking on north side of Alpine Rd.

Trip 1. A Loop Trip on Coal Mine Ridge

A delightful trip at any time, this loop tours a flowery garden in spring.
- **Distance:** 3.75-mile loop.
- **Time:** 2½ hours.
- **Elevation Gain:** 360'

TRAIL NOTES

The Old Spanish Trail for hikers and equestrians starts up through the woods opposite the parking area at Willowbrook Drive. When you reach a junction where the Toyon Trail turns right, take a few steps farther and bear right, uphill, on the Old Spanish Trail, under oaks and past small meadows. As you come out of the woods, the Old Spanish Trail turns right, paralleling the service road going uphill to a water tank, and then turns left, but you step onto the Coal Mine Trail, which continues across the meadow to the left of the big water tank. On the opposite ridge you can see the homes of Portola Valley Ranch, whose owners dedicated this open space to the town.

Ancient oaks arch over the Old Spanish Trail.

Beyond the water tank, the Coal Mine Trail goes into the woods and continues left past a connector to the Toyon Trail, your return route.

The Coal Mine Trail zigzags southeast uphill under oaks and bays to an opening in the trees where you will find the Vernal Pool, perhaps a sag pond, a sign of past earthquakes and land movements. Circle it carefully to avoid disturbing the pond plants at its edges. By summer the water will have evaporated, yet the plants have adapted to the dry summers and they return each year. Another ½ hour through the woods takes you to the high point of the trip. From the meadow here you can see the Bay and across to the eastern foothills (unless it's smoggy). In the foreground to the east the brush-covered ridge on the far side of Los Trancos Creek rises to join Monte Bello Ridge. As you enter this meadow look for the upper end of the Toyon Trail on your right. On your left is an ancient, wide-spreading live oak, a good, shady resting place. In spring you will be glad you made the final climb to this ridgetop meadow to see the carpet of lupine, pink mallow, forget-me-nots, dandelions, buttercups, cowslips and poppies.

You can return the way you came, or take the slightly longer 2¼-mile Toyon Trail back on the west side of the ridge. This is a narrow trail for hikers only (horses may use the Old Spanish and Coal Mine trails). Cut into the steep side of the ridge, it descends through an oak forest on a very gentle grade down into the canyon of Corte Madera Creek.

In about a mile along the Toyon Trail you come to a junction where the short connector to the lower water-tank meadow takes off. Continue straight ahead. You soon cross two wooden-plank bridges over little streams. Though the streams run only after a rain, there is moisture enough for a garden of maidenhair ferns lining their banks. The trail continues past a couple of sunny chaparral-covered slopes, then turns back into the woods of oaks, bays and buckeyes. Benches along the way invite you to sit and enjoy the view of grassy Windy Hill through the trees and the heavily forested ridges across the canyon. As you listen to the calls of birds, you may also hear the sounds of Corte Madera Creek below. Then continue downhill to the short trail that descends to the parking area at Willowbrook Road near the creek.

Trip 2. A Hike up the Old Spanish Trail and down the East Slopes of Coal Mine Ridge

From the top of the ridge you descend on the Arroyo Trail.
- **Distance:** 5-mile loop.
- **Time:** 3 hours.
- **Elevation Gain:** 360'

TRAIL NOTES

Start up the Old Spanish Trail as in Trip 1, but keep left (east) where the Coal Mine Trail goes uphill past the water tank. Our route on a service road goes through an oak glade on a gentle grade, then turns up through chaparral and oak woodland. In ½ mile we reach the hilltop meadow and meet the Coal Mine and Toyon trails. After a pause to catch your breath, or in spring to admire the flowers in the meadow, start down the Arroyo Trail, which heads down switchbacks on the east side of the ridge under spreading canyon oaks. You cross grasslands, and go through a eucalyptus grove before descending through oak-madrone woods along a fern-clad north slope to reach a bridge across a tributary of Los Trancos Creek.

Shortly beyond the bridge, the trail forks. Bear left and continue along the hillside for ½ mile to gravel-surfaced Bay Laurel service road. Cross it, turn left, uphill, on the trail beside the road, and go ¼ mile to an intersection where you rejoin the Old Spanish Trail. Turn downhill here and retrace your steps back to Willowbrook Drive.

Trip 3. The Larry Lane Trail
Map on page 203

This 1¾-mile loop trail climbs 500 feet from the floor of the valley halfway to Skyline Boulevard to a vista point. This public riding and hiking trail is dedicated as a memorial to Laurence W. Lane, who loved to ride these hills with his family and friends and who promoted horse trails, mostly along roads that were built in the Westridge subdivision and are maintained by a homeowners' association.

Looking north from Coal Mine Ridge.

The trail begins at Hayfields Road where there is limited parking at the first roadside pullout a block above Portola Road. On switchbacks the trail climbs past some homes along the way, so trail users are asked to stay on the trail at all times except at trailside rest areas. As the trial emerges from the woods it splits east and west, and then the branches meet on a traverse at the top of the hill. Here a magnificent oak spreads its ancient limbs over the trail. Benches along the way give you a rest on your climb and a place to enjoy the mountainside scene. Locked gates in the upper part of the trail lead into Woodside Trails Club paths for equestrians only.

Hound's tongue.

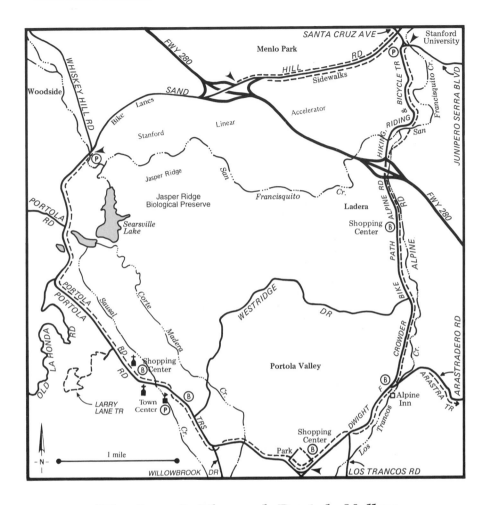

"The Loop"—Through Portola Valley, Woodside and Menlo Park

A roadside trail of nearly 12 miles goes past the community of Ladera, through Portola Valley and along the outskirts of Woodside and into Menlo Park. It includes off-the-road paved paths, unsurfaced horse and hiking trails and continuous bike lanes on road shoulders.

Jurisdiction: San Mateo County, Town of Portola Valley, Town of Woodside, City of Menlo Park.

Maps: *Tour of Historic Portola Valley*, USGS topos *Palo Alto* and *Mindego Hill*.

How To Get There: From I-280 take Alpine Rd exit, go north toward Palo Alto to parking areas at trail access points: (1) beside Alpine Rd south of Santa Cruz Ave/Junipero Serra Blvd intersection; (2) near San Francisquito Creek bridge opposite entrance to Portola Valley Training Center; (3) Town Center in Portola Valley.

- **Distance:** 12–mile loop; many convenient entry points allow trips of different lengths.
- **Time:** 6 hours—hikers; 1–2 hours—bicyclists and equestrians.
- **Elevation Gain:** Gentle grade.

TRAIL NOTES

The first two miles of trail were built in 1969 by San Mateo County under a federal program to encourage trail building in urban areas. This trail leaves from Alpine Road just south of the Santa Cruz/Junipero Serra Boulevard intersection, skirts the Stanford Golf Course and curves onto the old road fronting a small settlement formerly known as Stanford Weekend Acres. Opposite the P.V. Training Center (rear entrance to the Stanford Linear Accelerator), the trail leaves the road and crosses a bridge over San Francisquito Creek on the old road alignment.

San Francisquito Creek drains the area from the Phleger Estate and Huddart Park to the San Mateo County boundary. Just upstream from the bridge it is joined by smaller Los Trancos Creek. As the path comes back to Alpine Road it goes under I-280 and dips down toward the creek, where it has its own underpass below the freeway on-ramp.

The trail passes the Ladera community and a swim and tennis club, then enters the Portola Valley town limits and becomes the Dwight F. Crowder Memorial Bicycle Path. This trail was built in 1971 with memorial funds to honor a Portola Valley geologist, conservationist and bicycling enthusiast who worked long and successfully to get the trails plan adopted in newly incorporated Portola Valley. The path veers away from the road to skirt a meadow shaded by immense valley oaks, the memorial Dorothy Ford Park, which adjoins Kelley Park, where Alpine Little League plays baseball in the spring.

Again the path comes close to the road, but is shielded from it by trees and tall chaparral. This sunny stretch is welcome on winter walks. Crossing Arastradero Road, along which horse trails lead to Palo Alto and Los Altos Hills, you come to California's oldest roadhouse, the Alpine Inn. Formerly called Rossotti's, it is now a registered historical landmark. The bronze plaque embedded in a boulder by the entrance tells that the structure was built in the 1850s as a gambling retreat and a meeting place for Mexican Californios. It was strategically located on the earliest trail used by rancheros and American settlers crossing to the coast. It has continued to serve as a roadhouse and saloon to this day.

Once past the adjoining soccer field, you are headed straight toward the mountains. The weather on the dark-forested Skyline ridge ahead

The landmark Alpine Inn has refreshed its guests for over 100 years.

often gives early warning of changing weather in the valley—gathering clouds signal impending rain, blue haze heralds a smoggy day ahead and fog flows indicate cooler temperatures from the coast.

At the intersection of Los Trancos Woods Road, the path crosses to the other side of Alpine Road. By the redwood at the path's edge is a historical marker noting the home of Maximo Martinez, who in the 1830s received the grant of Rancho Corte de Madera, the first in San Mateo County. Three generations of Martinezes lived here in the house that remained until 1940. The path continues along Alpine Road to its intersection with Portola Road, where it ends in a charming little park planted by the Town of Portola Valley. Furnished with benches and graced by a fanciful iron deer, this park is a good place to picnic or to wait for the bus that stops at the corner.

An unpaved footpath and equestrian trail continues around "The Loop." Go west from the park at the corner of Alpine and Portola roads on the trail along the northeast side of Portola Road. After passing playing fields and orchards, the trail crosses the road at the stone gatehouse of the former Willow Brook Farm. Built in 1912 of wood faced with stones from Corte Madera Creek, this is the only structure left of the estate which with its mansion once dominated the valley.

Here Portola Valley widens and before you spread fields and orchards on the valley floor and unbroken views of the Santa Cruz Mountains. Going through the valley on foot allows you to appreciate the charm of this quiet rural scene. Right below your feet, nevertheless, is one of the most active earthquake faults in the country. Because of this seismic hazard, much of the valley floor is still planted to hay and fruit trees or used for riding rings. In the great earthquake of 1906 the land displacement in some places nearby was as much as 8 feet.

At the Jelich orchards you can buy fresh fruit in season. And farther on is the little Portola Valley schoolhouse, built in 1912. An interesting example of the mission-revival style popular at the turn of the century, it is now a historical landmark. The more modern buildings next to it, built as a school before earthquake hazards were fully recognized, currently house the Town Center, library and meeting rooms.

The little Portola Valley School no longer houses students, but it still intrigues architectural historians with its mission-revival style executed in redwood.

At the Village Square Shopping Center the path returns to the northeast side of the road. Beyond is the charming California mission-style Church of Our Lady of the Wayside. Built in 1912, it is a favorite subject of local art classes. For the next mile the trail follows along the fences of tree farms, orchards and estates.

Where Portola Road turns north at Old La Honda Road, you can see Searsville Marsh. Bordered by willows and cattails, it is a favorite resting place for ducks and other migrating waterfowl. Beyond the marsh Portola Road turns west but the path continues straight ahead along Sand Hill Road. At this junction you may want to cross the road to read the historic marker noting the lumberman's village that once stood here. John Sears, the first settler, came here in 1832. His hotel, a store, school and dwellings were removed as the water rose behind a new dam which created the lake we know as Searsville. From here to the junction of Whiskey Hill Road the path follows the fence of Stanford University's Jasper Ridge Biological Preserve. Somewhat removed from the road and its traffic, the path goes gently up and down through the trees.

There is no formal off-road path on Sand Hill Road between Whiskey Hill Road and I-280. Many hikers and joggers use the unpaved road shoulder. It is a favorite stretch for bicyclists because the wide bike lanes are uninterrupted by side roads.

The mile-long linear accelerator lies on the south side of the road beginning opposite the Whiskey Hill Road junction. Rising beyond is the rocky promontory of Jasper Ridge, Stanford's Biological Preserve, a protected treasure of unique flora and fauna. (See Appendix III for docent-led walks through the preserve.)

In summer and fall the pale gold fields of oat grass on both sides of the road are accented by dark-green valley oaks. This once-common kind of grassland scene, cherished by Californians, is fast disappearing. On the north side of Sand Hill Road, an equestrian center leases acreage for riding events. On the south side Christmas-tree growers lease many acres. Crossing the I-280 interchange is a hazard for bicyclists and pedestrians, and should not be attempted by equestrians.

From I-280 to Santa Cruz Avenue you walk on paved paths over knolls where office buildings and their parking lots are interspersed with open fields and stately oaks. The sidewalks on both sides of Sand Hill Road from the freeway to Santa Cruz Avenue are good cool-weather walks, with vistas of the rolling foothills and their forested mountain backdrop.

Near the Santa Cruz Avenue intersection you pass the tree-filled Buck estate, now willed to Stanford University. At the corner go east across the intersection with the traffic lights and take the paved path on the right to the bridge. Using the pedestrian tunnel under Junipero Serra Boulevard there, you reach the Alpine Road Hiking, Riding and Bicycle Trail entry—"The Loop's" starting point.

Whether taken in sections or in its entirety, this easily accessible and varied loop is an asset to Peninsula hikers, bicyclists and equestrians. It is a particular favorite of road bicyclists whose phalanx formations sweep through on their daily noon rides.

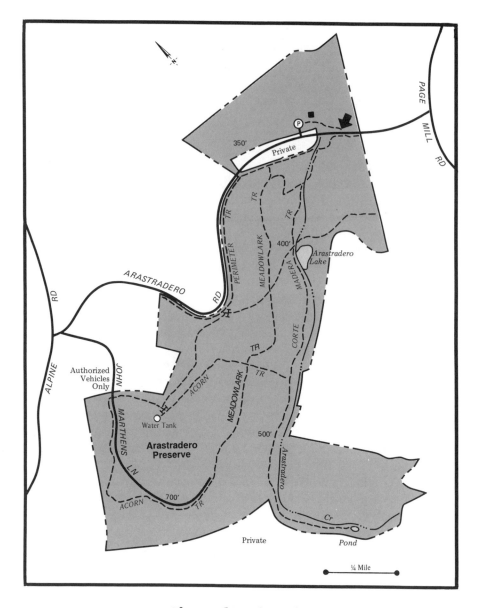

City of Palo Alto

Arastradero Preserve

For a glimpse of the rolling grasslands and magnificent oaks of foothill ranchlands, visit the City of Palo Alto's Arastradero Preserve. On the south side of Arastradero Road between Alpine and Page Mill roads, this 677-acre preserve is open daily to the general public. The preserve adjoins two large open-space areas—Palo Alto's Foothills Park on the south and Stanford lands west of I-280 on the north, although neither is accessible from the preserve.

More than 6 miles of trails, mostly former ranch roads, traverse the gentle hills and valleys of the preserve. Just minutes away from midpeninsula cities, it is easy to find quiet and solitude on a hike to nearby Arastradero Lake or to the oak-studded ridge at the south end of the preserve. Equestrians, especially, use the Perimeter Trail to make connections between Portola Valley and Los Altos Hills trails. A proposal for a trail from Arastradero Preserve up through Foothills Park along Page Mill Road to Los Trancos Open Space Preserve is being considered.

Jurisdiction: City of Palo Alto—415-329-2261.
Facilities: Trails for hikers, equestrians and bicyclists; restroom.
Rules: Open 8 A.M. until dusk. Dogs not allowed on weekends; permitted on leash only, Monday through Friday. No boating or swimming in the lake. Bicycles not permitted on the Perimeter Trail.
Maps: City of Palo Alto *Arastradero Preserve* and USGS topo *Palo Alto*.
How To Get There: From I-280 take Page Mill Rd south, turn right on Arastradero Rd and go ½ mile to preserve parking lot on north side of road. Take graveled path south from parking area and cross Arastradero Rd to reach preserve entrance.

Trip 1. Hike along Arastradero Creek to the Lake and up the Canyon to Its Headwaters

Try this hike in the early morning when ducks are paddling on the lake and birds are singing in the willows by the creek.

- **Distance:** 3½ miles round trip.
- **Time:** 2 hours.
- **Elevation Gain:** 350'

TRAIL NOTES

Start on the Corte Madera Trail, which leaves the preserve entrance beside Arastradero Creek. In late winter and in spring this can be a rushing stream, but by summer it is reduced to a trickle. The huge tree stumps on the far side of the creek are remnants of giant eucalyptuses that bordered an old ranch road, damaged during a serious fire here in 1985. Palo Alto is eliminating these alien trees from the preserve.

Beyond the creek crossing, a well-worn trail climbs up a short hill where brilliant orange poppies and blue lupines bloom profusely in spring. Stately white oaks with wide-spreading limbs dot the grasslands. As you approach the lake a graveled road takes off left, and almost immediately you come to the tree-shaded, reed-bordered lake. The

Mallard ducks nest at little Arastradero Lake.

slanting light of the morning sun streams through the trees, picking up the iridescent green of mallard ducks and the glossy shoulder patches of redwing blackbirds. If you are a fisherman, you may want to try your skill on the fish in this little lake.

Continuing on the Corte Madera Trail, you follow Arastradero Creek upstream along its willow-bordered course. Dense stands of trees clothe the hillsides east of the creek. Occasional oaks and some stands of buckeyes offer shade on the grassy slope west of the trail, and in spring flowers bloom in abundance. A haze of magenta clarkia covers the hillside in late June. As the creek bends east, so does the trail, until you come to a pond probably built for watering cattle.

A bit farther on in the ever-narrowing, moist canyon, a California dogwood thrives. Soon the trail ends, and your route becomes a utility service road. Retrace your steps to the preserve entrance.

Trip 2. Sample-All-the-Trails Loop

From creekside to topside this trip offers wide views and a stop in a quiet, wooded dell.

- **Distance:** 4-mile loop.
- **Time:** 2¼ hours.
- **Elevation Gain:** 400'

TRAIL NOTES

Begin on the Corte Madera Trail, as in Trip 1, until you reach the graveled road that takes off to the right near Arastradero Lake. Take this road through wide meadows, which in spring are filled with flowers. Shortly you meet the Meadowlark Trail and turn left (uphill) on it. Out on top of the rolling grasslands you may see red-tailed hawks, black-shouldered kites or northern harriers in their endless sky patrol for rodents and snakes. An occasional great blue heron wings overhead on its way to fish in the lake.

Crossing the Acorn Trail and still climbing the hill, you soon reach a barn at the crest of the hill. The City of Palo Alto in 1996 voted to demolish this barn and the nearby house. Past the handsome old barn, scheduled for demolition in 1997, the trail becomes a gated, graveled road. The trail changes its name at the gate, becoming the Acorn Trail, and turns off to the left side of the road. On it you descend past fields of oat grass dotted with ancient oaks and accented with bright flowers through spring and early summer. Just before a white-rail boundary fence the Acorn Trail goes right. Under a light forest cover you drop down to a grassy valley beside a little watercourse, where there is a remote dell for your knapsack lunch.

From this quiet place it takes only a few minutes continuing downhill to reach a graveled road. Instead of taking this road, you go right, through an opening in a nearby fence, and then immediately turn left, uphill, still on the Acorn Trail. Now you traverse a tree-shaded hillside where ferns and horsetails thrive and in spring deep-pink shooting stars bloom.

In a few minutes you reach the wide central plateau of the preserve. Southeast lies the dark shape of Black Mountain and north are the cities by the Bay's shore. On this plateau you may hear the meadowlark's call, even before you meet the Meadowlark Trail. Turn left on this trail and walk down the plateau past one trail junction to the Perimeter Trail. Then, bearing right on it, you pass the private property where barns and buildings were lost in the same 1985 fire that destroyed the eucalyptus trees. In ¼ mile on the Perimeter Trail you are back at the preserve entrance.

Foothills Park

The fifteen miles of trail through the woodlands, grasslands and chaparral-covered hills of this park are restricted to residents of the City of Palo Alto and their accompanied guests.

Jurisdiction: City of Palo Alto (Residents Only)—415-329-2261.
Maps: USGS topo *Mindego Hill* and maps available at park entrance.
How To Get There: From I-280 take Page Mill Rd south about 3 miles to park entrance.

TRAIL NOTES

The park, as stated in its brochure, "preserves 1400 acres of serenity and beauty on the fringes of a vast metropolitan area. Quiet oak-woodland, rolling grassland, rugged fields of chaparral and cool hollows studded with ferns and scented with bay comprise a diverse and inspiring natural scene. Superb vistas punctuate the park's picturesque setting between baylands and redwood forests."

Foothills Park is popular with Palo Alto residents, whose frequent visits number in the hundreds of thousands each year. Understandably, it arouses some envious thoughts in those living in neighboring communities, who may visit the park only as guests. However, the park, to quote the Palo Alto Municipal Code, "has been established as a nature preserve in order to conserve for the residents of the City the natural features and scenic values within the City boundaries, to protect and maintain the ecology of the area . . . . The fire hazard in Foothills Park is extreme and the population load in Foothills Park must be restricted and said park must be subject to reasonable closing hours and open only to residents of the City of Palo Alto. . . . "

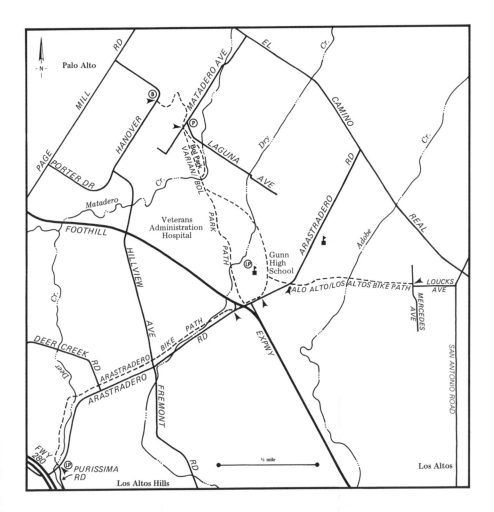

The Arastradero/Foothill Expressway Hub

Three paved paths radiate out from this busy intersection to quiet rural scenes. Though school children and commuters hurry along these convenient routes, you can enjoy a leisurely stroll on each and find creeks and beautiful trees along the way. Combining two of these trails provides an off-the-road route from Los Altos Hills or Los Altos to Palo Alto. Paths are open during daylight hours for pedestrians and bicyclists, closed to motorcyclists.

Jurisdiction: City of Palo Alto—415-329-2261.
How To Get There: From El Camino Real or Foothill Expwy in Palo Alto, take Arastradero Rd to Gunn High School. Parking limited during school hours.

Trip 1. Varian/Bol Park Path

On the west side of Gunn High School a path winds gently north to reach charming, secluded Bol Park and Hanover Street in Stanford Industrial Park.

- **Distance:** 2.8 miles round trip.
- **Time:** 1½ hours.

TRAIL NOTES

Starting from Arastradero Road in front of Gunn High School, go west around the corner of Miranda Way. Take the path that follows the school's western edge, passing playing fields and tennis courts on the former route of the Southern Pacific Railroad and the Peninsular Electric Railway on their runs to Los Gatos and San Jose. Though houses, industry and heavy traffic are now nearby, the City of Palo Alto has used this easement in a way that retains the feel of the open countryside that the early trains used to travel through. The green lawns of Bol Park and its magnificent oaks invite you to stop in this little park laid out along the banks of tree-bordered Matadero Creek.

Views to the west are dominated by ever-changing light patterns on the Peninsula foothills. Look up to Black Mountain, splendid in every season. A crystal-clear day reveals every canyon and ridge on its flank; a stormy one finds big billowy clouds hanging on its upper slopes.

Trip 2. Palo Alto/Los Altos Bike Path

A wide, paved path winds through the ¾-mile, landscaped right of way for the City of San Francisco's Hetch Hetchy aqueduct.

- **Distance:** 1½ miles round trip.
- **Time:** ¾ hour.

Motorcycle ban allows hikers and cyclists to pass.

TRAIL NOTES

A joint project of the cities of Palo Alto and Los Altos, the path starts from Arastradero Road opposite and just east of Gunn High School. A sign BIKE PATH, LOS ALTOS marks the entrance. Passing between the old trees and well-kept lawns of Alta Mesa Cemetery on the right and the expansive playing fields on the left, the path continues toward Los Altos. Much used by children on their way to school and by families on short strolls near their homes, this path also serves as a shortcut for commuters going to their jobs.

After crossing the bridge over Adobe Creek, the path passes backyard gardens where an occasional apricot tree, lonely remnant from Los Altos' former vast orchards, stands beside it. The path ends at a cross street, although city streets will take you to El Camino Real or San Antonio Road.

Trip 3. Arastradero Bike Path

A third walk follows Arastradero Road westward along the route of the Spanish timber haulers on a paved bike path to Purisima Road in Los Altos Hills.

- **Distance:** 3½ miles round trip.
- **Time:** 1¾ hours.

TRAIL NOTES

This path follows the route of one of the earliest roads on the Peninsula. Its name recalls the days when the Spanish hauled trees, cut in the forests of present-day Portola Valley, down this route to build the Santa Clara Mission. *Arrastradero* (the correct Spanish spelling uses a double "r") signifies a place where something is dragged along. Cars now speed along Arastradero on a divided road, but once again there is a place for those on foot.

For 1½ miles from the expressway the path goes past landscaped industrial buildings and parking lots on the north side of the road. However, beyond the industrial park, the path is routed away from Arastradero Road into the ravine beside the creek, where there is a peaceful scene of grassy hills, valley oaks and grazing horses. It terminates less than a mile from Los Altos Hills' and Palo Alto's big parks in the foothills. It was implemented in the late 1970s at the instigation of Los Altos Hills trails advocate Artemas Ginzton (see Town of Los Altos Hills). This is a short, pleasant walk for the rainy season, when it is good to have paving underfoot.

Town of Los Altos Hills

Map on pages 220–21

Los Altos Hills was settled by ranching families, who planted orchards on its sunny slopes and rode horseback through its wooded canyons. By the time the town was incorporated in 1956 there were many existing horse trails, which the town fathers kept as a nucleus for the extensive trail system still growing today.

Presently Los Altos Hills has about 95 miles of trails owned and maintained by the town. Nearly all that have been built since incorporation were acquired through the development process. As large properties were subdivided, trail routes were required to be set aside and trails constructed.

A glance at the town's Pathways Map shows that most of the trails run beside roads. However, on closer inspection some quite long routes are seen to be running along the backs of properties, following drainage patterns or linking the town's two large open space preserves, Byrne and Juan Prado Mesa preserves.

Byrne Preserve, now 79 acres, was named after an early settler, Col. Bernard Byrne, whose son donated the bulk of the land to the Nature Conservancy. In turn the conservancy gave the land to the Town of Los Altos Hills in 1967, and Col. Byrne's daughter then donated another 25 acres.

The adjoining Westwind Barn was built in the 1940s to house Morgan and Arabian horses. A subsequent owner, Countess Bessenyey, raised Hungarian thoroughbred horses there, and in 1975 the Town acquired the property. It now is operated by Friends of Westwind as a cooperative stabling facility.

Juan Prado Mesa Preserve, 13 acres in size, named for the original owner of the Rancho San Antonio land grant, was created in 1970 as part of the Dawson subdivision.

All of Los Altos Hills' pathways are open to the public, suitable mainly for hiking and horseback riding, but remember you are going through private property. Be courteous and respect residents' privacy. Described here are two walks you can take in this community, so completely subdivided, yet remarkably rural.

Jurisdiction: Town of Los Altos Hills—415-941-7222.
Maps: *Los Altos Hills Pathways*, USGS topos *Mindego Hill* and *Cupertino*.
Facilities: Paths for hikers, equestrians and bicyclists.

Rules: Observe common sense and courtesy. Bicyclists should yield to other users, and must stay on hard-surfaced roads and paths.

How To Get There: From I-280 take Magdalena Ave south 0.2 mile to first street on your right, Dawson Dr. Turn right and go 0.3 mile to the bottom of hill. Park on roadside, taking care not to block driveways or mailboxes.

Trip 1. Juan Prado Mesa Preserve

From a wooded neighborhood, climb to rolling grasslands.

- **Distance:** 1 mile round trip.
- **Time:** ½ hour.
- **Elevation Gain:** 120'

TRAIL NOTES

Start westward along a shady path marked by a wooden path post, walking between two houses where you must remember to respect the privacy of residents. Soon you are on an old roadbed running through the small canyon of an intermittent creek, shaded by live oaks, buckeyes, small redwoods and some black walnuts. There is so much foliage that the adjacent houses on the hills above you are invisible, although human activities are audible.

When you come out of the woods onto grasslands, you find the creek is henceforth confined in a man-made trench as it emerges from the pond of a 43-acre rock quarry, presently being subdivided into a housing development. The path skirts this quarry on the northeast and winds uphill across former grazing lands to Stonebrook Drive. When the quarry development is completed, it will connect by trail with MROSD's Rancho San Antonio Preserve.

Trip 2. Artemas Ginzton Pathway

How To Get There: From I-280 take El Monte exit west, go 0.5 mile, and then turn left (southwest) on Moody Rd. After 2.2 miles look for pathway sign on righthand bank and park at roadside pullout on opposite side of road.

Find a secret path that leads to glorious Bay views.

- **Distance:** 2.2 miles round trip.
- **Time:** 1½ hours.
- **Elevation Gain:** 330'

TRAIL NOTES

The Artemas Ginzton pathway was named in 1991 in honor of Los Altos Hills' premiere trails advocate, the person most responsible for including trails in the original design of the town at incorporation. A number of the town pathways were laid out by Mrs. Ginzton and the Town Pathways Committee. Later, she devoted her energies to Santa Clara County when she served on its Trails and Pathways Committee.

Starting northwest up the hill from Moody Road, the Artemas Ginzton Pathway parallels the road in an open, bay-tree forest. The hillside is full of springs that nourish the riparian vegetation in this intermittent branch of Adobe Creek. In May two species of brodiaea bloom, as well as apricot monkey flower and white yarrow.

After 0.3 mile you come to a four-way junction where the left route goes down a private road to Moody Road. The right-hand path, on which you will return, goes to Byrne Park Lane, and the path you take goes straight ahead to Westwind/Altamont. At 0.6 mile from where you started, you pass a bridge over the small creek on your left. This trail leads eventually to Page Mill Road. However, you keep to the right (east) toward Westwind/Altamont. You will pass another rather indistinct trail on your left, heading uphill to the Byrne Preserve, but your trip continues east. Pass open grasslands and then houses, skirt left by a vineyard and then go through a horse gate into 79-acre Byrne Preserve.

Here you can walk up through grasslands dotted with oaks to a 788-foot knoll to take in the 360° view. Looking clockwise from Windy Hill in the north, your eye follows landmarks from Montara Mountain to San Bruno Mountain, past San Francisco to Mt. Diablo in the East Bay and along the Diablo Range to Mt. Hamilton. Closer at hand Hoover Tower at Stanford University peeks up over grassy knolls, and the developed parts of San Mateo and Santa Clara counties spread before you.

In Byrne Preserve you are 1.1 miles from Moody Road. On your return trip retrace your route through the horse gate and continue straight onto Byrne Park Lane, following a roadside path to its cul-de-sac. A somewhat indistinct and very steep path leads down through the grasslands to a canyon trail which you follow to the four-way junction you passed on your way up. Take the lefthand route back to Moody Road, where creek dogwood's inconspicuous but very fragrant flowers bloom in May.

There are other adventures to be found in Los Altos Hills, so buy their Pathways Map and explore further on your own. On the other side of Moody Road is the entrance to Hidden Villa, a private, non-profit farm and environmental center, where hiking and equestrian trails lead to Monte Bello and Rancho San Antonio open space preserves. See pages 187 and 220.

Open Space Preserves and a County Park in Los Altos, Cupertino and Saratoga Foothills

Runners near Deer Hollow.

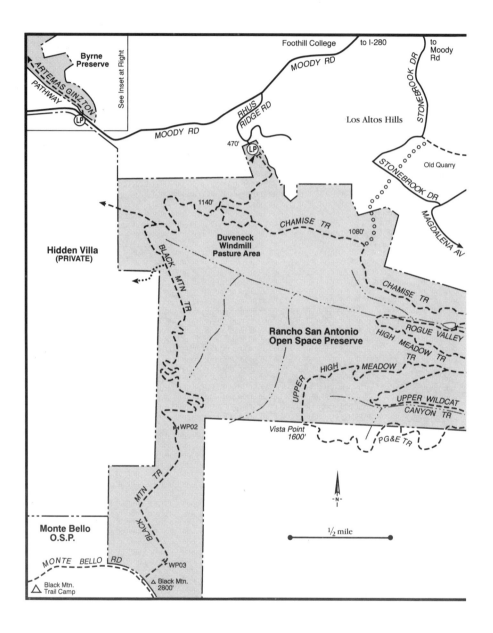

Rancho San Antonio County Park

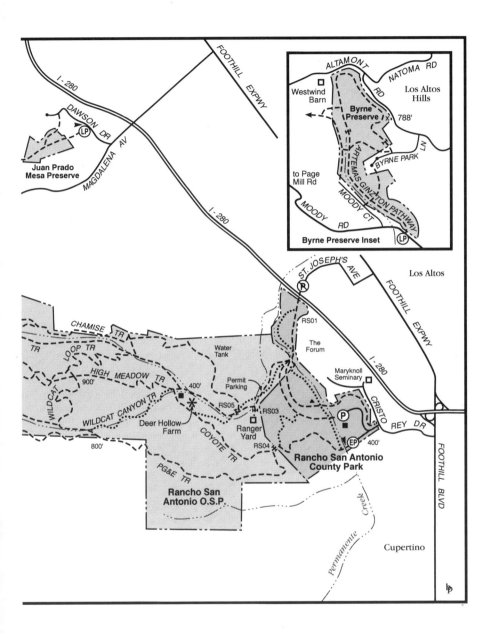

and Rancho San Antonio Open Space Preserve

This splendid foothill retreat consists of a 167-acre Santa Clara County park and a neighboring, 2135-acre Midpeninsula Regional Open Space District preserve. A diversity of trail environments, from spreading oaks and cool creeksides of the valley floor to dry chaparral and oak-madrone forests on the slopes of Black Mountain, makes this a place of endless interest. With the 1993 addition of the former quarry ridge lands, the Duveneck Windmill Pasture and the Preserve are linked by a 2.1-mile trail along the preserves eastern ridge.

Most of these lands were part of Rancho San Antonio, a Mexican land grant deeded to Juan Prado Mesa in 1839, whose boundaries ran from Adobe Creek to Stevens Creek. In 1860 the Grant brothers purchased much of the land included in the preserve site for a cattle ranch. Many of the original ranch buildings remain, adding to the pleasure of walks through the preserve.

The County Park entrance from Cristo Rey Drive off Foothill Boulevard just west of I-280 is the main entrance to both the park and the preserve. The park provides a paved bicycle path and trails for hikers and equestrians, two meadows for informal activities, model airplane flying area, a picnic area, parking for cars and horse trailers, and restrooms.

The City of Mountain View's Department of Parks and Recreation operates Deer Hollow Farm within Rancho San Antonio Open Space Preserve, using some of the old ranch buildings, and conducts programs for children. MROSD has occasional docent-led tours.

The accessibility and variety of the park and preserve's trails make them some of the most popular on the Peninsula for hikers, runners and equestrians.

Jurisdiction: Midpeninsula Regional Open Space District—415-691-1200 and Santa Clara County—408-358-3741.

Facilities: County Park: trails for hikers and equestrians that link to MROSD trails; picnic areas, two meadows for informal activities, and a model-airplane flying area; environmental education programs; parking for cars and horse trailers, restrooms. MROSD: trails for hikers and equestrians, Deer Hollow Farm.

Rules: Open dawn to dusk. Bicycles allowed only on paved path in County Park and on service road to Deer Hollow Farm. No dogs. Farm open Tuesday through Sunday, 8 A.M. to 4 P.M.

Maps: MROSD brochure, Santa Clara County brochure, and USGS topos *Cupertino* and *Mindego Hill*.

How To Get There: From I-280 take Foothill Blvd south. Immediately turn right on Cristo Rey Dr and go 1 mile to county park entrance. For trips in open space preserve use northwest parking area and take hiking or bicycle path to Deer Hollow Farm and preserve trails.

Trip 1. Deer Hollow Farm

A walk through Deer Hollow Farm gives children (and adults too) a chance to see farm animals and some of the Grant brothers' barns.

- **Distance:** 2.2 miles round trip.
- **Time:** 1½ hours.
- **Elevation Change:** Nearly level.

TRAIL NOTES

The farm buildings go back to the days of the Grant Ranch that thrived here over a hundred years ago. From the cattle chutes visible at the entrance to the preserve, to the barns and outbuildings at the farm, we have an opportunity to see a ranch complex, now rare, but once common in Santa Clara County. The board-and-batten white-washed redwood construction and functional design have a classic simplicity that delights the eye and appeals to photographers and painters. The high, airy feed barn at the far end of the farm is a fine example of the uncontrived grace of ranch architecture so characteristic of the county's rural past. The historic Grant Cabin, once inhabited by the foreman for the Grant family, has recently been restored using historic grant funds. For preserve visitors, the cabin's restored furnishings provide a glimpse of turn-of-the-century life.

Although the Deer Hollow Farm is closed to visitors except for the programs of the Mountain View Parks Department, from the pathway through the farm one can see the goats, pigs, chickens and other farm creatures. For school-group environmental-education programs run by the City of Mountain View, contact the Department of Parks and Recreation—415-903-6430.

Trip 2. Wildcat Canyon, Meadow Ridge, Rogue Valley Loop

This loop along the canyons and over Meadow Ridge is popular with hikers and runners.

- **Distance:** 5.6-mile loop.
- **Time:** 2 hours.
- **Elevation Gain:** 620'

TRAIL NOTES

Two new trails skirt Deer Hollow Farm on the western hillside to reach the trailhead just beyond the last barn: one, the Coyote Trail for hikers only, veers left off the preserve's main entrance trail, the other and longer, multi-use bypass trail leaves the utility service road higher on the ridge. At the junction after the farm, take the Wildcat Canyon Trail (for hikers only) to the left (southwest). You enter a cool, fern-walled, narrow canyon under the arching branches of dark bay trees, a quiet place remote from the suburban world only a mile or so away. After ½ mile the canyon

The feed barn at Deer Hollow Farm is the center for the children's programs of the Mountain View Park and Recreation Deptartment.

widens and the path rises gently to reach a junction with the Upper Wildcat Canyon Trail, on which you turn right (west). Follow this trail to the Wildcat Loop Trail and bear right (north).

A few easy switchbacks take you up a sunny, chaparral-covered slope where quail call from the cover of sagebrush and mountain mahogany beside the path. Soon the path levels off as it reaches Meadow Ridge above. Spring is a time to linger here to enjoy the flowers dotting the rounded grassy hills--bold yellow daisies of mule ears, orange poppies, purple brodiaea, dark-blue lupine, and patches of blue-eyed grass. You will find good views and fine places for lunch.

Although you could cut the trip short and return 1.1 miles down the High Meadow Trail from here, to continue this loop take the Wildcat Loop Trail north 0.9 mile down to Rogue Valley. The shady trail descends on long switchbacks through the woods, a pleasant route for a hot day. Oaks meet overhead and in the dampness of spring maidenhair ferns cover the banks. Each turn offers new glimpses of the valley below.

In ½ hour you are down in Rogue Valley, and bearing right (east) you go past the farm to the parking area.

Trip 3. Up Rogue Valley and back over the Ridge to Upper Wildcat Canyon.

Explore the upper valley and the canyons on either side of the ridge.
- **Distance:** 8-mile loop.
- **Time:** 4 hours.
- **Elevation Gain:** 600'

TRAIL NOTES

From the Deer Hollow Farm you have the choice of starting either up Rogue Valley or up Wildcat Canyon. However, from Rogue Valley you have a shady climb to the crest of Meadow Ridge, rather than climbing a sunny south-facing slope.

Going west up the valley by the creek, you soon come to tall bay trees, alders and maples. A dam impounds the creek to create a small reservoir. Farther upstream beyond the reservoir the maples are even taller, and like the others, they turn satisfyingly golden in fall. In 0.5 mile past the pond you come to a junction with an old ranch road and you turn onto it to reach the ridgetop. As you climb the mile up an easy grade, you begin to see across the canyon and beyond to the East Bay hills.

At the ridgetop trail junction the ranch road turns downhill back to the farm, but this trip continues uphill along the ridge. You look south toward Black Mountain and across Wildcat Canyon to the dark, wooded flank of the ridge between Wildcat and Permanente creeks. In 0.3 mile you come to another junction, where you leave the ridge and the road, which continues to the top of the preserve. Here you bear left along another old ranch road, the Upper Wildcat Canyon Trail, down into the canyon of the same name.

It is an easy descent into the tight canyon of Wildcat Creek. Thick stands of bays and oaks darken this steep canyon, making it a good route on warm summer days. The creek and the trail beside it drop rapidly for nearly a mile to a junction with the Wildcat Loop Trail on the south side of the ridge.

Near the junction, in late winter and early spring, the trail is brightened by the tiny, bright yellow blossoms of the uncommon shrub, leatherwood (*Dirca occidentalis*). Masses of this shrub along the canyon have the effect of a sprinkling of flecks of gold against the dark bay laurels. Where the canyon widens there are the pink blooms of wild currant. From the junction it is only about 1½ miles by one of the several routes back to the parking area.

Trip 4. Up the Meadow Trails to the Shoulder of Black Mountain

A dramatic hike to the 1600-foot heights of the preserve returns down the south side of the ridge.

- **Distance:** 8 miles round trip.
- **Time:** 4½ hours.
- **Elevation Gain:** 1200′

TRAIL NOTES

Park in the southernmost equestrian parking lot in the County park and go past the preserve entrance to start the climb beyond Deer Hollow Farm, taking the High Meadow Trail. A few turns up the buckeye-, oak- and madrone-covered slope bring you to the grassy expanse of the ridge, green and flower-covered in spring or golden as the season turns. From these 1000-foot heights you look down on densely settled Santa Clara Valley. In the other direction are the wooded slopes that rise to Black Mountain's 2800-foot summit.

Continue up the ridgetop past junctions with the trails to Rogue Valley and Upper Wildcat Canyon. Your trail up the mountain, the Upper High Meadow Trail, continues around bend after bend as it climbs. Views become more sweeping with each turn in the road. Across Wildcat Canyon you can see the utility service road which you will take on the return trip.

After another mile's climb you leave the grassy slopes as the road makes a sharp turn south into oak woods before circling a knoll at 1400 feet. Crowning the little knoll above the road are a few spreading oaks and a madrone. This is a dramatic place to pause or picnic. You can take in the whole Peninsula from here. Looking far north beyond San Bruno Mountain, you see the unmistakable outline of Mt. Tamalpais in Marin County. Black Mountain's summit, marked with antennas, is just visible above the southern ridge. Southeast lies the Santa Clara Valley.

After another ½ mile up the mountain, the trail turns east at the boundary of the preserve. Here you pick up the utility service road, known colloquially as the "PG&E Road," and start the return trip. From this vantage point you look straight down the wilderness of Wildcat Canyon. The road here is outside the preserve's boundaries, but it is used by hikers and equestrians.

Downhill all the way from here, you wind in and out of wooded ravines along the south edge of the preserve. The road banks are furrowed by so many deer trails that you know that a great number of these wild creatures live on Black Mountain. However, unless you are here in the early morning or evening you will see only the tracks they make on their way to water in the creeks below. Bobcats and mountain lions share this mountain too, but usually are too shy to make their presence known.

Stay on the utility road for 4 miles back to the County park and your parking place there.

Three Trips in the Duveneck Windmill Pasture Area

Map on pages 220–21

These 710 acres are part of the Rancho San Antonio Open Space Preserve. Lying immediately west of the original Rancho San Antonio preserve and extending south to the heights of Black Mountain, the Duveneck Windmill Pasture Area makes up one third of the preserve's total acreage. With the 1993 purchase of the acreage immediately east of the Windmill Pasture Area, there is now trail access to the main Rancho San Antonio Open Space Preserve and Rancho San Antonio County Park.

The original 430-acre Windmill Pasture was the generous gift of Frank and Josephine Duveneck to the Midpeninsula Regional Open Space District. The Duvenecks' Hidden Villa Ranch is well-known for its environmental education programs, its farm tours, its interracial summer camp and its youth hostel, the first in the West, which celebrated its 50th anniversary in 1987. Since the death of the Duvenecks, the Hidden Villa programs and its ranch and wilderness lands are owned and operated by a private, nonprofit corporation, the Trust for Hidden Villa. MROSD has an easement over 1435 acres of Hidden Villa's wilderness lands.

Hidden Villa Ranch is open during the school year, but closed during the summer camp period. Since the ranch is non-profit, an entrance fee is requested to help maintain its facilities. Its private trails are open to hikers and equestrians; no bicycles are allowed, except on the ranch entrance road.

Eight miles of trails wind through the Duveneck Windmill Pasture Area's fragrant bay-tree and oak woodlands, across sloping, grassy meadows, up the steep shoulder of Black Mountain and down to the floor of the rancho.

How To Get There: From I-280 take El Monte Ave exit west; just beyond Foothill College turn left on Moody Rd, then in 0.5 mile turn left on Rhus Ridge Rd. Continue for 0.2 mile, then turn right down to a small parking place at gated trail entrance.

Trip 1. A Short Hike to a Secluded Meadow

A half-hour's hike takes you to a high, hidden pasture in the shadow of Black Mountain.

- **Distance:** 2 miles round trip.
- **Time:** 1¼ hours.
- **Elevation Gain:** 500'

TRAIL NOTES

From the preserve entrance in a forested glade, take the trail, which is a patrol road, up a wooded canyon. In spring, flowers bloom along the trail, and ferns—wood fern, gold back and maidenhair—line the road banks. By summer the gold back and maidenhair have dried up, but the wood fern still clothes the hillsides with green.

As you round the last bend, pause on the threshold of the meadow, which the Duvenecks named the Windmill Pasture after an old windmill that stood until 1991. Behind you are the cities of the Santa Clara Valley. But take a few more steps along the trail and you'll find yourself in a secluded pasture remote from that urban scene. Handsome oaks border the pasture, and Black Mountain rises beyond.

This is a place to enjoy at your leisure. Short trails through the pasture invite you to explore it and to find hilltop spots to sit in the sun or watch the changing light on Black Mountain. Look along the lower border of the pasture for the sign that tells the story of the windmill.

In the mid-1800s the pasture was a part of the Rancho San Antonio, an early Mexican land grant. Before that time, these woodlands and meadows, so rich in fruits, berries, seeds and game, were the territory of the Ohlone Indians, who had a village beside Adobe Creek in the valley below. A summer day might have found them gathering seeds here or beating the grass to round up grasshoppers, which they considered a delicacy when lightly roasted.

Nowadays, early-rising residents with a thermos of coffee, a roll and an orange in a backpack find this a great site for a breakfast walk. And it is just right, too, for a leisurely picnic supper at the end of a warm summer day.

Trip 2. Trek to Black Mountain

From the Windmill Pasture hike up a steep trail to the highest mountain in the Sierra Morena.

- **Distance:** 8 miles round trip.
- **Time:** 5 hours.
- **Elevation Gain:** 2380'
- **Connecting Trails:** Monte Bello Open Space Preserve trails in Monte Bello Open Space Preserve.

TRAIL NOTES

This trail is closed to bicyclists and seasonally may be closed to equestrians. Plenty of water in your pack and an early start are requisites for this trip. From the Rhus Ridge parking area, take the 0.9-mile trail to the Windmill Pasture. After pausing there to survey the peak you will be climbing, veer right to dip into a shady oak woodland. Traverse a chaparral ridge and then go back into a clump of trees, where you watch for a trail junction on your left. Take this route, the Black Mountain Trail, through a swale that drains into one of Permanente Creek's tributaries. Keep left at the first trail junction and begin your steady upward climb.

Shortly, out on the open ridge that divides the drainages of Adobe and Permanente creeks, your views on both sides are of wilderness lands, too steep to have been farmed. Across the deep canyons to the left lie the High Meadow trails of Rancho San Antonio, now accessible from the Duveneck Windmill Pasture Area. To your right are the private wilderness lands of Hidden Villa.

Beautiful pink clusters of wild currant will delight you on an early spring trip, as well as graceful ferns on banks above the trail. Look for white limestone rocks of the kind mined in the Permanente cement quarry on the southwest side of Monte Bello Ridge.

After about 2½ miles of this unrelenting ascent with intermittent tree cover, you zigzag around switchbacks and wooded ravines dripping with winter rivulets. Here on a wide transverse ridge is a forest of tall madrones and oaks, where trailside glades, free of heavy underbrush, invite you to pause.

Tall towers anchored on this ridge support the power lines spanning the upper reaches of Adobe and Permanente Creek canyons and running northward on the east side of the ridge all the way to Woodside. You cross under the power lines and emerge from the woods on a broad, bare and steep service road cut through chaparral. Now, with communications towers in view and a second wind in your lungs, you head for the 2800-foot top of Black Mountain. From the summit there are marvelous views west into Stevens Creek Canyon and thousands of acres of open-space lands on the Skyline ridge. Turn around to behold the entire Bay Area spread out before you.

After a lunch break here you can explore the MROSD backpack camp, downhill to the west near the site of the old Morrell farmhouse on gated Monte Bello Road (see Trip 2, Monte Bello Open Space Preserve). With an advance reservation, you could stay there overnight. For your return trip, you could arrange a shuttle to meet you at the west entrance of Monte Bello Open Space Preserve on Page Mill Road or you could return the way you came. Whatever your route, you have the satisfaction of having climbed the highest mountain in the northern Santa Cruz Mountains.

Trip 3. Chamise Trail to Rogue Valley

Tread the high-line route from pasture to pond.
- **Distance:** 6.6 miles.
- **Time:** 4 hours.
- **Elevation Gain:** 500'

TRAIL NOTES

Start from the Rhus Ridge parking area and climb the steep road through oak woodland and patches of chaparral, as in Trip 1. If you take this trail in spring, note as you ascend, the small chinquapin trees beside the trail. Their slightly curled, yellow-backed leaves and prickly seed pods are easy to distinguish. Here too, are silk-tassel trees, another small tree that is easy to identify in spring by the long strand or tassel of gray-green flowers at the branch tips, that become berries in fall. You may also be lucky to spot some beautiful orange wind poppies waving gracefully in sunny openings.

When you reach the Windmill Pasture, bear left (east) on the well-worn trail crossing the upper meadow but below its oak-bordered ridge. At the end of the meadow you rise through a little gap and follow the wide Chamise Trail, an old road, that traverses the lands purchased from an adjoining landowner in 1993. From openings along the trail, there are glimpses of the midpeninsula and San Francisco Bay to the east. West lie the steep forested ridges enfolding Permanente Creek and its tributaries. Often in dense chaparral, occasionally you dip into oak woods. The trail takes its name from the tiny-leaved, erect, brownish green chaparral shrub that covers the slopes on the south side of the trail. In the company of manzanita and mountain mahogany, it makes a dense, prickly almost impenetrable cover, except for resident rabbits, quail, mice and voles.

Soon you begin a long, gradual descent and your view is down into the Rogue Valley, which lies at the base of a lovely east-facing ridge. You wind around little knolls and past some very badly eroded ridges below the trail. When you reach a trail junction, turn right (south) to reach the little pond which sits at the Rogue Valley Trail junction. You can see it before you reach it. Here beside its reed-lined waters you could stop for a snack before starting back up the hill. This valley, formerly occupied by horse stables and corrals, is being restored with native plants. The return trip on the south-facing ridge should be taken in the early morning or late afternoon of a summer day, but it is delightful on a sunny winter day.

Or you could continue on the Rogue Valley Trail, following it 1.1 miles to the Deer Hollow Farm to see the animals. From there it is 1 or 2 miles (depending on your route) to parking areas in Rancho San Antonio County Park, where you could have friends meet you for a picnic in the meadow.

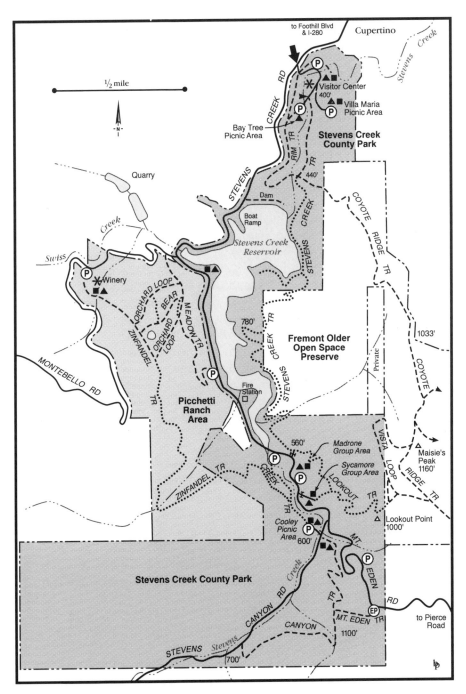

1/2 mile

to Foothill Blvd
& I-280

Cupertino

Stevens Creek

Visitor Center
400'

Villa Maria
Picnic Area

Bay Tree
Picnic Area

Stevens Creek
County Park

Quarry

440'

Dam

Boat
Ramp

Stevens Creek
Reservoir

Creek

Swiss

Winery

780'

Fremont Older
Open Space
Preserve

1033'

Picchetti
Ranch
Area

Fire
Station

MONTEBELLO RD

ZINFANDEL TR

560'

Madrone
Group Area

Maisie's
Peak
1160'

Sycamore
Group Area

Lookout Point
1000'

Cooley
Picnic
Area 600'

Stevens Creek County Park

CANYON RD

1100'

to Pierce
Road

STEVENS   Stevens

700'

Stevens Creek County Park and Picchetti Ranch Area

Stevens Creek County Park

The park encompasses a foothill canyon surrounding a reservoir fed by year-round streams. In an early description of this rugged area, Padre Pedro Font, a cartographer who accompanied Colonel Juan Bautista de Anza to California in 1776, wrote, "This place of San José de Cupertino has good water and much firewood, but nothing suitable for settlement because it is among the hills very near the range of the cedars . . . and lacks level land." Later, the Arroyo de San José de Cupertino, which included Stevens Canyon and the Villa Maria, was named Stevens Creek after Elisha Stephens (the spelling has been changed), who lived here in the 1850s. The Jesuits of the University of Santa Clara purchased the Villa Maria, a 30-acre farm and winery, in 1893. It contained a chapel, villa house, winery and barn, with grape vineyards and orchards of walnuts, apples and chestnuts. The buildings are gone, but remnants of the orchards and vineyards can still be seen.

Hiking trails originate from (1) the north entrance to the park off Stevens Canyon Road in what is known as the Villa Maria Area, below the dam and its spillway, and (2) upstream above the reservoir near the intersection of Stevens Canyon and Mt. Eden roads. In the north and south ends of the park are connections with trails in the adjoining Fremont Older Open Space Preserve. The new Zinfandel Trail (for hikers only) connects the park with the Picchetti Ranch Area of Monte Bello Open Space Preserve.

Jurisdiction: Santa Clara County—408-358-3741.

Facilities: Visitor center, picnic areas for families and groups, trails chiefly for hikers. Equestrians allowed on first part of Stevens Creek Trail and all of Mt. Eden Trail. Equestrian parking at Mt. Eden trailhead.

Rules: Open from 8 A.M. to ½ hour past sunset. No bicycles except on Rim Trail connection to Fremont Older Preserve's Coyote Ridge Trail. Pets on leash in picnic area, no pets on trails.

Maps: Santa Clara County brochure *Stevens Creek County Park*; MROSD brochures *Fremont Older OSP, Picchetti Ranch Area, Monte Bello OSP*; USGS topo *Cupertino*.

How To Get There: From I-280 take Foothill Blvd south, which becomes Stevens Canyon Rd, and reach north entrance of park in about 2 miles. For Villa Maria Area and visitor center, turn left at park entrance sign. For other trails, continue on Stevens Canyon Rd, which runs through the park and intersects Mt. Eden Rd near south end.

Trip 1. Hike to the Reservoir and Climb the Hills Above

From the visitor center the trail under the oaks rises on a gentle grade toward the dam and circles partway around the reservoir to the 2-mile Stevens Creek Trail.

- **Distance:** 2.7 miles one way.
- **Time:** 1½ hours.
- **Elevation Gain:** 200'

TRAIL NOTES

Start up the Stevens Creek Trail past the visitor center on an old roadbed under tall spreading oaks, climbing gently for 0.6 mile toward the dam. Near the spillway you pass a trail that goes left to the Coyote Ridge Trail in adjoining Fremont Older Open Space Preserve.

Beyond the spillway cross a small meadow on the 0.4 mile level, hikers-only trail that circles partway around the reservoir to its junction with the trail to Laurel Flat and the southern picnic areas. This pleasant walk through oak groves by the water makes an easy excursion for those who may not want to make the climb above the reservoir. The Stevens Creek Trail goes on around the reservoir for another 300 yards to an oak-shaded flat—a good place for a picnic.

But to continue over the hill above the reservoir, turn uphill onto a section of the Stevens Creek Trail, built in 1987–88 by volunteers under the sponsorship of the Trail Center. As the trail winds in and out of ravines through oak woodlands, you glimpse the water below through the trees. After rounding an open, chaparral-covered ridge, you walk on a fenced ledge above the reed-rimmed lake and descend into oak forest again near the upper end of the reservoir at Laurel Flat.

The trail ends above Stevens Canyon Road near a cluster of picnic areas. You can pick up the 0.7-mile Lookout Trail from here for a loop trip of 6 miles, returning to the visitor center by way of the Coyote Ridge Trail in Fremont Older Preserve (see Trip 1 in Fremont Older section, page 240).

Trip 2. Lookout Trail

A climb from Stevens Creek through the woods reaches ridgetop Lookout Point for views of Stevens Creek Canyon and Fremont Older Open Space Preserve, where you can walk on connecting trails.

- **Distance:** 1.4 mile round trip.
- **Time:** 1½ hours.
- **Elevation Gain:** 440'

TRAIL NOTES

Take Stevens Canyon Road past the reservoir and turn left into parking for the Madrone Picnic Area. Find the trail entrance behind the restrooms. The trail crosses a small ridge that separates this picnic area from the Sycamore Picnic Area. Another trail comes up from behind the Sycamore Picnic Area and joins this one about 200 yards up a small ravine.

Lookout Point has wide view into Fremont Older Preserve.

The trail, for hikers only, ascends a steep hill on switchbacks under oaks and toyons, a shaded walk for warm weather. In spring the hill is lush and green when ferns and undergrowth are fresh from the rains, and irises, wild currants and roses are in bloom. In fall and winter, toyons are bright with berries.

In 15 minutes you are at the first ridge, from which you can look south to the park's Mt. Eden Trail. Then, at the 1000-foot-high Lookout Point, you can see west far up the canyon and east over the Fremont Older Preserve. At Lookout Point go through the stile leading out of the park into the preserve. Before returning, walk along the ridge to a lunch spot overlooking the meadow, where you will often have the pleasure of watching horses cantering over the trails.

For a loop trip, continue across the meadow and up to the south Coyote Ridge Trail, a multi-use trail, and head north on it for 2½ miles back to the Stevens Creek Trail and the visitor center.

Trip 3. Creek Trail

This creekside trail is just right for a short walk before a picnic lunch.

- **Distance:** 1 mile round trip.
- **Time:** ½ hour.
- **Elevation Change:** Nearly level.

TRAIL NOTES

At the intersection of Stevens Canyon and Mt. Eden roads, find the hikers-only trail going downstream from the Cooley Picnic Area. This trail makes for a leisurely stroll under alders and sycamores. From parts of the trail you can look down from the high banks of the creek into its pools and watch for fish in its depths. If you see perched in a tree a blue-grey bird somewhat larger than a jay, with white stripes and a rumpled crest on his outsized head, it is a kingfisher, who is also watching for fish in the creek.

This trail ends at the creek, but in times of low water you can cross the creek to parking on Stevens Canyon Road, and you could extend your walk across the road on Trip 1 or 2.

Trip 4. To a Southern Ridgetop on Multi-Use Trails

The short Mt. Eden Trail leads to the Canyon Trail and over the ridge for striking views of the Santa Cruz Mountains.

- **Distance:** 1.6 miles round trip.
- **Time:** 1 hour.
- **Elevation Gain:** 300'

TRAIL NOTES

From the parking area off Mt. Eden Road at the south end of the park, the Mt. Eden Trail climbs south briefly, then levels off to a gentle grade heading northwest. It is an easy stroll under great bay trees and oaks. Blue wild lilacs bloom here in summer. In 0.2 mile you meet the Canyon Trail (a fire road), on which you turn left sharply (southwest) to climb a chaparral-covered slope. If you are picnicking at the Cooley or Canyon picnic area in the south end of the park, take the Canyon Trail to its junction with the Mt. Eden Trail and proceed as described here.

Along your way on the right is a great craggy limestone outcrop, a good place to pause for the views up the canyon and down the reservoir. In ¼ mile from the junction you reach the high point of the trail and sweeping vistas of the Santa Cruz Mountains. You can continue down the fire road if you welcome the exercise of the climb back. But you may want to linger near the summit, where there are several fine spots for spreading out your picnic.

Beyond the ridgetop the slopes are covered with oaks, bays and buckeyes. There are firs here and there on the way down to Stevens Canyon Road. However, there is no parking at the trail's lower end, so the trip should be taken as a round trip from Mt. Eden Road.

Picchetti Ranch Area, Monte Bello Open Space Preserve
Map on page 231

A visit to the Picchetti Ranch is an opportunity to enjoy the flavor of a foothill winery and ranch of the late 1800s, an experience now all but vanished. The ranch was in the Picchetti family from the 1870s until the Midpeninsula Regional Open Space District acquired it in 1978. Vincenzo Picchetti came to the Santa Clara Valley from Italy in 1872, and soon after bought the ranch and planted orchards and vineyards on its hillsides. Early family quarters, the family home, the winery and the orchards remain.

Today the buildings of the Picchetti Ranch form the centerpiece of the preserve. Listed in the National Register of Historic Places and in the Santa Clara County Resource Inventory, these buildings are being restored with grant funds for historic preservation. The first to be completed was the old brick winery in a joint project by MROSD and the lessee, the Stortz family. The family currently operates the Sunrise Winery on site and offers wine-tasting on Friday, Saturday, and Sunday from 11 to 3 (except holidays). Private parties may rent the building for special events. Call 408-741-1310. The inviting picnic tables and grounds are open to the public on Friday and Sunday 8 A.M.-4 P.M. and Saturday 11 A.M.-3 P.M.

Recent restoration of the large barn across the courtyard from the winery preserved much of the original siding and foundation rock work. The Stortz family, with grants for historic preservation, completed the fermentation building to be used in wine-making. MROSD finished restoring the original blacksmith shop, and the little Picchetti homestead house soon will be repaired as well.

The ranch's 372 acres extend past an old orchard and up gentle hills. Four miles of trails take you to oak groves, meadows and wooded slopes. A 10-minute spring stroll through a flowery orchard brings you to a small, tree-shaded pond. Another 5 minutes along the trail and you are in a parklike meadow dotted with oaks.

Jurisdiction: Midpeninsula Regional Open Space District—415-691-1200.

Facilities: Trails for hikers and equestrians, historic winery, wine tasting, picnic tables and restroom.

Rules: Except for winery and adjacent buildings, preserve open dawn to dusk. No dogs.

Maps: MROSD brochure *Picchetti Ranch Area, Monte Bello OSP* and USGS topo *Cupertino.*

How To Get There: From I-280 go right (south) on Foothill Expwy, which becomes Foothill Blvd. and then Stevens Canyon Rd. Continue about 3 miles beyond entrance to Stevens Creek Reservoir in Stevens Creek County Park. Just beyond a quarry on your right, turn right, uphill, onto Monte Bello Rd. and go ½ mile to Picchetti Ranch.

Trip 1. A Stroll to Picchetti Pond and a Hilltop View

A short easy trail takes you uphill through the old orchard.

- **Distance:** 1 mile round trip.
- **Time:** 45 minutes.
- **Elevation Gain:** 140'

TRAIL NOTES

Start from the parking lot to the right of the winery gate on a trail that crosses a bubbling stream, Swiss Creek, on a small bridge. You may be serenaded by the winery's resident peacocks. Take the old ranch road, now called the Zinfandel Trail, by the abandoned orchard, ignoring the first side road leading down to your left. After less than ½ mile you pass the north leg of the Orchard Loop Trail on your left, also an old road, and reach the Bear Meadow Trail that circles left around a small pond. This trail is for hikers only. Dried up in summer, this pond is home to a frog chorus in the rainy season, and nearby logs make pleasant seats for a picnic lunch.

Take this trail around to the east side of the pond to a fork, from which you take the lefthand trail that winds gently northeast to the summit of a small hill (elevation 1,000 feet). You will meet the righthand trail, the Bear Meadow Trail, later on this trip. Shaded by live oaks, this hill offers superb views in three directions. To the north is a quarry you passed on the road, where the machinery makes quite a noise on weekdays. Other noises you can hear on weekends are shots coming from the Sunnyvale Rod and Gun Club just east of the quarry. Beyond this quarry and through a gap in the northern ridge you can see buildings of the much larger Permanente Quarry in the hills behind Cupertino. Limestone from this quarry was used to make the cement for Shasta Dam in 1945. The East Bay is faintly visible through this gap on a clear day. Filling the foreground to the northeast are the Stevens Creek Dam and the reservoir behind it. Farther to the east are the slopes of Fremont Older Open Space Preserve. Think, as you survey all before you, that had not some foresighted people formed the Midpeninsula Regional Open Space District in 1972 the nearby hills would not have been preserved for future generations to walk on.

Descending east from the small hill be careful of your footing on this very steep trail. You join the north leg of the Orchard Loop Trail, a patrol road, and turn right (east) through chaparral vegetation. This stretch can be very hot in summer, but in spring the ceanothus blossoms fill the air with scent. After only ¼ mile you come to a junction where a patrol road leads left downhill to Monte Bello Road. This trip turns right on the Bear Meadow Trail (here a patrol road), and after about only 100 feet takes a foot trail going right uphill on which you can return to the pond and back the way you came.

To visit a lovely meadow and shady oak woodland from the Orchard Loop/Bear Meadow Trail junction described above, continue right on the Bear Meadow Trail and pass the foot trail that returns to the pond. On the right another foot trail bypasses the wide patrol road for a short distance, goes uphill, and then bends around to cross the patrol road to meander 0.7 mile southeast past an oak-bordered meadow and through the woods down to parking on Stevens Canyon Road opposite the reservoir.

Trip 2. The Zinfandel Trail to Stevens Creek County Park

Contour through forest and chaparral to the Cooley Picnic Area. This route circles around the hill behind the pond to views down the valley.

- **Distance:** 3.8 miles round trip.
- **Time:** 2 hours.
- **Elevation Loss:** 600′

TRAIL NOTES

Begin this trip from the winery parking lot on the 1.9-mile Zinfandel Trail as in Trip 1. If you do not wish to return the same way, you can leave another car at the Cooley Picnic Area in Stevens Creek County Park. (The entrance to this picnic area is on Stevens Canyon Road just west of the Mt. Eden Road intersection).

Passing the Picchetti Pond and the two ends of the Orchard Loop Trail patrol road, continue south over a bridge and through a stile on the Zinfandel Trail. This gently sloping trail leaves the meadows behind and enters thick woods. Multiple-trunked bay trees shade you on hot days. In chaparral-covered openings in the bay-tree forest occasional fir trees reach for the sky.

Pass several side creeks, rushing during winter rains, and keep a lookout past a small wooden bridge for a clump of California nutmeg trees on the downhill side of the trail. Note the very sharp needles shining in the canyon light. At the preserve boundary between Picchetti Ranch and Stevens Creek Park there is a good view of the Stevens Creek Dam and the reservoir, and the Santa Clara Valley spreading to the east. A trail in Fremont Older Open Space Preserve is visible on the opposite hillside, tempting you to extend your hike to that preserve.

Soon you begin to switchback down through former ranchlands, seeing a huge barn roof on private property below you. Some buildings of the Santa Clara County Park maintenance yard lie ahead; your trail, becoming very narrow, jogs left on a patrol road, and then the trail, much narrower, resumes on the right. (Note these turns carefully for your return trip.) You wind down through the forest to join the Creek Trail and turn right on it to reach the Cooley Picnic Area by Stevens Canyon Road.

Historic winery built by Picchetti family has been restored.

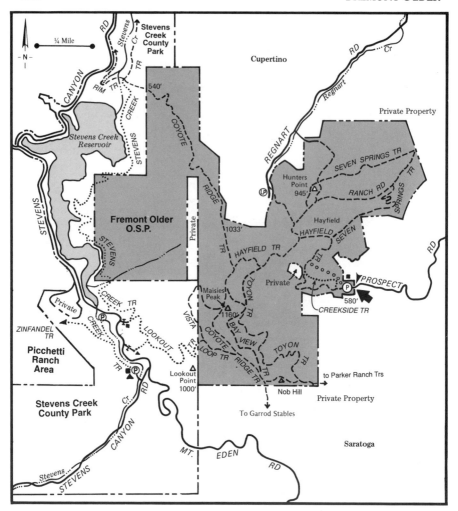

Fremont Older Open Space Preserve

The preserve is part of the old William Pfeffer Ranch, later owned by Fremont Older, a noted San Francisco newspaper editor, and his wife Cora Bagley Older. In the 1920s Mrs. Older designed their ranch home, known as "Woodhills," with a flat roof and many pergolas, a departure from the prevailing style of the times. The house, in a state of disrepair when the Midpeninsula Regional Open Space District acquired the ranch in 1975, was restored by a leaseholder and is now listed in the National Registry of Historic Places. Woodhills is open for occasional house tours. (Call the district for information on the tour schedule.)

Meanwhile 739 acres of the ranchlands are open to hikers, equestrians and bicyclists, who can take the old ranch roads that wind across the rolling hayfields to old orchards and climb its long central ridge. The preserve is heavily used by equestrians from nearby stables and by bicyclists who enjoy the challenge of its many hill climbs. Trails leading to streets in neighboring subdivisions have no designated parking areas.

Jurisdiction: Midpeninsula Regional Open Space District—415-691-1200.
Facilities: Trails for hikers, equestrians and bicyclists.
Rules: Open dawn to dusk. Approved helmets required for all bicyclists. Dogs on leash allowed on all Fremont Older trails.
Maps: MROSD brochure *Fremont Older OSP*, Santa Clara County *Stevens Creek County Park* and USGS topo *Cupertino*.
How To Get There: From I-280 go south on Hwy 85, take DeAnza Blvd/Saratoga Sunnyvale Rd exit and go south. Turn right on Prospect Rd and go 1.3 miles to MROSD parking area.

Trip 1. Coyote Ridge Trail to Stevens Creek County Park

For a hike with exhilarating views take the trail that climbs the steep west ridge of the preserve and then descends to Stevens Creek Park at the Villa Maria Area.

- **Distance:** 4.6 miles round trip.
- **Time:** 3 hours.
- **Elevation Gain:** 400'
- **Connecting Trail:** Stevens Creek Trail in Stevens Creek Park.

TRAIL NOTES

Hikers, equestrians and bicyclists leave the parking lot on a road that goes along the creek under oak and bay trees. However, when the new multi-use trail on the north side of the parking lot is completed, bicyclists must use this trail. Beyond the first bend in the road, hikers can take the marked Creekside Trail to the right and equestrians continue on the road. After about a 15-minute walk, hikers leave the creekside to emerge on the road, pass the multi-use trail on the right, and join all users on the Hayfield Trail, winding uphill. Beside rolling hayfields bear left past the Seven Springs Trail to a saddle. In spring the green of the sprouting grass in the fields is brilliant against the trunks of old fruit trees. As the oat grass dries, these round hills are golden and billowing for a brief time.

Turn left (southwest) at the saddle and go uphill on the ranch road lined with a few old walnut trees. On the way from the hayfields to the ridgetop you pass the Toyon Trail on the left, but you continue uphill on the ranch road. In a last steep climb from this junction you reach the Coyote Ridge Trail, running north and south along the spine of the preserve.

Bear right at the ridgetop to reach Stevens Creek Park. This trail goes through tall chaparral—wild cherry, wild lilac, mountain mahogany and

Baling hay on "The 80" in 1917.

scrub oak. This brush gives cover to any number of wild creatures, most of which you will not see because they are nocturnal or shy. But when the path is dusty or muddy, you can see by the tracks that it is a busy thoroughfare—the pointed, wedge-shaped hoof prints of deer, the pads of coyotes, the engaging little handlike prints of raccoons and bird tracks, particularly quail. You may even see these plump birds scurrying across the trail ahead of you. And remember, this is rattlesnake country.

Along with the tracks of small animals there will be horseshoe prints, bicycle-tire treads and marks of hiking boots. There are other signs of man, too, on the ridge. The preserve borders a residential subdivision, so in some places the trail is close to houses built on these hills.

As the trail turns and starts around a ridge toward Stevens Creek Canyon, the views of the valley and the mountains are sweeping—golf clubs, subdivisions and quarries below, straight ahead the hangars of Moffett Field, the San Francisco Bay and the East Bay hills. To the north-west Monte Bello Ridge rises from the bend in Stevens Creek and extends to its summit at Black Mountain. Its quarry-scarred face seen from the trail belies the name given to the ridge at a time long before our needs for cement and gravel resulted in the massive excavations. However, the rest of the ridge is beautiful indeed, and someday even this quarry will be grown over with chaparral and trees.

After 0.4 mile along the ridge the trail makes a switchback, and then it descends rapidly for 0.7 mile into Stevens Creek Park. A short, winding service road leads to the Stevens Creek Trail by the reservoir. Turn right on the Stevens Creek Trail toward the visitor center and perhaps have a creekside lunch in the shade at the nearby Villa Maria or Bay Tree picnic area. A car left at the Bay Tree parking lot could make this a shuttle trip and, of course, a much shorter hike.

For a longer trip you can take the Stevens Creek Trail south. At the first junction, one trail goes right partway around Stevens Creek Reservoir, but the hikers-only trail veers left up the hillside and down, returning to Fremont Older Open Space Preserve by way of the Lookout Trail, which connects to the Vista Loop Trail and then the southern Coyote Ridge Trail. This makes a loop, adding almost 5 miles to your trip. See Trip 2 below, and Trips 1 and 2, Stevens Creek Park, (see pages 232 and 233 for detailed directions and trip descriptions.)

Trip 2. Loop Trip South to Maisie's Peak

Skirt the east side of the southern ridge and return over the top of the preserve's highest point.

- **Distance:** 4½ miles round trip.
- **Time:** 2½ hours.
- **Elevation Gain:** 580'
- **Connecting Trail:** Lookout Trail west in Stevens Creek Park.

TRAIL NOTES

Start this trip as in Trip 1, turning left at the saddle. In about ¼ mile from the saddle, take the Toyon Trail, which veers left toward the stables and the southern ridges. Past tall eucalyptus and in and out of secluded canyons you contour along the east side of the ridge. In spring, pink-blooming wild currants and blue wild lilacs brighten the trail. Here and there blossoming fruit trees remind you of earlier ranching days.

At the first junction you can veer right on the Bay View Trail, staying high on the ridge and following it up and down over high vista points. Crowned with spreading oaks, these hilltops make good picnic destinations. However, if you take the lefthand fork and continue south on the Toyon Trail, you traverse a hillside of chaparral interspersed with patches of oaks. Then out in open, rolling meadowlands the Bay View and Toyon trails meet. From here the Bay View Trail continues 0.2 mile due south to the preserve boundary. The Toyon Trail circles east and then south, passes a gate into the preserve and then turns west over Nob Hill to rejoin the Bay View Trail at another gate on the southern preserve boundary. This loop is especially favored by riders from nearby stables.

If you eschew the Toyon Trail loop, continue south on the broad, well-used Bay View Trail to the south end of the preserve and turn north on the Coyote Ridge Trail. To reach the park's 1160-foot high point, stay on the broad ridgetop to a fork in the trail marked by a sign for Maisie's

Peak, named for Maisie Garrod. She and her brother, R. V. Garrod, purchased this property in 1910, grew hay, pastured horses and planted orchards here. Their heirs sold these southern ridgetop acres to the MROSD in 1980 but kept the property on which the present stables are located, just to the south.

A rocky trail goes straight up one side of the peak, but the 360° views from the fenced vista point are worth the steep climb. In the broad meadowlands west of and below the peak is the 1-mile Vista Loop Trail. Across the meadows to the southwest is Lookout Point, on the boundary between Stevens Creek Park and Fremont Older Preserve. A trail from the point joins the Vista Loop, which you take to reach the trail to Maisie's Peak. (See Trip 1 for a description of a loop trip through these parklands.)

Now, return to the trail from your summit climb and follow it north. At the second trail junction you turn right and descend on the Hayfield Trail past the old walnut trees, where deer often rest in the shade. At the saddle in the hayfields you turn right and return to the preserve entrance.

Trip 3. Hunters Point

This trip across hayfields to an apricot orchard is an easy walk, especially recommended for an early supper hike.

- **Distance:** 2 miles round trip.
- **Time:** 1 hour.
- **Elevation Gain:** 365'

TRAIL NOTES

Start from the Prospect Road parking lot, as in Trip 1. At the saddle in the hayfields turn right and take the trail to Hunters Point. You will pass two trails on the left that go down off the ridge, but you head straight for the hilltop, where the trees of an old apricot orchard still have a foothold. Here on the knoll called Hunters Point you can see the whole Santa Clara Valley spread out before you. To the west is the steep ridge that crosses the preserve; beyond are the heights of the Santa Cruz Mountains.

In summer, when the days are long, the short walk to Hunters Point is ideal for a picnic supper. With a festive spread in your pack you can walk to the top of the hill and have enough time left to enjoy a leisurely supper as you watch the sunset and its glow on the East Bay hills. When the lights begin to go on in the valley, it is time to pack up to get back to the parking lot by dusk, when the park closes.

Trip 4. Seven Springs Trail

Take a bypass trail and then climb to Hunters Point.

- **Distance:** 3.5-mile loop.
- **Time:** 2 hours.
- **Elevation Gain:** 365'

TRAIL NOTES.

Leave the parking lot and proceed toward the saddle on the Hayfield Trail as in Trip 1. As the trail curves left before reaching the saddle, look for the new Seven Springs Trail cutoff on your right. This trail is for hikers only until its new surface is compacted. Take this trail and contour north on it, first around a grassy knoll, then gently down through a shady forest kept green by underground springs, which give the trail its name and once provided water for adjacent ranches. Today houses fill former orchard lands, but moisture from the springs still seeps down to the canyon floor. Look for a small grove of sycamores on your right—you may spot a red-tailed hawk nesting near its top.

Reaching the valley and a patrol road leading from the preserve boundary, you cross through an old walnut orchard and start uphill toward Hunters Point. The Seven Springs Trail veers north a little and then climbs west up the nose of Hunters Point. Immediately after passing a side trail on the right, you come to a fork and follow the righthand trail to a hilltop encircled by large oak trees with a toyon understory. Beyond this tree-sheltered hilltop a small flat supports a little apricot orchard. A short, steep climb from the orchard brings you to Hunters Point and the downhill return to the parking area.

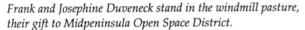

Frank and Josephine Duveneck stand in the windmill pasture, their gift to Midpeninsula Open Space District.

Forest Parks in Southwestern San Mateo County

The large parks southwest of the Skyline lie in the heart of a remarkable aggregation of stately redwoods and mixed hardwood forests midway between ridge and ocean. Creased by deep canyons where perennial streams flow west, these beautiful parks offer more than 14,000 acres of rugged mountainsides, superb second-growth and several virgin redwood groves, high ridges with ocean and mountain vistas, clear, deep pools in shady canyons and a network of interconnecting trails. Each of these parks has a fine interior trail system; now trails connect these parks east to the Skyline ridge and southwest to state parks in Santa Cruz County and thence to the sea.

The magnificent redwoods preserved in these parks were first noted by Fray Juan Crespi when traveling with Don Gaspar de Portolá on his search for Monterey Bay in 1769. Crespi described them as "very high trees of a red color, not known to us" and named them *palo colorado*, red tree.

Over the intervening years many botanists studied the trees, eventually assigning their qualities of great height and long life to the genus *sequoia*. It is generally thought that the Hungarian botanist Stephen Endlicher gave it this generic name in honor of the Cherokee nation chief, Sequoyah.

The trips described in these forest parks lead visitors on short nature walks and long-distance trails to behold splendid specimens of this remarkable tree.

Pescadero Creek County Park Complex

San Mateo County's three parks in the La Honda area are Pescadero Creek, Memorial, and Sam McDonald parks. Together they comprise some 8027 contiguous acres in the drainage basin of Pescadero Creek. They were acquired at different times but have interconnecting trails and share many characteristics. Each is typical of the Santa Cruz Mountains habitat—redwood and Douglas fir forests, mixed evergreen forests and dense riparian vegetation along the streams. Rainfall is heavy on this western side of the mountains, and most of the streams run year-round.

According to Frank Stanger's *Sawmills in the Redwoods*, logging began in this area when John Tuffley built a mill upstream from the town of Pescadero in 1856. Logging has occurred intermittently since then. However, due to its remote location, the area was never completely clear-cut. The difficulty of trips over the Santa Cruz Mountains on wagons hauled by oxen also prevented total clearing. But enterprising loggers, such as William Page, built a road over the Skyline to haul shingles to Mayfield and the Bayside. Other loggers hauled their shingles to Pigeon Point and sent them by boat to San Francisco.

Names of creeks and roads in the area remind us of the stalwart men and their families who built mills and established homes here. Blomquist and McCormick creeks were named for early mill owners. The steep hill between La Honda and Memorial Park known as Haskins Grade was once part of 500 acres owned by Aaron Haskins, who also had a mill on McCormick Creek. The road between Memorial and Pescadero parks was named for Henry Wurr, an immigrant from Germany who gave land for the Wurr School which remained in use until 1935.

Memorial Park, the first of the complex acquired by San Mateo County, owes its existence to Roy W. Cloud, the county superintendent of schools in the 1920s. When visiting schools in this outlying area, he was struck by the beauty of the forests and streams near the old Wurr School. In the Spring of 1923 he appealed to the County Board of Supervisors to buy land for a park here. After studying possible sites, a citizens committee recommended that the County buy 310 acres for $70,000, the beginnings of today's Memorial Park. It was named in honor of the San Mateo County men who lost their lives in World War I. During President Franklin Roosevelt's era veterans of World War I worked on WPA projects here building roads, picnic sites and restrooms, some of which remain today.

Sam McDonald Park, the wooded retreat of a longtime employee of Stanford University, was bequeathed to the university in 1957 and one year later purchased by San Mateo County. McDonald began buying land in the La Honda area in 1917 and eventually owned more than 400 acres along Alpine Creek in the northwest corner of today's park. McDonald, a descendant of slaves, was born in 1884 in Louisiana, and came to Mayfield (part of today's Palo Alto) in 1903. His first employment was at Stanford University as a teamster, from which he rose in over fifty years to become Superintendent of Athletic Grounds and Buildings. Sam McDonald was particularly fond of children, and he wanted his land to become a park for the benefit of young people. In 1976 the County bought additional acres southwest of McDonald's holdings and the 37-acre Heritage Grove Preserve, bringing the total acreage to today's 1002. It is most fitting that the campsites in this park that bears Sam McDonald's name can be reserved by organized youth groups only.

Pescadero Creek Park, the largest of the three, was purchased by the County following the controversy over plans to build a dam on the creek to supply water to the Pescadero area and to provide water-oriented recreation on a deep-water lake behind the dam. Proposed for the site of today's Worley Flat, this dam would have flooded the entire creek canyon, including some of today's Portola Redwoods State Park. In 1968 the County agreed to buy 4736 acres from the Santa Cruz Lumber Company in six yearly purchases through 1973. The company could take all the trees above 400 feet, the elevation of the proposed dam, in specified logging areas, beginning on the north side of the creek. San Mateo County had the option to purchase significant trees or outstanding groves of trees selected by the county forester before timber cutting by the company. Accordingly, during the three years following this agreement, San Mateo County purchased many of the park's monarch trees. Fortunately, many areas of the park were difficult for the loggers to reach and thus some trees that the county could not purchase were saved.

However, public opposition to the size and height of the dam, its flooding of many Portola State Park redwoods and its enormous cost delayed and finally brought a halt to plans for a dam. In March 1971 a new agreement provided that the county would purchase all remaining timber above the 400-foot level and the lumber company would cease all logging operations. Today, Pescadero Creek County Park's 46 miles of trails pass through impressive re-grown redwood and fir forests, especially along Jones Gulch and Towne creeks.

The Pescadero Creek County Park complex does not stand alone in southwestern San Mateo County. Surrounded by a tapestry of parks and preserves and a network of trails, this is indeed one of the most remarkable public open space areas in California. Immediately upstream on Pescadero Creek is the 2800-acre Portola Redwoods State Park, making a total of more than 10,000 acres of redwood environment for public use and enjoyment.

In addition, two long trails join these parks to other public open spaces. The 6.8-mile Basin Trail extends from Portola Redwoods through Pescadero Creek Park and on an easement through private lands reaches Big Basin Redwoods State Park in Santa Cruz County. Another long-distance trail links the Old Haul Road Trail in Pescadero Creek Park with the Slate Creek Trail in Portola Redwoods State Park, which connects to the Ward Road Trail in Long Ridge Open Space Preserve on the Skyline ridge. In the planning stage is a connection from Skyline Ridge Open Space Preserve down the Old Page Mill Road that could enter Portola Redwoods State Park at the Peters Creek Loop and continue to Pescadero Creek Park on the Pomponio or Old Haul Road trails. These existing and potential trail links will further enhance an already outstanding recreational experience and will provide backpacking routes that will challenge sturdy outdoor enthusiasts. Overnight stays in the trail camps in Portola Redwoods and Big Basin Redwoods state parks and in Pescadero Creek County Park can be reserved by calling each park's number listed in Appendix III of this guidebook.

Due to the parks' proximity to the Pacific Ocean, summer fogs and strong winter storms affect the parks' weather. Trails near creeks and under the redwood trees can be damp late into summer. Visitors should always carry extra sweaters and jackets. Spring and fall are delightful times to enjoy the trails, picnic sites and camping at the parks.

Jurisdiction: San Mateo County—415-363-4020; reservations—415-363-4021.

Facilities: Each park in the complex has different facilities, described under that park's description. The main office for the complex is at Memorial Park—415-879-0212. Trails for hikers, some trails for equestrians, picnic tables and campsites, group facilities by reservation and two trail camps.

Rules: Open 8 A.M. to sunset. Horses on designated trails only; bicycles on designated roads only; no dogs; no ground fires allowed. Reservations required for all organized youth groups, regardless of size or activity, group campsites and picnic areas, trail camps and Jack Brook Horse Camp. Reservations are not accepted for family camping and picnicking. Fees.

Maps: San Mateo County brochures *Pescadero Creek County Park, Memorial Park* and *Sam McDonald Park* and USGS topos *La Honda, Mindego Hill,* and *Big Basin.*

How To Get There: Access to Pescadero Creek County Park complex is along some rather tortuous roads—La Honda, Pescadero and Alpine roads—to five park entrances: (1) Sam McDonald Park—From Hwy 84 (La Honda Rd) in La Honda on west side of Skyline, turn left (southeast) on Pescadero Rd, go 1.1 miles to a triangular intersection with Alpine Rd, turn sharp right and continue 0.5 miles on Pescadero Rd to park entrance on right. (2) Pescadero Park, west entrance at Wurr Rd—Follow directions in (1) above, pass Sam McDonald Park and go about 4 miles to sign on left pointing straight ahead (west) to Memorial Park and another small street sign marking Wurr Rd. Turn left on Wurr Rd. and continue ¼ mile to Hoffman Creek Trailhead and a small parking area there. (3) Memorial Park—On Pescadero Rd pass the Wurr Rd sign and go straight ahead (west) ¼ mile to park entrance on left. (4) Pescadero Park, Tarwater Creek Trailhead—From Hwy 35 (Skyline Blvd) west of Palo Alto, take Alpine Rd south for 3.1 miles and bear right past Portola State Park Rd. Continue 0.4 mile to Camp Pomponio Rd, turn left onto it, continuing 1 mile to a small unpaved parking area on left just uphill from gated entrance to County Jail. (5) Trails in eastern part of park complex are also accessible from Portola Redwoods State Park (see page 271). From Hwy 1 take Hwy 84 to La Honda and follow Pescadero Rd as described above.

Coral bells and ferns thrive along Fall Creek's rocky bank in Pescadero Creek County Park.

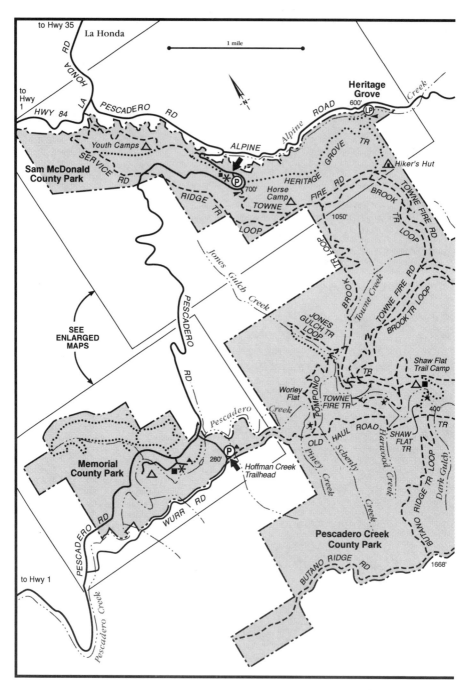

Pescadero Creek

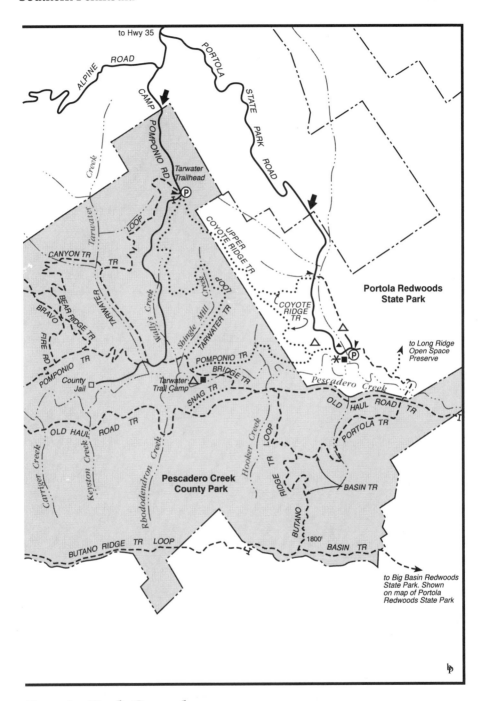

County Park Complex

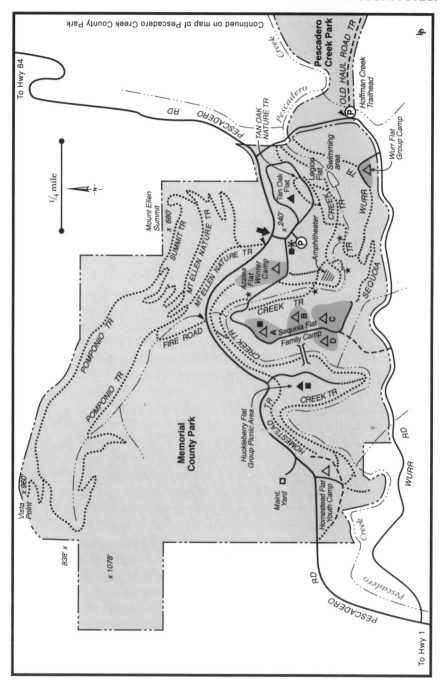

Memorial County Park

San Mateo County's oldest park lies on Pescadero Creek west of La Honda and east of Pescadero in the heart of majestic redwood forests. Its camping and picnicking facilities draw visitors year-round to enjoy the grandeur of the trees and the beauty of the creek environment. Under the high branches of the redwoods are pleasant campsites and picnic areas, set among shiny-leaved huckleberry bushes and tall ferns. Close to the park entrance is a visitor center which features the creek and redwood-forest plants and animals. Docent-led nature walks and evening camp-fires in summer help visitors appreciate the plants, animals, and history of the park.

This 500-acre park is laid out within the meanders of Pescadero Creek, a major year-round stream which rises southeast in the Santa Cruz Moun-tains and is joined by at least fifteen creeks on its long route to the ocean. In summer when water is lower the creek is dammed and warm enough to play in and a sandy beach on its north side near Legion Flat is popular for sunning in midday.

Steelhead, an anadromous trout species, swim upstream to spawn in the creek after fall rains and then return to the sea in the spring. Because this trout is protected, park naturalists carefully monitor the creek habitat, and they have enhanced it with logs placed vertically along the banks, rocks installed to form pools and native plants encouraged along its course. No fishing is allowed.

Approximately 10 miles of trail lead along the creek, through its redwoods and up to two vista points. Two nature trails, one of which is for the physically disabled, pass by outstanding natural features of the park. Connections to Pescadero Creek and Sam McDonald county parks' trails make Memorial Park an excellent starting point for day and over-night hiking trips.

Facilities: Trails for hikers, Tan Oak Trail for physically handicapped, two nature trails, camping and picnic sites for groups and families, visitor center. Evening programs at amphitheater and docent-led na-ture walks, June through Labor Day weekend.

Rules: Open year-round. Trails for hikers only. Reservations and fees are required; see Pescadero Creek County Park Complex rules. No dogs, no fishing, no horses.

Maps: San Mateo County brochure *Memorial Park* and *Pescadero Creek County Park* and USGS topo *La Honda*.

How to Get There: Follow the directions on pages 249–50 for access point (3).

Trip 1. Tan Oak Nature Trail

Follow the green rope to learn all about redwood country.

• **Distance:** 0.4 mile loop.

- **Time:** Allow ½ hour to read the pamphlet and absorb what is described.
- **Elevation Loss:** Very small.

TRAIL NOTES

From the Tan Oak Flat picnic area find the start of the trail just north of the parking area. This informative trail, accessible to wheelchair users and sight- and hearing-impaired persons, was laid out by Linda Wagner, a San Jose State University student, and implemented in 1980 by Bill Lawrence and Gary Woodhams, San Mateo County park rangers. A green rope laced through stout posts guides those with sight impairment.

On a short trail you can learn the secret of the redwood's long life and how plants adapt to the redwood's dense shade. See for yourself the park's tallest and oldest tree and stop at a meditation grove to admire a ring of ancient, burned-out redwoods. This grove was dedicated in 1957 by the California Daughters of the American Revolution and rededicated in 1994. When you recall the date of the Revolution, consider that these trees were probably standing here 1000 years before 1776.

After you have absorbed the redwood ecology, try some of the following trips around the park:

Trip 2. West Side Loop Trip on the Creek and Homestead Trails

Meander along and across Pescadero Creek and return under stately redwoods.

- **Distance:** 2.1-mile loop.
- **Time:** 1½ hours.
- **Elevation Change:** Relatively level.

TRAIL NOTES

Since the portable bridges over Pescadero Creek are removed during the rainy season, this hike is best done in summer or fall. From the park office follow the park road to Tan Oak Flat and take the Creek Trail on its east side. Shortly you make a sharp angle and the Creek Trail begins its westward route. Follow the trail past Legion Flat to the beach where Pescadero Creek is impounded for a swimming area in summer. (You can also reach this point by descending the wide stairs off the service road as it bends east.)

From the beach area take the trail along the bluff top to the amphitheater, where you can descend on steep steps to the creek or circle around the side of the amphitheater and pick up the Creek Trail going north. In times of low water, you can descend the steps to the creek, cross it on a portable bridge (removed in winter) or hop across on rocks, and continue downstream under overhanging willows and tanbark oaks. At the Sequoia Flat campsites, follow the road east to ford the creek that flows through a culvert. In winter, the creek overflows on a wide cement apron and this trail is impassable, so stay on the trail on the bank above the creek. On the north side of the creek the trail narrows to a bare 12 inches and threads along a steep, moist bank. When it crosses a wooden foot bridge over a small creek, look upstream to see Pomponio Falls tumbling down the bank.

Continuing on the Creek Trail you come to a steel bridge spanning the creek, which you can reach by climbing wooden steps up the hillside. If you go across the bridge (may be closed for repairs), you will be at Campground B, where there are restrooms and a phone. From the bridge high over the creek you can see the restoration work done to reinforce the creek banks and to improve the steelhead habitat.

Then return to the Creek Trail on the west side of the bridge and follow it around two bends to the Homestead Trail and begin the return leg of this loop trip. The Creek Trail often washes out in heavy winter rains, in which case take a trail across the picnic area to the Homestead Trail. Although you travel below Pescadero Road here, huckleberry bushes and graceful ferns screen the trail.

When you see a sign that points across Pescadero Road to the Pomponio Trail, you could walk up a few steps, cross the road, and take either the Mt. Ellen Summit Trail, the Mt. Ellen Nature Trail or the longer 3.5-mile Pomponio Trail Loop, which climbs to a vista point at an elevation of 995 feet. This Pomponio Trail commemorates a Native American turned "desperado," who holed up in this area in the 1820s. Pomponio Creek, which flows to the Coast from the heights northwest of the park, and the long Pomponio Trail, the former Boy Scout camp and the road to the Tarwater Trailhead in Pescadero Creek Park are named for this colorful, historic character. Unfortunately, the records of his 1824 court martial and execution in Monterey were lost in the 1906 San Francisco fire.

However, by continuing on the Homestead Trail you soon reach the Azalea Flat campgrounds and the service road, from which you can return to the amphitheater and go on to Tan Oak Flat. To add a short loop after this trip, you could descend to Pescadero Creek from the Creek/Tan Oak Nature Trail junction, turn left (east) on the Wurr Trail and wander for ½ mile through the redwoods on the south side of the creek. When you reach Wurr Road, walk north on it past an ancient barn, cross the bridge over the creek and immediately enter the park on the Creek Trail again. You soon pass a moss-covered stone structure, built by WPA crews during the Roosevelt years, still used as a water pumping station. Shortly you find the swimming beach and the stairs up to Tan Oak Flat, thus completing a full-scale exploration of this beautiful park's south side.

Trip 3. Mt. Ellen Trails

Try the Nature Trail Loop or climb to the Summit for mixed evergreen and chaparral environments and views north to Mindego Hill.

- **Distance:** 1 mile—Nature Trail; 1.6 miles—Summit Trail.
- **Time:** 1 hour, at least—Nature Trail; 1½ hours—Summit Trail.
- **Elevation Gain:** 200'—Nature Trail; 430'—to Mt. Ellen.

TRAIL NOTES

Carefully cross Pescadero Road and take the hikers-only trail uphill to the first junction. Turn left (northwest) here onto the Nature Trail and follow the numbered posts that point out the significant trees, plants and terrain you pass through, as well as describing the animals and birds that inhabit the park. At the junction where the Pomponio Trail goes off left, stay right on the Nature Trail. Then at the next junction, the Summit Trail goes left to reach the top of Mt. Ellen, but you arc right on the Nature Trail, zigzag around several switchbacks to the next junction, turn right and descend past the first Nature Trail sign to return to the park entrance. During the summer park naturalists lead interpretive hikes on this trail.

However, if you take the Summit Trail, you will climb up and around many switchbacks through the forest where blue lupines in spring and sticky monkey flower in summer grace the trailside. Shortly you will pass a left turnoff for the Pomponio Trail, which follows a narrow path along the southwest-facing hillside up to a high western viewpoint and returns down a broad service road. If you continue on the Summit Trail, zigzag back and forth uphill until you reach a fenced opening (not marked as the summit, but it may be) with a birdseye view north through the trees of Mindego Hill's grassy south side. Then undulate down and up on the ridge for 500 feet to another clearing with a worn sandstone base, where the view is limited.

It's downhill all the way from here, winding around many bends, switchbacking out into open grassland, and then back into an oak forest. If you take this trip early in the day or in the late afternoon, you will hear many species of birds calling, and if you stop beside the trail, you may see them flitting into trailside bushes and trees. After you pass the Nature Trail junctions, it is a quick descent through the redwoods to the Pescadero Road crossing and the park visitor center.

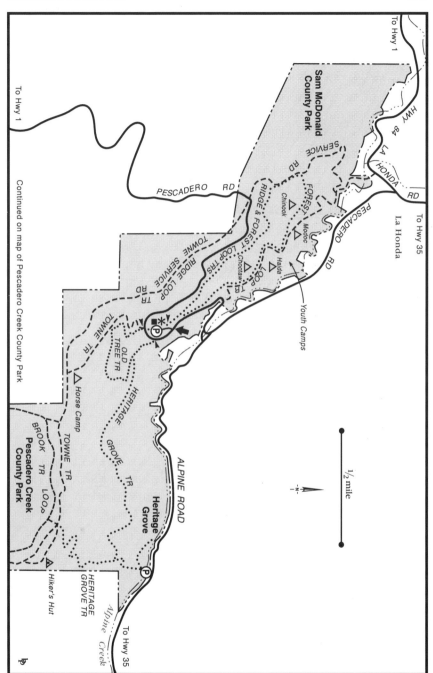

Sam McDonald County Park

This 1003-acre San Mateo County park, part of the Pescadero Creek
County Park complex, lies on both sides of meandering Pescadero Road

near La Honda. The 400 northeast-facing acres that drain into Alpine Creek are mostly redwood forest with understories of huckleberry, creambush and hazelnut and a lush ground cover of redwood sorrel. On the southeast side of Pescadero Road are the sunnier grasslands and oak/madrone woods on south-facing Towne Ridge. On the north side of this ridge lies the 38-acre Heritage Grove on the banks of Alpine Creek. Here are specimen old-growth redwoods and a fine second-growth redwood/fir forest preserved following a citizens fund drive that culminated in the County's acquisition of the grove. Parklands stretch from the grove west to Pescadero Road.

Trails for hikers loop through the redwood forest and pass the group campsites on the north side of Pescadero Road. On the south side trails wind through a stately redwood forest to the Heritage Grove and uphill to Towne Ridge and the Hikers Hut. Equestrians use the unpaved park service roads to reach both sides of the park and other trails in adjoining Pescadero Creek County Park.

A well-kept horse camp on Towne Ridge, named in honor of former parks and recreation director Jack Brook, is open by reservation for equestrians only.

Facilities: Trails for hikers and equestrians, picnic sites, group campsites reserved especially for youth groups, Hikers Hut and Jack Brook Horse Camp. Restrooms at park office and in campsites.
Rules: All youth groups must make reservations; picnic sites available on first-come, first-served basis. No dogs, no pets, no bicycles. Fee for group camping.
Maps: San Mateo County brochure *Sam McDonald Park* and *Pescadero Creek County Park*, USGS topos *La Honda* and *Mindego Hill*.
How To Get There: There are two access points: (1) Park office on Pescadero Rd—follow directions (1) on page 249; (2) Heritage Grove on Alpine Rd—go 1.2 miles east of Pescadero/Alpine Rd junction on south side of road.

Trip 1. Two Loop Trails North from Park Office

Find the Wolf Tree in a quiet redwood grove.

- **Distance:** 2.6-mile—Forest Loop; add 1 mile for service-road extension; 3.6-mile—Ridge Loop.
- **Time:** 1½ hours.
- **Elevation Gain:** 300′

TRAIL NOTES

Start this trip for hikers only on a trail to the right of the park office and walk immediately uphill under beautiful redwood trees. At the first junction turn left on the foot trail (bear right to reach the campsites) winding up and down past many burned-out shells of giant redwoods and some splendid living trees. Some of these long-lived trees are fire-scarred and others are hollow and yet still living. As you meander along the steep-sided trail, note the beautiful, graceful ferns flourishing in this shady forest. Ferns can prosper without much sunlight because they reproduce by spores instead of by pollination, which is dependent on insects and flowers. Because redwoods groves create dense shade, plants that don't need direct sunlight or insects to pollinate them can flourish.

Here and there are seats cut out of redwood stumps or into the middle of fallen logs, pleasant stopping places to contemplate the magnificent trees. After about a mile on this trail, look on your right for a fallen monarch, a branch of which resembles a wolf's head.

For the most part, the forest floor is covered with redwood and tan oak duff, often carpeted with three-leaved redwood sorrel enlivened with small pink-petalled blossoms in spring. Look for occasional hazelnut bushes overhanging the trail, whose velvety, light green leaves emerge in spring and whose nuts in fall become favorite food for squirrels. The shells can be found underfoot, but seldom on the bush.

After 1.3 miles you reach a junction where the Forest Loop Trail goes right and the Ridge Trail goes left. (See page 264 for Ridge Loop segment described briefly to this point in reverse.) Take the Forest Loop Trail (north), joining the unpaved service road for a very steep downhill stretch. Then watch on the right for a small sign pointing right to continue on the 2.6-mile Forest Loop Trail, which goes east to the Chinook camp-site. If you continue on the service road, you will have a longer loop hike north past the park's water-storage tank, then up, down and around bends heading north, then east to the banks of Alpine Creek. Here you are at the park boundary, where private homes sit below the road. Stay on the road as it turns south and climbs out of the creek canyon. Lovely five-fin-ger ferns drape the trailside, and trillium bloom here in spring—both plants that thrive in this moist, shady environment.

About ¼ mile after turning due south you enter the Modoc group site, where there are picnic tables, barbecues, restrooms and a little circle of log seats for evening gatherings. You follow the paved park road here past other group campsites with Native American names, such as Haida and Choctaw, above a near-vertical canyon wall. When you round the head of this deep canyon beyond the Choctaw camp, find the Forest Loop Trail leading off the road on your right, follow this foot trail uphill to the junction where you started this loop and then descend to the park office.

Trip 2. Big Tree Trail South from Park Office

Try this loop trail before a picnic at one of the tables in the redwoods.

- **Distance:** 1-mile loop.

- **Time:** ¾ hour.
- **Elevation Gain:** 200′

TRAIL NOTES

Begin from the southeast side of the parking area on a trail through the trees that quickly emerges at Pescadero Road. Carefully cross to the other side and step onto the Big Tree Loop Trail, part of the Towne Trail leading to Pescadero Park. Passing a picnic table on your left, begin your uphill trip under second-growth redwoods already reaching 150 feet skyward. Underfoot are branchlets and cones of the redwoods, making very pleasant footing. Pass a road to a few private inholdings in the park, and continue to a park sign on the right that points left to the Heritage Grove Trail and right to the Big Tree Trail. You take the latter one and climb steadily uphill on a shady north-facing slope. This is a lovely, cool hike on a hot day, with sunlight filtering through the trees and Steller's jays squawking in the canopy.

Continuing uphill, you bend south and then slowly descend west past a big green water tank. Paralleling the Towne Trail service road, you head downhill left (southeast), descend some steep steps, go around some switchbacks and finally reach the Big Tree. Stop here to admire its 15-foot diameter and its hollow core. Fire-scarred and open on two sides, this venerable giant is alive and well. Apparently when redwoods are burned, they tend to sprout from the base, which may account for the multiple, fused trunks.

You could stop for rest and a picnic lunch at a nearby picnic table, or cross Pescadero Road to where other tables under the trees offer a pleasant place to reflect on the wonders of these magnificent trees.

Trip 3. Heritage Grove Loop

After following a well-built hikers' trail to redwoods along Alpine Creek, you rise gradually to Towne Ridge and return downhill.

- **Distance:** 5-mile loop.
- **Time:** 2½ hours.
- **Elevation Gain:** 550′

TRAIL NOTES

This route on the north side of Towne Ridge, a cooler, more gradual, but longer way to the ridge and Hikers Hut than the Towne Trail (service road), starts as described in Trip 2. When you see the sign for the Heritage Grove pointing left, take that trail. Meandering through a forest of widely spaced redwoods and Douglas firs, you nip into little ravines, cross a stream with a little waterfall that is known as Gorge Creek and cross another intermittent but unnamed creek.

Where the trail bends north, you can hear Alpine Creek coursing over rocks and fallen trees at the bottom of the slope. There are stumps of cut redwoods with slots for springboards on which the early loggers stood to use a two-handled saw. Then after 1.2 miles you will see a sign on a hefty redwood post pointing left to the Heritage Grove. Five minutes take you to the fenced flat where the largest and best trees remain, thanks to citizen fund-raising and the County Board of Supervisors who purchased the grove. Beyond, down a pretty trail are two bridges over Alpine Creek and a small parking area on the creek side of Alpine Road. This short trail from Alpine Road makes an excellent introductory redwood-ecology walk.

Jack Brook Horse Camp.

After savoring the sight and sound of the creek and its riparian trees and shrubs, retrace your steps to the grove, and then turn left (due south) at the redwood signpost to begin the climb to Towne Ridge and the Hikers Hut. From here to the ridge you traverse a mixed forest of oaks, bays, maples, and some Douglas firs. Around a wide turn you pass a knoll where the canopy is high above the ground and the understory is a tangle of creambush, berry and honeysuckle vines, and hazelnut trees. This different environment might indicate a clear-cut or fire occurred here in recent past.

When you reach the ridgetop grasslands, look to your left for the ¼-mile trail through the woods to the Hikers Hut (see Pescadero Park Trip 2. Brook Trail Loop). After a short detour to experience the wonderful view across Pescadero Creek Canyon and up to Butano Ridge, you can return to the Towne Trail and go west ¾ mile to visit the Jack Brook Horse Camp. Although this is reserved for equestrians only, you can walk up to see the corrals, campsites and the little cottage that once belonged to the Towne family, who sold these 400 acres on the south side of the ridge to San Mateo County.

From the junction of the horse camp trail take the Towne Trail (service road) downhill along the west side of a redwood-filled canyon, pausing on the steep descent to savor the healthy trees whose tops tower high above the trail. At some point your eyes are almost at the level of the lower tree branches 100 feet above their trunks.

An alternate route to return to the park office follows the Ridge Trail out to Pescadero Road, crosses it, and mounts a few steps to reach the service road. Then you proceed downhill about 800 feet to the junction of the Forest Loop Trail. Turn right here and wind up and down along the 1.3-mile trail on the north-facing ridge to the park office (route described in reverse in Trip 1). This would add about 3 miles to your trip, but would make a fine overview of Sam McDonald Park.

Pescadero Creek County Park

This 6486-acre park, the keystone that ties Memorial and Sam McDonald parks together, encompasses seven miles of Pescadero Creek as it meanders through the canyon between Towne and Butano ridges. Joined by nineteen intermittent streams that tumble down the steep sides of these ridges, Pescadero Creek forms the centerpiece of the park. More than 40 miles of trail reach its highest points, follow its creeks and penetrate its great forests. When combined with the adjacent lands of Portola Redwoods State Park, this vast open space is premier country for long, strenuous hikes and horseback rides. Trails leading to the banks of Pescadero Creek offer short jaunts for casual walks. The canyons are heavily forested, especially on north-facing, 2,000-foot Butano Ridge, while the southwest-facing slopes of 1,200-foot Towne Ridge offer pockets of grassland with inspiring views in all directions. Included here are trips that sample Pescadero Creek Park's splendid, remote, almost-wilderness acres, less than an hour from the urban Bayside.

Facilities: Trails for hikers and equestrians, trail camps by permit from Memorial Park office.
Rules: Bicycles on Old Haul Road only. No dogs, no fires.
Maps: San Mateo County brochure *Pescadero Creek County Park*, USGS topos *La Honda*, *Mindego Hill* and *Big Basin*.
How To Get There: Follow directions on pages 249–50 to access points (2), (4) and (5).

Trip 1. A Short Walk to Pescadero Creek and Worley Flat

When the water level is low, take a backpack picnic to an easy destination for families with young children.

- **Distance:** 2 miles round trip to creek; 3 miles round trip to Worley Flat.
- **Time:** 1 to 2½ hours.
- **Elevation Gain:** 50′ to creek; 100′ to Worley Flat.

TRAIL NOTES

Choose a sunny day for this trip, pack a lunch, take dry socks and extra clothing and start from the Hoffman Creek Trailhead at the Wurr Road entrance to the park, access point (2) on page 249–50. You set off across a sturdy bridge over Hoffman Creek and pass a few picnic tables by a kiosk on your left. After orienting yourself at the park map here and learning about its wildlife, follow the wide, unpaved Old Haul Road. Still used for occasional logging on nearby private property, this road/trail undulates up and down through a clearing and a former orchard, then dips into redwoods on an easement through adjoining private lands, where second-growth trees are being harvested. Although the ancient redwood forest was logged many years ago, remnant stumps of old monarchs still stand beside the trail attesting to the size and grandeur of the ancient forest. Some trees are hollow and tempt little ones to crawl through. Others are blackened by fires of long ago.

About ½ mile through the cool forest you pass Piney Creek, after which watch for the signed Pomponio Trail turnoff on your left. As you drop down under a canopy of deciduous alder and willow trees to the creekside, you find a portable foot bridge (removed at high water) over Pescadero Creek. Here the creek tumbles over scattered rocks, tugs at clumps of graceful grasses, laps at mossy stream banks and brushes against willows that arch overhead. Here children can float leaf boats downstream, watch skeeter bugs on the water and see dragonflies flitting above the stream.

After a picnic in the shade at creekside or in the sunny meadow at Worley Flat, just another ten minutes up the Pomponio Trail, return on the Old Haul Road from a delightful children's outing.

Trip 2. Brook Trail Loop

Climb out of the creek canyon to sunny meadows and wide views.
- **Distance:** 8-mile loop.
- **Time:** 5 hours.
- **Elevation Gain:** 650'

TRAIL NOTES

Although this trip reaches many trail junctions which are well-marked, some signs may be obscured or missing. Begin at the Hoffman Creek Trailhead on Wurr Road [access point (2)] and follow the directions to Worley Flat as in Trip 1. Then continue on the Pomponio Trail past the wide, mowed meadow and curve right (east) across its north end. On the far side of the meadow follow the Pomponio Trail left onto a graveled tread and go uphill through oak woodland. Soon you cross a wide, closed-off trail, the former Jones Gulch Trail, and take the foot trail down a long traverse. In sunny patches look for blue iris blooming in spring and red rose hips and orange-red poison oak leaves in fall. On switchbacks you descend to the creek, which you can hear gurgling in the canyon after heavy rains.

After 1.6 miles from your starting point you reach another trail junction, where the sign tells you that the Pomponio Trail goes right and the Jones Gulch Trail goes left. Ahead of you is the Jones Gulch Bridge, which you will take to begin the Brook Trail Loop. Turn sharply left (north) at the junction, go right onto the bridge and you have reached a magical part of Pescadero Park. If you pause here under the towering redwood trees, look into the depths of the creek canyon carved out of Butano sandstone to see five-finger ferns and moss draping its high banks and little waterfalls dropping over fallen logs. Carpets of pink-flowered redwood sorrel adorn the forest floor in this idyllic spot—a cool destination for a hot day's hike.

Waterfall on Fall Creek.

In 500 feet you bear right on an unpaved patrol road, the unmarked Jones Gulch Trail, cross Towne Creek in a culvert, go 300 feet farther on the patrol road, and turn sharply left. On a rare, hot morning, it would be cooler to ascend the other side of the loop, which is shaded in the morning, and then descend on this side. A sign farther along the patrol road points right to the other leg of the loop.

Slowly climbing through a forest of ancient and second-growth trees on the west side of the Brook Trail Loop, you find new trees sprouting from fallen ones, tanbark oaks growing out of sawn-off redwoods and slanting light filtering through the forest canopy. You may be puzzled by the presence of an occasional monarch tree remaining near a clump of redwood stumps. A possible explanation is that some trees were too inaccessible, too scarred by fire or just too difficult to haul out of the forest.

About midway up the mountain the trail narrows and skirts a deep ravine, then makes 10 or 11 switchbacks through mixed forest to a chaparral clearing. From here you can look down into the deep, heavily wooded canyon of Towne Creek and east across it to the route of your return trip. To the south lies Butano Ridge rising above the Pescadero Creek Canyon. Then after more switchbacks through a forest of fir, oak and madrone, you emerge on a gentle grassy slope with a view of the Skyline ridge. (Occasionally, you can hear sounds of target practice from a gun club off Skyline Boulevard east of here.) Trail signs point south to destinations in Pescadero and Memorial parks and east to the Hikers Hut and the continuation of the Brook Trail Loop. In a few steps you are on a wide, unpaved road, which you can take, but you may prefer to stay on the foot trail which parallels this road around the head of the Towne Creek canyon. You are now in Sam McDonald County Park.

In about ½ mile look for the left turnoff sign (north) to the Hikers Hut. To reach this attractive Sierra Club hut, follow the trail ¼ mile uphill into the woods. Shortly you come to a sturdy cabin with a million-dollar view. Thanks to Ollie Mayer and a dedicated team of Sierra Club volunteers, this hut was imported from Denmark and assembled on this park site in 1977. You can reserve this hut for an overnight or a weekend by calling the Loma Prieta Chapter of the Sierra Club. (See Appendix III.) However, if you are just visiting for the day, you can sit on a log seat in front of the hut and enjoy the vista of forested Butano Ridge and Pescadero Creek canyon. After a rest and snack here, begin the next leg of your trip.

Return to the Brook Trail Loop and proceed downhill about ½ mile through a fir forest. When the trail crosses the patrol road, you can climb up to a ledge where two picnic tables and another fine view of southwestern San Mateo County's beautiful evergreen forests await you. Following this short digression, take the narrow foot trail through beautiful, quiet redwood groves on the west-facing side of the canyon. When you come to the Towne Fire Road, cross it, and at the next junction angle sharply right to stay on the Brook Trail Loop. If you go left and uphill from here, you will be on the Bear Ridge Trail, which is discussed in Trip 3.

For approximately ½ mile the Brook Trail Loop levels off, paralleling the fire road. Then it joins the road for about 500 feet, after which you leave the road, go right, uphill, and zigzag through deep redwood forest to another trail junction, where the Brook Trail Loop goes right onto the Pomponio Trail heading north. Shortly you cross another fire road, the Jones Gulch Trail, and continue to Grangers Bridge across Towne Creek, signed Elevation 270 feet. From this bridge you can look upstream to the confluence of Towne and Jones Gulch creeks. Little waterfalls drop into a pebbly pool shaded by huge redwoods, its banks festooned with graceful ferns. Just a bit farther is the Pomponio/Brook Trail junction where you began the Brook Trail Loop. Take a last look at the lively creek as it tumbles over a sandstone shelf, bounces off a fallen tree, and continues on its way to join Pescadero Creek.

Now you bear left on the Pomponio Trail, retrace your steps on a few switchbacks uphill, cross Worley Flat, and head southwest to the ford of Pescadero Creek. Shortly you reach the graveled Old Haul Road, where you turn right (west) to return to the Hoffman Creek Trailhead.

Trip 3. A Loop around the Tarwater Creek Basin

Explore up and down the east-facing slopes of the Tarwater Creek canyon.
- **Distance:** 5 miles.

- **Time:** 3 hours.
- **Elevation Loss:** 650' to trip's lowest point.

TRAIL NOTES

From the northeast corner of the park at the Tarwater Trailhead on Camp Pomponio Road, access point (5) on page 250, take the west leg of the Tarwater Trail Loop just across the road from the parking area. The first part of this trail is thoroughly described in the Tarwater Trail Loop write-up in Portola Redwoods State Park (see Trip 4, page 279).

When you reach the junction of the Tarwater and Canyon trails, bear right onto the Canyon Trail, an old logging road, and pause to admire the huge redwood tree on the left side of the trail. It must have been left by the loggers because of some defect or because the county purchased it during the negotiations for the park. A little farther along in the hushed silence of the ancient forest, descend to the Tarwater Creek crossing. You are now on the north side of a tributary of Tarwater Creek. In this canyon where horsetails, ferns and huckleberry thrive, begin a climb of several hundred feet on a narrow trail, closed to horses in wet weather. Switchbacks carry you up and up past a few pools in the creek, a huge logjam and a marshy spot where wild boars have been at work. From an elevation of about 900 feet you make a long climb south and then round a sharp switchback to look north through the trees to Towne Ridge and the houses along Alpine and Camp Pomponio roads.

About two hours from the trailhead you reach the Bear Ridge Trail and turn left (south) on it through a forest with a high canopy. Swing along on this trail up a little hump and then downhill to intersect the Bravo Fire Road, on which you descend briefly before angling left on the Bear Ridge Trail again. With the steep canyon of Tarwater Creek on your left, you contour along this hillside through big Douglas firs, then cross to the west side of the ridge.

After meeting a fence across an old trail, you pass the white plastic pipes where treated wastewater from the jail is sprayed on the hillside. This is not a good place to pause for lunch. Shortly you meet a trail junction and turn left (southeast) on the Pomponio Trail. If you go west on this trail, you reach the eight Shaw Flat Trail Camps, which are reservable by calling the Memorial Park office. You must carry your own water, food and sleeping bag; there are restrooms. However, if you are not going to Shaw Flat, follow the Pomponio Trail downhill into a huckleberry hollow and then out to the paved Camp Pomponio Road. Here a big sign tells you that the jail (a men's correctional center) is just west of here and only official visitors may enter. Therefore, go left, following the road across a steel-trussed bridge over Tarwater Creek, climb up a short hill, and turn left (north) around a split-rail fence onto the wide, west leg of the Tarwater Trail Loop.

Now you hike up a little rise, then drop down, but gradually ascend along the east bank of Tarwater Creek under tall redwoods and Douglas firs, with cut logs bordering much of the trail. In fall, there is often a beautiful display of shelf fungus in shades of salmon pink and cream on these logs. When you reach the Canyon Trail junction, bear right between redwood posts and retrace your steps to the Tarwater Trailhead where your trip began.

Trip 4. Butano Ridge Trail Loop

Innumerable switchbacks take you up and down on a day-long workout.
- **Distance:** 13.3 miles.
- **Time:** 8 hours.
- **Elevation Gain:** 1750'

TRAIL NOTES

Even if you don't take the entire loop, a climb partway up the western leg of this loop trail offers the experience of a second-growth forest relatively untouched since the logging of the late 1960s. With an early start from the Hoffman Creek Trailhead, access point (2) on page 249, you can do the uphill stretch in the cool of the morning. Carry extra sweaters, a windbreaker and plenty of water and food for this trek to the top of the ridge. In fall, days can be delightfully warm and sunny; summer can bring drippy fogs and chilly, damp days.

On the Old Haul Road you follow the same route as in Trips 1 and 2, but after reaching the Pomponio Trail turnoff, you continue another 1.5 miles, passing the marked crossings of Schenly and Harwood creeks. Occasional dense groves of alders fill hollows along the wide, unpaved road and ferns clothe its shady banks. But the stately redwoods are the main attraction along this road in the bottom of Pescadero Creek canyon.

Two trails cross to the north side of the creek—Towne Fire Road and the Shaw Flat Trail—and lead to the Shaw Flat Trail Camp on the Pomponio Trail. Just opposite the Shaw Flat Trail, look for the entrance to the western leg of the Butano Ridge Trail Loop on your right (south). Now you step onto this well-designed, comfortably graded trail that goes up and

Tall alders lean over Old Haul Road.

around ridges, between giant redwoods, past burned-out shells of monarch redwoods and continues zigzagging upward for nearly 2 miles. Underfoot your way is carpeted with duff and small branchlets; occasionally a tree root protrudes across the trail. About two thirds of the way up the mountain, you hit a southeast-trending ridge where there should be views of the coast, but thick, second-growth forest intervenes. However, you traverse this minor ridge until you finally reach the road on the ridgetop, the Butano Ridge Trail Loop.

This road follows the park boundary except for one Pescadero Creek County Park piece that extends downhill to the south. There may be a sunny spot along the ridge where a fallen log provides a resting place, although no picnic sites appear. The wide road continues in rollercoaster fashion for more than 2 miles until a gate bars further travel. Look on the left here for the Butano Ridge Trail Loop, which angles sharply uphill. When this trail levels off, you turn right (east) and contour under tall redwoods and Douglas firs until you reach a massive sandstone wall, at least 30 feet high and 150 feet long.

Shortly beyond this exposed sandstone is the Basin Trail sign on your right. From here it is 5.5 miles to Big Basin Redwoods State Park and 21 miles to Waddell Creek. (See Trip 7, Portola Redwoods State Park). Another sign points you sharply left on the Butano Ridge Trail Loop. Now you begin a series of innumerable switchbacks that carry you rapidly downhill in a lovely evergreen forest.

At the next trail junction take the left fork, the Butano Ridge Trail Loop. The right fork, the Portola Trail (also called the Basin Trail) will reach the Old Haul Road about a mile farther east and across from the trail into Portola Redwoods State Park. (See Trip 7 in that park.) Continuing on the Butano Ridge Trail Loop, you drop down into a damp little glade, then descend to a flatter area near the Old Haul Road. At the junction with this road are several wax myrtle trees that bear closely spaced, long, glossy, narrow leaves. At first glance these small trees could be mistaken for California bay trees, a much larger tree whose leaves have a distinctive, aromatic scent.

Now you turn left on the wide, graveled Old Haul Road and follow it uphill past Hooker Creek, the Snag Trail to the Tarwater Trail Camp on the right and Rhododendron Creek on the left. When you see the sign for Keyston Creek, look for a small waterfall upstream in a shady ravine. Then just past Dark Gulch, you will see the other leg of the Butano Ridge Trail Loop on which you started your climb to the ridgetop. From here you retrace your steps to the Hoffman Creek Trailhead, winding up and down some small hills, past exposed, fractured shale road cuts and under the redwood canopy to the broad clearing before crossing the Hoffman Creek bridge at the Wurr Road parking area.

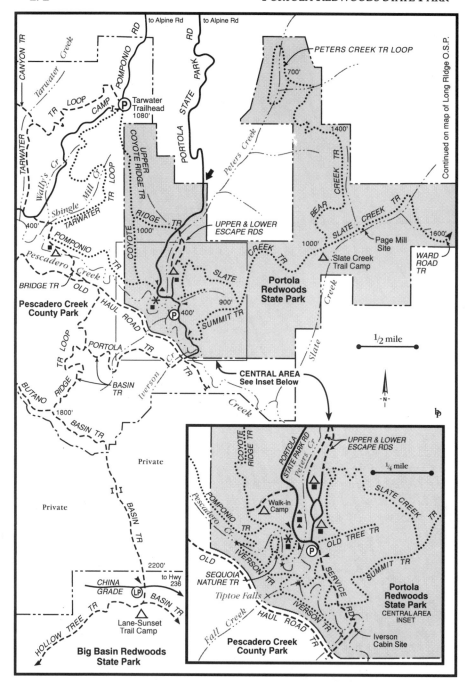

Portola Redwoods State Park

Portola Redwoods State Park's more than 2800 acres nestled at the
base of Butano Ridge lie along the northeast side of Pescadero Creek on

ridges bisected by Peters, Evans, Evergreen and Slate creeks. The park offers miles of hiking trails through stately redwoods and mixed ever-green forests. Some of the largest redwoods in San Mateo County can be found in the shady canyons. The park adjoins San Mateo County's 8027-acre complex of Pescadero Creek, Memorial, and Sam McDonald parks. On its northeast corner it abuts Long Ridge Open Space Preserve, which lies along the crest of the Santa Cruz Mountains amid thousands of acres of contiguous open space.

The first known European settler in this area, Christian Iverson, a former Pony Express rider, came here in the 1860s and built a small redwood cabin on a high bank above a meander of Pescadero Creek. The cabin, hard-hit by the earthquake of 1989, is slated for restoration using drawings of the original cabin developed by State Park volunteers.

After the Gold Rush, lumbermen came to this area seeking wood first to build and then rebuild San Francisco. They cut the giant redwoods along the streams and hillsides and made them into shingles and shakes, then hauled them by oxen teams over the Skyline ridge to the Embarcad-ero in present-day Palo Alto.

William Page, who lived in Searsville in present-day Woodside, devel-oped a mill on Peters Creek which was later moved to Slate Creek, the latter within today's park boundaries. The road he built from old May-field in today's Palo Alto, Page Mill Road, is still in use on the east side of Skyline Boulevard. Beginning on the west side of the Skyline, the Old Page Mill Road Trail descends 2 miles through Skyline Ridge Open Space Preserve and may continue as a public trail to the Peters Creek Loop in Portola Redwoods at a future date. This loop is about a mile upstream from the site of the original Page's Mill, now on private property.

In the early 20th century, San Francisco residents seeking quiet and relaxation in these magnificent forests established summer retreats here. John A. Hooper, a San Francisco banker who had moved to the former Mountain Home Ranch in present-day Woodside, built a large summer residence on Pescadero Creek. In 1924 a San Francisco Shrine group purchased 1600 acres in this area which were bought by the State of California in 1945. The Save-the-Redwoods League donated many acres in the last 50 years, swelling the present-day acreage to over 2800 acres. Today, hikers and campers drive the winding road to enjoy a dayhike or a picnic or to take a longer camping trip.

At the park office/visitor center are exhibits of the outstanding natural features of the park. Freeze-dried specimens of many animals and sam-ples of trees, flowers, and shrubs are displayed in life-like settings. Future plans call for increasing the number of exhibits.

Trails starting from the park office offer trips of one to 13 miles, some on short nature trails around Pescadero Creek, several on longer loop trips, and still other trails that connect to adjoining Pescadero Creek County Park, Long Ridge Open Space Preserve, and Big Basin Redwoods State Park. With the opening of the Basin Trail in 1995 and the proposed Butano Fire Trail Extension, there is the opportunity for extensive backpacking trips between Portola Redwoods State Park and other state and regional parks in the area.

Spring, summer, and fall are the best times for hiking, picnicking, and camping. The many campsites for families, groups, and backpackers willing to walk to trail camps are very popular during summer, especially on weekends. The campsites fill by reservations on all weekends between Memorial and Labor Day.

Dayhikers will find parking at pleasant picnic areas near the park office convenient to all the trailheads. Those who stay in the campsites can get an early start on long hikes to the outer edges of the park and on to neighboring parks. All trips in this park are described from the park office/visitor center at the creek level (400') and most go uphill from there. Following are seven trips of different length and difficulty to suit varying interests and abilities.

Jurisdiction: State of California, Department of Parks and Recreation—415-948-9098.

Facilities: Trails for hikers; visitor center, amphitheater; camping for families, groups and backpackers; picnic areas with barbecues, restrooms. Reservations: Destinet. Fee for parking and camping.

Rules: Hikers only on trails. Bicycles allowed on Old Haul Road Trail in adjacent Pescadero Creek County Park. No dogs on trails; allowed on leash in camp and picnic areas. Fishing prohibited in order to protect native steelhead trout population.

Maps: Portola Redwoods State Park brochure, USGS topos *Mindego Hill* and *Big Basin*.

How To Get There: From Hwy 35 (Skyline Blvd) west of Palo Alto, take Alpine Rd south for 3.1 miles to left turnoff onto Portola State Park Rd. Continue 3.4 miles to park office in visitor center, then proceed to parking areas nearby.

Trip 1. Exploring along Pescadero Creek

Meander down to the creek through tunnels of huckleberry bushes on the Sequoia and Iverson trails.

- **Distance:** Sequoia Trail, ¾-mile loop; Iverson Trail, 3-mile loop.
- **Time:** Sequoia Trail, ¾ hour; Iverson Trail, 1½ hours.
- **Elevation Change:** 90'

TRAIL NOTES

The Sequoia Trail, a must for understanding redwood-forest ecology,

Author Rusmore and redwood giant.

is well-described in the park brochure and is available at the park
office for a small price. After you
have wandered along this fascinating route and learned about
the soil, root system, and effects
of fire on these magnificent trees,
try your newfound knowledge
on the Iverson Trail. It begins just
a few yards north of the park office opposite the Madrone picnic
area. Turn left (northwest) onto
the trail and walk between tall
huckleberry shrubs under red-
barked madrone, mossy-trunked
Douglas fir, and good-sized
redwoods to a fenced overlook of
Pescadero Creek. At least 75 feet
below the steep canyon wall the
creek flows along its bed carved
over the centuries into sandstone
uplifted from under the Pacific Ocean. You follow the Iverson Trail left at
two junctions, the first where the Coyote Ridge Trail goes right and the
next where the Pomponio Trail also goes right.

Continuing downhill, sometimes descending steps braced by redwood planks, you go beside moss-covered logs edging the trail and arrive
at creek level. In summer portable wooden-plank bridges make its crossing easy. In winter these bridges are removed, and the creek can be
treacherously swift and full. On the other side you rise through the forest,
past a swampy area of serrated-edged grasses, to a junction with the
Sequoia Trail in a high huckleberry hollow. Proceeding straight ahead on
the Iverson Trail you climb switchbacks through redwoods of all ages,
some burned but still living, others with hollow cavities in their trunks, to
two lookouts over Pescadero Creek. Through openings framed by alders,
firs and tanbark oaks, you see and hear the creek far below.

At the next junction you can go left on an unnamed trail to cross
Pescadero Creek and return to the park office. If you go 0.15 mile straight
ahead, you cross Fall Creek on a little bridge and continue right to its
Tiptoe Falls. Here this lively creek drops over a corrugated shelf of shale
or sandstone into a lovely little pool in a basin flanked on two sides by
high rock walls clothed with overhanging ferns, shrubs, and trees.
Upstream in a narrow canyon the creek splashes over a jumble of fallen
logs, visible but inaccessible.

Leaving this cool canyon, return to the main trail by going to your right up a bank and through a grove of widely spaced, second-growth redwoods. Beyond is a group of ancient stumps with notches cut for inserting the springboards on which early loggers balanced to fell these huge trees. Shortly the Iverson Trail crosses a bridge over Iverson Creek and goes uphill to the park service road. Step out onto this road and turn left (north) to see, beside the trail, timbers remaining from Christian Iverson's 1860s cabin, which volunteers plan to rebuild in the near future.

To return to the park office, bear left on the trail (not shown on the park map) just beside a road barricade, descend along the east bank of Pescadero Creek, and then cross it on the service-road bridge. From here you can follow the paved road back to the park office, stopping at a fenced overlook to gaze again at the creek flowing below its high northeast canyon wall. Alternatively, you can follow the foot trail described in reverse in Trip 2, the Summit/Slate Creeks Loop. The trail junctions are marked along the service road.

Trip 2. Summit and Slate Creek Trails Loop

Climb out of the canyon through mixed evergreen and oak/madrone forests to experience fine views of Butano Ridge to the southwest.

- **Distance:** 2½-mile loop; add 1.2 miles for side trip to the Old Tree.
- **Time:** 1½ hours; add 30 minutes for side trip.
- **Elevation Gain:** 550'

TRAIL NOTES

From the park office turn right on the entrance road, cross the bridge over Peters Creek and turn right again. Just past the amphitheater the road becomes a service road for park vehicles only. Look on your right here for a trail that leads to Tiptoe Falls. On it you immediately step into an understory of shiny-leaved huckleberry bushes with long, pliant branches that grow under tall, second-growth redwoods. After 0.3 mile go left on a short trail back to the park service road and continue on it to an opening overlooking Pescadero Creek flowing 200 feet below in a sheer-sided canyon. Just beyond the overlook re-enter the forest on a trail where more huckleberries are interspersed with graceful fern fronds, long-leaved iris and climbing honeysuckle. On a series of small ups and downs you pass several double-trunked redwoods and one huge virgin redwood. When the trail again hits the service road, cross it and take the Summit Trail.

Shortly you come upon two water tanks, then switchback uphill past several redwoods scarred by fire, yet still living. As you gain elevation, there are tanoak, live oak, and madrone, some Douglas fir, and fewer redwood trees. Heading steadily upward you contour below a ridge and then hike atop a narrow, knife-edge ridge where cream-colored clusters of

Fremont lilies blossom in spring, and pink wild roses bloom on small-leaved, thorny bushes in summer. Then, as the trail curves east, you see south over a patch of chaparral—toyon, manzanita, chamise and honeysuckle—to densely-forested Butano Ridge. Here is a good rest stop, just a few feet from the summit at 950 feet.

From here you descend through redwoods to the junction of the Summit and Slate Creek trails. You could go northeast 1.3 miles on the Slate Creek Trail to the backpackers camp, the "Slate Creek Trail Camp," continue another ½ mile to Page's Mill Site and forge uphill 2½ miles more to the boundary of Long Ridge Open Space Preserve. However, to take the return leg of this loop trip, turn due north on the Slate Creek Trail.

Now traversing a west-facing ridge, you nip back into the heads of ravines, round bends, and get deeper into redwood forest. The Save-the-Redwoods League and the Sempervirens Fund long ago initiated a program through which donors can honor friends and family by dedicating a tree or a grove of trees. Here in Portola Redwoods State Park, you will pass several of these groves, preserved for all of us to enjoy. Money from these dedications goes to purchase more redwood acreage for the state park system.

When you reach a trail junction sign that points right, 0.3 mile to the campground, stay left and bear due south, contouring along a narrow trail with mossy banks.

Near Slate Creek Trail Camp.

Stay on this ridge through the redwoods for 0.5 mile. Here some recently fallen trees remain as seats beside the trail. At the next junction you can take the Old Tree Trail left (east) for a ½-mile round trip into a quiet canyon to see a grand old redwood giant, at least 12 feet in diameter, surrounded by a split-rail fence to preserve its fragile root system.

If you choose the Old Tree side trip, return to the Slate Creek Trail junction, continue straight ahead to the service road and go to your right on it to the park office. If you don't take the trip to the Old Tree, bear right (west) at the Old Tree Trail junction and go less than 0.2 mile to the park service road and then right to the park office.

Trip 3. Coyote Ridge Loop Trail and Upper Coyote Ridge Trail

You may not see coyotes, but these high grasslands are favorite hunting sites.

- **Distance:** 2.2 miles—Loop Trail, plus 4 miles round trip—Upper Coyote Ridge Trail.
- **Time:** 3 hours.
- **Elevation Gain:** 630'

TRAIL NOTES

Starting from the park office go left on the entrance road for about 30 feet, turn left on the Iverson Trail, and in 0.1 mile turn right onto the Coyote Ridge Loop Trail. Shortly you cross a paved road leading to the walk-in campsites and switch back uphill through oak- and bay-tree forest. As you climb, note the burnt trunks of still-living trees, and several redwoods that have developed double trunks, probably due to repeated stress from fires. Researchers now know that forests benefit from fire, since burning the undergrowth reduces competition so seedlings can flourish. It is also known that fire helps some seeds to sprout.

Shortly you reach a low ridge where a large fallen tree in a small clearing makes a pleasant place for a rest or early lunch. This would be a good short destination for a children's hike. In spring there are violets and trillium blooming, wind whispering in the trees and the scent of blossoming madrones.

Climbing steadily, you reach the junction of the two Coyote Ridge trails (elevation 960 feet), where you turn left onto the Upper Coyote Ridge Trail. This trip description will follow the Upper Coyote Ridge Trail, return to this junction and then descend on the other leg of the Coyote Ridge Loop Trail. If you eschew this 4-mile round trip, bear right and begin your descent to the park office following directions found later in this trip.

Bear left on the Upper Coyote Ridge Trail under large madrone trees, whose large, shiny-green leaves, orange-red berries, and rich, red-brown trunks add color to hillside trails. In a series of gentle ups and downs you traverse a long north-trending ridge, first on its west side, then on the east. From openings in the forest there are views of Butano Ridge southwest and of Towne Ridge north in Pescadero County Park. In summer, fog hangs over the beach beyond coastal ridges, sometimes enveloping not only this park but the entire western half of San Mateo County.

When the trail shifts to the east side of the ridgetop, you are in the hushed shade of great redwood, Douglas fir and bay trees. Near the boundary with Pescadero Creek County Park, look for a row of mossy green posts and a wire fence going east past two large "Bearing Trees." On one tree with a sign showing land-survey numbers, the tree's bark has grown around the fence wire, embedding it at least ten inches.

Now you walk along an open hillside above grasslands that drop into the Evans Creek Canyon. East across this canyon the Portola Park Road meanders along the ridge between Evans and Peters creeks. Beyond lie the high ridges forming the crest of the Santa Cruz Mountains. Continuing on this trail, you soon dip into oak woods and shortly arrive at a clearing where there is a small dirt parking lot on Camp Pomponio Road (gated downhill from here to the San Mateo County Jail), and the end of this trail.

You can rest in sun or shade here and then retrace your steps on the Upper Coyote Ridge Trail. As you step onto this trail, note on a nearby signpost that the Tarwater Trail Loop (see Trip 4) also reaches this parking area.

Returning to the Coyote Ridge Trail junction, look for the shade-loving maroon trillium in spring or the magenta masses of sun-loving clarkia in late spring and summer. At any season you can see graceful woodland grasses swaying in the breeze. When you reach the junction, angle sharply left and start your steep descent via numerous switchbacks. Along the way there is a charming little meadow ablaze with yellow, cream, pink, and blue wildflowers, still blooming when the authors visited here one August. On beyond, climb three steps cut into a tree fallen across the trail and then, in a deep ravine, cross a plank bridge over a little creek that splashes into a pool about 20 feet left of the trail. Abruptly you drop down to the main park road, cross it, descend wooden steps to a bridge over Evans Creek and shortly cross the longer Peters Creek bridge with chain-link fenced sides. With the sounds of rushing water filling the air, you reach the junction with the Slate Creek Trail (east) and the Upper Escape Road. Turn right (south) on the Upper Escape Road through a fine redwood grove and follow the fairly level road back to the campground and on to the park office.

Trip 4. Tarwater Trail Loop

Through forests and meadows a two-park sampler reaches a deserted barn and the source of the trail's name.

- **Distance:** 5 miles.
- **Time:** 3 hours.
- **Elevation Gain:** 630'

TRAIL NOTES

Although most of this trip is in Pescadero Creek County Park, beginning in Portola Redwoods State Park makes it possible to start uphill and end going down. Therefore, go a few steps north beyond the park office and take the Iverson Trail, which is just across the park entrance road from the Madrone picnic area. Follow the Iverson Trail past the first junction, where the Coyote Ridge Trail turns right. You continue on the Iverson Trail for 0.12 mile to the next junction, where you go straight onto the Pomponio Trail and the Iverson Trail goes left. Signs here indicate that Pescadero County Park is 0.5 miles, McDonald County Park 4.0 miles and Memorial Park, 7.0 miles. Signs also warn that the trail, which is narrow and has some steps, is unsafe for and closed to horses.

Shortly the Pomponio Trail widens and becomes an unpaved road as you enter Pescadero Creek County Park. Climbing gradually through Douglas firs, oaks, madrones and redwoods, you reach a big crossroads and another sign: left, on the Bridge Trail to the Old Haul Road Trail, among others, and right, continuing on the Pomponio Trail 0.1 mile to the Tarwater Trail Loop, which you take.

As you follow the wide Pomponio Trail, watch on your right for a small sign that marks the beginning of the narrow Tarwater Trail Loop. Step onto this hikers-only trail and into a dark grove of second-growth redwood trees. Ferns and moss-covered rocks line the trail and Shingle Mill Creek courses through and around the grove. This area, easily accessible to logging through the 1960s and early '70s, has regrown tall and dense since then. Huge stumps encircled by new growth attest to the size and tenacity of the ancient trees.

Now on an unpaved road, you swing west, cross Shingle Mill Creek enclosed in a culvert, and ascend past scattered woods and meadows. As you turn north, the banks on the right side of the road are chalky limestone, characteristic of many soils on the west side of Skyline. Still gaining elevation on this road, you come upon a tremendous old redwood perched at the top of the steep hillside on the left. At least 12 feet in diameter with a burned-out heart and two huge elbow-shaped limbs high above the ground, this ancient monarch is worth watching for.

After crossing the deep ravine of Wally's Creek, you might pause at a high, grassy meadow on the left which is bordered on the north by a fence and woods of oak and Douglas fir. Probably used as pastureland before the park acquisition, this meadow is now a good place for a picnic and offers views across the deep canyon of Pescadero Creek and its many tributaries to the wooded heights of Butano Ridge in the southwest. In meadows and clearings such as this, listen for birds singing and bees buzzing, and watch for dragonflies and colorful butterflies. Here too, you will find lovely spring wildflowers, and if you are very quiet, you may see deer browsing or rabbits scurrying into the brush.

Then continuing along the trail, you soon reach a gate at the parking area on Camp Pomponio Road where this leg of the Tarwater Trail Loop and the Upper Coyote Ridge Trail converge. Looking north from here, about 3 miles as the crow flies, you can see the rounded south side of

2143-foot Mindego Hill, creased by a big canyon and fringed with trees on its lower slopes.

To continue the loop, cross the road and take the signed Tarwater Trail Loop northwest about ¼ mile through open grassland to a sharp turn left, then meander along a narrower trail into a pretty oak/bay woodland. Emerging from the woods you follow the east edge of a long meadow, then cut across it to skirt the forest above a branch of Tarwater Creek. As you walk under the trees, continue around a huge, lone redwood and look for a side trail cutting over to a small building with corrugated tin roof under a cluster of tall eucalyptus trees, known as Tie Camp. Just a few steps lead you to it and a peek at the thick redwood sides and floors of this long-deserted dwelling, later used as a barn. The fence across the lower end of this meadow and bailing wire scattered about recall the days when a dairy farmer rented the site, kept goats and cows in the meadow and transported milk and cheese out of the canyon to local customers.

This barn is all that remains of an extensive layout for the Moore, Fisher and Troupe mill operation that cut redwood trees into railroad ties here in 1915–16. Some present-day residents of this area remember that descendants of the mill operators later came here for holidays in the new-growth redwoods. After exploring the exterior of this deserted site (not safe to enter it), get back on the main trail and contour around the barn's south side into a little swale where an early settler planted a double row of pear trees, now quite aged, and then switchback downhill into the shade of big redwoods.

The trail zigzags downhill through the redwoods past a horsetail-fringed wallow dug up and rooted in by wild pigs. Although these big creatures, descended from European pigs brought here for sport hunting, may not be in sight, respect them for their long teeth and unpredictable nature. At its junction with the Canyon Trail the narrow Tarwater Trail Loop widens, and you bear left (south) to continue this trip. However, if you go right (north) a short distance on the Canyon Trail, you will cross the main trunk of Tarwater Creek and discover the meaning of its name. Observe its surface for globs of thick, shiny, iridescent material. Clue: San Mateo County once had an exploratory lease with a petroleum company just southwest of here.

Now following the wide Tarwater Trail Loop, make a gentle rise and continue south about one mile through sizable redwoods above the east side of Tarwater Creek. Huckleberries, iris, and ferns line the trail's edge in this quiet woods. At the next junction, go through a gate in a split-log rail fence onto Camp Pomponio Road and turn left following the road (also the Pomponio Trail here) for about 200 feet. Then veer off right onto the narrow Pomponio/Tarwater Trail Loop. With another gate on your left, go right onto an unpaved road, still the Pomponio/Tarwater Trail

Loop, in a small clearing bordered by high ceanothus. Just watch the signs and remember to go generally east.

Soon you cross Wally's Creek, then Shingle Mill Creek, and note on your left the other leg of the Tarwater Trail Loop, on which you started several hours before. You now retrace your steps on the Pomponio Trail by going left on it at the Bridge Trail junction. As you wind through the forest of bay trees and redwoods, your path is littered with fallen leaves and branchlets. Soon the sign for Portola Redwoods park office assures you that it is 0.5 mile to the end of a very beautiful hike.

Trip 5. Peters Creek Loop

A full day's trip to Old Page Mill Road and spectacular redwoods spared in old logging days.

- **Distance:** 13+ miles round trip.
- **Time:** 8 or 9 hours.
- **Elevation Gain:** 1000'

TRAIL NOTES

Start this trip early in the day, take plenty of water and food and allow ample time to negotiate the steep climb out of Peters Creek on the return leg. You could spend the night at Slate Creek Trail Camp, 3 miles from the park office and do the 7-mile loop up and down to Peters Creek on the second day. The campsites can be reserved by calling the park office.

To begin this trip, take the Summit Trail, as in Trip 2, to its junction with the Slate Creek Trail. From this junction at 940 feet, go right (northeast) along an east-facing ridge under a high forest canopy of redwoods, Douglas firs, and occasional oaks growing in more open zones. In many places the huckleberries form high walls on either side of the trail, making it seem as if you were going through a leafy, green canyon. Gently gaining a little elevation, you swing around to the north-facing slope and in 1.3 miles you reach Slate Creek Trail Camp. Here six separate campsites with picnic tables screened by low native shrubs sit under high madrones and tan oaks. Unless all the campsites are occupied, this is a good place for an early lunch or snack before beginning the next uphill leg of your trip.

When you've explored a bit and are ready to start off, return to the junction where the Bear Creek Trail takes off north, and begin the 7-mile round trip to Peters Creek. The trail is an old jeep road that climbs around a west-facing knoll, swings east, and then north up a steep canyon above an intermittent creek, a tributary of Slate Creek. In a few places you must climb over fallen trees or go around big boulders, not serious obstacles on your steadily upward trek. Under redwoods at first, you eventually rise to more open country where firs, oaks and bays thrive and the old road ends at about the 1380-foot level.

From this point a narrow trail leaves the damp canyon and enters a high wooded bowl. You meander close to private property—stay on the trail through this area. Under tall Douglas firs and a dense tangle of berry vines, veer a bit west, and emerge in chaparral made up of hardy manzanita, chinquapin and some knobcone pines. These pines, which need fire to germinate their seeds, corroborate the authors' impression that fire must have cleared the old forest here. You are now at the highest point of your trip, about 1440 feet. From this chaparral area you can briefly look northwest to the ridge that Alpine Road traverses, the route you took to get to Portola Redwoods State Park.

Soon you traverse a forest of spindly Douglas firs, possibly the site of an old lumber camp (as evidenced by an old, tilted wooden privy) and proceed up and down a southwest-facing ridge to an opening high on its north side. Here are a few brief views of the Peters Creek Canyon, upstream from your intended destination.

Now you begin the downhill leg of your trip on a foot trail that can be slippery if the litterfall is damp or the soil muddy. On foggy days the air is fragrant with bay leaves crushed underfoot, and moisture drips from trees overhead. Steadily downward you go, zigzagging into and around ravines on a west-facing slope. Small cones of Douglas firs and acorns from tan oaks and live oaks litter the trail. After you cross a little plank bridge over Bear Creek, you make a sharp turn left (west), traversing a side slope above the creek thickly covered with fern fronds, redwood sorrel and trailing yerba buena.

Soon you are in the depths of a magnificent redwood grove at the confluence of Bear and Peters creeks. Here is a magical place of monarch redwoods, pervaded by a hushed silence broken only by the sounds of the creek slapping against rocks and tree roots, and tumbling over fallen logs and boulders. You can rock-hop the creek and make a loop around the grove to see more trees and the signs that honor families and organizations from whom donated funds purchased this land and preserved the trees. Then choose a fallen log on which to sit and contemplate why these trees, many at least 12 feet in diameter, are still standing. Perhaps it was too steep to haul the cut lumber or shingles out of here. Maybe the woodcutters saw flaws unperceived by today's hikers. Perhaps they were just tired of sawing these giant trunks by hand. Regardless, they are worth the trip to behold.

On your return you will be climbing the steepest part first—an elevation gain of 760 feet in about a mile. After you reach the trip's high point, it is almost all downhill. Allow plenty of time to enjoy the trees, flowers, ridges and canyons.

Trip 6. Uphill to Long Ridge Open Space Preserve

This trip is described in the Long Ridge chapter as an 8-mile, downhill-all-the-way excursion with car shuttle. When the Old Page Mill Road is opened as a trail all the way to the Peters Creek Loop in Portola Redwoods State Park, Trips 5 and 6 could be combined for an approximately 15-mile loop trip with an overnight at Slate Creek Trail Camp.

Trip 7. The Basin Trail to Big Basin Redwoods State Park

A surfeit of switchbacks up Butano Ridge leads to an easement trail through private land and thence to Big Basin Redwoods State Park.

- **Distance:** 6.8 miles.
- **Time:** 5 hours.
- **Elevation Gain:** 1917′

TRAIL NOTES

Although this trip for hikers and equestrians begins in Portola Redwoods State Park, the first half is mostly in Pescadero Creek County Park. However, starting from one of the Pescadero Park trailheads would add 3 to 6 miles to your trip. So, this trip description starts from the Portola Redwoods park office. Follow the service road to the right (east) and either take the foot trails described in Trip 2 or the service road past the Slate Creek Trail turnoff. Continue past the park maintenance area, cross Pescadero Creek and proceed on an elevated bank above a tight meander of the creek beyond the old Iverson Cabin site. Just 50 feet farther you enter Pescadero Creek County Park at the Old Haul Road. On the other side of this road/trail, pick up the Basin Trail (also called the Portola Trail) heading uphill under alders, toyons, and oaks. At first paralleling Iverson Creek, you then cross it and contour through a pretty dell under some second-growth redwoods enlivened in late summer by orange redwood lilies and yellow mimulus.

Following the east side of Fall Creek you climb steadily and then cross it in an opening in the forest. Just before the creek crossing is a lively little waterfall and farther upstream a cascade rippling over mossy rocks. Look here for blue-flowered iris and white-blossomed, fragrant azalea in spring. Around more zigzags and out on a few knolls you continue upward through redwood and Douglas fir forest.

When you reach a fork in the trail, go left on the Butano Ridge Loop Trail (the other fork heads north down to the Old Haul Road.) Now seriously climbing, you gain altitude at every switchback as you round shoulders of the ridge, go between great columns of redwoods, and pass burned shells of monarch trees. Here too, you will find small caves in great sandstone boulders worn away by wind, rain and chemical action. Look for trees growing out of the rock and other rocks that have broken loose and tumbled down the hillside.

Occasional madrone or tanoak trees have sprung up in gaps where old or diseased trees have fallen and left a clearing. But in general, this is a very shady redwood/fir forest, cool in summer, and exposed to ocean winds and fogs that condense on tree branches and fall on the ground (and on hapless hikers). This environment is just right for white milk-maids, creamy-white and maroon trillium in spring, pretty little bluebells in summer, and the predominant, evergreen huckleberry shrub.

At one of the numerous switchbacks look for a deep ditch that loggers once used to haul logs up the mountain on a cable attached to trees at top and bottom of the ridge. Near this ditch are cut ends of two large trees that were buried when the ditch was dug some 60 or 70 years ago.

View from the Scenic Overlook on the Basin Trail.

At the Basin/Butano Ridge Loop Trail junction, a sign tells you that the Basin Trail goes left 5.5 miles to Big Basin Redwoods State Park, while the Butano Ridge Loop Trail veers right, trending northwest to the ridgetop. This trail follows the unpaved Butano Ridge Road, and eventually descends to the Old Haul Road on a west segment of this trail. (See Trip 4 in Pescadero Creek County Park).

However, following the Basin Trail you turn left (southeast), round the nose of a ridge and contour 0.8 mile through scattered redwoods and Douglas firs to a small clearing, the Scenic Overlook, a good place for lunch with a view. If the day is fair, many high points along the Skyline ridge are visible from here—Mt. Melville in Russian Ridge Open Space Preserve, Lambert and Peters creek canyons, which feed into Pescadero

Creek, and the high grasslands in Long Ridge Open Space Preserve. Bring your binoculars to identify other features of the southern Peninsula.

The next leg of your trip, about 2 miles, ambles down and up along the ridgetop, gaining about 300 feet in elevation before reaching China Grade Road in Big Basin Redwoods State Park. After reaching the boundary of Pescadero Creek County Park, just 0.2 mile from the overlook, this segment of the Basin Trail goes through the private Redtree Properties L.P., formerly the Santa Cruz Lumber Company, which granted an easement to Sempervirens for a 15-foot-wide hiking and equestrian trail. No bicycles are allowed. Logging roads intersecting the trail are blocked off, but are used to haul logs during the regular harvesting season, which follows a 16-to 20-year sustained-yield cycle. Sempervirens Fund, the oldest land-conservancy organization in California, negotiated the arrangements for this important connector.

Volunteers from the Santa Cruz Mountains Trail Association under the direction of Tony Look, first executive director of Sempervirens Fund, and Robert Kirsch built this section of trail and volunteers patrol and maintain the trail as well. It undulates up and down along a ridgetop under Douglas firs and redwoods on a carpet of spent leaves. At a few points en route you can look east to other lands of the State Park System on Highway 9—Castle Rock and Big Basin—which descend from the Skyline ridge.

As you approach Big Basin Redwoods State Park, watch the signs for the China Grade Road trailhead and the boundary of the park. You can have a shuttle car waiting for you here, or if you carry your gear in your backpack, you can stay in nearby Lane-Sunset Trail Camp by making advance reservations with Big Basin Redwoods State Park. This trail can be taken in reverse by starting at the Basin Trail/China Grade Road junction for a mostly downhill trip.

Tony Look

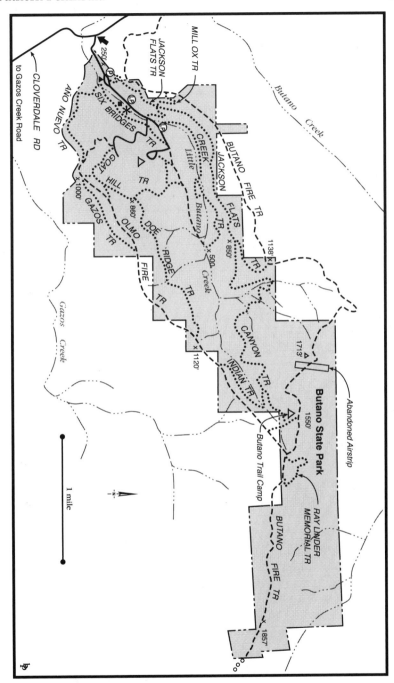

Butano State Park

Not the smallest or the largest of state parks, nor the most isolated, 3200-acre Butano State Park nevertheless has a special quality of solitude, and after short acquaintance one can get a feel for the whole park as a unit, despite its diverse habitats. Centered around the valley of Little Butano Creek, with riparian habitat along its banks, the slopes of the park rise gently on three sides, enclosing the park between ridges that form the watershed of this pretty stream.

Butano (the preferred pronunciation is "Boo-" with the accent on the first syllable) was first visited by Indians, who fished the stream, burned the underbrush to create open hunting and gathering grounds and were supplanted by more aggressive people of European descent. By the 1860s the Jackson family had settled on the northern or Jackson Flats side of the canyon, and the Taylor and Mullen families had settled on the southern, or Goat Hill, side. Together with Purdy Pharis, who also logged the El Corte de Madera and Purisima areas, the settlers logged the redwood forest in the canyon bottom until about 1900, taking all but a few of the forest giants. In the 1940s logging of giant Douglas firs took place, as testified to by some remaining stumps. Count the rings on younger fallen firs—you will find they are about 50 years old.

By the early part of the 20th Century most of the Butano and Little Butano Creek watersheds were owned by Timothy Hopkins, son of Mark Hopkins of "Big Four" fame. He left this property to Stanford University, and in the 1950s much of the area was sold to private parties. An active preservation effort resulted in the purchase by the State of California of the valley of Little Butano Creek for a state park. In 1961 Butano State Park became part of the state park system.

A paved road runs about a mile along the canyon floor, leading to the Ben Ries Campground (named after the park's first ranger, killed in an accident), and this road continues unpaved for service vehicles and hikers only, for another mile into the canyon. The other trails in the park all are narrow, for hikers only. Surrounding the park on the tops of the ridges are two fire roads: Butano Fire Road on the north, leads past an abandoned airstrip and turns east through the most recently acquired part of the park, Butano Crossing. The other fire road is Olmo Fire Road, running along the south ridge between Little Butano Creek and Gazos Creek drainages. Both these roads go through sections of private property.

A trail connection, for hikers and equestrians only, is proposed between Butano and Big Basin Redwoods state parks beyond Butano Crossing on an easement through private lands along the existing Butano Fire Trail.

Sempervirens Fund, a private land-conservancy which has acquired much of the land for Big Basin and Castle Rock state parks, recently bought a one-half interest in 1800 acres in the upper Gazos Creek drainage south of Butano State Park.

Jurisdiction: State of California Department of Parks and Recreation—415-879-2040.

Facilities: Trails for hikers, campground with 39 campsites, picnic area, trail camp with 8 sites.

Rules: Trails open dawn to dusk; no bicycles or horses; dogs on leash allowed in campground but not on trails. Camping reservations advised from April 1 through Labor Day by calling Destinet; day use and camping fees.

Maps: California State Parks *Butano State Park*, USGS topo *Franklin Point*.

How To Get There: Take Hwy 92 or Hwy 84 from I-280 to Hwy 1 on Coastside and turn south. At 4.6 miles south of Hwy 84 take Pescadero Rd east for 2.6 miles, turn right (south) on Cloverdale Rd and then go south 5 miles to park entrance on left (east).

Trip I. Circumnavigate the Park

Take the "high road" around the park, visiting all its habitats, on the Jackson Flats and Doe Ridge trails.

- **Distance:** 10.3 miles.
- **Time:** 5 to 6 hours.
- **Elevation Gain:** 1000'

TRAIL NOTES

From the entrance station parking lot take the Jackson Flats Trail heading north through second-growth Douglas fir and live oak trees following a gradual grade on the north side of the valley. After 10 minutes you enter second-growth redwood forest, and the trail widens to an old road paralleling the paved road below. In the open forest there are burned stumps, and the trail narrows to a single track.

Soon you pass a series of flat, swampy areas, probably the heads of large landslides. These wet areas are important winter breeding grounds for newts, where interesting marsh plants such as skunk cabbage and cattails flourish. Cross the Mill Ox Trail, which comes up from the valley floor on the right and joins the Butano Fire Road above.

After about 3 miles, at the junction where the Jackson Flats Trail veers left to join the Butano Fire Road, take the Canyon Trail to the right to circle around the head of the valley. Here at about 850 feet elevation, the vegetation changes significantly, from the fir- and redwood-forest you have been walking in. You are now on the Santa Margarita Formation of shale and sandstone, which forms great banks of gravelly material on which grow knobcone pines, oaks, manzanita and chinquapin. Notice also some California nutmegs, with sharp-tipped, shiny needles, a handsome small tree.

The Canyon Trail heads generally east, circling in and out of numerous small drainages. Some small redwood and fir trees are in the protected canyons, but the vegetation is mainly chaparral, with more nutmeg, manzanita and possibly a canyon or a maul oak. Views are to the east and south, looking across Little Butano Creek, and this south-facing slope is sunny and hot. Working up and down this slope, we have gone just under 6 miles to reach an elevation of 1250 feet when we meet the junction with the Indian Trail. The Canyon Trail goes left to the trail camp, which is charmingly situated in a grove of second-growth redwoods and Douglas firs. It has 8 primitive campsites with rustic tables and stools, lovingly hand-crafted and maintained by volunteers from the Sierra Club Singleaires. There are pit toilets but no water, and campfires are not allowed. From this trail camp you can stroll on the nearby Ray Linder Nature Trail, which is ¾ mile long.

Little Butano Creek.

Near the Canyon/Indian Trail junction is a footbridge across Little Butano Creek and a mossy sandstone seat, a convenient spot for lunch. The trickling stream is cooling on a hot day. This area, little visited by humans, has animal visitors—look for bobcat or gray fox tracks in the dust. Here you are at the edge of chaparral, with plentiful tan oak and huckleberry.

After only half a mile the Indian Trail ends at the Olmo Fire Road, on which you also can reach the trail camp by a roundabout route. The fire road is wide on the ridge, with splendid views to the south, west and north. Many bicycle tracks are on the road. After about ⅓ mile you reach the Doe Ridge Trail on the right; no bikes allowed. Here is an instant change of habitat. You are on the north-facing slope, in redwood- and fir-forest. This trail winds gently down and west to a junction with the Goat Hill Trail at 8.3 miles from the start of your trip.

Take the Goat Hill Trail right downhill to its junction with an unnamed trail leading to the Ben Ries Campground, and go left to the campground. There are 39 campsites in a nice open forest amid redwood trees and ferns. A nearby campfire center has benches facing a stage for interpretive programs. From the campground this trip continues west on a trail down an excessively steep grade to a side creek and a road leading to the ranger residences and the maintenance yard. Beyond this paved road the trail climbs up again just as steeply. Take heart, for you are nearing a different habitat at the end of your hike!

Passing the park office you join the Six Bridges Trail. This last stretch is through riparian vegetation along Little Butano Creek and its north-flowing tributaries, and there actually are six bridges amid the willows, maples, alders and herbaceous plants. This is sensitive habitat, so please stay on the trail. Note one huge fir tree that managed to survive the ax during earlier logging. This Six Bridges Trail would make a nice, easy stroll for a hot day.

At 10.3 miles from your start, you reach a junction with the Año Nuevo Trail going uphill to the left, and shortly thereafter you are at the entrance station. Pause to look into the little visitor center here; it is maintained by a volunteer group, part of the San Mateo Coast Natural History Association.

Trip 2. To an Overlook and Some Unusual Habitats

Climb the south rim of the park for great views and diverse vegetation.
- **Distance:** 3 miles.
- **Time:** 2½ hours.
- **Elevation Gain:** 750'

TRAIL NOTES

Park at the entrance station and take the Año Nuevo Trail on the south side, left of the small nature center. Start out through riparian vegetation and cross Little Butano Creek on a bridge, passing the Six Bridges Trail on your left. Climb uphill through cow parsnip, thimbleberry and wild cucumber spiraling around any nearby stem, and over tree roots through willows to reach a Douglas fir forest. In March forget-me-nots are in bloom along the trail (not native plants but brought here by European settlers) and red elderberry bushes are covered with white panicles of bloom. Large horsetails, an ancient plant from the Cretaceous period, are evidence that this trail has a number of springs to keep them moist year-round.

As you climb you can see through the trees all the way to the ocean, and long clusters of lichen on tree branches indicate how often ocean fogs invade this canyon. Rest on a handy bench to contemplate the view to the west. Here you see some landforms that are rather puzzling at first glance. Little Butano Creek emerges from its canyon and then turns sharply north before joining the main Butano Creek; together they flow a bit farther north before going west to the ocean. Parallel to Little Butano Creek is the intermittent stream, Arroyo de los Frijoles, dammed into two little lakes for irrigation. The direct entrance of these streams into the ocean is blocked by a 400-foot-high ridge called the Mesa, which apparently was formed by action of the San Gregorio Fault. Though low, this mesa tends to block some of the summer fogs and strong ocean winds from reaching Butano State Park. This ridge forms the centerpiece of a 5600-acre property on which POST has an option, some of which may become public open space linking Butano Park to the Coast.

Continue on excellent, short switchbacks and then a last steady pull to reach the Año Nuevo Overlook bench. This viewpoint is at 980 feet, and at one time commanded a bird's eye view of Año Nuevo Island to the south. The view now is somewhat obscured by growing forest, but there are many interesting things to look at from this spot. You will have taken about 40 to 50 minutes to climb to this point.

Stile cut in fallen tree.

As you rest, see how many of these plants you can identify from your seat on the bench: live oak, Douglas fir, madrone and tan oak trees; coffeeberry, huckleberry and ceanothus bushes; poison oak, blackberry and honeysuckle vines; strawberry, sword fern and Douglas iris plants.

Continue on the Año Nuevo Trail east along the ridge through a fir forest, with hazelnut shrubs just leafing out in March. Stroke their leaves—they feel like velvet. When you reach the Olmo Fire Road, you continue southeast along it to where the road has been cut into a shaley bank. In the spring elderberry bushes bloom in the valley below, and cream-colored zygadine lilies grow in the shade. Passing a trail to the right (not marked, and do not take it), you reach an intersection of the Goat Hill Trail Extension to the left and the Gazos Trail to the right. Go right (northeast) although the trail entrance is a little obscure, and travel on the Gazos Trail, paralleling the Olmo Fire Road but much above it. This is a sort of rollercoaster trail along the ridge, and has interesting views of the Coastside to the west and of the canyon of Gazos Creek to the south.

On the south slope of the ridge which the Gazos Trail follows is the same vegetation we saw in Trip l. Santa Margarita shale formation broken into small chips growing knobcone pines, chamise and bracken ferns, all adapted to hot, dry hillsides. Views east are of the forested Gazos Creek canyon.

When you reach the Olmo Fire Road and at the end of the Gazos Creek Trail, take this road left (west) and downhill steeply through fir forest. Note one giant fir with an 8-foot-thick trunk and four large trunks diverging from it. In ½ mile take the Goat Hill Trail connection downhill to the right, and descend on its righthand branch 0.9 mile to reach the maintenance road next to Little Butano Creek. From here you can either return along the trail discussed in Trip l, a little over a mile, or take the Little Butano Creek Loop described in Trip 3.

Trip 3. Little Butano Creek Trail

Stroll along the valley bottom through redwood forest.
- **Distance:** 2¼ miles.
- **Time:** 1½ hours.
- **Elevation Gain:** 30'

TRAIL NOTES

As you go northeast from the entrance kiosk, watch across the park road for an old wooden flume on the north side. This was built early in the 20th century to carry water from a small dam upstream to irrigate fields in private lands farther west. From the end of the paved road leading to Ben Ries Campground take the unpaved maintenance road, now named the Little Butano Creek Trail, east up the creek. The original redwood forest was logged in the 1800s, but second-growth redwoods and even a few giants missed by the loggers make this a shady and beautiful trail. The road is surfaced with needles and it winds down to the creek where redwood sorrel grows in the deep shade.

On the way you pass a new building used for water treatment. At a small dam on the creek is a building used to pump water from the creek to this treatment building for campground and residence use. After crossing Little Butano Creek on a footbridge, the trail goes downstream on the north bank past large redwood stumps and small redwood trees. *Trillium ovatum* blooms in spring, a three-petaled white flower atop three spade-shaped leaves. You can also find *Clintonia andrewsiana* in spring, with its lovely rose-purple flowers brightening the shade. The trail crosses on small bridges back and forth over the creek several times. See if you can spot a strange, huge redwood burl near the junction of an unused trail just south of one of these crossings.

Soon on the north side of the creek you reach a bench on which to rest while admiring the level area in this generally steep-sided canyon. Passing numerous side creeks bridged by board walks you reach a very boggy area where numerous yellow-flowered plants with huge leaves bloom in spring. This is yellow skunk cabbage, quite rare in California and known from only a few localities in the Santa Cruz Mountains growing in wet ground near perennial springs.

The trail crosses here to the south side of the creek, and 100 feet farther on reaches a paved road where there is a pullout for a few cars to park. Just ahead and downstream is the junction with the Mill Ox Trail, noted in Trip 1, and you can avoid returning on the pavement by going up this very steep trail to the Jackson Flats Trail, then returning to the entrance station. The Mill Ox Trail has a tunnel tree in this segment which could easily accommodate child adventurers.

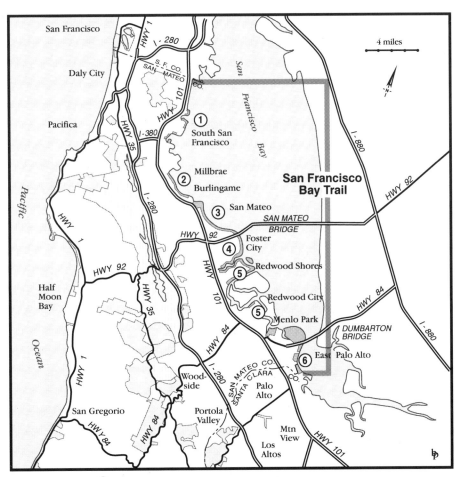

① Numbers in circles refer to Bay Trail text

Circled #   Park or Trail Name in Text
on Map

Circled # on Map	Park or Trail Name in Text
1	Brisbane, South San Francisco and San Bruno
2	Millbrae and Burlingame
3	Coyote Point County Recreation Area and City of San Mateo Parks
4	Foster City
5	Redwood City and Port of Redwood City
6	Menlo Park and East Palo Alto

San Francisco Bay Trail

Introduction

San Mateo County's trails by the Bay are as varied as its convoluted 100-mile shoreline. More than 40 miles of trail are in place and more are planned. Although there are a number of gaps between these trails, a Bay-Area-wide plan for bicycle and hiking trails circling the Bay envisions a continuous trail down San Mateo County's Bay shoreline.

Today landscaped paths overlook blue Bay waters that reflect massive airline buildings and tall storage tanks. Promenades edge lawns by restaurants and hotels. Paths through neighborhood Bayside parks are busy with bicyclists and strollers. Trails over a reclaimed trash mountain give walkers a perspective on the geometry of salt ponds below. Boardwalks beside sloughs take birdwatchers through wide expanses of marshes to find avocets, willets, and long-billed egrets probing for food in the mud.

The original Bay margin from the rocky promontory of Candlestick Point to Coyote Point was a series of low points of land and protected coves. South of Coyote Point to Palo Alto were broad marshes crossed by sloughs extending as much as 3 miles into the Bay.

More than two hundred years ago when Spanish explorers came up the Peninsula, they found the marshes an impassable barrier and followed inland paths worn by Indians on the solid ground near the alignment of present-day El Camino Real. From their villages on creeks, Indians traveled in reed boats, finding abundant fish, shellfish, and birds along sloughs.

During Spanish and Mexican times the boat trip to San Francisco from landings along navigable sloughs was easier than travel on the rough, muddy roads. Then Anglos built more landings and channeled sloughs to improve shipping, and by 1863 a railroad extended to San Jose. Here and there the newcomers drained the marshes for pastures and crops, and around the turn of this century built dikes around marshes to impound Bay waters for salt ponds.

As Peninsula communities grew, marshes gave way to subdivisions, industrial parks, and freeways. The Bay's edges became sites of city dumps, sewage-treatment plants and an international airport. The Bay became smaller and more polluted. Concern for the Bay and recognition of the values of marshlands gave rise to a Save-The-Bay campaign that resulted in passage of the Bay Conservation and Development legislation in 1968. This law not only limited filling of the Bay but also required public access to the Bay.

A trend toward trails by the Bay gained added momentum from the 1987 state legislation that mandated a plan for a continuous recreational corridor with a bicycle and hiking trail around San Francisco and San Pablo bays by 1989.

From Candlestick State Recreation Area just north of the county boundary down to the international airport several segments of trail take bicyclists and walkers beside the Bay waters. As construction continues in Brisbane and in South San Francisco, gaps in the trail will be filled. South of the airport through Burlingame are only a few breaks in the landscaped paths. From Coyote Point Recreation Area down San Mateo's shore and around Foster City a bicyclist can ride an unbroken paved shoreline path for 12 miles. Now a bridge over Belmont Slough connects these paths to the long levee path around Redwood Shores. From Redwood Shores to Menlo Park there are significant gaps in the Bay Trail, but pleasant paths front the Port of Redwood City. From Menlo Park to the Dumbarton Bridge some trail segments are in place and others are planned. These trails would complete an unbroken bicycle path to Palo Alto in Santa Clara County. From there continuous paths extend to Moffett Field.

By the late 1990s we can look forward to trails from San Francisco down the Peninsula to the South Bay at Alviso. Traversing these trails we can appreciate the magnificent setting of San Francisco Bay, enclosed and delineated by the Coast Range mountains. Bicyclist, runner, walker and neighborhood stroller can enjoy the outlook across broad marshes or open water.

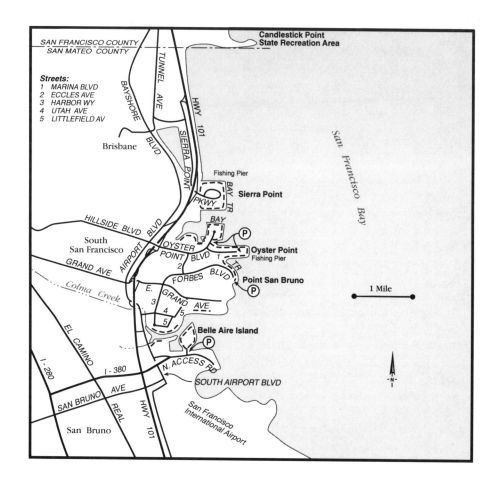

Brisbane, South San Francisco and San Bruno

Brisbane

At the Sierra Point industrial park, sidewalks along the main roads and a paved path on the riprap seawall take the bicyclist and the walker out to a marina and a fishing pier. Although no trail exists from the Candlestick Point State Recreation Area at the San Francisco boundary south along the Bay east of the Bayshore Freeway causeway, bicyclists can ride in the bike lanes along Marina Boulevard west of the freeway to reach Sierra Point.

Circling Sierra Point

A walk or a bicycle ride around the landscaped perimeter of an industrial park takes you to the edge of the Bay.

Facilities: Landscaped picnic areas and restrooms, paved paths for pedestrians and bicyclists.
Map: USGS topo *San Francisco South.*
How To Get There: From Bayshore Hwy 101: Southbound—Take Sierra Point Pkwy exit, go south and then go under freeway onto Marina Blvd. Follow it east to any of several parking bays facing marina at north and south ends. Northbound—Take Bayshore Blvd exit, cross over freeway, turn south and go 1000 feet to left turn onto Sierra Point Pkwy. Go north under freeway, turn right on Marina Blvd and continue to parking bays.

- **Distance:** 1½-mile loop.
- **Time:** 1 hour.

TRAIL NOTES

Walk down to the quayside promenade from your parking area to enjoy the boating scene—sailors working on their boats, others lunching on deck or motoring out to set sail on the open Bay. Over the masts you see Mt. Diablo rising above its foothills. South across the cove another yacht harbor, the Oyster Point Marina, adjoins yet another industrial park. From the marina take the paved path north to the fishing pier and continue west around the shoreline of Sierra Point. One gets a sense of spaciousness here beside the expanse of Bay water.

Past high-rise office buildings the path deadends below Bayshore Freeway at a small fisherman's park. To complete the circle around Sierra Point, retrace your steps to the first path on the right and continue on the paved sidewalks toward the south shoreline. You will cross palm-lined, sidewalk-bordered Sierra Point Parkway, which offers a shorter route back to the marina parking. However, if you continue to the south shore, you'll find the unpaved route along the riprap seawall easily passable on foot. This shore is more protected from strong Bay winds than the north shore.

South San Francisco

Map on page 298

From the trail around Sierra Point in Brisbane through South San Francisco to the San Francisco International Airport, there are altogether more than 5 miles of Bayside paths. They take you on a number of short trips beside yacht harbors, through Point San Bruno Park, along Colma Creek and around Belle Air Island. Because of the present gaps between completed trails, these trails are more interesting for walkers than bicyclists. However, as new building construction fronting the Bay is approved, trails will be required and gaps will be filled.

Trip 1. A Stroll around Oyster Point and Its Yacht Harbors

This walk takes in quayside boating activity and offers long views over the open water.

Jurisdiction: Oyster Point Marina, San Mateo County Harbor District; Oyster Cove Marina, part of private industrial park.
Facilities: Fishing pier, parks, two marinas, picnic areas, restrooms. Paved pedestrian and bicycle paths.
Map USGS topo *San Francisco South.*
How To Get There From Bayshore Hwy 101: Southbound—Take Airport Blvd. south and turn east on Oyster Point Blvd. After 0.9 mile turn right on Marina Blvd. and go through marina to public parking area near fishing pier. Northbound—Take Airport Blvd. exit, immediately turn left (north), go 0.2 mile, turn right (northeast) on Gateway Blvd. and continue 1 mile to Oyster Point Blvd. Turn right (east), continue to Marina Blvd. and follow directions above. Day use fee.

- **Distance:** 4 miles round trip.
- **Time:** 2 hours.

TRAIL NOTES

From the parking area walk out onto the fishing pier, installed by the San Mateo County Harbor District and the California Department of Fish and Game. At your approach, flotillas of white-faced black coots swimming near the pier take off with noisy flapping of wings and splashing, yet they barely leave the water. Soon they settle again, resuming their search for food beneath the surface.

From the pier walk around to the south side of the point on a path at the top of the sloping bank for a spectacular vista of Bay and distant mountains. The 80-foot tree-topped knoll of Coyote Point juts out into the Bay and the 182-foot hill above Point San Bruno stands just across the cove from you. The ridges of the Santa Cruz Mountains that you see above you on the west extend from San Bruno Mountain in the near foreground to Black Mountain in the south.

Your path curves right, crosses the road to the Harbormaster's office and returns beside the marina to the pier. On the path beside the marina you pass a fleet of boats berthed in the East Basin behind the breakwaters. Near the fishing pier you will find picnic tables tucked behind protective plantings.

A trail continues west from the Harbormaster's office for ½ mile to the West Basin, and then north past the swimming beach to the wide, paved paths around the office and industrial parks of Oyster Point. Now you walk on a wide, landscaped, paved path marked public trail at the edge of the Bay. Flanked by acres of parking lots, the high-rise buildings in this industrial park are deserted on weekends. From the benches along the trail you can see downtown San Francisco and, across the Bay, the wooded ridgetops behind Oakland and Berkeley. Just a few feet beyond the seawall white-winged terns wheel and dive for fish.

Continue around to the Oyster Cove Marina west of the point, where the blue of canvas sail covers repeats the blue roofs of the adjoining buildings. The trail goes around the marina past a strip of marsh and mudflat where avocets and egrets stand on long, thin legs. Two 8-foot slabs of marble placed beside the trail serve as benches from which to observe the marsh life. Shortly beyond the marsh the paved path terminates. Marina parking is permitted only on weekends and holidays. Then you can park at this end of the trail and do this trip in reverse.

On the way back to your car you see different views of harbor and Bay. You may also see sunbathers and swimmers enjoying the beach just south of the high-rise buildings. This little beach, one of only two Bayside bathing sites in San Mateo County, is protected from the harshest northwest winds.

Trip 2. Point San Bruno Paths

The views are splendid from this short stretch of trail.

Facilities: Picnic tables, parcourse.
How To Get There: Follow directions in Trip 1 to Oyster Point Blvd, turn right (south) on Eccles Blvd and go to Forbes Blvd. Go east on Forbes Blvd to its intersection with Pt. San Bruno Blvd. Here is a little park Bayward from a large industrial plant complex. Ten parking spaces at this plant are reserved for midweek trail users. On weekends there are many parking places available close to the trail.

- **Distance:** 2 miles round trip.
- **Time:** ½ hour.

TRAIL NOTES

At Point San Bruno is a tiny park of manicured lawns, cypress trees, picnic tables and paths. In an ideal location for workers in the nearby commercial and industrial buildings and for weekend visitors, the park's

Picnic tables at Point San Bruno overlook the Bay.

graveled trails wind among lava boulders and seabreeze-tolerant plantings close to the Bay.

From the park, where a parcourse begins, paths lead north to the other exercise stops and to Bayside picnic tables and benches. At the end of the trail, although there is no path, you can walk north on a little pebbled beach at low tide to the park at the Oyster Point Marina. Here at the water's edge the resting shorebirds—egrets, gulls and willets—will fly off before you get close enough for a picture, no matter how quietly you advance.

Trip 3. Some Short Walks on the Trails beside Colma Creek

Views of marshes and the open Bay reward you for seeking out the several short paths along the banks of Colma Creek.

Facilities: Paved path for pedestrians, benches.
How To Get There: From Bayshore Hwy 101: (1) North bank Colma Creek; Southbound—Take Airport Blvd south to South Airport Blvd and continue east of Hwy 101 to Utah Ave, where you turn east. Shortly after crossing Colma Creek, turn south on Harbor Way. At curve where street name changes to Littlefield Ave, turn right onto 20-foot-wide access road to parking behind commercial buildings beside trail. Northbound—Take San Bruno Ave Ext. exit, turn left (northwest) on South Airport Blvd, turn east on Utah Ave and follow directions above. (2) South bank Colma Creek: Follow directions for

north bank Colma Creek to reach South Airport Blvd east of Hwy 101, turn east on Belle Air Rd, and then turn left into parking area for large discount store.

- **Distance:** Two paths, round trips of 1½ miles and 1 mile.
- **Time:** ¾ hour and ½ hour.

TRAIL NOTES

For the first stroll, on the north bank of the wide channel of Colma Creek and its fringes of marsh, park behind the commercial buildings at Harbor Way and step across the railroad tracks to the trail. Surfaced with blue rock and removed from the buildings, the trail runs through a broad band of fill for about ¾ mile. At high tide the creek is full to its pickleweed-and-cordgrass borders. Ducks, mudhens and seagulls near the banks dive for food in the water. At low tide, flocks of sandpipers and willets scamper at water's edge ready to pluck worms or clams from the mud.

As you walk east beyond the mouth of the creek, a few low islets of marsh dot the water, havens for the waterfowl. Across the channel lies the SamTrans maintenance facility on Belle Air Island and beyond is the San Francisco International Airport.

The trail is interrupted for a short stretch, but it can be reached again from the end of Haskins Way, which runs south from East Grand Avenue. Boulders and huge blocks of cement between the industrial buildings and the trail make convenient perches for Bayside viewing. Here the creek widens and you look out to the open waters of the Bay, across to Hayward and south to the airport. The expanse of water is a tranquil scene, attracting workers from nearby plants.

Another stroll, particularly suited to those who stay in the airport inns of South San Francisco or who shop at the discount store, is a ½-mile paved path along the landscaped south bank of Colma Creek. It begins east of the bridge over Colma Creek on South Airport Boulevard, edges the parking areas and skirts the back of the store. Then it goes through a narrow, fenced aisle adjacent to the Water Quality Control Plant. Notable are the salt-tolerant plantings of native shrubs, yellow lupine, gray salt bush and daisylike grindelia, or yellow gum plant. When these plants mature, this will be a pleasant path for noon-hour exercise or an after-shopping stretch.

Trip 4. A Parcourse and Hike on Belle Air Island

This well-surfaced loop path offers views of creek, Bay and airport activity as well as a fitness course.

Facilities: Paved path for pedestrians and bicyclists, picnic tables, parcourse, benches.

How To Get There: From Bayshore Hwy 101: Southbound—Follow directions for Trip 3 to South Airport Blvd, continue south to North Access Rd and go east. Turn left (north) on causeway to SamTrans facility on Belle Air Island. Park on left side of entrance. Northbound— Take San Bruno Ave Ext. east, turn left (north) on South Airport Blvd and go right (east) on North Access Rd. Turn left (north) on causeway to parking.

Distance: 1-mile loop.

Time: ½ hour to walk, longer if you use the parcourse.

TRAIL NOTES

This little island, now connected to North Access Road by a causeway, is circled by a paved path and parcourse built for the employees of the SamTrans maintenance station but also open to the public. The island lies off the mouth of Colma Creek between Point San Bruno's industrial-park development and the airport. The large-scaled white buildings with their blue and red trim lend a lively air to the island.

The path circling Belle Aire Island includes a parcourse.

To the left of the entrance is parking for the public. By the water's edge young trees frame picnic tables for lunching in the sun. The 1-mile landscaped path has enough parcourse equipment along the way to keep the SamTrans staff in top condition. Benches at intervals accommodate those not so exercise-minded who want to enjoy the views of water and bird life. A run around the path is enlivened by the sight of planes from the airport taking off just beyond the tanks and hangars, by the view of ducks and coots feeding in the creek channel and, on still days, by the reflections of the strong patterns of the industrial plants in the water.

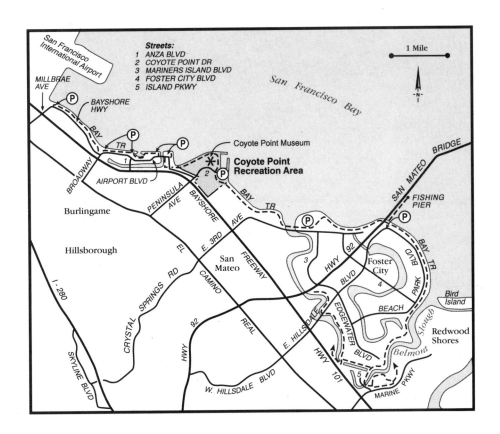

Millbrae and Burlingame

Though not continuous, paths follow the Bayside from Millbrae Avenue south to the west end of Coyote Point Recreation Area. Where the waterside path is interrupted, pedestrians can use the sidewalks along Bayshore Highway and Airport Boulevard and bicyclists can ride in the bike lanes. Millbrae's Bayfront Park sits just south of the airport. Burlingame, one of the first cities in San Mateo County to meet BCDC's public shoreline access requirements, has waterfront walkways along much of its 3 miles of Bay frontage. These paths cross bridges over sloughs, pass an array of hotels and restaurants and reach parks with lawns, trees and playgrounds. Described here are two walks along the Millbrae and Burlingame shoreline.

Facilities: Paved paths for bicyclists and pedestrians. Fishing pier, benches, restrooms. Some paths lighted in the evening.
Map: USGS topo San Mateo.
How To Get There: There are two public parking areas: (1) North

Shoreline: From Bayshore Hwy 101 take Millbrae Ave. exit, go east and turn right (south) on Bayshore Hwy (frontage road). Past Cowan Rd turn left into first parking lot north of high-rise hotel on Bay. (2) South Shoreline: Southbound—From Bayshore Hwy 101 take Broadway exit, go under freeway overcrossing, turn right (north) on Rollins Rd and immediately turn right (east) onto overcrossing. After crossing freeway, turn right onto Bayshore Hwy (frontage road) and go 0.1 mile. Turn left (east) on Airport Blvd, which curves south around Burlingame's Bayside Park. At Anza Blvd turn left toward Bay and continue to signed shore parking areas near hotels beside Bay. Northbound—From Bayshore Hwy 101 take Anza Blvd exit, go east on it across Airport Blvd to designated parking areas as described in directions above.

Trip 1. North Shoreline—Millbrae Avenue to Broadway

This walk takes you across two marshy inlets and in front of Bayfront establishments before continuing on sidewalks to the south-shoreline paths.

- **Distance:** 2 miles round trip.
- **Time:** 1 hour.

TRAIL NOTES

When you step out of your car at the north end of the hotel parking area [(1) in the directions above] you look across a cove to the San Francisco Airport runways and their extensions. Start your walk by going north along the cove for a few hundred yards toward Millbrae Avenue to the handsome redwood pedestrian/bicycle bridge spanning an inlet. The marsh-bordered inlet attracts shorebirds, particularly the snowy white egret. Beyond the bridge a walkway continues through Millbrae's Bayfront Park to Millbrae Avenue. From benches here a visitor sees almost constant feathered- and metal-winged aerial activity accompanied by a cacophony of bird cries and engine roars.

If you turn southward from the hotel parking lot, take the paved landscaped path beside the Bay that winds along past hotels and in front of car-rental establishments and motor inns. The restaurants beyond here, set back from the zigzag seawall, will install a path when the seawall is replaced.

For now, leave the Bayfront, go back out to the Bayshore Highway sidewalk and cross the pedestrian/bicycle bridge over the mouth of Mills Creek at Burlingame's Shoreline Bird Sanctuary. From this bridge you have an outstanding vista of tidal marsh and open Bay. The paved path continues on the south side of the creek in front of restaurants, hotels and businesses as far as One Bay Plaza, almost 1 mile from your starting point. You can retrace your steps from here or take the sidewalk along Bayshore Highway to continue south.

Mills Creek enters the Bay, with airport in distance.

Trip 2. Stroll Along the South Shoreline– Broadway to Coyote Point Recreation Area

Take this delightful Bayfront walk following a paved path fringed by lawns, shrubs and trees and furnished with benches facing the Bay.

- **Distance:** 4 miles round trip.
- **Time:** 2 hours.

TRAIL NOTES

At the parking area at Anza Blvd, [(2) in directions above] BCDC signs note that the landscaped area and path curving along the Bay's edge in both directions is public shore. To the west the path goes in front of high-rise hotels and commercial buildings. Beyond these structures you must cross Airport Boulevard and use the path there for 1000 feet, then return to the Bay's edge for ¼ mile Bayward of Burlingame's Bayside Park. The path ends just beyond the park, near the Broadway exit from Highway 101.

If you go in the other direction from the Anza Blvd. parking area and east of the first high-rise hotel, you will find pleasant, landscaped paths along the Bay and around the Anza Lagoon linking hotels and restaurants. These paths, well-lighted in the evening, make for delightful strolls. The Bay waters reflect lights from the airport and shorefront hotels. Around the lagoon pathside lights shimmer on the water.

For a daytime walk from the Anza Blvd. parking area you will find a fishing-access pier arcing out over the water. Even if you don't care about fishing, you can sit on the nearby benches and watch the fishermen's attempts to hook a big one. There are fish-cleaning sinks here and a restroom.

Where the Bayfront path meets the mouth of the lagoon, a striking pedestrian bridge vaults across the inlet, taking you to a shoreside restaurant on the other side. Here is 2-hour public parking at Bay View Place, from which you could start a walk.

Continuing farther east along the water, you can make your way along a strip of land in front of undeveloped property and soon come to the inlet for the Burlingame Recreation Lagoon. The lagoon, a slough resculptured by fill, is edged with cordgrass and pickleweed and inhabited by snowy white egrets stalking fish and frogs. Moored at the mouth of this lagoon is an old Oakland ferry, the Frank M. Coxe, once refurbished as a restaurant, now apparently derelict. Plantings edge the Bay and a parking area provides another access to the Bay Trail. The paved path resumes here, extending to the vehicle bridge across the inlet. On the far side and south along the waterfront a broad band of fill behind the seawall serves as an unpaved path.

Along the seawall at the point where it angles south is yet another access point, a paved parking area edged with plantings and picnic tables provided by San Mateo County and the Anza Corporation, known as Fisherman's Park. Fishermen cast their lines from the seawall, and on breezy days windsurfers skim the waters of the cove between here and Coyote Point. You can make your way along a rough path by the riprap seawall for 0.3 mile, paralleling Airport Boulevard. Then turn east to follow the paved Coyote Point Park paths.

You have come 2 miles from your starting point at Anza Blvd, but if you want to walk or ride your bicycle farther, there are many miles of continuous, paved trails farther down the Bay.

The San Francisco Bay Conservation and Development Commission requires public access at intervals along the bay.

Coyote Point County Recreation Area and City of San Mateo Parks

Map on page 305

Six miles of continuous paved paths edge San Mateo and Foster City's Bayfront from Coyote Point Recreation Area to Little Coyote Point at the San Mateo/Hayward Bridge. These paved paths for runners, walkers and bicyclists connect four parks, passing a bathing beach, marshes and a yacht harbor.

Maps: San Mateo County *Coyote Point County Recreation Area* and USGS topo *San Mateo*.

How To Get There: Access points from north to south from Bayshore Highway 101: (1) Coyote Point Recreation Area—(a) Southbound—Take Poplar Ave exit, turn right on Humboldt, right on Peninsula Ave and go across freeway to park entrance; (b) Northbound—Take Dore Ave exit, turn left on North Bayshore Blvd. and proceed to Coyote Point Dr and park entrance. (2) Harborview Park—From North Bayshore Blvd, south of Coyote Point Dr, turn east on Monte Diablo Ave to its end. Limited on-street parking, access to trail on levee. (3) Ryder Park—Take East Third Ave exit from Bayshore Freeway for ½ mile to limited parking on left. (4) Tidelands Park—Take East Third Ave exit from Bayshore Freeway to parking on north side of E. Third Ave near bridge over Marina Lagoon.

Trip 1. An Outing on Trails through Coyote Point Recreation Area South to San Mateo Creek

This trip can be a leisurely stroll on part of the trail or a vigorous round trip through the park and along the high dike path to Ryder Park by the creek. For bicyclists it can be part of a 12-mile round trip ride to the San Mateo/Hayward Bridge.

Jurisdiction: County of San Mateo—415-363-4020 and City of San Mateo—415-377-4640.

Facilities: Coyote Point Recreation Area—Bathing beach with showers, restrooms; picnic areas with barbecues; playgrounds; Coyote Point Museum; yacht harbor. Access for physically limited. City of San Mateo—Two city parks with picnic areas and play equipment.

Rules: Coyote Point Recreation Area—Fee. Open sunrise to sunset. No pets allowed. City parks—Open until 9 P.M.

- **Distance:** 6 miles round trip.
- **Time:** 3 hours.

TRAIL NOTES

Coyote Point Recreation Area, the County of San Mateo's 670-acre park, has a 2-mile shorefront trail, as well as a network of interior trails. The shorefront trail is for pedestrians only, but bicyclists can use a paved path that skirts the south edge of the park and emerges at its easternmost tip near a restored marsh.

For this trip drive to Coyote Point Recreation Area's west parking area near the beach promenade. Pick up the broad, paved path and follow it eastward along the swimming beach. The beach at Coyote Point Recreation Area and the point itself are almost the only remaining fragments of the county's original shoreline. Here by the beach are a bathhouse, a special ramp for physically limited swimmers' access, picnic areas, and playing fields. After this promenade reaches the tree-topped knoll in the center of the park, it follows the bluff to two observation platforms overlooking the Bay. From the first you look northwest through the trees to the San Francisco Airport; from the second platform you see sailboats cutting through the water, and below you are more boats at their berths in the yacht harbor.

Atop the eucalyptus-covered knoll you'll find the Coyote Point Museum, the only Bay interpretive facility in San Mateo County. Don't miss the permanent exhibits about Bay ecology, featuring dioramas of birds in the marshes and aquariums of marine life.

Continuing through the park you descend past the yacht harbor to an elegant little marsh, restored and now attracting resident shorebirds and migratory waterfowl. At the marsh you are 2 miles from the parking area. You could turn around and retrace your steps or continue down the 1-mile dike trail of Shoreline Park.

The City of San Mateo's Shoreline Park extends east from the Coyote Point marsh on a straight dike under the power lines. On top of the dike the paved path is popular with walkers, runners, bicyclists and children in strollers. Close to neighboring homes and adjacent to Harborview and Ryder parks, Shoreline Park provides occasional benches from which to enjoy the Bay and the bird life in the band of marsh beside the dike. When you reach Ryder Park, you may want to explore the trail that continues ½ mile upstream beside San Mateo Creek.

Trip 2. A Walk or Bicycle Ride from Ryder Park to the San Mateo/Hayward Bridge

Past a mountain of trash, beside a healthy marsh and atop a seawall this trip takes you on San Mateo and Foster City's paths to the bridge.

Jurisdiction: San Mateo and Foster City.

- **Distance:** 6 miles round trip.
- **Time:** 3 hours on foot; 1½ hours by bicycle.

TRAIL NOTES

You can begin this trip at either Ryder or Tidelands park, or start on the far side of the San Mateo Bridge in Foster City. It is described here from Ryder Park.

On the southeast side of Ryder Park, San Mateo Creek flows into the Bay 7 miles from its source behind Crystal Springs Dam in the foothills. Spanning the creek is a handsome bridge which leads to a mile-long path around the future Seal Point Park, a mound created over the years from the city's refuse. Now the landscaped path around this landfill offers unobstructed views of the open Bay.

As the path returns to East Third Avenue another pedestrian/bicycle bridge crosses the wide inlet to Seal Lagoon, now called Marina Lagoon. It's worth a stop here to see the flocks of shorebirds wheel and dive over the mouth of the lagoon. Then continue past the broad marsh, its colors subtly changing from green in spring to red-brown in fall.

As you continue east on the trail beside East Third Avenue, you see across the street the green lawns and curving paths of San Mateo's Tidelands Park. Past the park you enter Foster City, where the Bay Trail stays on a levee next to East Third Avenue for about a mile. The path stays inland past an area of new construction, along the Bay beside a golf course and then near Foster City Boulevard it follows the Bay's edge on top of a seawall for the last ¾ mile before the San Mateo Bridge. On this exposed section of the trail, waves splash against the rocks and invigorating breezes blow off the water. Several access ramps offer windsurfers starting points for Bay sails.

After passing under the bridge you come to the San Mateo County Fishing Pier, a windswept section of the old low-level bridge, now much favored by fishermen. Also fishing are the black-winged cormorants and the slender-winged terns you may see flying overhead.

You've come 3 miles from Ryder Park beside San Mateo Creek. You can retrace your steps from here or follow 6 more miles of trail circling Foster City. There is ample parking south of the bridge and a few picnic tables.

Foster City

Map on page 305

From the San Mateo/Hayward Bridge the Bay Trail continues around the perimeter of Foster City. You can walk or ride a bicycle for more than 6 miles circling the city. Marshland, where resident shorebirds congregate and migratory waterfowl rest and nest, lies between the path and the Bay.

Foster City, once a marsh and tidelands threaded by a system of sloughs, is now a city of homes and apartments, shopping centers and office complexes. In mitigation for the taking of these wetlands, BCDC required public access and marsh restoration at the Bay's edge.

Facilities: Paved paths on levees for pedestrians and bicyclists. City parks nearby with restrooms, picnic tables and play areas.
Rules: Open during daylight hours.
Maps: USGS topos *San Mateo* and *Redwood Point*.
How To Get There: From Bayshore Hwy 101 take Hwy 92 east. Turn right (southeast) on Foster City Blvd and then left (north) on East Hillsdale Blvd. This street becomes Beach Park Blvd, which you follow to a parking area on left side of road near San Mateo/Hayward Bridge.

Trip 1. Circling the City on Foot or Bicycle

Walking along beside the Bay in the company of runners, bicyclists, joggers and people pushing baby carriages, you will find a fascinating and diverse marine setting.

- **Distance:** 6+ miles one way.
- **Time:** As long as you can spend.

TRAIL NOTES

Starting from the San Mateo/Hayward Bridge, the Bay Trail is on a levee above the adjacent city street. Bayward, the tall transmission towers provide perches for birds. Especially noticeable are the large black birds sitting with outstretched wings—diving cormorants, whose feathers need occasional drying, unlike other waterfowl. An offshore lagoon is often filled with birds resting on the mudflats or probing the shallow waters with their long beaks. Avocets, distinguished by their black-and-white striped wings, sweep the water with upturned bills. The plain gray willet also has black and white stripes on its wings, seen only when it flies.

As the trail curves around the city, it leaves the water's edge, then returns to border Belmont Slough for 2 miles. This slough is a rich birding area, where great blue herons and white egrets stand tall in the marsh grasses. The tidal changes from ebb to flood attract a range of birds—those that dive in the water for their food and those that probe the mudflats.

After the path leaves Belmont Slough, it takes two courses—one follows a levee and continues north along Marina Lagoon, the former Seal Slough, until it reaches East Hillsdale Boulevard. The City of San Mateo's intermittent paths on the north side of Highway 92 follow Marina Lagoon back to Tidelands Park on East Third Avenue. The other course continues along the Bay's circuitous shoreline, following the path southwest to Island Park (near the Belmont Sports Complex). Here it crosses a bridge over the slough to a paved trail adjacent to the parkway that circles the high-rise Oracle buildings in Redwood Shores.

In the lee of Coyote Point, boats find safe moorage.

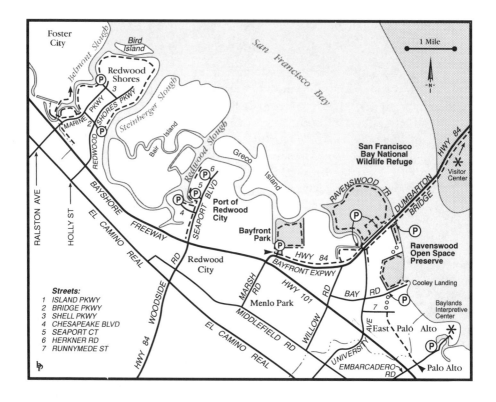

Redwood City and Port of Redwood City

Paths circle the island between Belmont and Steinberger sloughs. Once marshland, most of the island is now filled and developed as Redwood Shores, but a rim of protected marsh lies outboard of the levee. The levees here are being raised and then the Bay Trail will be constructed inboard of the levees. Several platforms will be built to provide views of marsh and Bay. The connection between the southwest end of the Redwood Shores Trail and Bair Island Road is proposed to follow levees Bayward of Highway 101 on Inner Bair Island.

Short paved paths along the south bank of Redwood Slough take walkers to the Port of Redwood City and its marinas. From the historic embarcadero on this slough in the mid-1800s, logs from the Pulgas Redwoods were rafted or sailed by schooner to build Gold Rush San Francisco. Today the Port of Redwood City accommodates seagoing vessels and its marinas berth hundreds of yachts.

In granting a 1984 permit for an additional wharf at the port, BCDC required public access to the slough. Now small parks and wharf-side paths invite visitors to watch port activities. A pleasant park by a new boat ramp was included in 1986 improvements at the port's marina.

Jurisdiction: Redwood City and Port of Redwood City.
Facilities: Pathways for pedestrians and bicyclists. Restrooms at parks and Port of Redwood City Marina. Handicapped access at Marina.
Rules: Open 8 A.M. to dusk. Marsh by path is protected by California Fish and Game Department. No dogs on path. Port open 8 A.M. to 5 P.M.
Map: USGS topo *Redwood Point*.
How To Get There: From Bayshore Hwy 101: (1) Redwood Shores—Take Marine Pkwy or Redwood Shores Pkwy (Holly Street) exit and park either at one of small parks along Oracle Pkwy which circles Oracle buildings, along Marine Pkwy or at Mariner Park at southeast end of Bridge Pkwy, one block southeast of Redwood Shores Pkwy. (2) Port of Redwood City: Southbound—Take Woodside Rd exit, then go east under freeway to Seaport Blvd and continue east to parking on Chesapeake Dr or Seaport Ct; Northbound—Take Seaport Blvd exit and go to parking areas.

Trip 1. A Bicycle Ride, Run or Stroll Along the Redwood Shores Levee

Around Redwood Shores between Belmont and Steinberger sloughs a nearly 10-mile levee path follows much of the perimeter of the island. Bayward, Bird Island, a band of protected marsh washed by the tides, provides habitat for waterfowl.

- **Distance:** 10 miles one way.
- **Time:** 5 hours.

TRAIL NOTES

Start at one of the public parks edging the pathway. Along this levee top, fringed with a band of protected marsh, you find a variety of seabirds and shorebirds, both resident and migrant. In winter months the sloughs are a resting place for ducks on their way down the Pacific Flyway. Watch the waters for the great flat-bodied skates that inhabit the sloughs. Along the path is low-growing saltbush, which is host to the fingernail-sized pygmy blue butterfly.

The bicyclist or the energetic walker who gets to the outer rim of the unpaved path will see Bird Island across a slough. From the height of the levee you can see over the green cordgrass of Bird Island to the blue Bay beyond. The island is a protected avian habitat, a nesting ground for snowy egrets and herons.

Among many species of shorebirds, the least tern nests here, an endangered species on the California coast. This tern looks like a small, slender gull with a slightly forked tail. Also nesting here is the cosmopolitan Caspian tern, gull-sized with a red beak. These terns are fishers, so you may see them plunging headlong into the water for their prey.

The nearly 10 miles of paths circling much of this island provide bicyclists a good ride, runners a satisfying workout and walkers and birdwatchers trips of any length to suit their inclination.

Trip 2. The Port of Redwood City

Strolls to delightful urban seascapes await you at the municipal marina and the Port of Redwood City.

TRAIL NOTES

Several short strolls around the port are described here. Each takes off from Seaport Boulevard. On your way to the Port you will note beside Seaport Boulevard a paved and landscaped path on your right, a good walk on the edge of a salt pond.

For the first stroll turn left at Chesapeake Boulevard, a new, tree-lined street leading to an industrial park. Look for the small park to your right as you reach the yacht basin. Turn into the parking space by the small, two-story building that houses the offices of the Port of Redwood City's Harbormaster. At the park are tables by the water for lunch or checkers and a long bench for sheltered sunning or boat watching. Beyond are piers and a launching ramp. Across a narrow channel are berthed large yachts in surprising variety.

From the paved court of the little park and up a short flight of steps, a three-block-long boardwalk leads back out to Seaport Boulevard. This raised walk covers a slurry pipe from the salt pond to the salt company. From the walk you have more views of yachts across the channel. On a strip of marsh below, you may see great blue herons stalking fish.

After lunch in the sun and a walk down the boardwalk and back, you can move on to the next marine stroll. Turning left from Seaport Boulevard onto Seaport Court, you will find parking, two restaurants, trees, an exercise course and an 800-foot strip of flower-bordered lawn beside Redwood Creek. Across Redwood Creek rises the pile of salt at the former Leslie Salt Works, now Cargill.

The last stroll is along the wharves of the Port of Redwood City. Go two long blocks farther down Seaport Boulevard and turn left at Herkner Road. Check in with the attendant at the port gate and go on to the parking lot as directed. The port is open from 8 A.M. to 5 P.M. You will see by the ship channel the little Bay Access Park, with flower beds and benches from which to watch the action in the channel. Immediately downstream you may find a seagoing freighter or two tied up at the wharf, lending deep-sea flavor to this outing. Unless the vessel is loading or unloading, you can walk along the wharf beside it. The cargo might be redwood logs or scrap iron from a 25-foot-high pile by the wharf.

In the other direction a short path leads up the channel (left) to more wharves—for the Geodetic Survey ship and often for large yachts from other ports. It is the Bay Conservation and Development Commission requirements for public access that result in waterside parks and paths such as these all around the Bay.

Menlo Park and East Palo Alto

Map on page 314

The City of Menlo Park's Bayfront Park and the Bay Trail to Highway 84 are close to populous neighborhoods and to many offices and plants. Noontime runners and families on weekend excursions find interest in the ever-changing marsh and Bay life. Although there are two short gaps in the Bay Trail south of Highway 84, most of the route is complete.

Jurisdiction: Caltrans, San Mateo County, Midpeninsula Regional Open Space District, cities of Menlo Park and East Palo Alto.

Facilities: Pedestrian and bicycle paths, benches, and parking.

Rules: Bayfront Park open dawn to 5 P.M. Dogs allowed on leash. Bayfront Expressway path and Ravenswood Open Space Preserve open dawn to dusk.

Map: MROSD map and USGS topos *Palo Alto* and *Mountain View.*

How To Get There: From Bayshore Hwy 101: (1) Bayfront Park—Turn north on Marsh Rd, cross Bayfront Expwy to parking. The Bay Trail beside Bayfront Expwy and the Ravenswood Trail can also be reached from Hwy 84 at its junction with University Ave. Park at shore access area adjacent to Sun Microsystems on north side of Hwy 84 or at generous parking area at Ravenswood Pier (now closed) at east end of frontage road on south side of Hwy 84; (2) Southern Ravenswood Open Space Preserve and Bay Trail—Take Hwy 84 east, turn south on University Ave, then go east on Bay Rd to its end at Cooley Landing and a parking area; (3) In Palo Alto, go east on Embarcadero Rd to Geng Rd, then north to parking at Baylands Athletic Center.

Trip 1. Bayfront Park—A Hike over the Hills or a Run by the Slough

Easy paths over gentle hills bring you to new views over marsh and Bay.

- **Distance:** 2-mile loop.
- **Time:** 1 hour.
- **Elevation Change:** Relatively level.

TRAIL NOTES

The 130-acre Bayfront Park at the end of Marsh Road, created on top of many years' accumulation of municipal refuse, brings us fresh views of the Bay from trails on its landscaped heights. From experimental plantings of salt-tolerant trees, small forests are springing up on the hills.

Several miles of paths wind over the slopes and a 2-mile trail circles the park just above the marsh.

The park is surrounded by marshes and sloughs. Along Flood Slough to the left of the entrance road, ebb tide leaves mudflats by its banks, attracting white egrets. You cannot miss the lovely great white egret, standing nearly 3 feet tall, and the smaller snowy egret, which nests in reeds and cordgrass in the marsh and searches for fish in the shallows. To the right of the road is a small tidal pool with islands where ducks swim and broad mudflats where sanderlings and willets find food.

From the parking area a gate on your right leads to paths over the hillsides. From the vantage point of the modest elevation of the park you can see the Santa Cruz Mountains from San Bruno Mountain down to Mt. Umunhum.

To the north is an expanse of marsh and Bay. Salt ponds below reflect in their waters their end product, the tall pyramids of salt at Redwood City. West are the curves of West Point Slough marking the landward boundary of Greco Island, one of the largest areas of natural marsh in the South Bay.

A walk along the paths through the park is enlivened by a unique garden of "word rock poems." Read the sign at the main entrance for keys to the symbolism of the clusters of rocks you pass. Put in place by the Menlo Park Environmental and Beautification Committee in collaboration with artist Susan Dunlap, "the rocks are carefully selected to support and translate the true meaning of each word."

A walk eastward leads to a saddle, but continue over the hill beyond. If you go north through the saddle, your senses will be assailed by occasional rumblings and whiffs of gas from a methane-recovery plant operating on the site of the former sewage-treatment plant. However, this operation is temporary, a part of the process of creating a park from the dump. Meanwhile some of the profits from the operation go toward completion of the park.

In addition to paths over the hills, the 2-mile trail around the park by the slough is a popular route for runners, who can enjoy a glimpse of marsh life along the way.

Trip 2. The Bay Trail from Marsh Road to Dumbarton Bridge

Try these trails by marsh, slough and Bay waters for birdwatching, brisk walks and jogging.

- **Distance:** Bayfront Trail—5 miles round trip; Ravenswood Trail—4-mile loop.
- **Time:** Bayfront Trail—1½–2 hours; Ravenswood Trail—1–1½ hours.

- **Connecting Trails:** Trails in Bayfront Park, trail in northern Ravenswood OSP and bicycle lanes on Dumbarton Bridge (Highway 84).

TRAIL NOTES

This trip combines two trails–the 2½-mile Bayfront Trail, which runs along the marshlands next to the Bayfront Expressway and around the perimeter of the Sun Microsystems complex to the University Avenue/Highway 84 junction; and the Ravenswood Trail, which makes a 4-mile loop northeast from that junction following Ravenswood Slough, circles a salt pond to the Bay's edge, then returns to a trail along Highway 84 that skirts around a fenced utility substation and firefighters training center and leads back to the University Avenue junction. During the fall hunting season some sections of this trail are open only to hunters.

Popular with noontime runners from nearby offices and with those who want a longer run than the 2-mile path around Bayfront Park, this long stretch of Bay Trail is also an important link to bicycle lanes across the Dumbarton Bridge and to trails in the San Francisco Bay National Wildlife Refuge. A freeway overpass from the SFBNWR leads to Coyote Hills Park of the East Bay Regional Parks District. A bicycle trail from there goes all the way to Niles Canyon.

Negotiations have long been under way to close two gaps in the Bay Trail route south of the Highway 84 approach to the Dumbarton Bridge: the first is between the existing trails in the north and south sections of Ravenswood Open Space Preserve; the second gap is between the southern Ravenswood Preserve entrance at Bay Road and the existing surfaced trail from Palo Alto that ends at Runnymede Street. When these gaps are closed, there will be a continuous trail from Menlo Park's Bayfront Park to Mountain View's Shoreline Park.

The first leg of this Bay Trail route south of Highway 84 is an existing ½-mile levee trail running due south in the northern section of the Ravenswood Open Space Preserve that ends at the preserve boundary. Unobstructed Bay views east and the sight of myriad birds on the salt ponds and mudflats are your rewards for taking this short trip. It can be reached from access (1) at the Ravenswood Pier, page 318. (The pier itself is closed.)

Until the expected trail connections are completed south from Highway 84, the best Bay Trail access is from the second leg of the route at Bay Road in the southern section of the Ravenswood Open Space Preserve, described in Trip 3 below.

Trip 3. A Walk North in Ravenswood Open Space Pres around a Restored Marsh

On paths and boardwalks past tidal marsh, open water and a slough yo the opportunity to examine the variety of bird life.

- **Distance:** 2.4 miles round trip.
- **Time:** 1 hour.

TRAIL NOTES

To reach this preserve see directions for access (2) page 318. Ravenswood Open Space Preserve a small viewing plaza and bench ne the parking lot overlook the channel of a slough. From the plaza you lo across the Bay toward the narrows where Dumbarton Bridge and a abandoned railroad bridge cross to Fremont. The north side of historic Cooley Landing is approximately the original shoreline. Early settlers envisioned that it would become the South Bay's leading port when scow schooners carried wheat and hay to San Francisco from what was called Ravenswood Wharf. Lester Cooley purchased it in 1863 and renamed it Cooley's Landing. The grain warehouse and brick plant he built nearby failed in the 1880s when Redwood City developed its wharves farther north. Immediately north across the water is the high land of Coyote Hills Park of the East Bay Regional Parks District.

The plaza is a good point for starting the trip by the salt pond on the north side of the slough. Cross the bridge over the slough and follow the levee path straight ahead. The slough follows around the bend in the levee. Bayward is one of the many salt ponds that ring the South Bay. Under auspices of the Coastal Conservancy and MROSD the outer levee was breached and now the tides flood the pond, restoring it to a tidal marsh. This path is surfaced for bicycle riding as far as a bench and viewing platform on the levee.

The viewing platform is a good vantage point from which to watch ducks and other water birds dabble or dive for food. At low tide when mudflats rim the marsh, look for the long-billed and long-legged shore-birds that find crabs, snails and mollusks in the shallows. When you have identified, or just enjoyed watching, the bird life, return along the edge of the slough to the bridge where you started.

Trip 4. Walk or Bike to Palo Alto from Ravenswood Open Space Preserve

Enjoy the panoramic views over this great expanse of restored tidal marsh.

- **Distance:** 2 miles round trip.
- **Time:** 1 hour.

TRAIL NOTES

One of the outstanding views of marsh and Bay is from the paths along the marshes of Laumeister and Faber tracts. These lands, purchased by Palo Alto in the 1960s, were restored by breaching the levees. The expanse of cordgrass, at first glance appearing unbroken to the Bay's edge, is in fact a network of small, meandering sloughs. At low tide these ribbons of mud are alive with snails, mollusks and worms. Incoming tides bring nourishing sediments to plants of the marsh. The cordgrass, one of the most productive of all plants and an air purifier, removes much carbon dioxide and gives off much oxygen.

The marsh is home to many small and inconspicuous birds and animals. You may not see the shy and endangered harvest mouse, but keep an eye out for the chicken-sized but well-camouflaged clapper rail.

Marsh inhabitants that you can spot even at a distance, of course, are the common egret, 3 feet tall, and the smaller snowy egret. Happily their numbers are increasing here. Once nearly extinct, they are now common sights, thanks to the Audubon Society, which campaigned for their survival after they were nearly hunted out of existence for their beautiful nuptial feathers.

From Bay Road to Runnymede Street there is no official trail, but the old 0.4-mile levee is usable to reach the surfaced trail. The path down the marsh makes a slight bend at Runnymede Street, then goes straight toward San Francisquito Creek, the San Mateo County boundary. You will see the row of trees bordering the channel of the creek out to the Bay. The trail crosses the creek, then continues at the edge of Palo Alto's Golf Course to Geng Road. There is parking here, and a connection to Palo Alto's long Baylands Trail, on which you can bicycle all the way to Mountain View's Shoreline.

Great white egret

San Mateo Coast Beaches and Coastal Trail

Introduction

Extending more than 40 miles from San Francisco south to Santa Cruz County, this dramatic shoreline is dotted with sandy beaches, accented with rocky points, and indented by several relatively quiet bays. Along this southeast-trending coastline runs the Pacific Coast Highway, State Route 1, almost always in view of the sea and never more than 2 miles inland. This route is justly famous for its magnificent views of the surf, and its easily seen beaches and bluffs along the route.

Historically, the Coastside was used by the Spanish Franciscan missionaries for grazing cattle; few crops were grown. After Mexican independence from Spain in 1821 lands belonging to the missions of Dolores in San Francisco and Santa Cruz on the coast were divided into private *ranchos*, the names of which still lie on the land. Some of these Mexican *ranchos* became towns (San Gregorio and Pescadero, for example), others became state parks (Butano and Año Nuevo), but the leisurely life of the *rancheros* did not last long. By 1843, Americans were challenging the Mexican authority. They soon took over the government and the land, by fair means or foul, and intensive grazing use of the land was replaced by more intensive agriculture. The relatively level creek bottoms and coastal bluffs were planted in row crops.

Because this coast is situated across the Santa Cruz Mountains from the center of Bay Area population, and because its agriculture is profitable, most of the Coastside has been sparsely settled and today many miles of coastline remain open. As a result, most of the beaches are public and there is frequent coastal access. However, with increasing Bay Area population, pressure to develop housing has begun to fill open lands, particularly in the Half Moon Bay area. The public is fortunate that so many miles of undeveloped coastline and uninterrupted ocean views remain.

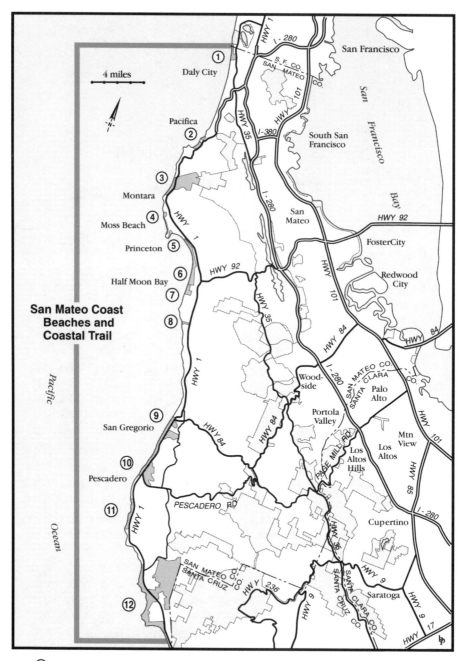

4 miles

Daly City

Pacifica

Montara

Moss Beach

Princeton

Half Moon Bay

**San Mateo Coast
Beaches and
Coastal Trail**

San Gregorio

Pescadero

San Francisco

S. F. CO.
SAN MATEO CO.

South San
Francisco

San Mateo

FosterCity

Redwood
City

Wood-
side

Portola
Valley

Palo
Alto

Mtn
View

Los
Altos
Hills

Los
Altos

Cupertino

Saratoga

SAN MATEO CO.
SANTA CLARA CO.

SAN MATEO CO.
SANTA CRUZ

SANTA CLARA CO.
SANTA CRUZ CO.

Pacific

Ocean

San
Francisco

Bay

HWY 1

I - 280

HWY 35

I - 380

HWY 101

I - 280

HWY 92

HWY 1

HWY 92

HWY 101

HWY 84

HWY 1

HWY 35

HWY 84

HWY 84

I - 280

PAGE MILL RD

HWY 1

PESCADERO RD

HWY 35

HWY 85

I - 280

HWY 101

HWY 84

HWY 9

HWY 236

HWY 9

HWY 9

HWY 17

(1) Numbers in circles refer to San Mateo Coast Beaches and Coastal Trail text

San Mateo Coast Beaches and Coastal Trail

San Mateo Coast Beaches and Coastal Trail

Circled # on Map	Park or Trail Name in Text
1	Thornton State Beach
2	Pacifica City and State Beaches
3	Gray Whale Cove and Montara State Beach
4	James V. Fitzgerald Marine Reserve
5	Pillar Point Marsh and Harbor
6	Half Moon Bay State Beaches
7	Poplar County Beach
8	Cowell Ranch State Beach
9	San Gregorio and Pomponio State Beaches
10	Pescadero State Beach and Marsh
11	Pebble Beach to Bean Hollow State Beach
12	Año Nuevo State Reserve and Coastal Access

A segment of the California Coastal Trail, one of four long north-south trails in San Mateo County, is proposed to extend from Fort Funston on the county boundary with San Francisco to Año Nuevo, close to the Santa Cruz County boundary. Here is an opportunity to walk, ride a bicycle or a horse within sight and sound of the sea. The long-term goal of the Coastal Trail is to provide a continuous route along the California coast, connecting beaches and recreation sites in 15 counties on the bluffs or rocky shores, over the sand dunes, or, where necessary, inland from Highway 1 along local, lightly traveled streets. The Coastal Trail segment is part of the adopted San Mateo County Trails Plan, is identified in the statewide trails plan, and is part of the Joint Access Program of the state's Coastal Conservancy and the California Coastal Commission.

A non-profit organization based in Sonoma County, Coastwalk, is dedicated to introducing the public to this spectacular shore and to completing the Coastal Trail along its 1100 miles from the Oregon border to Mexico. Already long stretches of this trail exist for multi-day hikes; there are many opportunities for shorter day hikes. Coastwalk schedules day and week-long hikes in one or more coast counties each summer. Hikers carry their personal belongings, but their camping gear and a hearty meal await them at day's end.

In San Mateo County, the State of California, the County and a city own and operate many beaches for all to enjoy. A few beaches are privately owned or operated. All public beaches are accessible from Highway 1 by trail, from a roadside pullout or from a designated parking area. Most public beaches charge a modest parking fee and many have self-registration kiosks to accept fees. Camping is available at the Half Moon Bay State Beaches.

In addition to the public agencies that have secured beaches and coastside lands west of Highway 1, private, non-profit organizations and land trusts are active in buying still-private lands that might be lost to the public domain. Cowell Ranch State Beach is a case in point (see page 341). Other non-profit groups are the Pacifica Land Trust, which purchased the San Pedro Point lands that soon will be open for public use; Sempervirens Fund, which has bought land in the Gazos Creek drainage; and the Peninsula Open Space Trust, which has an option on eight square miles inland from Pigeon Point, some of which will be retained in agriculture, some will be dedicated for public parkland. The Save-the-Redwoods League has purchased sizable redwood groves which are now state park lands. Active on the state and national levels as well, are the Trust for Public Land and The Nature Conservancy.

The California Coastal Conservancy, brought into being by the Coastal Act of 1976 and funded by three state bond acts, works to aid local governments in the planning, developing and funding for coastal access and land acquisition. This legislation limited coastal development west of Highway 1 to facilities that are visitor-serving, and required that public access be available where development was allowed.

On clear days the vista of the intense blue sea, broken by a succession of white-crested waves, stretches far beyond the shore. Onshore, sandpipers and willets search for unwary crabs and clams. Grebes and terns dive for fish in the water. Offshore is a parade of ships of all sizes from huge tankers and fishing vessels to recreational sailboats. Gray whales pass by on their annual migration from the Bering Sea to calving grounds in Baja California. On foggy days the scene changes—it becomes more closed in, the sea and sky are leaden, and the air is damp. Nevertheless, a vigorous walk along the strand or on a bluff-top trail can bring a sense of solitude and peace. On a stormy day the sight and sound of huge waves crashing on the shore remind one of the immense power of the sea ceaselessly eating away at the bluffs.

Visitors to San Mateo coast beaches should be aware that the water is very cold, the surf is treacherous due to hazardous rip currents, and there are no lifeguards on duty. High tides even in summer can completely inundate many beaches. Sudden rogue waves can sweep people off exposed rocks. When planning a beach walk, consult tide tables in local newspapers.

See Appendix III for San Mateo Coast Beaches' phone numbers.

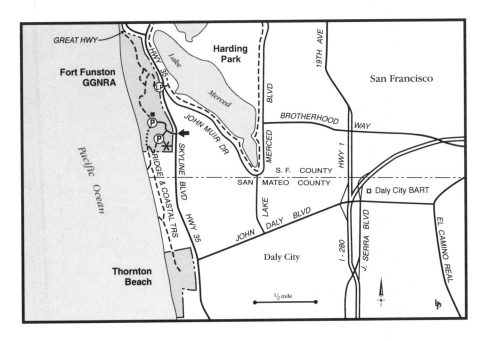

Fort Funston to Thornton State Beach

Slated to become part of the Golden Gate National Recreation Area, this remnant of state beach is a half-mile collection of sand dunes below the bluffs seaward of Skyline Boulevard in Daly City. It is flanked on the north by the Olympic Club's ocean golf course and at low tide by narrow, sandy beaches extending south to Mussel Rock. A segment of the Bay Area Ridge Trail follows a 1.2-mile sandy trail up and down the dunes from Fort Funston in San Francisco south to Thornton Beach. At this writing, this trip is accessible from Fort Funston in San Francisco only, making it a 2.4-mile round trip.

This stretch of beach is managed by the Golden Gate National Recreation Area, which operates the Fort Funston facility. Here are visitor center, native plant nursery, viewing deck with benches in protected nooks, a hang-glider launching site, trails, picnic tables, water, phone, restrooms, and parking. Fort Funston is open from sunrise to sunset. Dogs must be on leash or under voice control and owners must pick up pet litter. Fort Funston—415-556-8642; 415-239-2366.

To get to Fort Funston from the north, take Highway 35 (Skyline Boulevard) to Lake Merced and after passing John Muir Drive, go 0.1 mile, and turn right (west) into Fort Funston. At the road fork, bear right and continue to an extensive parking area. From the south, take Highway

35 (Skyline Boulevard) north to John Muir Drive, make a U-turn at the signal, go south on Skyline Boulevard 0.1 mile, and turn right (west) into Fort Funston.

From the bluffs at Fort Funston, stairs and a sand-ladder lead down to the beach where the Bay Area Ridge Trail heads south. Overhead hang-gliders and para-gliders join pelicans and seagulls as they soar with the winds. Around you on the dunes in spring and summer is a restored native garden of blooming wildflowers in many hues—crimson Indian paintbrush, yellow blossomed, gray-leaved lizardtail, purple sand verbena and lavender sea daisy. When the tide is out, you can take a stroll beside the sea to find shells of many shapes, crabs skittering at the edge of an oncoming wave and scattered flotsam and jetsam brought in on the tide.

When you reach a long, high dune paralleling the shore, you rise to its crest to find windswept Monterey pines and a couple of picnic tables in its lee. These are all that remain from the days when Thornton Beach had a fine entrance road down to picnic areas and camping sites along the shore. Heavy storms battering the coast in the 1980s and the run-off from city streets eroding the bluffs brought the demise of the beach facilities.

Here is the place to turn around and head north to Fort Funston and its bluff-top viewing deck. From there you can look north to Pt. Reyes, west to the Farallones, and south to San Pedro Point in Pacifica. Almost the entire expanse of sandy beaches that you see in either direction is in the public domain.

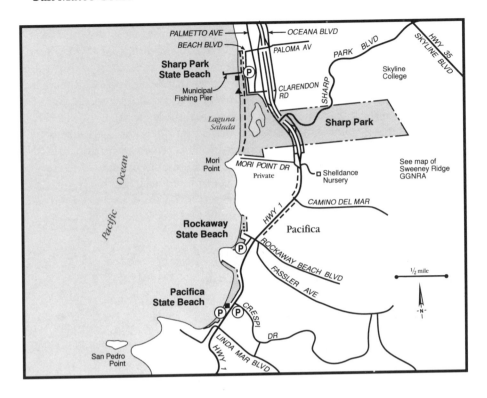

Pacifica Beaches

Curving beaches between rocky points adjacent to Highway 1 beckon visitors to sandy coves and rolling surf. The northernmost beach is the City of Pacifica's Sharp Park Beach and farther south are the Pacifica State Beaches, all managed by the City of Pacifica—415-738-7380. The Coastal Trail follows the shore with a few detours back to sidewalks along Highway 1.

A public beach and ocean-front trail stretch for a mile along Pacifica's Sharp Park district. From north of Paloma Avenue to Clarendon Road, the wide, paved ½-mile trail runs behind a sturdy sea wall bolstered with huge boulders. After the trail passes the Pacifica pier, a generous landscaped border of lawn separates Beach Boulevard and parking bays from the trail. Occasional picnic tables and barbecues, benches, and tall, square columns topped with attractive light fixtures invite visitors and residents to enjoy this beach and open space.

Beyond Clarendon Road, where there is limited street parking, the trail rises to the top of a bulwark of boulders topped with loose earth, which protects the Sharp Park Golf Course from the ravages of winter storms. This public course built around Laguna Salada and several other lagoons fills the land back to Highway 1 and extends east toward the GGNRA lands on Sweeney Ridge. The elevated trail overlooking the ocean continues past the golf course to the north side of Mori Point, where it follows Mori Point Road out to Highway 1, then continues on a paved sidewalk on the west and then the east side of the highway.

Around the point and a deserted limestone quarry is the Rockaway Beach section of Pacifica, where public beaches are accessible north and south from Rockaway Beach Boulevard. At the mouth of small streams at each end of this beach are little coves tucked between two rocky points. North of the boulevard are limited parking and a short section of paved ocean-front trail fenced with nautical rope. At the south end are changing rooms, a few benches, a mowed lawn and parking.

Surfer catches a nice one at Rockaway Beach.

A fence surrounds the ridge south of Rockaway and no sidewalk edges the busy highway. But immediately south of this rocky point is a State of California, wide, 1½-mile long sandy beach with dunes anchored by beach grass and ice plant at its north end. Farther south, accessible from Linda Mar Boulevard, are generous parking areas and restrooms. This a favorite surfing beach, where the black, wet-suited surfers bobbing over swells and gliding down waves look like seals at play.

On clear days, the sea sparkles and waves crash on the shore, seagulls wheel over the picnic tables, and children search for shells and make sand castles. The State of California and the City of Pacifica are well on the way to connecting these beaches by walks and trails to form a continuous waterfront experience for coastal enthusiasts. Some wide trails are open to bicyclists.

No trail presently extends south from the Pacifica State Beaches to Gray Whale Cove, although several old trails over San Pedro Mountain, at present in private ownership, join the existing 3.2-mile Old Pedro Mountain Road in McNee Ranch (see page 52).

Gray Whale Cove State Beach

Map on page 52

This clothing-optional beach is operated by a concessionaire who charges an admission fee. A small parking area is situated on the east side of Highway 1. It is extremely dangerous to cross the highway on foot or to turn left out of this parking area. Up a few steps from the parking area is the mile-long Gray Whale Cove Trail, which contours along the ridge south to the McNee Ranch entrance. Slightly north of and below the trail is the infamous Devil's Slide, which persists in falling off into the sea, taking parts of Highway 1 with it.

Montara State Beach

Map on page 52

Just across Highway 1 from the McNee Ranch entrance is this lovely, mile-long, wide beach of golden sand and rolling surf. From a small, unpaved parking area on the west side of the highway steps lead down the side of a ravine to the beach, where Martini Creek drops into the sea. Long walks along this broad strand, strewn with bits of sea plants and creatures tossed on shore by the waves, bring views of the rocky points both north and south. Parking is also available at the south end of the beach, where there is a public restroom, and until 5 P.M. you also can park beside the restaurant there.

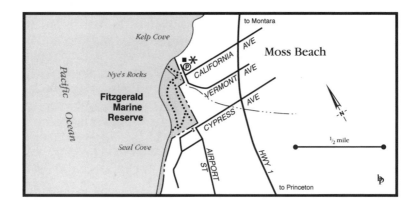

Fitzgerald Marine Reserve

This San Mateo County Marine Reserve in Moss Beach extends along the Coast for 3 miles and out into the ocean for 1000 feet, from north of California Avenue south to Pillar Point. Established in 1969 at the urging of then Supervisor James V. Fitzgerald, it is now a San Mateo County Parks Reserve affiliated with the State of California Department of Fish and Game. The reserve is open from sunrise to sunset and docent trips are offered under the auspices of San Mateo County's Coyote Point Museum.

To get there from Highway 1 north of Half Moon Bay, take California Avenue west to North Lake Street and turn right. There is parking for 42 cars and an additional area accommodates 20 cars along North Lake Street. No tidepool animals, shells or rocks may be taken, but fishing is permitted with a fishing license for various fish, eels and abalone. No dogs allowed.

From the visitor center and parking area a wide, paved path descends beside San Vicente Creek to the beach and tidepools. At low tide when the rocky shale shelf is exposed, visitors can carefully walk on it to observe the complex and fragile marine community in the pools and on the rocks. The area between high and low tide is home to many endangered species and to a great variety of seaweed, crabs, sponges, sea anemones, starfish and fish.

County biologists are conducting long-range studies of roped-off test plots on the rocks to determine the health of this reserve. By counting the species in a square-meter test and a control plot, researchers expect to identify how the reserve's marine life is regenerating from past abuse. Begun in 1994, these studies will continue over a five- or six-year period. Variables affecting marine life include wave conditions and human visitation. Biologists are noticing an improvement in visitor behavior—now most visitors observe, photograph, or draw, but don't take specimens.

Just offshore on Nye's Rock is a resident colony of 300 harbor seals.

Visitors can often hear their gruff barking and see them hauled out on the rocks or swimming in the lagoon between the rock and shore.

When the tide is out, the sandy beach is accessible for strolls along the water, but visitors should be mindful that high tides almost obliterate the beach. Check the tide tables posted at the visitor center or those published daily in local newspapers. Photos from 1911 show a large sand dune situated between the ocean and the present shoreline. Probably, cliff modifications by homeowners and breakwaters constructed along the coast have caused this change.

When you have checked out the tidepools and the coastal strand, try a ½-mile bluff-top walk south from the visitor center. Take the trail toward the beach and turn left on a bridge over San Vicente Creek. Climb through coastal shrubs lining the trail to the flat bluff-top, where spring wildflowers bloom and a wide view of the coast spreads before you.

From here at low tide look just north of the main entry trail for a geologic syncline, identified by several exposed concentric rings of Pleistocene shale grouped around some large table rocks. Earth movements along the Seal Cove Fault, a part of the San Andreas Fault system that enters the sea here, lifted the coastline up against Montara Mountain. To the northeast you can see the long sweep of this mountain forming a backdrop for this coastal area. At high tide large combers roll in to inundate and continually batter all these ancient rocky protrusions.

After you have oriented yourself on the bluffs, walk south into the cypress grove and follow the trail as it meanders through the trees. The first inhabitants of this coast, an ancient people dating back an estimated 6000 years, left middens that recently were discovered. Later people, the Ohlones, came to the Coast from the Bayside to fish and hunt, but apparently did not live here. Now, 135,000 people come each year to wander the bluffs, enjoy the views and explore the marine life in the tidepools. About 20% of these visitors are school children.

Continuing through the trees, the trail soon dips down to the former lands of Reverend Arthur Smith of Oakland, where three large palm trees and remnants of foundations mark the location of his large, Victorian summer residence. A fence just beyond the wooden steps that lead down to Seal Cove Beach marks the end of the trail. Return along the bluff for different views or follow a trail east to an opening in the fence and traverse the trail along the course of the Seal Cove Fault back to the visitor center.

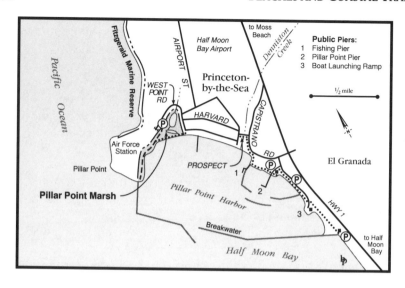

Pillar Point Marsh and Harbor

Pillar Point's 175-foot ridge topped by its antenna is the dominant feature of the middle coastline of San Mateo County. On its northwest side is the Fitzgerald Marine Reserve, on its heights is a United States Air Force tracking station and in the sheltering arm of its southwest side are the Pillar Point Harbor and the Pillar Point Marsh.

The 35-acre freshwater Pillar Point Marsh nestled within the protective arm of the Pillar Point promontory is now flourishing after years of neglect. Fed by a clear creek flowing through willow trees and tall grasses, this marsh is a resting place for migratory birds winging along the Pacific Flyway and home to many species of year-round resident birds. At any time of year, even the casual visitor will see snowy-white egrets resting on reeds patiently watching for a meal of frogs or other marsh-dwellers. Especially in spring, red-wing blackbirds trill their mating calls from perches on cattails and flash their red shoulder patches as they fly low across the marsh.

To reach the marsh from Highway 1 in Princeton, just north of Half Moon Bay, take Capistrano Road west past the yacht harbor to Prospect Way and turn left. Go right on Broadway and immediately turn left on Harvard Avenue. At the end of Harvard, turn right on West Point Avenue, go 0.5 mile around the marsh and turn left into the parking area.

A graveled trail edges the west side of the marsh and continues along the base of Pillar Point to the west breakwater. En route you can scan the relatively calm harbor for terns and pelicans diving for unwary fish or see marbled godwits and sandpipers searching for clams in the shallow, quiet water of the harbor's shore. Bring your binoculars and a bird book to identify these and many other birds as you rest on one of the benches along the route. Out in the harbor you may notice seagulls perched atop a raft which is an abalone nursery. From the west breakwater, you can walk around the bluff on the beach to an area called Mavericks, where huge combers send saltwater spray skyward as they collide with Sail Rock. Watching experienced surfers ride these waves past rocky protrusions is a fascinating culmination of your walk.

On your return to the marsh, you can walk east on its sandy beach almost to the Romeo Pier, a private loading dock for the fishing industry. A beautiful northwest backdrop for this moon-shaped harbor is the long arm of Montara Mountain.

Pillar Point Harbor

For many years fishermen and farmers on the Coastside struggled to get their fish and produce to market in San Francisco from the small communities west of the Santa Cruz Mountains. Repeatedly they petitioned the county supervisors and the national government to help build a safe harbor. Finally, after World War II, Pillar Point was designated as a harbor to be implemented by the Army Corps of Engineers and managed by San Mateo County Harbor District. When the harbor was completed in 1961, it quickly was discerned that the great outer arms of the breakwater were insufficient to deflect the strong winter storms coming in past Pillar Point. A long west arm was added to the breakwater, but still the inner harbor was too exposed. After the addition of an interior breakwater in 1982, the small-boat anchorage is safe now and filled with local fishing vessels and pleasure craft.

A Stroll Along the Waterfront at Princeton-by-the-Sea.

To see commercial and recreational fishermen bring in their catch at San Mateo County's only ocean port, begin your 1-mile walk from the generous parking areas just southwest of the signalized intersection at Highway 1 and Capistrano Road. Saunter down to the busy port and follow the walkway northwest around the inner anchorage. Here boats of all sizes and shapes sport all manner of masts—some with navigation gear, some with yachting colors. You can walk out on Johnson Pier to see the fishing fleet landing its catch or walk northwest of the anchorage to the public fishing pier where young and old try their luck with pole and reel or hand line and sinker.

Continue your stroll north to the sidewalk along Capistrano Road, where public picnic tables offer views of the harbor and restaurants sell prepared meals of the day's catch. Follow the path to Prospect Way and across the mouth of Denniston Creek—once the area's clear, clean water supply—which now flows ignominiously in culverts to its outlet here.

Return to the inner anchorage, pass the parking areas and take an informal path southeast beside the road to the boat-launching ramp. From there a broad, paved walkway proceeds beside the beach to the east breakwater. En route this path passes a long ramp to a bluff-top restaurant. Beyond the breakwater there is no formal path along the surfers' beach. However, at Mirada Road and Highway 1 it is possible to use paths and sidewalks to reach the next paved segment of the Coastal Trail at Arroyo en Medio, described next in the Half Moon Bay State Beaches section of this guide.

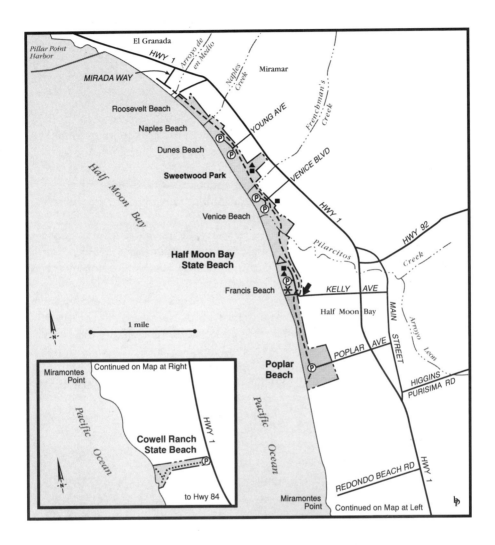

Half Moon Bay State Beaches

A paved trail runs for almost 3 miles through the California State Beaches at Half Moon Bay. Laid out east of the parking areas and camp-sites and behind the dunes, it crosses two major Coastside streams and several intermittent rivulets. At all beaches there is a fee for day-use at convenient parking areas and for camping facilities. You can walk, bike or ride a horse within sight and sound of the sea.

This trip is described from south to north, since parking is best at the southernmost beach. From Highway 1 south of Half Moon Bay, take Kelly Avenue west to Francis Beach, pick up the Coastside Trail just east of the parking and campground areas and head north under a sheltering row of Monterey cypress trees. In this park a low chain-link fence separates the bicycling and hiking trail from the horse trail. Equestrians reach the trail from Kelly Avenue, not from the park.

At the end of the campground swing left around the park maintenance area and note a trail to the beach between the sand dunes and then find another on the right leading to a creek crossing for horses, but continue on the main trail. When you step onto the metal bridge spanning Pilarcitos Creek, look for a bronze plaque honoring John Hernandez, a Half Moon Bay resident, who was instrumental in developing this Coastside Trail. From this bridge you can see the swollen creek rushing to the ocean after winter storms, or at other times a smaller creek lazily meandering through the willows that crowd its banks.

Continuing north you pass fields of yellow lupine, low-growing coyote bush, bright orange poppies, and yellow mustard and oxalis. Soon you reach Venice Beach, accessible from Highway 1 on Venice Boulevard, where there are ample parking and restrooms.

Wherever a creek flows into the sea, the dunes are lower, and views from the trail expand. You can usually find a little path out to the bluffs or down to the beach to fully experience the continuous crashing of waves on the shore, seagulls wheeling overhead and salty ocean breezes blowing in your face. Especially in winter you will find numerous shorebirds searching the shore for clams. Shell and driftwood hunting are also best in winter after heavy storms.

Pilarcitos Creek flows into Half Moon Bay.

After passing the stables at Sea Horse Ranch, you cross a metal bridge spanning Frenchmans Creek and reach Sweetwood Park, a grassy meadow protected by a semicircle of venerable Monterey cypresses and Monterey pines. These trees, sculpted by years of onshore winds, once sheltered a seaside home. Today picnic tables, barbecues and restrooms nestle among the trees. Take the narrow path along the high north bank of Frenchmans Creek to find a few benches and a bluff-top trail with dramatic views of seagoing vessels, sailboats and fishing boats not too far offshore.

Although you can follow a narrow trail along the cliffs, the wide Coastside Trail continues from the east end of the meadow to Dunes Beach. Here an extensive parking area is accessible from Highway 1 via Young Avenue. From the bluffs here your views extend north to prominent Pillar Point and south along the curve of the shoreline to Miramontes Point. Easily distinguished by its huge communications screen and white government buildings atop a mesa, Pillar Point shelters within the curve of its south side the Pillar Point harbor for small craft, protected by a breakwater. Here too is the waterfront interpretive trail at Pillar Point Marsh and a cluster of marine-related buildings and restaurants.

Continuing to the northernmost parking area on this trail at Roosevelt Beach, (accessible from Highway 1 via Roosevelt Boulevard) you find high dunes, partially planted with dune grass, and a well-defined trail to the beach. An unnamed creek meanders along Naples Beach and empties into the bay. (This creek, though unnamed on the topographic map, is locally known as Naples Creek.) From here it is less than ½ mile to the end of the trail. On your way you pass a group of brown-shingled condominiums on the bluff-top and emerge at the outflow of Arroyo en Medio. In severe storms of recent years old Highway 1 in this location was washed out, but this trail uses the remaining half of its bridge to cross over the sheer-sided creekbed. This segment of the Coastside Trail officially ends here, although you can walk farther north along ocean-front Mirada Road for another half mile.

Poplar County Beach

Map on page 337

South from the Half Moon Bay State Beaches at Kelly Avenue the coastal terraces and sandy beaches extend approximately 1½ miles to the end of Redondo Beach Road. No established trails traverse the bluffs from Kelly Avenue to Poplar Beach, but many informal paths thread through tall grass dotted with spring wildflowers and introduced mustard. Barbara Vander Werf notes in her charming book *The Coastside Trail Guidebook* that the crumbling concrete rings you pass here are remnants of a World War II practice range on which guns were mounted to aim at targets at sea. You may be joined by cavalcades of horseback riders from nearby stables as you stroll along this sea terrace or even on the beach.

If you continue along the relatively level sea terrace, you arrive at Poplar Avenue, where there is an unsurfaced parking lot and a ramp down to the beach. Use this ramp to continue south. A stroll or brisk walk, except at very high tides, is quite possible all the way to the rounded (*redondo* in Spanish) points seen on the topo maps at the end of Redondo Beach Boulevard. Beyond here the surf washes close to shore and crashes against the rocks at the foot of the cliffs. Serious erosion at the mouth of an intermittent creek here makes cliff access hazardous, so retrace you steps northward.

As you go east on Poplar Avenue, note the yellow house with wide roof overhang on Railroad Avenue south of Poplar. Once the depot for the Ocean Shore Railroad, it is now a private home. This railroad, which ran from 1907 until 1920, was planned to extend from San Francisco to Santa Cruz. But the tracks never bridged the gap between Tunitas Creek, 8 miles south of Half Moon Bay, and Davenport Landing. However, passengers were transported by Stanley Steamer on a scenic ride across the unfinished section. On several beaches remnants of this historic route are visible.

Cowell Ranch State Beach
Map on page 337

This picturesque little beach is now a State of California beach, having been acquired and developed as part of a larger purchase by the Peninsula Open Space Trust. It lies on the west side of Highway 1 just south of the Half Moon Bay city limits, and at its well-marked entrance you will find a parking area, a restroom and an interpretive signboard. On one side of the sign are details of the POST acquisition; the other side tells the history of the land, from Indian habitation through whalers to settlers of European descent.

A wide, half-mile-long, level, graveled path from the parking area traverses the coastal terrace out to the cliff overlooking the sea. Along the path are benches of recycled material and more interpretive signs. To the south are fenced agricultural fields. In one place the fence is interrupted by a delightful wrought-iron gate decorated with a humpbacked whale design.

At the cliff end of the path is a circular vista point, surrounded by a wooden railing, where there are more interpretive signs, benches and another restroom. From this point are splendid views of the Coast, with the long arm and radar tower of Pillar Point prominent in the north. South of the point is a protected harbor-seal breeding ground—the rocks offshore and the beach are off-limits to humans. Read the interpretive signs to learn the story of these large mammals.

From the vista point a long flight of steps leads north to a small, curving, golden-sand beach. Tucked up against the tall cliffs, it is one of the more protected beaches along the San Mateo Coast.

South of the Cowell Ranch beach access area on both sides of Highway 1 are 1197 acres of farmland, which POST sold to local farmers in the early '90s subject to conservation easements for the preservation of agriculture. Easements on the bluffs south of the vista point reserved for future trails were donated by POST to the State. However, these easements cannot be activated until money for fencing and appropriate trail construction is available. POST also donated to the Coastal Conservancy the 5-acre historic Purissima (early spelling) Townsite, situated on the northeast corner of present-day Purisima Creek Road and Highway 1. Only the foundations of the former Dobbel mansion remain on the southeast corner of Purisima Creek Road, but a double row of cypress trees defines the curving driveway. The site can be identified by Monterey cypresses and pines bordering its frontage on Highway 1, but brambles and vinca have taken over the land.

San Gregorio and Pomponio State Beaches

These two beaches are popular destinations for daytime visitors (open 8 A.M. to sunset) from the Bayside; San Gregorio has a large parking lot, with a self-service fee structure (called an "iron ranger") and restrooms. This beach is just south of the intersection of La Honda Road with Highway 1, at the point where San Gregorio Creek runs into the ocean.

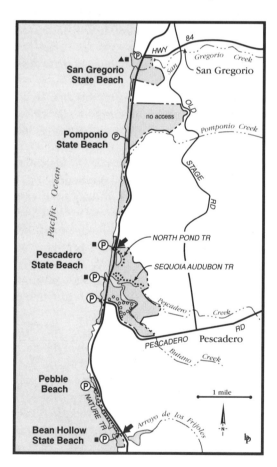

This large beach, with a cave under the cliff at its north side, tempts the visitor to walk south for long distances. Swimming here is not advisable, due to the strong undertow, which has been known to pull people out to sea. Driftwood and all sorts of interesting detrita lie at the tide line; flocks of sandpipers skitter in and out of the waves. There is always something interesting to find or to watch at this wide and beautiful beach. On the grassy strip beside the parking area is a historic marker noting that Captain Gaspar de Portolá and his party of Spanish explorers camped here for three days in October 1769. Although they missed the object of their search—Monterey Bay—they later found San Francisco Bay.

Pomponio State Beach is only about 1½ miles to the south, and could be called a part of San Gregorio Beach, since their sands are contiguous. A walk between the two would be an exhilarating experience when the surf is calm, the tide is low and the clouds are scudding fast from the west.

Pescadero State Beach and Pescadero Marsh
Map on page 342

Near the town of Pescadero (Spanish for the fishing place) are Pescadero Beach and Marsh, welcome resources for the recreationist and the nature lover. Pescadero State Beach's 2 miles of sandy beach, dunes and rocky outcroppings lie on the west, or ocean, side of Highway 1, and its 500 acres of marsh preserve are on the east side. The estuary of Butano and Pescadero creeks, a protected habitat for both migrating and resident birds and fish, can be observed from trails on your own or on nature walks guided by rangers.

In the early years of this century, European farmers who had settled in Pescadero drained much of the original marsh and used the area for agriculture. Owned by the Nunziatti family, the marshy areas remaining were managed after World War II by Tom Phipps as a hunting club. Migrating birds were the quarry, as well as ducks and Asian pheasants raised specifically for hunting. In the 1960s members of the Sequoia Audubon Society realized what a valuable habitat the marshland was and raised money to buy part of the land from the Nunziatti family. During the early 1970s the state parks acquired this nucleus of Pescadero Marsh, and continued acquisition until today the state owns 90% of the original marshland. Conservation easements on farming lands to the east were negotiated by POST. A marsh restoration effort is ongoing, managed by the state, and the Sequoia Aubudon Society has been commemorated with a trail named for them, which they still maintain. Pescadero Marsh, one of the premier birding spots in the county, is the only sizable estuarine marsh between Bolinas Lagoon and Elkhorn Slough.

Jurisdiction: State of California, Department of Parks and Recreation—415-879-2170.
Facilities: Beach for sunbathing, fishing; trails for nature study. Docent-led, 2-mile hikes leave every Saturday at 10:30 A.M. and Sunday at 1 P.M. from first parking lot south of Highway 1 bridge.
Maps: State parks brochure *San Mateo Coast State Beaches*, and *Pescadero Marsh Natural Preserve*, USGS topo *San Gregorio*.
Rules: Open 8 A.M. to sunset. Trails for hikers only. Hunting and dogs not allowed in preserve; dogs on beach, leashed only. Boats not allowed in sloughs during nesting season, March through August.
How to Get There: Take Hwy 1 south from Half Moon Bay for 17

miles. The state beach has three parking lots, all on ocean side of Hwy 1: (1) north of Pescadero Creek Bridge, (2) and (3) south of bridge, all with restrooms.

Trip 1. Sequoia Audubon Trail

Follow Pescadero Creek upstream to the end of the preserve.
- **Distance:** 2½ miles round trip.
- **Time:** 1½ hour.

Park at the first lot south of the creek on the west side of the highway, where you will find a restroom and the meeting place for the nature walks. Cross the highway bridge on a safe sidewalk on the west side, then go left down to the beach and under the bridge to reach the Sequoia Audubon Trail. On the dunes note that native dune grass planted to replace the invasive foreign ice plant is doing well.

At a junction with a trail leading left, on which you will return, you reach a signboard, which has information about spawning steelhead and advisories to boaters. From here go straight ahead on the Sequoia Audubon Trail, passing on your right an unsigned track leading to a shingled beach on Pescadero Creek itself. This estuary with calm waters and small beach might be a safe and pleasant place to swim on a hot day, avoiding the dangerous cold undertow of the ocean beach itself. The main Sequoia Audubon Trail soon reaches another junction, where on the left there is a bridge over a slough and a viewing platform. This area of the marsh is being managed by state scientists so that various sloughs, dikes and tidal gates keep water in the marsh and the pond for a longer period. Here you may see egrets feeding, herons stalking their prey or a pair of cinnamon teal ducks paddling through the water.

This trip continues straight (east) on the Sequoia Audubon Trail along a levee next to the slough. You are several hundred feet north of the main Pescadero Creek at this point. Along the way pass a huge, sprawling eucalyptus whose branches crawl along the ground, inviting climbers of all ages. Soon you reach a bench near the creek where you can view the marsh extending to the south. Look for some wood-rat nests in the thick willows, and for more benches by Pescadero Creek.

After about a mile, retrace your steps from the far end of the Sequoia Audubon Trail to the viewing platform and bridge that you passed earlier. Here take the righthand trail going northwest. You will see bushes of twinberry, a member of the honeysuckle family, which has reddish-yellow flowers in spring and black berries in fall. In damp areas there is yellow cinquefoil, a rose family relative with feathery leaves. Shortly you find another viewing bench, where you turn left (south) to return to the signboard, go under the bridge and on to the parking area.

Trip 2. North Pond Trail

Explore the quiet, east side of a restored marsh.

- **Distance:** 1 mile round trip.
- **Time:** ¾ hour.

Access to the North Pond Trail is somewhat hazardous. Park at the northernmost Pescadero Beach parking lot and scurry carefully across the highway, where traffic is fast and dangerous. This trail goes around the north and east sides of North Pond, reaching a small slough on the south side. You rise higher on the North Pond Trail, and get a splendid vista of the entire marsh, the two tributary creeks, the pond with its resident and migrating birds and the ocean to the west. Binoculars and bird books are essentials for this hike. Here you get a feeling for what the Coastside looked like before the Europeans arrived. The Pescadero Marsh is a special place, thanks to the foresighted members of the Audubon Society for their restoration work.

On this trip, you must return the way you came.

Pescadero Marsh.

Pebble Beach to Bean Hollow
Map on page 342

Stroll along a rocky, wave-swept coast
- **Distance:** 1 mile.
- **Time:** ½ hour.

Pebble Beach just south of Pescadero Creek has long been popular because of the unusual shiny pebbles that coat its strand. This was a popular destination in the 19th century when Pescadero had a brief fame as a summer resort. Visitors from San Francisco and the San Mateo County Bayside would stay at hotels in the little town of Pescadero and, according to a tourist guide of the time, collect pebbles form the beach. The guide noted: "Near the town is the famous Pebble Beach where agates, opals, jaspers, and carnelians, of almost every conceivable color, are found in great abundance, with a natural polish imparted by the action of the waves."

At Pebble Beach now, instead of nearby large hotels, is a parking lot with restrooms, and steps leading down to the small but beautiful beach. Collecting pebbles is no longer permitted, nor should one disturb the nearby tidepools or the interesting honeycomb-shaped rocks on the beach. But somewhat sheltered by the rocky points at each end, this beach is a protected place to splash in the water, with little of the undertow problems found at most coastal beaches.

Leading south from Pebble Beach is a narrow foot trail which runs 1 mile to Bean Hollow Beach through low-growing coastal-scrub vegetation. In spring the flowers blooming along this trail are magnificent. The trail runs within sight and sound of Highway 1, thereby somewhat diminishing its feeling of wildness, but if you look seaward, the coastal bluffs and offshore rocks lead your eye out to the ocean. Here you may see fishing boats hovering offshore or large container ships sailing along the horizon. If you are lucky, you may spot the spray of passing whales during their annual, December to March, migration along the coast.

There are no beaches along this stretch of trail, but the tidally exposed rocks are used extensively by fishermen. From an occasional small pull-out along the highway a fisherman's footpath runs down to the shore. Your trail crosses many small arroyos on wooden bridges, and posts with numbers indicate locations for a nature trail's points of interest.

At Bean Hollow State Beach, your trail descends the bank to the sand and crosses this small, sheltered beach to the south side, where on the bluff you find another parking lot with restrooms, and some picnic tables.

A one-hour round trip on this trail would be pleasant, or you can divide your party, one member driving south to pick you up at the next beach.

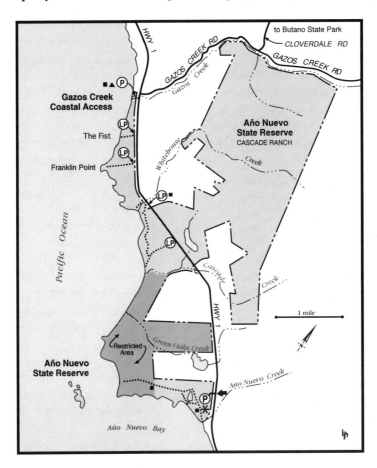

Año Nuevo State Reserve and Coastal Access

Best known for its northern elephant seal rookery, this interesting unit of the state park system has extremely varied natural features as well as human history that will fascinate all visitors. The State of California purchased Año Nuevo Island and a strip of adjacent mainland in 1958 to create the reserve, which now has been expanded to include over 4000 acres of coastal mountains, bluffs, dunes and beaches. The section of the reserve where the elephant seals breed is restricted to public access by guided tours (from December 1 to March 31) or by permit (from April 1 to November 30). Park rangers and docents are in the reserve to assist visitors in the restricted area. No access is allowed to Año Nuevo Island.

Named for the new year in 1603 by the party of Spanish explorer Sebastián Vizcaíno, who sailed past at that season, this coastal area had long been inhabited by Indians who hunted, fished and gathered shellfish from the sea. After the founding of Mission Santa Cruz 19 miles to the south, the Indians were greatly reduced in numbers due to their contact with Europeans. The Año Nuevo lands were used for pasturage, then became part of a private Mexican rancho in 1842, and eventually some of the land was purchased by the Steele brothers, who operated a dairy farm at Año Nuevo. Some of the park buildings, including the visitor center, a former barn, are relics of this period.

The main entrance to Año Nuevo State Reserve is on Highway 1, 30 miles south of Half Moon Bay and 19 miles north of Santa Cruz. At the entrance station (fee) there is a parking area with restrooms, and here the visitor is informed about where to go for the guided walk of the elephant-seal rookery. Reservations are recommended well in advance and can be made beginning in October by calling Destinet. Further information can be found at the Ranger office. Guided walks are provided by the State of California Department of Parks and Recreation. The San Mateo Coast Natural History Association has published an excellent booklet which is invaluable for a visitor taking the self-guiding nature walk from April through November. This guide book will not attempt to replicate the information in this booklet, but describes other trails in the Año Nuevo State Reserve that visitors will enjoy.

Lands on the northeast side of Highway 1 that are part of Año Nuevo State Reserve are not developed for public use at this time. Some old farm roads are used for ranger patrol—for example, at Old Woman Creek, off Gazos Creek Road—but these roads are gated to prevent public vehicle access.

Five Walks to Año Nuevo Beaches

There are five places along Highway 1 between the Año Nuevo main entrance and Gazos Creek that provide public access to the Coastside. About 6 miles north of the reserve is the Cascade Creek Trail. Here are a parking lot and a trail that crosses about a mile of grassland toward the southwest, with views of Año Nuevo Island at the end of the curving coast. There is native bunchgrass and prostrate coyote brush, and signs of a controlled burn, performed in the winter to rid the area of invasive, prickly gorse bushes. A row of eucalyptus and cypress trees remains from a windbreak planted years ago to shelter agricultural fields. You will note a marshy area at the delta of Cascade Creek, where once stood a dam to impound water for irrigation in the summer. This marsh is now splendid bird habitat. Here you are at the northern border of the closed area of Año

Nuevo Reserve; go anywhere you want to the north, but not to the south. A lovely, lonely beach is at the foot of the bluffs at the end of this trail, but it is covered at high tide.

A trail along the bluff goes north to the next beach access points at Whitehouse Creek, which are only 0.4 mile north. If you return to Highway 1 and drive, you will find two roadside parking areas here, one on the south, one on the north side of Whitehouse Creek. No house remains, but there is evidence of early settlement here—Monterey pine and eucalyptus trees and non-native gorse bushes. The south side trail crosses fields to join the Cascade Creek Trail and reaches the coastal bluffs beside the steep gulch of Whitehouse Creek.

Trails wind through the dunes to Año Nuevo beaches.

The north-side trail winds around in the grasslands, but it is easy walking and inspires one to run and enjoy the fresh breezes and sunshine (you would not want to come here on a foggy day; the trails are too indistinct and the bluffs too sudden!). Look here for sea otters resting in the kelp beds off the rocky shore, and marvel at how the sea has carved off a rocky "sea stack" just beyond the cliff. This stack has a grassy thatch on top, remnant of the coastal prairie.

About one mile farther north is the Franklin Point Trail. This trail is marked by a unique wooden sculpture which resembles a fist; in fact the rangers call it "The Fist." There actually are two small pullouts here, not far apart. The terrain here is markedly different from that of the grasslands farther south. This is an area of sand dunes with marshlands in between, all covered with dense vegetation of dune grass, coyote brush, wild strawberry, lizard tail, yarrow and in very wet areas, lush cinquefoil plants, a yellow-flowered member of the rose family. The trail to the beach is not very well defined, and goes through some wet areas. We do not recommend leaving the trail, as the undergrowth is difficult to walk through, and susceptible to damage. This is marvelous habitat for all kinds of animals. Northern harriers, red-tailed hawks and other raptors are continually gliding overhead looking for their next meal.

After you have walked about half a mile from the highway, you reach the dunes near Franklin Point, and can see to the north a long sandy beach stretching all the way to Gazos Creek, the north end of Año Nuevo State Reserve. Much of this beach is covered at high tide, but at low tide it is perhaps one of the least-visited and private beaches on the San Mateo Coast. It is not only humans that find this a secluded beach; when the authors visited it in March 1996 they were astonished to find on the smooth sand a set of sea-turtle tracks leading toward the ocean from a conspicuous mound of sand. A female turtle had come ashore in the night and laid her eggs, covered them with her flippers and gone back to sea! This is a rare event on this part of the California coast. The turtle probably was either a Pacific Ridley or a leatherback turtle, and it is important to make sure that there remain such quiet, protected beaches for these giant creatures to use.

The northernmost coastal access in Año Nuevo Reserve is at Gazos Creek. From here "The Fist" is visible about 1 mile to the south. The parking area at Gazos Creek has restrooms and steps down to the beach, and the signs say: NO VEHICLES, DOGS, FIRES OR CAMPING. It is across the highway from the Campbell Soup Company's mushroom factory, on the north side of Gazos Creek Road. You can walk south along the beach, looking for lavender sand verbena, wild cucumber and buttercups blooming in spring. A coastal trail shown on the Año Nuevo map that is purported to start from this beach has not been maintained for many years, and one should not attempt to walk south except at low tide on the beach itself. The parking and beach access trails described above are used mainly by fishermen. Other visitors too will find this an exhilarating way to experience the uncrowded parts of California's coast.

Acknowledgments

In the course of hiking all the trails and writing this expanded, third edition of *Peninsula Trails* we have experienced cooperation and assistance from many people—more than we can name here. We thank our families and friends who accompanied us on the hikes or drove shuttles to trail's end. To our delightful women's hiking group, the Walkie-Talkies, thanks for exploring new trails and revisiting old favorites with us. We are very grateful to our friend Bob Brown, who corrected some geologic faults in our manuscript.

To all the public agencies, their directors, staff and rangers, we say a hearty thank you, especially to: Golden Gate National Recreation Area—Brian O'Neill, Superintendent, and Stephen Prokop, Ranger; California Department of Parks and Recreation—Donald Murphy, Director, and the Bay Area and Santa Cruz Mountains District Rangers Chet Bardo, David Horvitz, Holly Hueneman, Sandy Jones and Leander Tamoria; Midpeninsula Regional Open Space District—Craig Britton, General Manager, Malcolm Smith, Public Affairs, Randy Anderson, Del Woods, and Mary de Beauvières, Planners, John Escobar, Operations Manager, and David Sanguinetti and Dennis Danielson, Rangers; San Mateo County Parks and Recreation Division—Patrick Sanchez, Director, Bob Emert, Superintendent (retired), and Robert Breen, Charles Brock, Lynn Fritz, Dennis Hanley, John Kenney, David Moore, Tom O'Connor and Ronald Weaver, Rangers; Santa Clara County Parks and Recreation Department—Paul Romero, Director, David Pierce, Mark Frederick and Ruth Shriber, Planners; Town of Los Altos Hills Pathways Committee—Les Earnest, Chairman. Their lively interest and generous contributions of up-to-date information, photographs, maps and trail data were indispensable.

To the Peninsula's outstanding longtime land trusts—Peninsula Open Space Trust, Audrey Rust, Director, and Sempervirens Fund, Verlyn Clausen, Director—we owe our gratitude for their help with maps, field trips and photos. We are grateful to Claude A. (Tony) Look, for initiating California Trail Days and for establishing the California Trails and Greenways Foundation to carry on this yearly event.

We wish to thank photographers Ann Duwe, Kenneth Gardiner, the Garrod family, Lynn Gibbons, Karl H. Riek and Charles Willard. We acknowledge the kindness of Nancy Woodward, who made her husband Sheldon's photographs available to us, photographers for the above-listed public agencies, land trusts, Hidden Villa, and the Woodside History Committee, all of whom generously contributed photographs.

We are especially grateful to Thomas Winnett, Editor and Publisher of Wilderness Press, who has worked long and patiently with us during the production of this edition of *Peninsula Trails*, and to his capable staff, Noëlle Imperatore, Anne Iverson, Larry Van Dyke, and Caroline Winnett. We enjoyed working with our cartographer, Ben Pease, whose expertise and on-the-ground knowledge were invaluable.

Jean Rusmore   Frances Spangle
Betsy Crowder   San Rafael, California
Portola Valley, California   January 17, 1997
January 16, 1997

Photo Credits

Mary de Beauvières – 102
Frank Bevans, MROSD – 137
Carolyn Caddes, MROSD – 116, 177, 188, 245
Crocker Land Co. – 35
Betsy Crowder – 275, 290
Alice Cummings, MROSD – 160
Ann Duwe – 19
Kenneth Gardiner – 322
Garrod family – 242
Lynn Gibbons – 40
Mary Hale, MROSD – 171, 180
Hidden Villa Archives – 18
Charlotte MacDonald, MROSD – 191, 195, 224, 234, 239
Midpeninsula Regional Open Space District – 104, 109, 149, 165
Karl H. Riek – 37
Jean Rusmore – 20, 26, 46, 49, 66, 67, 85, 93, 116, 119, 125, 130, 155, 162, 199, 202, 251, 263, 270, 277, 285, 286, 292, 298, 302, 307, 313, 323, 330, 338, 349
San Mateo County – 57
Frances Spangle – 24, 72, 74, 87, 90, 131, 134, 144, 210, 214, 304
State of California Department of Parks and Recreation – 99
Charles Willard – 267
Joe Hallett/Woodside History Committee – 117
Sheldon Woodward – 6, 58, 88, 141, 201, 205, 206, 345

List of Maps

Appendix I

TRAILS FOR DIFFERENT SEASONS AND REASONS
*Outstanding Outings

FOR THE SEASONS

SPRING—FABULOUS FLOWER FIELDS
*Edgewood County Park and Natural Preserve—Serpentine Loop Trail
Monte Bello OSP—Bella Vista Trail and Monte Bello Road
Rancho San Antonio Preserve—High Meadow and Upper High Meadow
Trails, Trip to a Secluded Meadow (Duveneck Windmill Pasture Area)
*Russian Ridge OSP—Bay Area Ridge Trail (south end) and
    Ancient Oaks Trail
*San Bruno Mountain Park—Summit Loop Trail
San Mateo Coast—Ocean bluffs and coastal terraces
Windy Hill—Connector trail from picnic area to Windy Hill Loop

SHADY TRAILS FOR HOT SUMMER DAYS
*Butano State Park—Little Butano Creek Trail
*Huddart Park—Lower Richards Road Trail along West Union Creek
Memorial County Park—Homestead Trail
Pescadero Creek County Park—Loop around the Tarwater Creek Basin
Phleger Estate—Miramontes Trail
*Portola Redwoods State Park—Iverson and Old Tree trails
Purisima Creek Redwoods OSP—Redwood Trail
Ridge/Skyline Trail
San Pedro Valley Park—Old Trout Farm Trail
Town of Portola Valley—Toyon Trail
Upper Stevens Creek Park—Trail to Grizzly Flat

FALL COLOR—*California Gold on Maple, Alder and Hazelnut Trees*
Coal Creek OSP—Trip 3, Upper Alpine Road Trail
Huddart Park—Crystal Springs Trail
*Monte Bello OSP—Canyon Trail, Stevens Creek Nature Trail
Pescadero Creek Park—Old Haul Road
*Sam McDonald Park—Heritage Grove Trail
Stevens Creek Park—Stevens Creek Trail
*Upper Stevens Creek Park—Alternate Trail and
    Table Mountain Trail: black oaks
Windy Hill OSP—Windy Hill Loop Trail

WINTER WALKS ON SURFACED PATHS—
For a breath of air between showers
Arastradero/Foothill Expressway Hub Trails
Bay Trails—most are surfaced
*Coastal Trail—Half Moon Bay Beaches
    Pillar Point Marsh and Harbor
    Pacifica City Beach
Laurelwood Park

San Bruno Mountain Park—Bog Trail and Guadalupe Trail
*Sawyer Camp Trail
"The Loop" through Portola Valley, Woodside and Menlo Park

HOW FAR IS IT? FROM SHORT WALKS TO LONG HIKES

SHORT WALKS ON NEARLY LEVEL TRAILS—*Less than five miles*
All Coastal Trails
*Año Nuevo State Reserve—Cascade Creek Trail
    Whitehouse Creek Trails
Arastradero/Foothill Expressway Hub Trails
Burleigh Murray Ranch Park—A Historic Ranch Trip
Butano State Park—Little Butano Creek Trail
Crystal Springs Trail—Highway 92 to Edgewood Road
Junipero Serra Park—Live Oak Nature Trail
Laurelwood Park—Main paved trail from Shasta Drive
Los Altos Hills—Artemas Ginzton and Juan Prado Mesa pathways
Memorial Park—West Side Loop Trip on Creek and Homestead Trails
Pescadero Creek Park—Short Walk to Pescadero Creek
Purisima Creek Redwoods OSP—Redwood Trail
Rancho San Antonio Park and Preserve—Trail to Deer Hollow Farm,
    Rogue Valley Trail
San Andreas Trail
San Bruno Mountain Park—Saddle Loop Trail
San Pedro Valley Park—Weiler Ranch Road, Trail to Old Trout Farm
*Sawyer Camp Trail—short round trips from south end
Skyline Ridge OSP—Loop trip around Alpine Lake
Stevens Creek Park—Trails from Mt. Eden Road to Canyon Trail junction,
Creek Trail
*The Bay Trails
"The Loop"— any segment along Alpine, Portola or Sand Hill roads
Thornewood OSP—Trip to a Historic Lake

LONG HIKES—*Five to ten miles*
Butano State Park—Trip 1, Circumnavigate the Park
El Corte de Madera OSP—Loop Trip on Gordon Mill and
    Lawrence Creek trails
    El Corte de Madera Creek/Resolution Trail Loop
Fremont Older OSP to Stevens Creek Park round trip
Half Moon Bay State Beaches—Coastside Trail round trip
Huddart Park—All-Day Hike Circling the Park; main entrance to Purisima
    Creek Redwoods Preserve's west entrance on Dean, Crystal Springs
    and Purisima Creek trails—with car shuttle
*Long Ridge Preserve to Portola Redwoods State Park or
    Long Ridge to Pescadero Trail Camp
*Pescadero Creek Park—Brook Trail Loop
    Tarwater Creek Basin Loop
    Tarwater Trail Loop
Phleger Estate—Climb to the Crest of the Santa Cruz Mountains
Portola Redwoods Park
    Coyote Ridge Trail to Tarwater Trailhead, round trip
    Portola Redwoods to Big Basin

Purisima Creek Redwoods Preserve
  Trip 2, Loop Trip from North Ridge
  Trip 3, Grabtown Gulch and Bald Knob Loop
  Trip 4, Bay Area Ridge Trail
Rancho San Antonio Preserve—Loop Trip on Deer Hollow, Meadow Ridge
  and PG&E trails
Russian Ridge Preserve—Bay Area Ridge Trail round trip
  Round trip to Mindego Ridge
San Bruno Mountain Park—Summit Loop and East Ridge Hike
Saratoga Gap to Monte Bello Preserve Page Mill entrance
Sawyer Camp Trail
Skyline Ridge Preserve—Bay Area Ridge Trail round trip
  *Bay Area Ridge Trail to Saratoga Gap through Long Ridge Preserve
Ridge/Skyline Trail
Sweeney Ridge—Mori Ridge Trail to Discovery Site round trip
  Ridge Trail from Milagra Ridge to Portola Gate and return
Waterdog Lake, Sheep Camp and Crystal Springs trails to Edgewood Road
Windy Hill OSP—Windy Hill Loop Trail
Wunderlich Park—Figure-Eight Loop Trip

*LOOP TRIPS THROUGH SEVERAL PARKS OR PRESERVES:
Upper Stevens Creek Park through Monte Bello and Long Ridge
  preserves—Charcoal Road, Canyon, Grizzly Flat, Peters Creek,
  Long Ridge Road trails; bicyclists start from Grizzly Flat
Monte Bello Preserve through Skyline Ridge, Russian Ridge and Coal Creek
  preserves on Stevens Creek Nature, Skid Road, Ridge trails, Meadow
  and Upper Alpine Road trails and Monte Bello Trail; equestrians and
  bicyclists use Canyon instead of Stevens Creek Nature Trail
Monte Bello Preserve through Skyline Ridge and Long Ridge preserves
  and Upper Stevens Creek Park on Stevens Creek Nature Trail, Skid Road,
  Ridge Trail south, Grizzly Flat and Canyon trails; equestrians and
  bicyclists use Canyon instead of Stevens Creek Nature Trail
Stevens Creek Park through Fremont Older Preserve on Lookout,
  Coyote Ridge and Stevens Creek trails

EXPEDITIONS—*Trails combined for trips of more than ten miles*
Belmont to Wunderlich Park main entrance—a 2-day trip for groups
  (reservations required) with car shuttle—Waterdog Lake, Sheep Camp,
  Crystal Springs trails to Huddart Park trail camp for overnight;
  next day, Crystal Springs, Skyline and Alambique trails to Wunderlich
  Park main entrance on Woodside Road
Butano Park—Circumnavigate the Park
Duveneck Windmill Pasture Area through Monte Bello OSP to Saratoga Gap
  on Black Mountain, Indian Creek, Canyon and Saratoga Gap trails or
  take in reverse, overnight at Hidden Villa Hostel or Black Mountain Trail
  Camp and return next day
Highway 92/Cañada Road to Wunderlich Park Skyline Boulevard entrance
  on Crystal Springs and Skyline trails (with car shuttle)
Huddart Park main entrance to Purisima Creek Redwoods Preserve west
  entrance and return—on Dean, Crystal Springs, Skyline and Purisima
  Creek trails; or take in reverse and overnight at Huddart Park trail camp
  (group reservations required)
Long Ridge Preserve to Big Basin—2- or 3-day hike with overnights in
  Portola Redwoods and Big Basin

Pescadero Creek County Park—Trip 4, Butano Ridge Trail Loop
Portola Redwoods to Big Basin round trip
Sam McDonald to Big Basin on Towne Ridge, Brook, Pomponio, Iverson
    and Basin trails with car shuttle
San Andreas, Sawyer Camp trails round trip
Skyline Trail from Huddart Park to Wunderlich Park round trip

DOWNHILL ALL THE WAY—*With a car shuttle*
*Basin Trail to Portola Redwoods
Coal Creek Preserve— Upper Alpine Road from Page Mill Rd. or Skyline
    Blvd. to lower entrance gate
Huddart Park—From Skyline Blvd. entrance on Chinquapin Trail to
    Miwok picnic area
Junipero Serra Park— Quail Loop Trail from upper picnic area on to lower
    picnic areas or continue to San Bruno City Park
Long Ridge Preserve—Downhill to Portola Redwoods
*San Bruno Mountain Park—Either leg of Summit Loop Trail from top
    of mountain
Sheep Camp Trail to Cañada Road
Waterdog Lake Trail from St. James Road to Lyall Road
Windy Hill Preserve—From Skyline Blvd. entrances on Spring Ridge,
    Hamms Gulch or Razorback Ridge trails to Alpine or Portola roads
*Wunderlich Park—Skyline Blvd. entrance to Woodside Road on Alambique
    Trail, or Skyline, Alambique and Bear Gulch trails

SPECIAL DESTINATIONS

VIEW POINTS—*Trips to high places for around-the-compass vistas*
Butano Park—Trip 2. To an Overlook
Edgewood Park—Serpentine Trail
El Corte de Madera Preserve—Trip 1. Loop Trip to Vista Point
Fremont Older Preserve—Trips to Hunters Point and South to Maisie's Peak
*La Honda Creek Preserve—A Trip down the Meadows for a Coastside View
Long Ridge Preserve—Bay Area Ridge Trail, Ward Road to Portola
    Redwoods
Los Trancos Preserve—Loop Trip on Franciscan and Lost Creek Trails
McNee Ranch—To Montara Mountain's North Peak
Monte Bello Preserve—Indian Creek or Bella Vista Trail to Black Mountain
Picchetti Ranch Area—Trip to a Hilltop
Purisima Creek Redwoods Preserve—Bald Knob Trail
Rancho San Antonio Preserve—Up the Meadow Trails to Shoulder
    of Black Mountain
    Duveneck Windmill Pasture Area—Trek to Black Mountain
Russian Ridge Preserve—Bay Area Ridge Trail Trip
*San Bruno Mountain Park—Summit Loop Trip
San Pedro Valley Park—Hazelnut Trail
    Montara Mountain and Brooks Creek Falls Trails
Sheep Camp Trail
Skyline Ridge Preserve—Bay Area Ridge Trail
Stevens Creek Park—Lookout Trail to Lookout Point, Canyon Trail
Sweeney Ridge—Portolá Discovery Site
*Windy Hill Preserve—Summit Hike on Anniversary Trail
Wunderlich Park—Alambique or Bear Gulch trails to "The Meadows"

ALMOST WILDERNESS—*yet so close to home*
    *Butano Park—Circumnavigate the Park
    El Corte de Madera Preserve—Loop Trip into Preserve's Southern Canyons
    Huddart Park—Trails in upper park
    Monte Bello Preserve—Canyon Trail
    *Pescadero Creek Park—A Loop Around the Tarwater Creek Basin
        Brook Trail Loop
    *Portola Redwoods Park—Peters Creek Loop Trip
    Purisima Creek Redwoods Preserve—Whittemore Gulch Trail,
        Bald Knob Trail
    Rancho San Antonio Preserve—Wildcat Loop Trail
        Meadow Trails to Shoulder of Black Mountain
    Wunderlich Park—Circle Trip to "The Crossroads"

CREEKSIDE TRAILS—*By pools and riffles, with rocks and overhanging trees*
    Burleigh Murray Ranch Park
    Butano Park—Six Bridges Trail from Nature Center
    El Corte de Madera Preserve—El Corte de Madera Creek Trail
    Huddart Park—Richards Road and Crystal Springs trails along
        West Union Creek
    Laurelwood Park
    Memorial Park—Creek and Homestead Trails
    Mills Canyon Nature Area
    Monte Bello Preserve—Stevens Creek Nature Trail
    *Pescadero Creek Park—Trip 1 and Brooks Trail Loop
    *Portola Redwoods Park—Sequoia and Iverson Trails
    Purisima Creek Redwoods Preserve—Purisima Creek Trail
    Rancho San Antonio Preserve—Wildcat Loop Trail
    Sam McDonald Park—Forest Loop Trail Ext.
        *Heritage Grove Trail on Alpine Creek
    San Pedro Valley Park—Old Trout Farm Trail
    Stevens Creek Park—Creek Trail
    Stulsaft Park—Arroyo Agua de Ojo
    Windy Hill Preserve—Eagle Trail on Windy Hill Loop

GLIMPSES OF 19th CENTURY RANCHES—*Orchards, vineyards, cattle grazing and haying*
    Burleigh Murray Ranch Park
    Fremont Older Preserve
    Picchetti Ranch Area
    Purisima Creek and El Corte De Madera preserves; Huddart and
        Wunderlich parks; Phleger Estate—sites of early logging camps
    Rancho San Antonio Preserve—Deer Hollow Farm and Grant Cabin
    Skyline Ridge Preserve

MEADOWS AND HILLTOPS FOR KITE FLYING, HAWK WATCHING, Or PEACEFUL PICNICKING
    Coal Creek Preserve—Meadow Trail
    Fremont Older Preserve—Hunters Point
    *La Honda Creek Preserve—Trail through the Meadow
    Long Ridge Preserve—Hickory Oak Trail
    Los Trancos Preserve—Page Mill Trail

Monte Bello Preserve—Indian Creek Trail, Knolls near Page Mill Road
Pescadero Park—Brook Trail Loop
Pulgas Ridge Preserve
Rancho San Antonio Park and Preserve—Wildcat Loop Trail
    To the Duveneck Windmill Pasture
*Russian Ridge Preserve—To the Slopes of Mindego Hill
San Bruno Mountain Park
Sheep Camp Trail
Sweeney Ridge
Windy Hill Preserve—Anniversary Trail, Spring Ridge Trail
Wunderlich Park—"The Meadows" and Upper Meadow on Skyline Trail

NATURE TRAILS AND SELF-GUIDING TRAILS
*Huddart Park—Chickadee Trail
Junipero Serra Park—Live Oak Nature Trail
*Los Trancos Preserve—Self-guiding and Docent Trips on
    San Andreas Fault Trail
*Memorial Park—Tan Oak and Mt. Ellen Nature trails
Monte Bello Preserve—Stevens Creek Nature Trail
Portola Redwoods Park—Sequoia Trail
Rancho San Antonio Preserve—Docent trip to Deer Hollow Farm
San Bruno Mountain Park— Bog Trail

TRAILS ON HISTORIC ROUTES
Alpine Road Hiking, Riding and Bicycle Trail
Arastradero Bike Path
Coal Creek Preserve—Upper Alpine Road
Coastal Trail—Portolá expedition camp site at San Gregorio Beach
Huddart Park—Richards Road Trail, Summit Springs Trail
*McNee Ranch—Old San Pedro Mountain Road
Purisima Creek Redwoods—Purisima Creek Trail
Sawyer Camp Trail
Sheep Camp Trail
*Skyline Ridge Preserve—Old Page Mill Road
*Sweeney Ridge—Portolá Discovery Site of S.F. Bay

BIRDWATCHING
All Bay Trails—*By marshes and sloughs*
All Coastal Trails—*From rocky cliffs, on sandy shores and beside marshes*
See *Meadows* above

TRAILS THROUGH FANTASTIC FORESTS—*Once logged, now regrown*
Butano Park
El Corte de Madera Preserve
Huddart Park
*Pescadero Creek Park Complex
Portola Redwoods Park
*Purisima Creek Redwoods Preserve
Ridge/Skyline Trail from Huddart to Wunderlich Park
Windy Hill Preserve
*Wunderlich Park

TRAILS TO WONDERFUL WATERFALLS—
Look for these after heavy winter rains

Butano Park—Circumnavigate the Park
Los Trancos Creek Preserve
Memorial Park—Pomponio Falls
*Pescadero Creek Park—Jones Gulch and Towne Creek
*Portola Redwoods Park—Tiptoe Falls
Upper Stevens Creek Park—Cascades and falls on Table Mountain Trail

HIKING TRAILS OPEN FOR BICYCLISTS, EQUESTRIANS AND WHEELCHAIR USERS

FOR BICYCLISTS
On Paved Paths
Almost all the Bay Trails
Arastradero Hub Trails
Half Moon Bay State Beaches—Coastside Trail
Rancho San Antonio County Park—To Deer Hollow Farm
San Andreas Trail
San Bruno Mountain Park—Radio Road to summit
Sawyer Camp Trail
Sweeney Ridge—Sneath Lane
"The Loop"

On Unpaved Service and Fire Roads; consult text for certain other trails
(Closed after rains)

Arastradero Preserve—All trails except the Perimeter Trail
Burleigh Murray Ranch
Coal Creek Preserve
El Corte de Madera Preserve—All trails but footpath to Sandstone
    Formation
Fremont Older Preserve—All trails but footpath from Prospect Road
Long Ridge Preserve
Los Trancos Preserve—Page Mill Trail
Monte Bello Preserve—All trails but Stevens Creek Nature Trail
Pescadero Creek Park—Old Haul Road
Purisima Creek Redwoods Preserve—All trails except Soda Gulch,
    Balk Knob and North Ridge footpath
Russian Ridge Preserve—All trails except Ancient Oaks and north end
    of Bay Area Ridge Trail
San Pedro Valley Park—Weiler Ranch Road
Skyline Ridge Preserve—All except hikers' alternate Ridge Trail routes
    and Alpine Pond Loop
Sweeney Ridge—All except Ridge Trail north from Mori Ridge Trail junction
    to Skyline College
Upper Stevens Creek Park—Uphill only on Table Mountain/Charcoal Rd.
Windy Hill Preserve—Spring Ridge Trail and Fence Line Trail

EQUESTRIAN TRAILS (**equestrian parking)
              (Some trails closed in wet weather)

Arastradero Preserve
Coal Creek Preserve
Crystal Springs Trail

Edgewood Park
El Corte de Madera Preserve
Fremont Older Preserve—Except for Foot Trail from Prospect Road
Half Moon Bay State Beaches—Coastside Trail
Huddart Park**
Long Ridge Preserve
Los Trancos Preserve—Page Mill Trail only
Monte Bello Preserve**—All trails except Stevens Creek Nature Trail
Pescadero Creek Park
Poplar Beach
Pulgas Ridge Preserve
Purisima Creek Redwoods Preserve—Except for Whittemore Gulch,
    Soda Gulch and Grabtown Gulch trails
Rancho San Antonio**—Except Wildcat Canyon Trail
Russian Ridge Preserve—No exit to Langley Hill Road at this writing
Sam McDonald County Park—except Heritage Grove, Big Tree
    and Forest Loop trails
Skyline Trail
Sweeney Ridge—All except Ridge Trail north from Mori Ridge Trail junction
    to Skyline College
The Loop—Alpine, Portola and Sand Hill Road trails
Windy Hill Preserve
Wunderlich Park**

FOR WHEELCHAIR USERS—*Level, surfaced paths*
Alpine Road Hiking, Riding and Bicycle Trail (some parts)
Coyote Point Recreation Area
Huddart Park—Chickadee Trail
Laurelwood Park, Shasta Street entrance
Palo Alto/Los Altos Bike Path
Pulgas Ridge Preserve—Cordilleras Trail
Purisima Creek Redwoods—Redwood Trail
Rancho San Antonio Park and Preserve (Call MROSD for permit parking)
San Andreas Trail, north end
San Bruno Mountain—Bog Trail and Guadalupe Trail
The Bay Trails—most are surfaced and almost level
Varian/Bol Park Path

SPECIAL OCCASIONS

OUTINGS WITH YOUNG CHILDREN—
A birthday party with no crumbs on the rug.
Short walks, picnic tables and restrooms nearby
*Coyote Point Recreation Area and Museum
Edgewood Park Day Camp Area
Fitzgerald Marine Reserve
Huddart Park
Junipero Serra Park
Laurelwood Park
Memorial Park
Oyster Point Marina and Beach
Point San Bruno Park
Purisima Creek Redwoods Preserve—Redwood Trail
*Rancho San Antonio Park

Sam McDonald Park
San Bruno Mountain Park
San Mateo Coast Beaches—Pescadero, Pebble Beach, Bean Hollow,
    Fitzgerald Marine Reserve, Half Moon Bay Beaches
*San Pedro Valley Park
Sierra Point Marina
Stevens Creek Park—Bay Tree, Cooley, and Villa Maria Picnic Areas
Stulsaft Park
The Bay Trail—At parks along the trail

OVERNIGHT IN THE PARKS AND PRESERVES—
*Youth groups and backpack camps by reservation and
nearby hostels (reservations recommended)*
Butano Park—camping
Half Moon Bay State Beaches—car camping
Hidden Villa Hostel (closed in summer)
Huddart Park—groups
Junipero Serra Park—youth groups
Memorial Park—groups
Montara Lighthouse Hostel
Monte Bello Preserve—backpackers
Pescadero Creek Park—Shaw Flat and Tarwater Trail Camps
Pigeon Point Lighthouse Hostel
Portola Redwoods Park—camping and Slate Creek Trail Camp
Sam McDonald Park—youth groups
San Bruno Mountain Park—youth groups

PARKS AND PRESERVES WITH MUSEUMS AND VISITOR CENTERS
Butano Park—Nature Center
Coyote Point Recreation Area—Coyote Point Museum
Portola Redwoods Park
San Pedro Valley Park
Skyline Ridge Preserve—Daniels Nature Center
Stevens Creek Park

ROUTES TO REMOTE and ANCIENT REDWOODS—
Can you see the treetop?
La Honda Creek Preserve—Trail to the Big Tree
Long Ridge to Portola Redwoods—Ward Road and Slate Creek Trails
*Memorial Park—Tan Oak Trail
Methuselah Tree—On east side of Skyline Boulevard opposite
    El Corte de Madera gate CM02 and uphill from Ridge/Skyline Trail
Pescadero Creek Park—Brook Trail and Butano Ridge Loop Trails
*Portola Redwoods Park—Peters Creek Loop Trip, Old Tree
    and Slate Creek Trails
Purisima Creek Redwoods Preserve—Lower Whittemore Gulch Trail
*Sam McDonald Park—Big Tree Trail, Heritage Grove Trail

Appendix II
Recommended Reading

History
Bogart, Sewall, *Lauriston; an Architectural Biography of Herbert Edward Law*, Portola Valley: Alpine House Publications, 1976.
Brown, Alan K., *Sawpits in the Spanish Redwoods, 1787-1849*, San Mateo: San Mateo County Historical Association, 1966.
_____, *Place Names of San Mateo County*, San Mateo: San Mateo County Historical Association, 1975.
Chase, J. Smeaton, *California Coast Trails*, Boston: Houghton Mifflin Co. 1913. Reprinted, Palo Alto: Tioga Publishing Co., 1987.
Cupertino Chronicle, Cupertino: California History Center, De Anza College, Local History Studies, Vol. 19, 1975.
Fava, Florence M., *Los Altos Hills, A Colorful Story*, Woodside: Gilbert Richards Publications, 1976.
Margolin, Malcolm, *The Ohlone Way, Indian Life in the San Francisco-Monterey Bay Area*, Berkeley: Heyday Books, 1978.
Marinacci, Barbara and Rudy, *California's Spanish Place-Names*, San Rafael: Presidio Press, 1980.
Morrall, June, *Half Moon Bay Memories; The Coastside's Memorable Past*, El Granada: Moonbeam Press, 1987.
Regnery, Dorothy F., *An Enduring Heritage, Historic Buildings of the San Francisco Peninsula*: Stanford: Stanford University Press, 1976.
Stanger, Frank M., *South From San Francisco, San Mateo County, California, Its History and Heritage*, San Mateo: San Mateo County Historical Association, 1963.
_____, *Sawmills in the Redwoods, Logging on the San Francisco Peninsula, 1889-1967*, 2nd printing, San Mateo: San Mateo County Historical Association, 1992.
VanderWerf, Barbara, *Montara Mountain*, El Granada: Gum Tree Lane Books, 1994.
_____, *The Coastside Trail Guidebook*, El Granada: Gum Tree Lane Books, 1995.

Natural History
California Natural History Guides, Berkeley: University of California Press.
Berry, William D. and Elizabeth, *Mammals of the San Francisco Bay Region*, 1959.
Ferris, Roxana S. *Native Shrubs of the San Francisco Bay Region*, 1968.
Gilliam, Harold, *Weather of San Francisco Bay Area*, 1966.
Grillos, Steve J., *Ferns and Fern Allies of California*, 1966.
Howard, Arthur D., *Evolution of the Landscape of the San Francisco Bay Region*, 1972.
Metcalf, Woodbridge, *Native Trees of the San Francisco Bay Region*, 1959.
Sharsmith, Helen K., *Spring Wildflowers of the San Francisco Bay Region*, 1965.
Smith, Arthur C., *Introduction to the Natural History of the San Francisco Bay Region*, 1959.

Stebbins, Robert C., *Reptiles and Amphibians of the San Francisco Bay Region*, 1960.

_____, *Trees of the West*, Blaine: Hancock House Publishers, 1992.

Birding at the Bottom of the Bay, 2nd ed., Palo Alto: Santa Clara Valley Audubon Society, 1990.

Conradson, Diane R., *Exploring Our Baylands*. Newark: San Francisco Bay Wildlife Society, 1996.

Crittenden, Mabel, and Dorothy Telfer, *Wildflowers of the West*, Blaine: Hancock House Publishers, 1992.

Lyons, Kathleen and Mary Beth Cuneo-Lazaneo, *Plants of the Coast Redwood Region*, Los Altos: The Looking Press, 1988.

McClintock, Elizabeth, Paul Reeberg and Walter Knight, *A Flora of the San Bruno Mountains*, Sacramento: California Native Plant Society, 1990.

Pavlik, Bruce, and Pamela Muick, Sharon Johnson, and Marjorie Popper, *Oaks of California*, Los Olivos: Cachuma Press, Inc. and California Oak Foundation, 1991.

Peterson, Roger Tory, *A Field Guide to Western Birds*, 3rd ed., Boston: Houghton Mifflin Company, 1990.

Scott, Shirley, *Field Guide to the Birds of North America*, 2nd ed., Washington, D.C: National Geographic Society, 1987.

San Francisco Peninsula Birdwatching, San Mateo: Sequoia Audubon Society, 1996.

Thomas, John Hunter, *Flora of the Santa Cruz Mountains of California*, Stanford: Stanford University, Press, 1961.

Uvardy, Miklos D. F., *The Audubon Society Field Guide to North American Birds*, New York: Alfred A. Knopf, 1977.

Guidebooks

California State Coastal Conservancy, *San Francisco Bay Shoreline Guide*, Berkeley: University of California Press, 1995.

Doss, Margot Patterson, *Bay Area at Your Feet*, Rev. ed. San Francisco: Don't Call It Frisco Press, 1987.

Hosler, Ray, *Bay Area Bike Rides*, San Francisco: Chronicle Books, 1990.

Rusmore, Jean, *The Bay Area Ridge Trail*, Berkeley: Wilderness Press, 1995.

Spangle, Frances and Jean Rusmore, *South Bay Trails*, 2nd ed. Berkeley: Wilderness Press, 1989.

Taber, Tom, *The Expanded Santa Cruz Mountains Trail Book*, 7th ed. San Mateo: The Oak Valley Press, 1994.

Whitnah, Dorothy L. *An Outdoor Guide to the San Francisco Bay Area*, 5th ed. Berkeley: Wilderness Press, 1989.

Appendix III

INFORMATION SOURCES ON PARKS, PRESERVES, TRAILS AND TRAIL ACTIVITIES

Public Agencies

National Park Service, Western Region
Golden Gate National Recreation Area
Fort Mason
San Francisco, CA 94123
  415-556-0561
Fort Funston Visitor Center
  415-239-2366

San Francisco Bay National Wildlife
  Refuge
P.O. Box 524
Newark, CA 94560
  415-792-2222

State of California, Department of Parks
  and Recreation
Bay Area District
  415-330-6300
See individual parks in text
See San Mateo Coast Beaches below
Reservations, Destinet
  800-444-7275

California State Coastal Conservancy
1330 Broadway, Suite 1100
Oakland, CA 94612
  510-286-0151

Midpeninsula Regional Open Space
  District
333 Distel Circle
Los Altos, CA 94022
  415-691-1200

San Mateo County Parks and Recreation
  Department
County Government Center
590 Hamilton St.
Redwood City, CA 94063
  415-363-4020
Reservations
  415-363-4021

Santa Clara County Parks and Recreation
  Department
298 Garden Hill Drive
Los Gatos, CA 95031
  408-358-3741
Reservations
  408-358-3751

San Mateo Coast Beaches
  Fort Funston and Thornton State Beach
    415-239-2366
  Pacifica City and State Beaches
    415-738-7380
  Montara State Beach
  Half Moon Bay State Beaches
  Cowell Ranch State Beach
    415-726-8819
  James V. Fitzgerald Marine Reserve
  Pillar Point Marsh
  Poplar County Beach
    415-728-3584
  San Gregorio and Pomponio State
    Beaches
  Pescadero State Beach and Marsh
  Pebble Beach and Bean Hollow Beach
    415-879-2170
  Año Nuevo State Reserve and Coastal
    Access
    415-879-2025

City Parks Departments

Atherton	415-325-4457
Belmont	415-595-7441
Brisbane	415-467-6330
Burlingame	415-696-3770
Daly City	415-991-8001
East Palo Alto	415-953-3100
Foster City	415-345-5731
Half Moon Bay	415-726-8297
Los Altos Hills	415-941-7222
Menlo Park	415-858-3470
Millbrae	415-259-2360
Mountain View—	
Deer Hollow Farm	415-903-6430
Pacifica	415-738-7380
Palo Alto	415-329-2261
Portola Valley	415-851-1700
Redwood City	415-780-7250
San Bruno	415-877-8868
San Carlos	415-802-4382
San Mateo	415-377-4640
South San Francisco	415-877-0560
Woodside	415-851-6790

Transportation Agencies Serving Parks and Preserves

BART 415-992-2278
. . . . 510-465-2278
San Francisco Municipal Railway—MUNI 415-673-6864
Samtrans (San Mateo County Transit District) 800-660-4287
Santa Clara County Transportation Agency . . . 800-894-9908

Transportation Guides

Metropolitan Transportation Commission, *Regional Transit Guide*, 9th ed.,
Oakland: Metropolitan Transportion Commission, 1996.
Bay Area Open Space Council and Greenbelt Alliance, *Transit Outdoors,
The Public Transit Guide to San Francisco Bay Area Regional Parks*, San Francisco:
Greenbelt Alliance, 1995.

Organizations Sponsoring Group Hikes, Bicycle and Horseback Rides, Interpretive Trips, Trail Maintenance Days

Many public agencies offer docent-led nature walks and occasional trail maintenance days. Consult the agency near you from the above list. In addition, local
and statewide nonprofit groups sponsor outdoor trips for environmental education and enjoyment, such as the following groups:

American Youth Hostels
  Santa Clara Valley Chapter 408-293-3787
  San Francisco Chapter 415-771-7277
American Volkssport Association 415-871-1608
Anza Trail 415-744-3968
Audubon Society—Bird walks
  Sequoia Chapter 415-345-3724
  Santa Clara Valley Chapter 408-252-3747
Bay Area Orienteering Club 408-255-8018
Bay Area Ridge Trail Council—Quarterly
Outings Calendar of guided trips 415-391-9300
Bay Trail 510-464-7935
Bicycle Groups, e.g. California Association of Bicycle Organizations,
  East Bay Bicycle Coalition, ROMP, Western Wheelers
California Native Plant Society, Santa Clara Valley Chapter . 415-856-2636
California Trail Days—4th Saturday & Sunday of April . . 415-948-1829
. . . . 800-325-2843
Coastwalk 707-829-6689
Community Colleges—Some offer group hiking classes:
  Skyline, San Mateo, Cañada, Foothill, DeAnza
Companions of the Trail 408-379-4809
Environmental Museums—
  California Academy of Sciences 415-750-7145
  Coyote Point Museum 415-342-7755
Filoli Center—Docent tours of wildland area . . . 415-364-2880
Golden Gate National Park Association 415-776-0693
Hiking Clubs—e.g. Sierra Club, American Volkssport
Horsemen's Associations—e.g. San Mateo County Volunteer Horse Patrol,
  San Mateo County Horsemen's Assn.
Marine Science Institute—Discovery Voyage,
  mostly for school groups 415-364-2760

Peninsula Open Space Trust 415-854-7696
Pescadero Marsh Natural Preserve 415-879-2170
Santa Cruz Mountains Natural History Association . . . 408-335-3174
   or Dial-A-Hike 415-948-9198
Santa Cruz Mountains Trail Association 415-968-2412
Sempervirens Fund 415-968-4509
Senior Centers—Some offer group walks: call cities
Sierra Club—Local chapters offer hiking, bicycling,
   backpacking, climbing and kayaking trips
   Loma Prieta Chapter 415- 390-8411
The Nature Conservancy 415-281-0423
The Trail Center—A 4-county non-profit, volunteer trail
   information and trail maintenance clearinghouse . . 415-968-7065
Women's Outdoor Network—Recreation resource for
   active Bay Area women 415-494-8583
Youth Groups—Boy Scouts, Girl Scouts, and Campfire units
   and YMCA, YWCA

Websites Keyed to Recreation

Golden Gate National Recreation Area—http://www.nps.gov/goga
Midpeninsula Regional Open Space District—www.openspace.org
The Trail Center—http://www.businessweb.com/trailcen

NOTE: **415** area code numbers for most of San Mateo County
   will change in August 1997 to **650**

Index

Numbers in **boldface** refer to the primary entry for that area.